THE COMMON LAW

Law & Society Series

Ancient Law
Henry Sumner Maine
with an introduction by Dante J. Scala

An Introduction to the Sociology of Law
Nicholas S. Timascheff
with an introduction by A. Javier Treviño

Common Law
Oliver Wendell Holmes
with an introduction by Randall G. Sheldon

Critique of the Legal Order
Richard Quinney
with an introduction by Randall G. Sheldon

Fundamental Principles of the Sociology of Law
Eugen Ehrlich
with a new introduction by Klaus A. Ziegert

Penal Philosophy
Gabriel Tarde
with a new introduction by Piers Beirne

Punishment and Social Structure
Georg Rusche and Otto Kirchheimer
with a new introduction by Dario Melossi

Sociology of Law
Georges Gurvitch
with a new introduction by Alan Hunt

The General Theory of Law and Marxism
Evgeny Bronislavovich Pashukanis
with a new introduction by Dragan Milovanovic

The Social Reality of Crime
Richard Quinney
with a new introduction by A. Javier Treviño

THE COMMON LAW

Oliver Wendell Holmes, Jr.

With a new introduction by **Tim Griffin**

Routledge
Taylor & Francis Group
LONDON AND NEW YORK

Originally published in 1881 by Little, Brown, and Company.
Published 2005 by Transaction Publishers

Published 2019 by Routledge
2 Park Square, Milton Park, Abingdon, Oxon OX14 4RN
52 Vanderbilt Avenue, New York, NY 10017

First issued in hardback 2019

Routledge is an imprint of the Taylor & Francis Group, an informa business

Library of Congress Catalog Number: 2004046050

Library of Congress Cataloging-in-Publication Data

Holmes, Oliver Wendell, 1841-1935.
The common law / Oliver Wendell Holmes ; with a new introduction by Tim Griffin.
p. cm.—(Law & society series)
Originally published: Cambridge, Mass. : Belknap Press of Harvard University Press, 1963, in series: The John Harvard library.
Includes bibliographical references and index.
ISBN 0-7658-0827-7 (pbk. : alk. paper)
1. Common law. I. Title. II. Law and society series.

K588.H65 2004
340.5'7—dc22 2004046050

ISBN 13: 978-1-138-53478-0 (hbk)
ISBN 13: 978-0-7658-0827-1 (pbk)

CONTENTS

THE COMMON LAW

LECTURE V

THE BAILEE AT COMMON LAW

LECTURE VI

POSSESSION

LECTURE VII

CONTRACT.—I. HISTORY

LECTURE VIII

CONTRACT.—II. ELEMENTS

LECTURE IX

CONTRACT.—III. VOID AND VOIDABLE

LECTURE X

SUCCESSIONS.—I. AFTER DEATH.—II. INTER VIVOS

LECTURE XI

SUCCESSIONS.—II. INTER VIVOS

INTRODUCTION TO THE TRANSACTION EDITION

THE COMMON LAW is Oliver Wendell Holmes' most sustained jurisprudential work. In it the careful reader will discern traces of his later thought as found in both his judicial opinions and other writings, such as *The Path of Law*. However, the book can be difficult because Holmes' objective is not always clear. I hope that this introduction will shed new light on the work. Accordingly, I begin with a brief account of Holmes' life and the influences that played a role in shaping his thought. I then turn to a discussion of the larger concerns of *The Common Law* as well as certain of the significant particulars of his presentation that bear on it. Finally, I consider the relevance of Holmes' position for contemporary legal theory. Although *The Common Law* is difficult, students of law and jurisprudence will doubtless find their effort in working through it highly rewarding.

I

Oliver Wendell Holmes, Jr. was born on May 8, 1841 into a prominent Boston family. His maternal grandfather, Charles Jackson, had served as a justice on the Supreme Judicial Court of Massachusetts. His father, Oliver Wendell Holmes, Sr., was a physician as well as a noted literary figure. In short, Holmes was born into a successful and well-established professional family.

As a young man Holmes was something of an idealist. He was, for example, passionately dedicated to the abolitionist cause and contemplated devoting himself to the study of philosophy. Neither of these positions was in accordance with his father's views or wishes for him. Nonetheless, in pursuit of the first of these ideals, abolitionism, Holmes enlisted in the Union army after his graduation from Harvard in 1861. He was commissioned a lieutenant in the Twentieth Massachusetts Volunteer Infantry and by the time he left the military in 1864, he had been involved in some of the worst fighting of the Civil War, had been wounded three times, and had been promoted to the rank of lieutenant colonel.

Holmes' military involvement may have taken much of the wind out of his idealist sails. This is hardly surprising given the divisive nature of the Civil War, and his firsthand witness of the cost, in this case in human suffering and life, of ideals, however worthy. This is not to suggest that the abolitionist cause was not just or that Holmes regretted his involvement in it. At least to my knowledge he never expressed any regrets. It has been noted, however, that the post-bellum Holmes was much more skeptical, if not cynical, about reform movements than the ante-bellum Holmes had been.

After his military service, Holmes considered various options before finally resolving to study law. In particular, he gave serious thought to pursuing a vocation in philosophy. In the end, he chose to enter Harvard Law School. He completed his legal studies and began to practice law in 1866. However, he remained interested in philosophy and in 1868 he began participating in the Metaphysical Club of Cambridge whose membership included such notable philosophical figures as Charles Sanders Peirce, Chauncey Wright, and William James. This association had a pronounced influence on the development of Holmes' theory of law.

Such were the events that shaped Holmes' outlook. From 1866 to the early 1880s his vocational focus was the law. In addition to his law practice, he was made a lecturer at Harvard Law School and coeditor of the *American Law Review*. In 1872 he married Fanny Bowditch Dixwell; that union would endure until her death in 1929. In 1873 Holmes published an edited version of *Kent's Commentaries on the Law*. Shortly thereafter, he began work on *The Common Law*, which appeared in 1881. The publication of this volume earned Holmes the rank of Professor of Law at Harvard Law School.

Holmes remained in this position for only one year. He resigned upon accepting an appointment as associate justice on the Supreme Judicial Court of Massachusetts, bringing to a close his brief stint as a practicing lawyer, academic, and scholar.

Holmes was sworn in as an associate justice of the Supreme Judicial Court of Massachusetts in 1883. In 1899 he was appointed the Court's chief justice. In 1902, after serving nineteen years on Massachusetts' highest court, President Theodore Roosevelt appointed Holmes an associate justice of the Supreme Court of the United States. He remained in that position until his retirement from the Court in 1932. He died on March 6, 1935 and was buried beside his wife in Arlington National Cemetery.

During his lengthy tenure on the U.S. Supreme Court, Holmes displayed those characteristics that earned him the title "The Great Dissenter." It is important to note that Holmes did not receive this title because he dissented often, particularly by contemporary standards, but because he dissented effectively. In his dissenting opinions he often exhibited prescience for later developments by the Court—indeed, many of his important dissenting opinions were vindicated by subsequent Court opinions. Of course, it is difficult to say whether this success was owed to Holmes' aptitude for anticipating the direction in which the Court would move—an aptitude that Holmes would find among the most admirable for a legal thinker—or whether it was owed to the persuasiveness of his dissenting arguments. In all likelihood, his success was a matter of his powers of both prediction and persuasion.

It is noteworthy that the seeds of some of Holmes' most notable opinions are already present in *The Common Law*. For example, in his celebrated dissenting opinion in *Lochner v. New York* (1905), Holmes challenged the Court's position that the Due Process clause of the Fourteenth Amendment contained, by implication, substantive principles discoverable by means of reason. There is a clear relationship between this position and his rejection of the idea that the common law could be organized by means of philosophical principles or theories. To Holmes' way of thinking, judges must decide cases on the basis of facts—widely conceived so as to include considerations of social policy. Significantly, these attitudes already figure prominently in *The Common Law*, to which I now turn.

II

Holmes greatly desired to make his mark as an author and scholar, and *The Common Law* was to be his vehicle for doing so. As noted above, prior to undertaking this project, he had edited *Kent's Commentaries on the Law*. Although the latter may have left him somewhat disillusioned with the state of the common law, it likely made him aware of the strengths of the common law system as well. In particular, he realized that the common law cannot be organized in accordance with one or another philosophical position. On the contrary, to attempt to impose order in this way would essentially compromise the common law's integrity. Thus, while it is possible to *discern* order in the actual workings of the common law, it would be a mistake to attempt to impose order on it from without so as to make it correspond to preconceived philosophical opinions. On this point, Holmes' position stood in stark contrast to that of many of his contemporaries.

At the time Holmes was writing *The Common Law*, there were movements afoot, in both America and England, to significantly reform the common law. The chief advocates of these movements, the utilitarians and the neo-Kantians/Hegelians, came from radically different camps. They agreed, however, that the common law was too disorderly and unsystematic to secure the larger aims for which a legal system exists. In particular, a crucial aim of the legal system is the imposition of order on society. However, the common law system itself seemed to lack order; the provisions of the law were therefore established on a case-by-case basis by judicial decisions.

Thus the difficulty, as the reformers saw it, was that the common law is a body of rules promulgated by judges in response to the particular facts of a given dispute. They recognized, of course, that a judge's decision is not entirely arbitrary. Common law judges must answer to precedent or *stare decisis*—the "rule of law" established in prior relevant judicial opinions. However, the determination of precedent is a tricky business in itself. There is, for example, the problem of determining exactly what the rule of law articulated in a prior case is—a task that is far more difficult than it might seem—and worse yet, there is always a question about whether a precedent case is relevant given the inevitable differences in fact situations between it and the case under consideration. Thus a common law judge must determine how closely the facts of the case under consideration match those of the precedent. If the facts in the prior decision are too remote, then the rule of the prior case may be disregarded or, in the language of the courts, "distinguished." Now obviously this is far more of an art than a science, and there is significant room for a judge's particular prejudices to enter into his interpretation and application of precedent. Thus, for those concerned with order and clarity, the common law appears sloppy and murky indeed.

Nor is the problem merely a matter of theoretical elegance and intellectual aesthetics. A more important concern is that individuals and the society as a whole rely on the law in ordering their affairs. But the fact that the common law allows so much room for judicial innovation makes its outcomes less predictable than they ought to be. This state of affairs is particularly scandalous in areas such as torts and criminal law, in which one who is held liable may suffer pecuniary losses or the loss of freedom. But the problem is not confined to these areas. Uncertainty in the law impacts the areas of property and contract as well; areas in which it is critical that one be able to rely on clearly defined rules to order one's affairs.

These are significant concerns, and Holmes' efforts to defend the common law system may seem surprising in light of them. However, he was convinced that the common law system possessed virtues that were overlooked or misunderstood by its critics. He held, moreover, that the concern for order of the sort envisioned by its critics was too simplistic. Thus, at the outset of *The Common Law* he observes that "[t]he object of this book is to present a general view of the Common Law. To accomplish this task, other tools are needed besides logic. It is something to show that the consistency of a system requires a particular result, but it is not all. The life of the law has not been logic: it has been experience" (p. 5). It is a mistake, Holmes thought, to attempt to impose an *a priori* order onto the common law simply for the sake of obtaining a rational legal order. There is more at stake than either logical consistency or certainty. The legal system must allow for the inevitable changes in society.

Of course, Holmes is not advocating the absence of order. His point is rather that there is order inherent in the common law that its critics have failed to notice. Furthermore, this order is more comprehensive, and therefore superior, to that which might be provided by a philosophical system such as utilitarianism or Kantianism. Thus, he continues, "[t]he felt necessities of the time, the prevalent moral and political theories, intuitions of public policy, avowed or unconscious, even the prejudices which judges share with their fellow-men, have had a good deal more to do than the syllogism in determining the rules by which men should be governed" (p. 5). In short, the aims of the law would not be met by a system in which the rule of law could be deduced as a conclusion from a syllogism, for such reasoning would not be responsive to the practical imperatives of society.

These remarks suggest that the law must be responsive primarily to pragmatic needs of the time, as disclosed in the thoughts, feelings, and even the prejudices that judges share with the general public. Indeed, a judge's ability to make decisions that are relevant to the community's current needs, by Holmes' reckoning, is one of the strengths of the common law. However, he is mindful of the threat that judicial innovation may pose to the stability of the legal system. As noted above, individuals need to rely on the law if they are to order their affairs in accordance with it. For Holmes, this reliability, or as he would prefer, predictability, is inherent in the common law's precedential structure. Thus, he completes his thought by indicating the important role of history in the eventual outcome of a judge's decision-making process: "The substance of the law at any given time pretty nearly corresponds, so far as it goes, with what is then understood to be convenient; but its form and machinery, and the degree to which it is able to work out desired results, depend very much upon its past" (p. 5).

Thus in the opening paragraph of *The Common Law*, Holmes provides a sketch of his general position. He is concerned to establish that the common law is able to meet the changing needs of society while preserving continuity with the past in order to enable individuals to rely upon it. A common law judge must be creative, then, both in determining the society's current needs, and in discerning how best to address these needs in a way that is continuous with past judicial decisions. In this way, the law evolves by moving out of its past, adapting to the needs of the present, and establishing a direction for the future. And to Holmes' way of thinking, this approach is superior to imposing order in accordance with a philosophical position or theory because the law would thereby lose the flexibility required of it in responding to the needs and demands of the disputing parties as well as the society as a whole.

III

Many of Holmes' remarks in *The Common Law* seem to suggest that he is on a crusade to rid the law of philosophy. However, one must be careful not to make too much of his apparent distrust of philosophy. While it is true that he was opposed to the positions of those, such as the utilitarians and Kantians, who wished to reform the common law system in accordance with abstract principles, Holmes was by no means adverse to the application of philosophy to law. On the contrary, *The Common Law* owes a considerable debt to philosophy; a debt that one is apt to miss by taking Holmes' negative remarks too seriously.

As we have seen, Holmes was well grounded in philosophy and a member of the celebrated Cambridge Metaphysical Club, from which sprang the philosophical tradition known as "pragmatism." Whether Holmes' participation in the Metaphysical Club was the ultimate source of his philosophical conviction, his jurisprudence clearly bears the marks of pragmatism.

There are a number of pragmatist themes evident in *The Common Law*. First, pragmatism takes an empirical approach and emphasizes that experience is the ultimate source of knowledge. However, experience so conceived is not static, nor does it come piecemeal as many empiricists had maintained. Rather, experience is continuous. There is regularity in the experience of the environment that quite naturally leads to regularity in responses to it. And as responses to the environment become more patterned, predictions are possible. There is, then, a reciprocal relationship between the environment and the individual.

This point is closely related to a second important feature of pragmatism, namely, that the function of knowledge is successful adaptation to the environment. In this respect, knowledge is not a matter of grasping timeless truths or reporting the contents of immediate experience. Rather, it is a matter of moving forward to successfully encounter the environment. Consequently, knowledge is future-oriented, enabling the individual to anticipate future experience and accommodate to it. Yet while the *purpose* of knowledge is to enable one to anticipate changes in the environment and adjust to them, the *source* of knowledge is past experience.

Thus on both the frontside and the backside of knowledge one finds experience. Past experience shapes an individual in such a way that future experience may be anticipated. When one's expectations are borne out by subsequent experience, the tendency to reproduce the expectation becomes more pronounced. On the other hand, when the anticipated experience fails to materialize, the discomfort so occasioned results in an investigation to discover the source of the problem.

A third aspect of pragmatism is that it is primarily a philosophical method. As initially conceived by Charles Sanders Peirce, the acknowledged founder of the pragmatist movement, pragmatism is a thesis about the meaning of theoretical terms. In order to properly analyze a theoretical term, Peirce maintained, it is necessary to look at the experience to which it is connected. The outcome of experience is the test of the meaning of the term.

A further element of the pragmatist picture, and the final one that I shall mention in connection with this discussion, is the profound debt it owes to the theory of evolution. The influence of Darwin's theory on pragmatism is discernible in a number of places. First, as noted above, knowledge is conceived as part of an individual's "natural history," so to speak. It enables the individual to "adapt" to the environment and, on the basis of regularity in past experience, to anticipate the future. Second, an implication of the evolutionary position is that human beings are continuous with nature. Hence, a pragmatist rejects any conception that looks upon human beings as independent or outside of the natural order. Human beings may be more sophisticated than other creatures, but the fact remains that the principles by which human beings are acted upon by the world and in turn act upon it are continuous with those of other creatures. Third, it follows that those activities and institutions peculiar to human beings are also continuous with the natural order and explicable by similar principles. Finally, as with nature, human activities and institutions are always in the process of growth and change. Indeed, that which does not grow or change is dead. A human institution, particularly one like the law that guides human conduct, is useful only if it can adapt to meet the changing needs of the human community.

These features of pragmatism are all present in *The Common Law*. Indeed, it seems that pragmatism offers a near perfect explanatory framework for conceptualizing the common law. First, the common law is grounded in experience. The "law" in this system arises out of a particular controversy between (generally) two parties. The decision in the case is, accordingly, conditioned by the facts at issue and previous rules of law that are also owed to the facts of a specific case.

Second, it relies upon continuity in experience and in the similarity between situations giving rise to the controversy. It is this similarity that makes the doctrine of precedent effective. In a related way, continuity explains the manner in which the law grows and evolves. There is not a complete break between past and present, and yet the past is not perfectly replicated in the present. Accordingly, precedents are slowly extended and expanded to adapt to present circumstances. These features of experience explain, in turn, how it is that the common law is able to accommodate both the change that is necessary for adaptation and the regularity that is necessary for ordering one's affairs. Changes in the common law are typically slow, and its course of evolution is therefore predictable. And this is as one would expect, since the judge who decides a particular controversy is part of the environment and milieu that gave rise to it.

Third, the common law is fundamentally methodological. This does not mean, of course, that particular decisions are not based on abstract principles. However, the principles that inform particular decisions have arisen out of collective experience. They are not, then, read into the law antecedently but emerge from the experiences of the society, of which the judge is a member. This inductive aspect of the common law explains, in large part, Holmes' rejection of the idea that substantive philosophical or moral principles should be introduced as a means of ordering the common law system. The desire to do so displays, to his way of thinking, blindness to the proper role of principles in the law and, moreover, would curtail the law's natural evolution.

As we have seen throughout this discussion, the most pronounced feature of the common law, according to Holmes, is that it is ever changing and adapting to meet current societal needs. In this respect, not surprisingly, the common law mirrors the evolution of species. In the latter case, alterations in the environment produce innovations in biological species with the result that their subsequent generations are better acclimated to the natural habitat. There is, of course, no final fixed form, for the species so altered is also part of the environment. Consequently, one species' advance may serve as a catalyst for subsequent changes in the environment and so on. There are no sharp breaks in the process. Rather, the process of evolution is continuous in both space and time. That is, the modifications of evolution occur in an environment over time. There is no starting over—nature begins with what is present and adjusts accordingly. The result is that the innovations to a species may be such that progeny bear little resemblance to their ancestor.

According to Holmes, the law evolves in much the same way. The social environment—the economic, moral, and political milieu—that is, the background of legal intervention, alters over time. Therefore, in order to remain responsive to this social environment, the law must change as well. But, of course, the law is also part of this environment and impacts it. There is, then, a continual reciprocity between the law and the social arrangements in which it is contextualized. And, as with the evolution of species, there is no starting over. Rather, in most cases, a judge takes existing legal concepts and principles, as these are memorialized in precedent, and adapts them, often unconsciously, to fit the requirements of the case and present social conditions.

Holmes' commitment to pragmatism and evolutionary theory inform both the polemical and positive contents of *The Common Law*. As concerns the former, he was convinced that the utilitarian and Kantian/Hegelian theorists were mistaken about the common law system because they were insensitive to the actual processes that underlie it. Utilitarians were inattentive to the historical character of legal change. For this reason, although utilitarian virtues of utility and expediency are critical factors in a judge's decision, considerations of precedent and compatibility with previous cases are important as well. An uncritical and ahistorical application of the principle of utility to a particular controversy might produce unintended consequences that could significantly disrupt the social order.

Holmes is similarly critical of the tendency of Continental legal theorists who followed in the traditions of Kant and Hegel. These thinkers saw the law as a properly intellectual exercise that *ought* to be regulated by rationally deduced principles. Even the Hegelians, who placed such great emphasis on history, saw history as little more than a backdrop against which reason worked out its principles. In contrast, for Holmes history is important because change occurs only within a temporal framework, and while not random—change results from identifiable causes—it is not "rational" either. There is no preconceived end to which history is moving. History is rather an account of adjustments occasioned by the felt necessity of ever-changing circumstances.

Holmes' application of the theory of evolution is important for his positive contributions to legal theory as well. First, much of his discussion in *The Common Law* is devoted to the explication of legal expressions and concepts. He engages in this analysis in order to illustrate how the common law's application of these expressions and concepts has evolved. Thus the terms used in resolving earlier disputes may come to have different scope and meaning when employed in later opinions. Second, Holmes is concerned to show that the common law is an effective instrument for responding to and producing social change. When seen in this light, the application of the theory of evolution to the legal system is normative as well as descriptive. That is, it does not merely explain how the law grows and adapts in response to social change, but it establishes the law as a means of effecting such change in its own right.

With this as background it may be useful to examine a particular example of this evolutionary approach from *The Common Law*.

IV

While Holmes' theoretical commitments are not wholly absent from *The Common Law*, they are largely implicit. He does not develop his general position in a systematic way; rather he focuses instead on concepts, e.g., liability, in the respective areas of the law, e.g., torts, and traces the evolution of those concepts. He describes this evolutionary process in the following way:

> The customs, beliefs, or needs of a primitive time establish a rule or a formula. In the course of centuries the custom, belief, or necessity disappears, but the rule remains. The reason which gave rise to the rule has been forgotten, and ingenious minds set themselves to inquire how it is to be accounted for. Some ground of policy is thought of, which seems to explain it and to reconcile it with the present state of things; and then the rule adapts itself to the new reasons which have been found for it, and enters on a new career. (p. 8)

Holmes' intent is to expose the workings of this process. However, as noted, his aim is not merely descriptive. Rather, once the common law's process of evolution is properly understood, judges will be in a position to guide the process instead of being guided by it. Thus, while "hitherto the process has been largely unconscious," Holmes maintains that "[i]t is important, on that account, to bring to mind what the actual course of events has been. If it were only to insist on a more conscious recognition of the legislative function of the courts...it would be useful...." (p. 32). For Holmes, this means that judges will be in a position to consciously employ considerations of social policy in making their decisions. Of course, precedent will continue to play an important role in guiding the judicial decision-making process, but judges are not bound by precedents that no longer serve the public interest. Therefore, Holmes concludes, "[w]hen we find that in large and important branches of the law the various grounds of policy on which the various rules have been justified are later inventions to account for what are in fact survivals from more primitive times, we have a right to reconsider the proper reasons, and, taking a broader view of the field, to decide anew whether those reasons are satisfactory" (p. 33).

Such a position may sound surprising given Holmes' rejection of theoretical intrusions into the law. However, there is an important difference, for whereas the concern of a judge committed to a philosophical, political, or ideological position is the consistency of the outcome of a case with that position, the concern of a judge following Holmes' approach is to produce a beneficial social outcome to the extent that is possible. It is also worth noting that although a judge may have philosophical commitments that influence the final decision in a case, these commitments are part of the judge's milieu and not an external standard by which to measure the particular judicial outcome or the legal system itself. That is to say, philosophy and philosophical commitments are no more privileged in particular judicial decisions or the law in general than are other features of the environment in which a case is decided.

Holmes' treatment of the concept of liability—in both civil and criminal law—may serve to illustrate this point. His view, contrary to that prevailing at the time, is that the apparent moral elements of liability are vestiges of an early period of the law's development. Thus, in contrast to legal theorists who maintain that the focus on intention in the assignment of liability is an important and fairly late development in law, Holmes insists that the law's evolution has moved increasingly away from such "internal" considerations as concern with motives and intentions, and towards "external" considerations such as how the average person of reasonable intelligence would act; what level of care the average person would exercise in a given situation; whether the average person would have foreseen the harm produced by a particular course of action; and so on.

Holmes reasons as follows: Vengeance, or the desire for it, is among the most basic motives to justice and redress; it is a natural response when one is intentionally harmed by another. However, intention in this case is critical, and without it, vengeance is not justified. When liability is thus circumscribed many of the harms one receives are without remedy. After all, many, if not most, harms are caused by carelessness rather than intention. As the law evolved, it gradually made provision for rectifying these harms and it did so in a way that focuses on the harm itself and the way in which it results rather than on the mental state of the agent whose action produced the harm. Consequently, as noted above, the foreseeability that the harm would occur, that is to say, the likelihood that harm would result from a particular action, becomes more important than the offender's reasons for acting.

In the early chapters of *The Common Law* Holmes identifies the steps in the evolution of legal liability. First, vengeance involved physical violence in response to an intentional harm: the perpetrator, whether human or not, received corporeal punishment. However, this response was less than satisfactory because (1) it provided no remedy to the victim apart from the satisfaction of revenge, and (2) it often resulted in an inequitable loss of property. Consider, for example, a premodern agrarian society operating under such a rudimentary system of redress. In such a society, if my horse breaks free and tramples a neighbor's chickens, the remedy is to destroy the horse that caused the harm. And yet, in this case both my neighbor and I are losers. My neighbor loses insofar as the death of the horse does not replace the loss of the chickens, and I lose because the horse was valuable to me. Indeed, the horse's value to me is probably far greater than the value of the chickens my neighbor lost. Now, by tweaking this situation, by making me responsible (liable) for the horse's actions and allowing me to compensate my neighbor for the lost chickens, a better outcome is secured. This solution seems simple enough, but it does involve important innovations. In particular, it requires that liability is extended to one who has not acted and, therefore, does not have the necessary intention to justify vengeance. In fact, as the owner of the horse, I not only lack the necessary "internal" mental state to justify vengeance, my liability does not owe to any mental state at all. It owes rather to the absence of a mental state—presumably negligence or a lack of care on my part to ensure that my property does not harm another. Thus the assignment of liability to me in this case is a legal fiction. I am not, strictly speaking, liable because I do not have the requisite mental state for liability.

With this outcome, both my neighbor and I (not to mention the horse) are better off than with the doctrine that requires a mental state for the assignment of liability. In addition, the community as a whole benefits from this extension of the notion of liability. First, because it establishes a more desirable outcome for parties involved in future cases of this sort. Second, and more importantly, because in such a community a resource like my horse contributes to the commonweal. A judge is justified in considering this concern for social policy because the outcome and the reasoning of the case extend, by means of precedent, to the entire society, and because my neighbor and I (the parties) are members of that society.

One final comment is in order before moving to the concluding section of this introduction. It should be apparent from the foregoing that

Holmes regards a common law judge's role as necessarily involving a legislative element. That is, in fact, the key feature distinguishing a common law tradition from the tradition of civil codes. Thus, although a judge does not enact legislation in the same way that a legislature does, a judge is no less concerned about the social implications of the decision in the case before her, and to ignore these implications is an injustice to the disputing parties (as members of the society) as well as the society as a whole. However, a common law judge must decide the case on the basis of the facts with which she is presented, as well as the relevant precedents and any relevant legislation. This feature of judicial decision-making often leads to the extension or modification of such concepts as "liability," and such extensions/modifications are one of the ways by which the common law evolves.

V

Holmes' legacy and that of *The Common Law* are difficult to measure. He continues to be an important figure in the philosophy of law, though perhaps more on the strength of his judicial opinions and the small work *The Path of Law*. This is unfortunate because, as I mentioned at the beginning, *The Common Law* is Holmes' most systematic jurisprudential work, and therefore provides a more thorough basis for comprehending and evaluating his position than do his other writings or his judicial opinions.

In this connection, *The Common Law* may help to explain the divergence of opinions about Holmes and his jurisprudence. There are those, for example, who extol Holmes as a progressive and a forerunner of such innovative legal approaches as the Critical Legal Studies movement. There are others, however, who regard Holmes' legal theory as offensive in its aristocratic and totalitarian tendencies. There is some basis for these diverse attitudes but there is also much in them that is oversimplified and inaccurate.

First, it is true that Holmes was a central figure in the American movement known as Legal Realism, and it is true that that movement influenced the development of Critical Legal Studies (CLS). On the whole these movements, and particularly the latter, are associated with progressive agendas. According to most CLS scholars, law is a social institution subject to all the prejudices and limitations of the society of which it is a part. Thus, one of the central themes of the CLS approach is that the judges who decide cases are typically members of the dominant class.

Not surprisingly, then, considerations of social standing, broadly conceived to include socioeconomic status, race, gender, etc., inform judicial decisions and thereby the law's form and substance. It is therefore wrong, the Critics maintain, to suppose that the rulings of the legal system are neutral or that they represent justice for everyone. In most cases, much to the discredit of the system and the disadvantage of those who are not members of the dominant class, the law serves to maintain the status quo. And this is not what one would expect or hope for in the legal system of a liberal democratic society.

Holmes would agree with much of the CLS position. Certainly on the level of description he would agree that judges are members of the dominant class and that their decisions reflect the prejudices and interests of that class. However, for Holmes this is an inevitable feature of the law and not necessarily an evil that needs to be corrected. Indeed, there is reason to believe that his commitment to Social Darwinism would lead him to assert that this situation is merely the outcome of evolutionary forces and ought not to be tampered with. In any case, Holmes' major concern was not to eradicate judicial prejudice or to level the playing field, so to speak. The larger concern for Holmes is that judges and legal theorists refrain from introducing external standards into the common law system by implementing global philosophical or ideological positions, whether progressive or conservative.

Second, there is some reason to suppose that Holmes' jurisprudence might lend itself to a kind of tyranny of the majority. He is not progressive about individual rights or the protection of the minority. Thus, in defending deterrence as a ground for punishment, he asserts that "the dogma of equality makes an equation between individuals only, not between an individual and the community" (p. 37). And, as part of the same discussion he responds to the Kantian objection that one should never treat another only as a means to an end by observing that "[i]f a man lives in society, he is liable to find himself so treated" (p. 38). Thus, while certain of Holmes' most notable dissenting opinions seem to advance progressive outcomes, the grounds for these outcomes were the benefits to the society and not the protection of individual rights.

This criticism is certainly valid, and one cannot read *The Common Law* without being struck by Holmes' pronounced preference for the societal good over individual interests. Still, his position in this regard is hardly simplistic. He recognizes that society benefits only when individuals are afforded certain legal rights. For example, freedom in the expression of alternative and unpopular opinions is necessary, according to Holmes, because such freedom advances the cause of society by introducing competition into the realm of attitudes and opinions. In short, it seems that Holmes avoids totalitarianism because, if for no other reason, he recognizes that the societal good (generally) requires individual rights.

Without question, the position presented in *The Common Law* is somewhat dated. In particular, the Social Darwinism to which Holmes subscribed has been discredited, and much of the common law system has now been codified. These facts notwithstanding, Holmes' position is important both because it is historically significant and because it continues to present a viable challenge to the omnipresent tendency to reconstitute the legal system to conform to one or another philosophical or ideological viewpoint. This tendency is currently manifest in the endorsement by many liberals of Rawlsian neo-Kantianism, as well as by many conservatives, who advocate a reading of the U.S. Constitution that is informed by the framers' "original intent." I think it is fair to say that Holmes would regard both of these partisan inclinations as mistaken. The liberal one because it seeks to impose an order that is foreign to the common law and that would curtail or artificially modify its growth and development; the conservative tendency because it assumes, wrongly, that the meaning of the terms and principles of the Constitution are static and fixed rather than living and therefore evolving. Regardless of how one feels about these issues, it is important to recognize the challenge that Holmes' thinking presents to such inclinations, and there is no better way of appreciating that challenge than by working through *The Common Law*.

TIM GRIFFIN

CAMBRIDGE, MASSACHUSETTS, February 2004.

THE COMMON LAW

PREFACE

This book is written in pursuance of a plan which I have long had in mind. I had taken a first step in publishing a number of articles in the American Law Review, but I should hardly have attempted the task of writing a connected treatise at the present time, had it not been for the invitation to deliver a course of Lectures at the Lowell Institute in Boston. That invitation encouraged me to do what was in my power to accomplish my wish. The necessity of preparing for the Lectures made it easier to go farther, and to prepare for printing, and accordingly I did so. I have made such use as I thought fit of my articles in the Law Review, but much of what has been taken from that source has been rearranged, rewritten, and enlarged, and the greater part of the work is new. The Lectures as actually delivered were a good deal simplified, and were twelve in number. The twelfth, however, was a summary of the foregoing eleven, and has been omitted, as not necessary for a reader with the book before him.

The limits of such an undertaking as the present must necessarily be more or less arbitrary. Those to which I have confined myself have been fixed in part by the limits of the course for which the Lectures were written. I have therefore not attempted to deal with Equity, and have even excluded those subjects, like Bills and Notes, or Partnership, which would naturally require an isolated treatment, and which do not promise to throw light on general theory. If, within the bounds which I have set myself, any one should feel inclined to reproach me for a want of greater detail, I can only quote the words of Lehuërou, "Nous faisons une théorie et non un spicilège."

O. W. HOLMES, Jr.

Boston, February 8, 1881.

LECTURE I

EARLY FORMS OF LIABILITY

THE object of this book is to present a general view of the Common Law. To accomplish the task, other tools are needed besides logic. It is something to show that the consistency of a system requires a particular result, but it is not all. The life of the law has not been logic: it has been experience. The felt necessities of the time, the prevalent moral and political theories, intuitions of public policy, avowed or unconscious, even the prejudices which judges share with their fellow-men, have had a good deal more to do than the syllogism in determining the rules by which men should be governed. The law embodies the story of a nation's development through many centuries, and it cannot be dealt with as if it contained only the axioms and corollaries of a book of mathematics. In order to know what it is, we must know what it has been, and what it tends to become. We must alternately consult history and existing theories of legislation. But the most difficult labor will be to understand the combination of the two into new products at every stage. The substance of the law at any given time pretty nearly corresponds, so far as it goes, with what is then understood to be convenient; but its form and machinery, and the degree to which it is able to work out desired results, depend very much upon its past.[a]

In Massachusetts to-day, while, on the one hand, there are a great many rules which are quite sufficiently accounted for by their manifest good sense, on the other, there are some which can only be understood by reference to the infancy of procedure among the German tribes, or to the social condition of Rome under the Decemvirs.

[a] [Imagination of men limited—can only think in terms of the language they have been taught. Conservative instinct.]

I shall use the history of our law so far as it is necessary to explain a conception or to interpret a rule, but no further. In doing so there are two errors equally to be avoided both by writer and reader. One is that of supposing, because an idea seems very familiar and natural to us, that it has always been so. Many things which we take for granted have had to be laboriously fought out or thought out in past times. The other mistake is the opposite one of asking too much of history. We start with man full grown. It may be assumed that the earliest barbarian whose practices are to be considered, had a good many of the same feelings and passions as ourselves.

The first subject to be discussed is the general theory of liability civil and criminal. The Common Law has changed a good deal since the beginning of our series of reports, and the search after a theory which may now be said to prevail is very much a study of tendencies. I believe that it will be instructive to go back to the early forms of liability, and to start from them.[b]

It is commonly known that the early forms of legal procedure were grounded in vengeance. Modern writers have thought that the Roman law started from the blood feud, and all the authorities agree that the German law began in that way. The feud led to the composition, at first optional, then compulsory, by which the feud was bought off. The gradual encroachment of the composition may be traced in the Anglo-Saxon laws,[1] and the feud was pretty well broken up, though not extinguished, by the time of William the Conqueror. The killings and house-burnings of an earlier day became the appeals of mayhem and arson. The appeals *de pace et plagis* and of mayhem became, or rather were in substance, the action of trespass which is still familiar to lawyers.[2] But as the compensation recovered in the appeal was the alternative of vengeance, we might expect to find its scope limited to the scope of vengeance. Vengeance imports a feeling of blame, and an opinion, however distorted by passion, that a wrong has

[b] [If successful result scientific in only proper sense—and this work is necess. prelim. to any serious codification or legislative working over of the substance.]

[1] E. g. Ine, c. 74; Alfred, c. 42; Ethelred, IV. 4, § 1.

[2] Bract., fol. 144, 145; Fleta, I. c. 40, 41; Co. Lit. 126 *b;* Hawkins, P. C., Bk. 2, ch. 23, § 15.

been done. It can hardly go very far beyond the case of a harm intentionally inflicted: even a dog distinguishes between being stumbled over and being kicked.

Whether for this cause or another, the early English appeals for personal violence seem to have been confined to intentional wrongs. Glanvill [3] mentions mêlées, blows, and wounds,—all forms of intentional violence. In the fuller description of such appeals given by Bracton [4] it is made quite clear that they were based on intentional assaults. The appeal *de pace et plagis* laid an intentional assault, described the nature of the arms used, and the length and depth of the wound. The appellor also had to show that he immediately raised the hue and cry. So when Bracton speaks of the lesser offences, which were not sued by way of appeal, he instances only intentional wrongs, such as blows with the fist, flogging, wounding, insults, and so forth.[5] The cause of action in the cases of trespass reported in the earlier Year Books and in the Abbreviatio Placitorum is always an intentional wrong. It was only at a later day, and after argument, that trespass was extended so as to embrace harms which were foreseen, but which were not the intended consequence of the defendant's act.[6] Thence again it extended to unforeseen injuries.[7] [e]

It will be seen that this order of development is not quite consistent with an opinion which has been held, that it was a characteristic of early law not to penetrate beyond the external visible fact, the *damnum corpore corpori datum*. It has been thought that an inquiry into the internal condition of the defendant, his culpability or innocence, implies a refinement of juridical conception equally foreign to Rome before the Lex Aquilia, and to England when trespass took its shape. I do not know any very satisfactory evidence that a man was generally held liable either in Rome [8] or England for the accidental consequences even of his own act. But whatever may have been the early law, the foregoing account shows the starting-point of the system with

[3] Lib. I. c. 2, *ad fin.*
[4] Bract., fol. 144 *a*, "*assultu præmeditato.*"
[5] Fol. 155; cf. 103 *b*.
[6] Y. B. 6 Ed. IV. 7, pl. 18.
[7] Ibid., and 21 H. VII. 27, pl. 5.
[e] [do not mean that limit to wilful wrongs conscious & theoretical, but unconscious result of mode in wh. law appeared and gradually extended its sphere.]
[8] D. 47. 9. 9.

which we have to deal. Our system of private liability for the consequences of a man's own acts, that is, for his trespasses, started from the notion of actual intent and actual personal culpability.

The original principles of liability for harm inflicted by another person or thing have been less carefully considered hitherto than those which governed trespass, and I shall therefore devote the rest of this Lecture to discussing them. I shall try to show that this liability also had its root in the passion of revenge, and to point out the changes by which it reached its present form. But I shall not confine myself strictly to what is needful for that purpose, because it is not only most interesting to trace the transformation throughout its whole extent, but the story will also afford an instructive example of the mode in which the law has grown, without a break, from barbarism to civilization. Furthermore, it will throw much light upon some important and peculiar doctrines which cannot be returned to later.

A very common phenomenon, and one very familiar to the student of history, is this. The customs, beliefs, or needs of a primitive time establish a rule or a formula. In the course of centuries the custom, belief, or necessity disappears, but the rule remains. The reason which gave rise to the rule has been forgotten, and ingenious minds set themselves to inquire how it is to be accounted for. Some ground of policy is thought of, which seems to explain it and to reconcile it with the present state of things; and then the rule adapts itself to the new reasons which have been found for it, and enters on a new career. The old form receives a new content, and in time even the form modifies itself to fit the meaning which it has received. The subject under consideration illustrates this course of events very clearly.

I will begin by taking a medley of examples embodying as many distinct rules, each with its plausible and seemingly sufficient ground of policy to explain it.

A man has an animal of known ferocious habits, which escapes and does his neighbor damage. He can prove that the animal escaped through no negligence of his, but still he is held liable. Why? It is, says the analytical jurist, because, although he was not negligent at the moment of escape, he was guilty of remote heedlessness, or negligence, or fault, in having such a creature at all. And one by whose fault damage is done ought to pay for it.

A baker's man, while driving his master's cart to deliver hot rolls of a morning, runs another man down. The master has to pay for it. And when he has asked why he should have to pay for the wrongful act of an independent and responsible being, he has been answered from the time of Ulpian to that of Austin, that it is because he was to blame for employing an improper person. If he answers, that he used the greatest possible care in choosing his driver, he is told that that is no excuse; and then perhaps the reason is shifted, and it is said that there ought to be a remedy against some one who can pay the damages, or that such wrongful acts as by ordinary human laws are likely to happen in the course of the service are imputable to the service.

Next, take a case where a limit has been set to liability which had previously been unlimited. In 1851, Congress passed a law, which is still in force, and by which the owners of ships in all the more common cases of maritime loss can surrender the vessel and her freight then pending to the losers; and it is provided that, thereupon, further proceedings against the owners shall cease. The legislators to whom we owe this act argued that, if a merchant embark a portion of his property upon a hazardous venture, it is reasonable that his stake should be confined to what he puts at risk,—a principle similar to that on which corporations have been so largely created in America during the last fifty years.

It has been a rule of criminal pleading in England down into the present century, that an indictment for homicide must set forth the value of the instrument causing the death, in order that the king or his grantee might claim forfeiture of the deodand, "as an accursed thing," in the language of Blackstone.

I might go on multiplying examples; but these are enough to show the remoteness of the points to be brought together.—As a first step towards a generalization, it will be necessary to consider what is to be found in ancient and independent systems of law.[d]

[d] [I propose to show that the true bond of union of all these is not to be found in the various grounds of policy wh. have been mentioned but in one wh. is com. to them all.]

There is a well-known passage in Exodus,[9] which we shall have to remember later: "If an ox gore a man or a woman, that they die: then the ox shall be surely stoned, and his flesh shall not be eaten; but the owner of the ox shall be quit." When we turn from the Jews to the Greeks, we find the principle of the passage just quoted erected into a system. Plutarch, in his Solon, tells us that a dog that had bitten a man was to be delivered up bound to a log four cubits long. Plato made elaborate provisions in his Laws for many such cases. If a slave killed a man, he was to be given up to the relatives of the deceased.[10] If he wounded a man, he was to be given up to the injured party to use him as he pleased.[11] So if he did damage to which the injured party did not contribute as a joint cause. In either case, if the owner failed to surrender the slave, he was bound to make good the loss.[12] If a beast killed a man, it was to be slain and cast beyond the borders. If an inanimate thing caused death, it was to be cast beyond the borders in like manner, and expiation was to be made.[13] Nor was all this an ideal creation of merely imagined law, for it was said in one of the speeches of Æschines, that "we banish beyond our borders stocks and stones and steel, voiceless and mindless things, if they chance to kill a man; and if a man commits suicide, bury the hand that struck the blow afar from its body." This is mentioned quite as an every-day matter, evidently without thinking it at all extraordinary, only to point an antithesis to the honors heaped upon Demosthenes.[14] As late as the second century after Christ the traveller Pausanias observed with some surprise that they still sat in judgment on inanimate things in the Prytaneum.[15] Plutarch attributes the institution to Draco.[16]

In the Roman law we find the similar principles of the *noxæ deditio* gradually leading to further results. The Twelve Tables (451 B.C.) provided that, if an animal had done damage, either the animal was to be surrendered or the damage paid for.[17] We

[9] xii. 28.

[10] θ', ix., Jowett's Tr., Bk. IX. p. 437; Bohn's Tr., pp. 378, 379.

[11] θ', xv., Jowett, 449; Bohn, 397.

[12] ια', xiv., Jowett, 509; Bohn, 495.

[13] θ', xii., Jowett, 443, 444; Bohn, 388.

[14] Κατὰ Κτησιφ. 244, 245.

[15] 1. 28 (11).

[16] Solon.

[17] "Si quadrupes pauperiem fecisse dicetur actio ex lege duodecim tabularum descendit; quæ lex voluit, aut dari [id] quod nocuit, id est, id animal,

learn from Gaius that the same rule was applied to the torts of children or slaves,[18] and there is some trace of it with regard to inanimate things.

The Roman lawyers, not looking beyond their own system or their own time, drew on their wits for an explanation which would show that the law as they found it was reasonable. Gaius said that it was unjust that the fault of children or slaves should be a source of loss to their parents or owners beyond their own bodies, and Ulpian reasoned that *a fortiori* this was true of things devoid of life, and therefore incapable of fault.[19]

This way of approaching the question seems to deal with the right of surrender as if it were a limitation of a liability incurred by a parent or owner, which would naturally and in the first instance be unlimited. But if that is what was meant, it puts the cart before the horse. The right of surrender was not introduced as a limitation of liability, but, in Rome and Greece alike, payment was introduced as the alternative of a failure to surrender.

The action was not based, as it would be nowadays, on the fault of the parent or owner. If it had been, it would always have been brought against the person who had control of the slave or animal at the time it did the harm complained of, and who, if any one, was to blame for not preventing the injury. So far from this being the course, the person to be sued was the owner at the time of suing. The action followed the guilty thing into whosesoever hands it came.[20] And in curious contrast with the principle as inverted to meet still more modern views of public policy, if the animal was of a wild nature, that is, in the very case of the most ferocious animals, the owner ceased to be liable the moment it escaped, because at that moment he ceased to be owner.[21] There seems to have been no other or more extensive liability by the old law, even where a slave was guilty with

---

quod noxiam commisit; aut estimationem noxiæ offerre." D. 9. 1. 1, pr.; Just. Inst. 4. 9; XII Tab., VIII. 6.

[18] Gaii Inst. IV. §§ 75, 76; D. 9. 4. 2, § 1. "Si servus furtum faxit noxiam ve noxit." XII Tab., XII. 2. Cf. Just. Inst. 4. 8, § 7.

[19] D. 39. 2. 7, §§ 1, 2; Gaii Inst. IV. § 75.

[20] "Noxa caput sequitur." D. 9. 1. 1, § 12; Inst. 4. 8, § 5.

[21] "Quia desinit dominus esse ubi fera evasit." D. 9. 1. 1, § 10; Inst. 4. 9, pr. Compare *May* v. *Burdett*, 9 Q. B. 101, 113.

his master's knowledge, unless perhaps he was a mere tool in his master's hands.[22] Gaius and Ulpian showed an inclination to cut the *noxæ deditio* down to a privilege of the owner in case of misdeeds committed without his knowledge; but Ulpian is obliged to admit, that by the ancient law, according to Celsus, the action was noxal where a slave was guilty even with the privity of his master.[23]

All this shows very clearly that the liability of the owner was merely a way of getting at the slave or animal which was the immediate cause of offence. In other words, vengeance on the immediate offender was the object of the Greek and early Roman process, not indemnity from the master or owner. The liability of the owner was simply a liability of the offending thing. In the primitive customs of Greece it was enforced by a judicial process expressly directed against the object, animate or inanimate. The Roman Twelve Tables made the owner, instead of the thing itself, the defendant, but did not in any way change the ground of liability, or affect its limit. The change was simply a device to allow the owner to protect his interest.[24]

But it may be asked how inanimate objects came to be pursued in this way, if the object of the procedure was to gratify the passion of revenge. Learned men have been ready to find a reason in the personification of inanimate nature common to savages and children, and there is much to confirm this view. Without such a personification, anger towards lifeless things would have been transitory, at most. It is noticeable that the commonest example in the most primitive customs and laws is that of a tree which falls upon a man, or from which he falls and is killed. We can conceive with comparative ease how a tree might have been put on the same footing with animals. It certainly was treated like them, and was delivered to the relatives, or chopped

[22] D. 19. 5. 14, § 3; Plin. Nat. Hist., XVIII. 3.

[23] "In lege antiqua si servus sciente domino furtum fecit, vel aliam noxiam commisit, servi nomine actio est noxalis, nec dominus suo nomine tenetur." D. 9. 4. 2.

[24] Gaius, Inst. IV. § 77, says that a noxal action may change to a direct, and, conversely, a direct action to a noxal. If a *paterfamilias* commits a tort, and then is adopted or becomes a slave, a noxal action now lies against his master in place of the direct one against himself as the wrong-doer. Just. Inst. 4. 8, § 5.

to pieces for the gratification of a real or simulated passion.[25]

In the Athenian process there is also, no doubt, to be traced a different thought. Expiation is one of the ends most insisted on by Plato, and appears to have been the purpose of the procedure mentioned by Æschines. Some passages in the Roman historians which will be mentioned again seem to point in the same direction.[26]

Another peculiarity to be noticed is, that the liability seems to have been regarded as attached to the body doing the damage, in an almost physical sense. An untrained intelligence only imperfectly performs the analysis by which jurists carry responsibility back to the beginning of a chain of causation. The hatred for anything giving us pain, which wreaks itself on the manifest cause, and which leads even civilized man to kick a door when it pinches his finger, is embodied in the *noxæ deditio* and other kindred doctrines of early Roman law. There is a defective passage in Gaius, which seems to say that liability may sometimes be escaped by giving up even the dead body of the offender.[27] So Livy relates that, Brutulus Papius having caused a breach of truce with the Romans, the Samnites determined to surrender him, and that, upon his avoiding disgrace and punishment by suicide, they sent his lifeless body. It is noticeable that the surrender seems to be regarded as the natural expiation for the breach of treaty,[28] and that it is equally a matter of course to send the body when the wrong-doer has perished.[29]

[25] LL. Alfred, c. 13; 1 Tylor, Primitive Culture, Am. ed., p. 285 *et seq.*; Bain, Mental and Moral Science, Bk. III. ch. 8, p. 261.

[26] Florus, Epitome, II. 18. Cf. Livy, IX. 1, 8, VIII. 39; Zonaras, VII. 26, ed. Niebuhr, vol. 43, pp. 98, 99.

[27] Gaii Inst. IV. § 81. I give the reading of Huschke: "Licere enim etiam, si fato is fuerit mortuus, mortuum dare; nam quamquam diximus, non etiam permissum reis esse, et mortuos homines dedere, tamen et si quis eum dederit, qui fato suo vita excesserit, æque liberatur." Ulpian's statement, in D. 9. 1. 1, § 13, that the action is gone if the animal dies *ante litem contestatam*, is directed only to the point that liability is founded on possession of the thing.

[28] "Bello contra fœdus suscepto."

[29] Livy, VIII. 39: "Vir . . . haud dubie proximarum induciarum ruptor. De eo coacti referre prætores decretum fecerunt 'Ut Brutulus Papius Romanis dederetur.' . . . Fetiales Romam, ut censuerunt, missi, et corpus Brutuli exanime: ipse morte voluntaria ignominiæ se ac supplicio subtraxit. Placuit cum corpore bona quoque ejus dedi." Cf. Zonaras, VII. 26, ed.

The most curious examples of this sort occur in the region of what we should now call contract. Livy again furnishes an example, if, indeed, the last is not one. The Roman Consul Postumius concluded the disgraceful peace of the Caudine Forks (*per sponsionem,* as Livy says, denying the common story that it was *per fœdus*), and he was sent to Rome to obtain the sanction of the people. When there however, he proposed that the persons who had made the contract, including himself, should be given up in satisfaction of it. For, he said, the Roman people not having sanctioned the agreement, who is so ignorant of the *jus fetialium* as not to know that they are released from obligation by surrendering us? The formula of surrender seems to bring the case within the *noxæ deditio.*[80] Cicero narrates a similar surrender of Mancinus by the *paterpatratus* to the Numantines, who, however, like the Samnites in the former case, refused to receive him.[81]

It might be asked what analogy could have been found between a breach of contract and those wrongs which excite the desire for vengeance. But it must be remembered that the distinction between tort and breaches of contract, and especially between the remedies for the two, is not found ready made. It is con-

---

Niebuhr, vol. 43, p. 97: Τὴν αἰτίαν τοῦ πολέμου 'Ρουτούλῳ ἀνδρὶ δυνατῷ παρ' αὐτοῖς ἐπιγράφοντες· οὐ τὰ ὀστᾶ, ἐπεὶ φθάσας ἐκεῖνος διεχειρίσατο ἑαυτὸν, διέῤῥιψαν. See further Livy, V. 36, "postulatumque ut pro jure gentium violato Fabii dederentur." and Ib. I. 32.

[80] Livy, IX. 5, 8, 9, 10. "Nam quod deditione nostra negant exsolvi religione populum, id istos magis ne dedantur, quam quia ita se res habeat, dicere, quis adeo juris fetialium expers est, qui ignoret?" The formula of surrender was as follows: "Quandoque hisce homines injussu populi Romani Quiritium fœdus ictum iri spoponderunt, atque ob eam rem noxam nocuerunt; ob eam rem, quo populus Romanus scelere impio sit solutus, hosce homines vobis dedo." Cf. Zonaras, VII. 26, ed. Niebuhr, vol. 43, pp. 98, 99.

[81] De Orator. I. 40, and elsewhere. It is to be noticed that Florus, in his account, says *deditione Mancini expiavit*. Epitome, II. 18. It has already been observed that the cases mentioned by Livy seem to suggest that the object of the surrender was expiation, as much as they do that it was satisfaction of a contract. Zonaras says, Postumius and Calvinus εἰς ἑαυτοὺς τὴν αἰτίαν ἀναδεχομένων. (VII. 26, ed. Niebuhr, Vol. 43, pp. 98, 99.) Cf. ib. p. 97. Compare Serv. ad Virg. Eclog. IV. 43: "In legibus Numæ cautum est, ut si quis imprudens occidisset hominem pro capite occisi et natis [agnatis? Huschke] ejus in concione offerret arietem." Id. Geor. III. 387, and Festus, *Subici, Subigere.* But cf. Wordsworth's Fragments and Specimens of Early Latin, note to XII Tab., XII. 2, p. 538.

ceivable that a procedure adapted to redress for violence was extended to other cases as they arose. Slaves were surrendered for theft as well as for assault; [32] and it is said that a debtor who did not pay his debts, or a seller who failed to deliver an article for which he had been paid, was dealt with on the same footing as a thief.[33] This line of thought, together with the quasi material conception of legal obligations as binding the offending body, which has been noticed, would perhaps explain the well-known law of the Twelve Tables as to insolvent debtors. According to that law, if a man was indebted to several creditors and insolvent, after certain formalities they might cut up his body and divide it among them. If there was a single creditor, he might put his debtor to death or sell him as a slave.[34]

If no other right were given but to reduce a debtor to slavery, the law might be taken to look only to compensation, and to be modelled on the natural working of self-redress.[35] The principle of our own law, that taking a man's body on execution satisfies the debt, although he is not detained an hour, seems to be explained in that way. But the right to put to death looks like vengeance, and the division of the body shows that the debt was conceived very literally to inhere in or bind the body with a *vinculum juris*.

Whatever may be the true explanation of surrender in connection with contracts, for the present purpose we need not go further than the common case of *noxæ deditio* for wrongs. Neither is the seeming adhesion of liability to the very body which did the harm of the first importance. The Roman law dealt mainly with living creatures,—with animals and slaves. If a man was run over, it did not surrender the wagon which crushed him, but the ox which drew the wagon.[36] At this stage the notion is easy to understand. The desire for vengeance may be felt as strongly

[32] D. 9. 4. 2.

[33] 2 Tissot, Droit Penal, 615; 1 Ihering, Geist d. Röm. R., § 14; 4 id. § 63.

[34] Aul. Gell. Noctes Attici. 20. 1; Quintil. Inst. Orat. 3. 6. 84; Tertull. Apol., c. 4.

[35] Cf. Varro, De Lingua Latina, VI.: "Liber, qui suas operas in servitute pro pecunia, quam debeat, dum solveret Nexus vocatur."

[36] D. 9. 1. 1, § 9. But cf. 1 Hale, P. C. 420.

against a slave as against a freeman, and it is not without example nowadays that a like passion should be felt against an animal. The surrender of the slave or beast empowered the injured party to do his will upon them. Payment by the owner was merely a privilege in case he wanted to buy the vengeance off.

It will readily be imagined that such a system as has been described could not last when civilization had advanced to any considerable height. What had been the privilege of buying off vengeance by agreement, of paying the damage instead of surrendering the body of the offender, no doubt became a general custom. The Aquilian law, passed about a couple of centuries later than the date of the Twelve Tables, enlarged the sphere of compensation for bodily injuries. Interpretation enlarged the Aquilian law. Masters became personally liable for certain wrongs committed by their slaves with their knowledge, where previously they were only bound to surrender the slave.[37] If a pack-mule threw off his burden upon a passer-by because he had been improperly overloaded, or a dog which might have been restrained escaped from his master and bit any one, the old noxal action, as it was called, gave way to an action under the new law to enforce a general personal liability.[38]

Still later, ship-owners and innkeepers were made liable *as if* they were wrong-doers for wrongs committed by those in their employ on board ship or in the tavern, although of course committed without their knowledge. The true reason for this exceptional responsibility was the exceptional confidence which was necessarily reposed in carriers and innkeepers.[39] But some of the jurists, who regarded the surrender of children and slaves as a privilege intended to limit liability, explained this new liability on the ground that the innkeeper or ship-owner was to a certain degree guilty of negligence in having employed the services of bad men.[40] This was the first instance of a master being made unconditionally liable for the wrongs of his servant. The reason given for it was of general application, and the principle expanded to the scope of the reason.

[37] D. 9. 4. 2, § 1.

[38] D. 9. 1. 1, §§ 4, 5.

[39] D. 4. 9. 1, § 1; ib. 7, § 4.

[40] Gaius in D. 44. 7. 5, § 6; Just. Inst. 4. 5, § 3.

The law as to ship-owners and innkeepers introduced another and more startling innovation. It made them responsible when those whom they employed were free, as well as when they were slaves.[41] For the first time one man was made answerable for the wrongs of another who was also answerable himself, and who had a standing before the law. This was a great change from the bare permission to ransom one's slave as a privilege. But here we have the history of the whole modern doctrine of master and servant, and principal and agent. All servants are now as free and as liable to a suit as their masters. Yet the principle introduced on special grounds in a special case, when servants were slaves, is now the general law of this country and England, and under it men daily have to pay large sums for other people's acts, in which they had no part and for which they are in no sense to blame. And to this day the reason offered by the Roman jurists for an exceptional rule is made to justify this universal and unlimited responsibility.[42]

So much for one of the parents of our common law. Now let us turn for a moment to the Teutonic side. The Salic Law embodies usages which in all probability are of too early a date to have been influenced either by Rome or the Old Testament. The thirty-sixth chapter of the ancient text provides that, if a man is killed by a domestic animal, the owner of the animal shall pay half the composition (which he would have had to pay to buy off the blood feud had he killed the man himself), and for the other half give up the beast to the complainant.[43] So, by chapter thirty-five, if a slave killed a freeman, he was to be surrendered for one half of the composition to the relatives of the slain man, and the master was to pay the other half. But according to the gloss, if the slave or his master had been maltreated by the slain man or his relatives, the master had only to surrender the slave.[44] It is interesting to notice that those North-

[41] D. 4. 9. 7, pr.

[42] See Austin, Jurisp. (3d ed.) 513; Doctor and Student, Dial. 2, ch. 42.

[43] Cf. L. Burgund. XVIII.; L. Rip. XLVI. (al. 48).

[44] See the word *Lege*, Merkel, Lex Salica, p. 103. Cf. Wilda, Strafrecht der Germanen, 660, n. 1. See further Lex Salica, XL.; Pactus pro tenore pacis Child. et Chloth., c. 5; Decretio Chlotharii, c. 5; Edictus Hilperichi,

ern sources which Wilda takes to represent a more primitive stage of German law confine liability for animals to surrender alone.[45] There is also a trace of the master's having been able to free himself in some cases, at a later date, by showing that the slave was no longer in his possession.[46] There are later provisions making a master liable for the wrongs committed by his slave by his command.[47] In the laws adapted by the Thuringians from the earlier sources, it is provided in terms that the master is to pay for all damage done by his slaves.[48]

In short, so far as I am able to trace the order of development in the customs of the German tribes, it seems to have been entirely similar to that which we have already followed in the growth of Roman law. The earlier liability for slaves and animals was mainly confined to surrender; the later became personal, as at Rome.

The reader may begin to ask for the proof that all this has any bearing on our law of to-day. So far as concerns the influence of the Roman law upon our own, especially the Roman law of master and servant, the evidence of it is to be found in every book which has been written for the last five hundred years. It has been stated already that we still repeat the reasoning of the Roman lawyers, empty as it is, to the present day. It will be seen directly whether the German folk-laws can also be followed into England.

In the Kentish laws of Hlothhære and Eadric (A. D. 680)

---

cc. 5, 7; and the observations of Sohm in his treatise on the Procedure of the Salic Law, §§ 20, 22, 27, French Tr. (Thevenin), pp. 83 n., 93, 94, 101–103, 130.

[45] Wilda, Strafrecht, 590.

[46] Cf. Wilda, Strafrecht, 660, n. 1; Merkel, Lex Salica, Gloss. *Lege*, p. 103. Lex Saxon. XI. § 3: "Si servus perpetrato facinore fugerit, ita ut a domino ulterius inveniri non possit, nihil solvat." Cf. id. II. § 5. Capp. Rip. c. 5: "Nemini liceat servum suum, propter damnum ab illo cuilibet inlatum, dimittere; sed juxta qualitatem damni dominus pro illo respondeat vel eum in compositione aut ad pœnam petitori offeret. Si autem servus perpetrato scelere fugerit, ita ut a domino pænitus inveniri non possit, sacramento se dominus ejus excusare studeat, quod nec suæ voluntatis nec conscientia fuisset, quod servus ejus tale facinus commisit."

[47] L. Saxon. XI. § 1.

[48] Lex Angl. et Wer. XVI.: "Omne damnum quod servus fecerit dominus emendet."

it is said, "If any one's slave slay a freeman, whoever it be, let the owner pay with a hundred shillings, give up the slayer," &c.[49] There are several other similar provisions. In the nearly contemporaneous laws of Ine, the surrender and payment are simple alternatives. "If a Wessex slave slay an Englishman, then shall he who owns him deliver him up to the lord and the kindred, or give sixty shillings for his life."[50] Alfred's laws (A. D. 871–901) have a like provision as to cattle. "If a neat wound a man, let the neat be delivered up or compounded for."[51] And Alfred, although two hundred years later than the first English lawgivers who have been quoted, seems to have gone back to more primitive notions than we find before his time. For the same principle is extended to the case of a tree by which a man is killed. "If, at their common work, one man slay another unwilfully, let the tree be given to the kindred, and let them have it off the land within thirty nights. Or let him take possession of it who owns the wood."[52]

It is not inapposite to compare what Mr. Tylor has mentioned concerning the rude Kukis of Southern Asia. "If a tiger killed a Kuki, his family were in disgrace till they had retaliated by killing and eating this tiger, or another; but further, if a man was killed by a fall from a tree, his relatives would take their revenge by cutting the tree down, and scattering it in chips."[53]

To return to the English, the later laws, from about a hundred years after Alfred down to the collection known, as the laws of Henry I., compiled long after the Conquest, increase the lord's liability for his household, and make him surety for his men's good conduct. If they incur a fine to the king and run away, the lord has to pay it unless he can clear himself of complicity. But I cannot say that I find until a later period the unlimited liability of master for servant which was worked out on the Continent, both by the German tribes and at Rome. Whether the principle when established was an indigenous growth, or whether the last step was taken under the influence of the Roman law, of which

[49] C. 3; 1 Thorpe, Anc. Laws, pp. 27, 29.
[50] C. 74; 1 Thorpe, p. 149; cf. p. 118, n. *a*. See LL. Hen. I., LXX. § 5.
[51] C. 24; 1 Thorpe, p. 79. Cf. Ine, c. 42; 1 Thorpe, p. 129.
[52] C. 13; 1 Thorpe, p. 71.
[53] 1 Tylor, Primitive Culture, Am. ed., p. 286.

Bracton made great use, I cannot say. It is enough that the soil was ready for it, and that it took root at an early day.[54] This is all that need be said here with regard to the liability of a master for the misdeeds of his servants.

It is next to be shown what became of the principle as applied to animals. Nowadays a man is bound at his peril to keep his cattle from trespassing, and he is liable for damage done by his dog or by any fierce animal, if he has notice of a tendency in the brute to do the harm complained of. The question is whether any connection can be established between these very sensible and intelligible rules of modern law and the surrender directed by King Alfred.

Let us turn to one of the old books of the Scotch law, where the old principle still appears in full force and is stated with its reasons as then understood.[55]

"Gif ane wylde or head-strang horse, carries ane man against his will over an craig, or heuch, or to the water, and the man happin to drowne, the horse sall perteine to the king as escheit.

"Bot it is otherwise of ane tame and dantoned horse; gif any man fulishlie rides, and be sharp spurres compelles his horse to take the water, and the man drownes, the horse sould not be escheit, for that comes be the mans fault or trespasse, and not of the horse, and the man has receaved his punishment, in sa farre as he is perished and dead; and the horse quha did na fault, sould not be escheit.

"The like reason is of all other beastes, quhilk slayes anie man, [It is added in a later work, "of the quhilk slaughter they haue gilt,"[56]] for all these beasts sould be escheit."

"The Forme and Maner of Baron Courts" continues as follows:—

"It is to witt, that this question is asked in the law, Gif ane

[54] Cf. Record in Molloy, Book 2, ch. 3, § 16, 24 Ed. III.: "Visum fuit curiæ, quod unusquisque magister navis tenetur respondere de quacunque transgressione per servientes suos in navi sua facta." The Laws of Oleron were relied on in this case. Cf. Stat. of the Staple, 27 Ed. III., Stat. 2, c. 19. Later the influence of the Roman law is clear.

[55] Quon. Attach., c. 48, pl. 10 *et seq*. Cf. The Forme and Maner of Baron Courts, c. 62 *et seq*.

[56] Forme and Maner of Baron Courts, c. 63.

lord hes ane milne, and any man fall in the damne, and be borne down with the water quhill he comes to the quheill, and there be slaine to death with the quheill; quhither aught the milne to be escheit or not? The law sayes thereto nay, and be this reason, For it is ane dead thing, and ane dead thing may do na fellony, nor be made escheit throw their gilt. Swa the milne in this case is not culpable, and in the law it is lawfull to the lord of the land to haue ane mylne on his awin water quhere best likes him." [57]

The reader will see in this passage, as has been remarked already of the Roman law, that a distinction is taken between things which are capable of guilt and those which are not,—between living and dead things; but he will also see that no difficulty was felt in treating animals as guilty.

Take next an early passage of the English law, a report of what was laid down by one of the English judges. In 1333 it was stated for law, that, "if my dog kills your sheep, and I, freshly after the fact, tender you the dog, you are without recovery against me." [58] More than three centuries later, in 1676, it was said by Twisden, J. that, "if one hath kept a tame fox, which gets loose and grows wild, he that hath kept him before shall not answer for the damage the fox doth after he hath lost him, and he hath resumed his wild nature." [59] It is at least doubtful whether that sentence ever would have been written but for the lingering influence of the notion that the ground of the owner's liability was his ownership of the offending thing and his failure to surrender it. When the fox escaped, by another principle of law the ownership was at an end. In fact, that very consideration was seriously pressed in England as late as 1846, with regard to a monkey which escaped and bit the plaintiff.[60] So it seems to be a reasonable conjecture, that it was this way of thinking which led Lord Holt, near the beginning of the last century, to intimate that one ground on which a man is bound at his peril to restrain cattle

[57] C. 64. This substantially follows the Quoniam Attachiamenta, c. 48, pl. 13, but is a little clearer. *Contra*, Fitzh. Abr. *Corone*, pl. 389, 8 Ed. II.

[58] Fitzh. Abr. *Barre*, pl. 290.

[59] *Mitchil* v. *Alestree*, 1 Vent. 295; s. c. 2 Lev. 172; s. c. 3 Keb. 650. Cf. *May* v. *Burdett*, 9 Q. B. 101, 113.

[60] *May* v. *Burdett*, 9 Q. B. 101.

from trespassing is that he has a valuable property in such animals, whereas he has not in dogs, for which his responsibility is less.[61] To this day, in fact, cautious judges state the law as to cattle to be, that, "if I am the owner of an animal in which by law the right of property can exist, I am bound to take care that it does not stray into the land of my neighbor."[62]

I do not mean that our modern law on this subject is only a survival, and that the only change from primitive notions was to substitute the owner for the offending animal. For although it is probable that the early law was one of the causes which led to the modern doctrine, there has been too much good sense in every stage of our law to adopt any such sweeping consequences as would follow from the wholesale transfer of liability supposed. An owner is not bound at his peril to keep his cattle from harming the neighbor's person.[63] And in some of the earliest instances of personal liability, even for trespass on a neighbor's land, the ground seems to have been the owner's negligence.[64]

It is the nature of those animals which the common law recognizes as the subject of ownership to stray, and when straying to do damage by trampling down and eating crops. At the same time it is usual and easy to restrain them. On the other hand, a dog, which is not the subject of property, does no harm by simply crossing the land of others than its owner. Hence to this extent the new law might have followed the old. The right of property in the offending animal, which was the ancient ground of responsibility, might have been adopted safely enough as the test of a liability based on the fault of the owner. But the respon-

[61] *Mason* v. *Keeling*, 12 Mod. 332, 335; s. c. 1 Ld. Raym. 606, 608.

[62] Williams, J. in *Cox* v. *Burbidge*, 13 C. B. N. S. 430, 438. Cf. Willes, J. in *Read* v. *Edwards*, 17 C. B. N. S. 245, 261.

[63] *Mason* v. *Keeling*, 1 Ld. Raym. 606, 608.

[64] In the laws of Ine, c. 42 (1 Thorpe, Anc. Laws, 129), personal liability seems to be imposed where there is a failure to fence. But if an animal breaks hedges the only remedy mentioned is to kill it, the owner to have the skin and flesh, and forfeit the rest. The defendant was held "because it was found that this was for default of guarding them, . . . for default of good guard," in 27 Ass., pl. 56, fol. 141, A. D. 1353 or 1354. It is much later that the reason is stated in the absolute form, "because I am bound by law to keep my beasts without doing wrong to any one." Mich. 12 Henry VII., Keilway, 3 *b*, pl. 7. See, further, the distinctions as to a horse killing a man in Regiam Majestatem, IV. c. 24.

sibility for damage of a kind not to be expected from such animals is determined on grounds of policy comparatively little disturbed by tradition. The development of personal liability for fierce wild animals at Rome has been explained. Our law seems to have followed the Roman.

We will now follow the history of that branch of the primitive notion which was least likely to survive,—the liability of inanimate things.

It will be remembered that King Alfred ordained the surrender of a tree, but that the later Scotch law refused it because a dead thing could not have guilt. It will be remembered, also, that the animals which the Scotch law forfeited were escheat to the king. The same thing has remained true in England until well into this century, with regard even to inanimate objects. As long ago as Bracton,[65] in case a man was slain, the coroner was to value the object causing the death, and that was to be forfeited as deodand "*pro rege.*" It was to be given to God, that is to say to the Church, for the king, to be expended for the good of his soul. A man's death had ceased to be the private affair of his friends as in the time of the barbarian folk-laws. The king, who furnished the court, now sued for the penalty. He supplanted the family in the claim on the guilty thing, and the Church supplanted him.

In Edward the First's time some of the cases remind us of the barbarian laws at their rudest stage. If a man fell from a tree, the tree was deodand.[66] If he drowned in a well, the well was to be filled up.[67] It did not matter that the forfeited instrument belonged to an innocent person. "Where a man killeth another with the sword of John at Stile, the sword shall be forfeit as deodand, and yet no default is in the owner." [68] That is from a book written in the reign of Henry VIII., about 1530. And it has been repeated from Queen Elizabeth's time [69] to within one hundred

[65] Fol. 128.

[66] Cf. 1 Britton (Nich.), 6 *a, b,* 16 (top paging 15, 39); Bract., fol. 136 *b;* LL. Alfred, c. 13 (1 Thorpe, Anc. Laws, p. 71); Lex Saxon., Tit. XIII.; Leg. Alamann., Tit. CIII. 24.

[67] Fleta, I. 26, § 10; Fitzh. Abr. *Corone,* pl. 416. See generally Staundforde, P. C., I. c. 2, fol. 20 *et seq.;* 1 Hale, P. C. 419 *et seq.*

[68] Doctor and Student, Dial. 2, c. 51.

[69] Plowd. 260.

years,[70] that if my horse strikes a man, and afterwards I sell my horse, and after that the man dies, the horse shall be forfeited. Hence it is, that, in all indictments for homicide, until very lately it has been necessary to state the instrument causing the death and its value, as that the stroke was given by a certain penknife, value sixpence, so as to secure the forfeiture. It is said that a steam-engine has been forfeited in this way.

I now come to what I regard as the most remarkable transformation of this principle, and one which is a most important factor in our law as it is to-day. I must for the moment leave the common law and take up the doctrines of the Admiralty. In the early books which have just been referred to, and long afterwards, the fact of *motion* is adverted to as of much importance. A maxim of Henry Spigurnel, a judge in the time of Edward I., is reported, that "where a man is killed by a cart, or by the fall of a house, or in other like manner, and the thing in motion is the cause of the death, it shall be deodand." [71] So it was said in the next reign that "omne illud quod movet cum eo quod occidit homines deodandum domino Regi erit, vel feodo clerici." [72] The reader sees how motion gives life to the object forfeited.

The most striking example of this sort is a ship. And accordingly the old books say that, if a man falls from a ship and is drowned, the motion of the ship must be taken to cause the death, and the ship is forfeited,—provided, however, that this happens in fresh water.[73] For if the death took place on the high seas, that was outside the ordinary jurisdiction. This proviso has been supposed to mean that ships at sea were not forfeited; [74] but there is a long series of petitions to the king in Parliament that such forfeitures may be done away with, which tell a different story.[75] The truth seems to be that the forfeiture took place, but in a different court. A manuscript of the reign of Henry VI.,

[70] Jacob, Law Dict. *Deodand*.
[71] Y. B. 30 & 31 Ed. I., pp. 524, 525; cf. Bract., fol. 136 *b*.
[72] Fitzh. Abr. *Corone*, pl. 403.
[73] Bract. 122; 1 Britton (Nich.), top p. 16; Fleta, I. c. 25, § 9, fol. 37.
[74] 1 Hale, P. C. 423.
[75] 1 Rot. Parl. 372; 2 Rot. Parl. 345, 372 *a*, *b*; 3 Rot. Parl. 94 *a*, 120 *a*, 121; 4 Rot. Parl. 12 *a*, *b*, 492 *b*, 493. But see 1 Hale, P. C. 423.

only recently printed, discloses the fact that, if a man was killed or drowned at sea by the motion of the ship, the vessel was forfeited to the admiral upon a proceeding in the admiral's court, and subject to release by favor of the admiral or the king.[76]

A ship is the most living of inanimate things. Servants sometimes say "she" of a clock, but every one gives a gender to vessels. And we need not be surprised, therefore, to find a mode of dealing which has shown such extraordinary vitality in the criminal law applied with even more striking thoroughness in the Admiralty. It is only by supposing the ship to have been treated as if endowed with personality, that the arbitrary seeming peculiarities of the maritime law can be made intelligible, and on that supposition they at once become consistent and logical.

By way of seeing what those peculiarities are, take first a case of collision at sea. A collision takes place between two vessels, the Ticonderoga and the Melampus, through the fault of the Ticonderoga alone. That ship is under a lease at the time, the lessee has his own master in charge, and the owner of the vessel has no manner of control over it. The owner, therefore, is not to blame, and he cannot even be charged on the ground that the damage was done by his servants. He is free from personal liability on elementary principle. Yet it is perfectly settled that there is a lien on his vessel for the amount of the damage done,[77] and this means that that vessel may be arrested and sold to pay the loss in any admiralty court whose process will reach her. If a livery-stable keeper lets a horse and wagon to a customer, who runs a man down by careless driving, no one would think of claiming a right to seize the horse and wagon. It would be seen that the only property which could be sold to pay for a wrong was the property of the wrong-doer.

But, again, suppose that the vessel, instead of being under lease, is in charge of a pilot whose employment is made compulsory by the laws of the port which she is just entering. The Supreme Court of the United States holds the ship liable in this instance also.[78] The English courts would probably have decided

[76] 1 Black Book of the Admiralty, 242.
[77] Cf. *Ticonderoga*, Swabey, 215, 217.
[78] *China*, 7 Wall. 53.

otherwise, and the matter is settled in England by legislation. But there the court of appeal, the Privy Council, has been largely composed of common-law lawyers, and it has shown a marked tendency to assimilate common-law doctrine. At common law one who could not impose a personal liability on the owner could not bind a particular chattel to answer for a wrong of which it had been the instrument. But our Supreme Court has long recognized that a person may bind a ship, when he could not bind the owners personally, because he was not their agent.

It may be admitted that, if this doctrine were not supported by an appearance of good sense, it would not have survived. The ship is the only security available in dealing with foreigners, and rather than send one's own citizens to search for a remedy abroad in strange courts, it is easy to seize the vessel and satisfy the claim at home, leaving the foreign owners to get their indemnity as they may be able. I dare say some such thought has helped to keep the practice alive, but I believe the true historic foundation is elsewhere. The ship no doubt, like a sword,[79] would have been forfeited for causing death, in whosesoever hands it might have been. So, if the master and mariners of a ship, furnished with letters of reprisal, committed piracy against a friend of the king, the owner lost his ship by the admiralty law, although the crime was committed without his knowledge or assent.[80] It seems most likely that the principle by which the ship was forfeited to the king for causing death, or for piracy, was the same as that by which it was bound to private sufferers for other damage, in whose hands soever it might have been when it did the harm.

If we should say to an uneducated man to-day, "She did it and she ought to pay for it," it may be doubted whether he would see the fallacy, or be ready to explain that the ship was only property, and that to say, "The ship has to pay for it," [81] was simply a dramatic way of saying that somebody's property was to be sold, and the proceeds applied to pay for a wrong committed by somebody else.

It would seem that a similar form of words has been enough to satisfy the minds of great lawyers. The following is a passage

[79] Doctor & Student, Dial. 2, c. 51. [80] 1 Roll. Abr. 530 (C) 1.
[81] 3 Black Book of Adm. 103.

from a judgment by Chief Justice Marshall, which is quoted with approval by Judge Story in giving the opinion of the Supreme Court of the United States: "This is not a proceeding against the owner; it is a proceeding against the vessel for an offence committed by the vessel; which is not the less an offence, and does not the less subject her to forfeiture, because it was committed without the authority and against the will of the owner. It is true that inanimate matter can commit no offence. But this body is animated and put in action by the crew, who are guided by the master. The vessel acts and speaks by the master. She reports herself by the master. It is, therefore, not unreasonable that the vessel should be affected by this report." And again Judge Story quotes from another case: The thing is here primarily considered as the offender, or rather the offence is primarily attached to the thing."[82]

In other words, those great judges, although of course aware that a ship is no more alive than a mill-wheel, thought that not only the law did in fact deal with it as if it were alive, but that it was reasonable that the law should do so. The reader will observe that they do not say simply that it is reasonable on grounds of policy to sacrifice justice to the owner to security for somebody else, but that it is reasonable to deal with the vessel as an offending thing. Whatever the hidden ground of policy may be, their thought still clothes itself in personifying language.

Let us now go on to follow the peculiarities of the maritime law in other directions. For the cases which have been stated are only parts of a larger whole.

By the maritime law of the Middle Ages the ship was not only the source, but the limit, of liability.[83] The rule already prevailed, which has been borrowed and adopted by the English statutes and by our own act of Congress of 1851, according to which the owner is discharged from responsibility for wrongful acts of a

[82] *Malek Adhel*, 2 How. 210, 234.

[83] 3 Kent, 218; Customs of the Sea, cap. 27, 141, 182, in 3 Black Book of the Admiralty, 103, 243, 345. [In many writers the liability of the ship appears as secondary—esp. where the Roman law comes in, e. g. Script de jure nautico, passim; ib. p. 671, Curicke, Jus mar Hanseat tit. 10, art. 2. The essential question is not the original but the modern form of the doctrine and the source of that.]

master appointed by himself upon surrendering his interest in the vessel and the freight which she had earned. By the doctrines of agency he would be personally liable for the whole damage. If the origin of the system of limited liability which is believed to be so essential to modern commerce is to be attributed to those considerations of public policy on which it would now be sustained, that system has nothing to do with the law of collision. But if the limit of liability here stands on the same ground as the *noxæ deditio*, it confirms the explanation already given of the liability of the ship for wrongs done by it while out of the owner's hands, and conversely the existence of that liability confirms the argument here.

Let us now take another rule, for which, as usual, there is a plausible explanation of policy. Freight, it is said, is the mother of wages; for, we are told, "if the ship perished, if the mariners were to have their wages in such cases, they would not use their endeavors, nor hazard their lives, for the safety of the ship."[84] The best commentary on this reasoning is, that the law has recently been changed by statute. But even by the old law there was an exception inconsistent with the supposed reason. In case of shipwreck, which was the usual case of a failure to earn freight, so long as any portion of the ship was saved, the lien of the mariners remained. I suppose it would have been said, because it was sound policy to encourage them to save all they could. If we consider that the sailors were regarded as employed by the ship, we shall understand very readily both the rule and the exception. "The ship is the debtor," as was said in arguing a case decided in the time of William III.[85] If the debtor perished, there was an end of the matter. If a part came ashore, that might be proceeded against.

Even the rule in its modern form, that freight is the mother of wages, is shown by the explanation commonly given to have reference to the question whether the ship is lost or arrive safe. In the most ancient source of the maritime law now extant, which has anything about the matter, so far as I have been able to discover,

[84] 3 Kent's Comm. 188.

[85] *Clay* v. *Snelgrave*, 1 Ld. Raym. 576, 577; s. c. 1 Salk. 33. Cf. Molloy, p. 355, Book II, ch. 3, § 8.

the statement is that the mariners will lose their wages when the ship is lost.[86] In like manner, in what is said by its English editor, Sir Travers Twiss, to be the oldest part of the Consulate of the Sea,[87] we read that "whoever the freighter may be who runs away or dies, the ship is bound to pay the mariners." [88] I think we may assume that the vessel was bound by the contract with the sailors, much in the same way as it was by the wrongs for which it was answerable, just as the debtor's body was answerable for his debts, as well as for his crimes, under the ancient law of Rome.

The same thing is true of other maritime dealings with the vessel, whether by way of contract or otherwise. If salvage service is rendered to a vessel, the admiralty court will hold the vessel, although it has been doubted whether an action of contract would lie, if the owners were sued at law.[89] So the ship is bound by the master's contract to carry cargo, just as in case of collision, although she was under lease at the time. In such cases, also, according to our Supreme Court, the master may bind the vessel when he cannot bind the general owners.[90] "By custom the ship is bound to the merchandise, and the merchandise to the ship." [91] "By the maritime law every contract of the master implies an hypothecation." [92] It might be urged, no doubt, with force, that, so far as the usual maritime contracts are concerned, the dealing must be on the security of the ship or merchandise in many cases, and therefore that it is policy to give this security in all cases; that the risk to which it subjects ship-owners is calculable, and that they must take it into account when they let their vessels. Again, in many cases, when a party asserts a maritime lien by way of contract, he has improved the condition of the thing upon

[86] "Ans perdront lurs loers quant la nef est perdue." 2 Black Book, 213. This is from the Judgments of the Sea, which, according to the editor (II., pp. xliv., xlvii.), is the most ancient extant source of modern maritime law except the decisions of Trani. So Molloy, Book II. ch. 3, § 7, p. 354: "If the ship perishes at sea they lose their wages." So 1 Siderfin, 236, pl. 2.

[87] 3 Black Book, pp. lix., lxxiv.

[88] 3 Black Book, 263. It should be added, however, that it is laid down in the same book that, if the vessel is detained in port by the local authorities, the master is not bound to give the mariners wages, "for he has earned no freight."

[89] *Lipson* v. *Harrison*, 2 Weekly Rep. 10. Cf. *Louisa Jane*, 2 Lowell, 295.

[90] 3 Kent's Comm. (12th ed.), 218; ib. 138, n. 1.

[91] 3 Kent, 218.

[92] *Justin* v. *Ballam*, 1 Salk. 34; s. c. 2 Ld. Raym. 805.

which the lien is claimed, and this has been recognized as a ground for such a lien in some systems.[93] But this is not true universally, nor in the most important cases. It must be left to the reader to decide whether ground has not been shown for believing that the same metaphysical confusion which naturally arose as to the ship's wrongful acts, affected the way of thinking as to her contracts. The whole manner of dealing with vessels obviously took the form which prevailed in the cases first mentioned. Pardessus, a high authority, says that the lien for freight prevails even against the owner of stolen goods, "as the master deals less with the person than the thing." [94] So it was said in the argument of a famous English case, that "the ship is instead of the owner, and therefore is answerable." [95] In many cases of contract, as well as tort, the vessel was not only the security for the debt, but the limit of the owner's liability.

The principles of the admiralty are embodied in its form of procedure. A suit may be brought there against a vessel by name, any person interested in it being at liberty to come in and defend, but the suit, if successful, ending in a sale of the vessel and a payment of the plaintiff's claim out of the proceeds. As long ago as the time of James I. it was said that "the libel ought to be only against the ship and goods, and not against the party." [96] And authority for the statement was cited from the reign of Henry VI., the same reign when, as we have seen, the Admiral claimed a forfeiture of ships for causing death. I am bound to say, however, that I cannot find such an authority of that date.

We have now followed the development of the chief forms of liability in modern law for anything other than the immediate and manifest consequences of a man's own acts. We have seen the parallel course of events in the two parents,—the Roman law and the German customs,—and in the offspring of those two on English soil with regard to servants, animals, and inanimate things. We have seen a single germ multiplying and branching into products as different from each other as the flower from the root. It hardly remains to ask what that germ was. We have seen

[93] D. 20. 4. 5 & 6; cf. Livy, XXX. 38.

[94] Pardessus, Droit. Comm., n. 961.

[95] 3 Keb. 112, 114, citing 1 Roll. Abr. 530.

[96] Godbolt, 260.

that it was the desire of retaliation against the offending thing itself. Undoubtedly, it might be argued that many of the rules stated were derived from a seizure of the offending thing as security for reparation, at first, perhaps, outside the law.[97] That explanation, as well as the one offered here, would show that modern views of responsibility had not yet been attained, as the owner of the thing might very well not have been the person in fault. But such has not been the view of those most competent to judge. A consideration of the earliest instances will show, as might have been expected, that vengeance, not compensation, and vengeance on the offending thing, was the original object. The ox in Exodus was to be stoned. The axe in the Athenian law was to be banished. The tree, in Mr. Tylor's instance, was to be chopped to pieces. The slave under all the systems was to be surrendered to the relatives of the slain man, that they might do with him what they liked.[98] The deodand was an accursed thing. The original limitation of liability to surrender, when the owner was before the court, could not be accounted for if it was his liability, and not that of his property, which was in question. Even where, as in some of the cases, expiation seems to be intended rather than vengeance, the object is equally remote from an extrajudicial distress.

The foregoing history, apart from the purposes for which it has been given, well illustrates the paradox of form and substance in the development of law. In form its growth is logical. The official theory is that each new decision follows syllogistically from existing precedents. But just as the clavicle in the cat only tells of the existence of some earlier creature to which a collarbone was useful, precedents survive in the law long after the use they once served is at an end and the reason for them has been forgotten. The result of following them must often be failure and confusion from the merely logical point of view.

On the other hand, in substance the growth of the law is legislative. And this in a deeper sense than that what the courts declare to have always been the law is in fact new. It is legislative in its grounds. The very considerations which judges most rarely

[97] 3 Colquhoun, Roman Civil Law, § 2196.
[98] Lex Salica (Merkel), LXXVII.; Ed. Hilperich., § 5.

mention, and always with an apology, are the secret root from which the law draws all the juices of life. I mean, of course, considerations of what is expedient for the community concerned. Every important principle which is developed by litigation is in fact and at bottom the result of more or less definitely understood views of public policy; most generally, to be sure, under our practice and traditions, the unconscious result of instinctive preferences and inarticulate convictions, but none the less traceable to views of public policy in the last analysis. And as the law is administered by able and experienced men, who know too much to sacrifice good sense to a syllogism, it will be found that, when ancient rules maintain themselves in the way that has been and will be shown in this book, new reasons more fitted to the time have been found for them, and that they gradually receive a new content, and at last a new form, from the grounds to which they have been transplanted.

But hitherto this process has been largely unconscious. It is important, on that account, to bring to mind what the actual course of events has been. If it were only to insist on a more conscious recognition of the legislative function of the courts, as just explained, it would be useful, as we shall see more clearly further on.[99]

What has been said will explain the failure of all theories which consider the law only from its formal side, whether they attempt to deduce the *corpus* from *a priori* postulates, or fall into the humbler error of supposing the science of the law to reside in the *elegantia juris*, or logical cohesion of part with part. The truth is, that the law is always approaching, and never reaching, consistency. It is forever adopting new principles from life at one end, and it always retains old ones from history at the other, which have not yet been absorbed or sloughed off. It will become entirely consistent only when it ceases to grow.

The study upon which we have been engaged is necessary both for the knowledge and for the revision of the law.

However much we may codify the law into a series of seemingly self-sufficient propositions, those propositions will be but a phase in a continuous growth. To understand their scope fully,

[99] See Lecture III., *ad fin.*

to know how they will be dealt with by judges trained in the past which the law embodies, we must ourselves know something of that past. The history of what the law has been is necessary to the knowledge of what the law is.

Again, the process which I have described has involved the attempt to follow precedents, as well as to give a good reason for them. When we find that in large and important branches of the law the various grounds of policy on which the various rules have been justified are later inventions to account for what are in fact survivals from more primitive times, we have a right to reconsider the popular reasons, and, taking a broader view of the field, to decide anew whether those reasons are satisfactory. They may be, notwithstanding the manner of their appearance. If truth were not often suggested by error, if old implements could not be adjusted to new uses, human progress would be slow. But scrutiny and revision are justified.

But none of the foregoing considerations, nor the purpose of showing the materials for anthropology contained in the history of the law, are the immediate object here. My aim and purpose have been to show that the various forms of liability known to modern law spring from the common ground of revenge. In the sphere of contract the fact will hardly be material outside the cases which have been stated in this Lecture. But in the criminal law and the laws of torts it is of the first importance. It shows that they have started from a moral basis, from the thought that some one was to blame.

It remains to be proved that, while the terminology of morals is still retained, and while the law does still and always, in a certain sense, measure legal liability by moral standards, it nevertheless, by the very necessity of its nature, is continually transmuting those moral standards into external or objective ones, from which the actual guilt of the party concerned is wholly eliminated.

LECTURE II

THE CRIMINAL LAW

In the beginning of the first Lecture it was shown that the appeals of the early law were directed only to intentional wrongs. The appeal was a far older form of procedure than the indictment, and may be said to have had a criminal as well as a civil aspect. It had the double object of satisfying the private party for his loss, and the king for the breach of his peace. On its civil side it was rooted in vengeance. It was a proceeding to recover those compositions, at first optional, afterwards compulsory, by which a wrong-doer bought the spear from his side. Whether, so far as concerned the king, it had the same object of vengeance, or was more particularly directed to revenue, does not matter, since the claim of the king did not enlarge the scope of the action.

It would seem to be a fair inference that indictable offences were originally limited in the same way as those which gave rise to an appeal. For whether the indictment arose by a splitting up of the appeal, or in some other way, the two were closely connected.

An acquittal of the appellee on the merits was a bar to an indictment; and, on the other hand, when an appeal was fairly started, although the appellor might fail to prosecute, or might be defeated by plea, the cause might still be proceeded with on behalf of the king.[1]

The presentment, which is the other parent of our criminal procedure, had an origin distinct from the appeal. If, as has been thought, it was merely the successor of fresh suit and lynch law,[2] this also is the child of vengeance, even more clearly than the other.

[1] Cf. 2 Hawk. P. C. 303 *et seq.*; 27 Ass. 25.
[2] 2 Palgrave, Commonwealth, cxxx., cxxxi.

The desire for vengeance imports an opinion that its object is actually and personally to blame. It takes an internal standard, not an objective or external one, and condemns its victim by that. The question is whether such a standard is still accepted either in this primitive form, or in some more refined development, as is commonly supposed, and as seems not impossible, considering the relative slowness with which the criminal law has improved.

It certainly may be argued, with some force, that it has never ceased to be one object of punishment to satisfy the desire for vengeance. The argument will be made plain by considering those instances in which, for one reason or another, compensation for a wrong is out of the question.

Thus an act may be of such a kind as to make indemnity impossible by putting an end to the principal sufferer, as in the case of murder or manslaughter.

Again, these and other crimes, like forgery, although directed against an individual, tend to make others feel unsafe, and this general insecurity does not admit of being paid for.

Again, there are cases where there are no means of enforcing indemnity. In Macaulay's draft of the Indian Penal Code, breaches of contract for the carriage of passengers, were made criminal. The palanquin-bearers of India were too poor to pay damages, and yet had to be trusted to carry unprotected women and children through wild and desolate tracts, where their desertion would have placed those under their charge in great danger.

In all these cases punishment remains as an alternative. A pain can be inflicted upon the wrong-doer, of a sort which does not restore the injured party to his former situation, or to another equally good, but which is inflicted for the very purpose of causing pain. And so far as this punishment takes the place of compensation, whether on account of the death of the person to whom the wrong was done, the indefinite number of persons affected, the impossibility of estimating the worth of the suffering in money, or the poverty of the criminal, it may be said that one of its objects is to gratify the desire for vengeance. The prisoner pays with his body.

The statement may be made stronger still, and it may be said, not only that the law does, but that it ought to, make the gratification of revenge an object. This is the opinion, at any rate, of two authorities so great, and so opposed in other views, as Bishop Butler and Jeremy Bentham.[3] Sir James Stephen says, "The criminal law stands to the passion of revenge in much the same relation as marriage to the sexual appetite."[4]

The first requirement of a sound body of law is, that it should correspond with the actual feelings and demands of the community, whether right or wrong. If people would gratify the passion of revenge outside of the law, if the law did not help them, the law has no choice but to satisfy the craving itself, and thus avoid the greater evil of private retribution. At the same time, this passion is not one which we encourage, either as private individuals or as law-makers. Moreover, it does not cover the whole ground. There are crimes which do not excite it, and we should naturally expect that the most important purposes of punishment would be coextensive with the whole field of its application. It remains to be discovered whether such a general purpose exists, and if so what it is.[a] Different theories still divide opinion upon the subject.

It has been thought that the purpose of punishment is to reform the criminal; that it is to deter the criminal and others from committing similar crimes; and that it is retribution. Few would now maintain that the first of these purposes was the only one. If it were, every prisoner should be released as soon as it appears clear that he will never repeat his offence, and if he is incurable he should not be punished at all. Of course it would be hard to reconcile the punishment of death with this doctrine.

[3] Butler, Sermons, VIII. Bentham, Theory of Legislation (Principles of Penal Code, Part 2, ch. 16), Hildreth's tr., p. 309.

[4] General View of the Criminal Law of England, p. 99.

[a] [Such purpose if it does exist must have a most important bearing on principles of liability. For instance if prevention be ground of punish. the man may be punished consistently with theory when the state of his conscience at the time of his act was such as to make pun. imposs. on a theory of retribution and undesirable on a theory of vengeance. Accord. the discussion of the purpose of pun. will lead directly into the discussion of the principles of liab. wh. are the main object. I shall try to show that the purp. is prev. & that in acc. with this standard are general—starting with ethical notions & working to object. standards—viz. in 1st stage what is wrong in av. man—2d definition of this by experience determ. degree of danger.]

The main struggle lies between the other two. On the one side is the notion that there is a mystic bond between wrong and punishment; on the other, that the infliction of pain is only a means to an end. Hegel, one of the great expounders of the former view, puts it, in his quasi mathematical form, that, wrong being the negation of right, punishment is the negation of that negation, or retribution. Thus the punishment must be equal, in the sense of proportionate to the crime, because its only function is to destroy it. Others, without this logical apparatus, are content to rely upon a felt necessity that suffering should follow wrong-doing.

It is objected that the preventive theory is immoral, because it overlooks the ill-desert of wrong-doing, and furnishes no measure of the amount of punishment, except the lawgiver's subjective opinion in regard to the sufficiency of the amount of preventive suffering.[5] In the language of Kant, it treats man as a thing, not as a person; as a means, not as an end in himself. It is said to conflict with the sense of justice, and to violate the fundamental principle of all free communities, that the members of such communities have equal rights to life, liberty, and personal security.[6]

In spite of all this, probably most English-speaking lawyers would accept the preventive theory without hesitation. As to the violation of equal rights which is charged, it may be replied that the dogma of equality makes an equation between individuals only, not between an individual and the community. No society has ever admitted that it could not sacrifice individual welfare to its own existence. If conscripts are necessary for its army, it seizes them, and marches them, with bayonets in their rear, to death. It runs highways and railroads through old family places in spite of the owner's protest, paying in this instance the market value, to be sure, because no civilized government sacrifices the citizen more than it can help, but still sacrificing his will and his welfare to that of the rest.[7]

If it were necessary to trench further upon the field of morals,

[5] Wharton, Crim. Law, (8th ed.) § 8, n. 1.

[6] Ibid., § 7.

[7] Even the law recognizes that this is a sacrifice. *Commonwealth* v. *Sawin*, 2 Pick. (Mass.) 547, 549.

it might be suggested that the dogma of equality applied even to individuals only within the limits of ordinary dealings in the common run of affairs. You cannot argue with your neighbor, except on the admission for the moment that he is as wise as you, although you may by no means believe it. In the same way, you cannot deal with him, where both are free to choose, except on the footing of equal treatment, and the same rules for both. The ever-growing value set upon peace and the social relations tends to give the law of social being the appearance of the law of all being. But it seems to me clear that the *ultima ratio*, not only *regum*, but of private persons, is force, and that at the bottom of all private relations, however tempered by sympathy and all the social feelings, is a justifiable self-preference. If a man is on a plank in the deep sea which will only float one, and a stranger lays hold of it, he will thrust him off if he can. When the state finds itself in a similar position, it does the same thing.

The considerations which answer the argument of equal rights also answer the objections to treating man as a thing, and the like. If a man lives in society, he is liable to find himself so treated. The degree of civilization which a people has reached, no doubt, is marked by their anxiety to do as they would be done by. It may be the destiny of man that the social instincts shall grow to control his actions absolutely, even in anti-social situations. But they have not yet done so, and as the rules of law are or should be based upon a morality which is generally accepted, no rule founded on a theory of absolute unselfishness can be laid down without a breach between law and working beliefs.

If it be true, as I shall presently try to show, that the general principles of criminal and civil liability are the same, it will follow from that alone that theory and fact agree in frequently punishing those who have been guilty of no moral wrong, and who could not be condemned by any standard that did not avowedly disregard the personal peculiarities of the individuals concerned. If punishment stood on the moral grounds which are proposed for it, the first thing to be considered would be those limitations in the capacity for choosing rightly which arise from abnormal instincts, want of education, lack of intelligence, and all the other defects which are most marked in the criminal classes. I do not say that they should not be, or at least I do not need to for my argument. I do not say that the criminal law does more good than harm. I only say that it is not enacted or administered on that theory.

There remains to be mentioned the affirmative argument in favor of the theory of retribution, to the effect that the fitness of punishment following wrong-doing is axiomatic, and is instinctively recognized by unperverted minds. I think that it will be seen, on self-inspection, that this feeling of fitness is absolute and unconditional only in the case of our neighbors. It does not seem to me that any one who has satisfied himself that an act of his was wrong, and that he will never do it again, would feel the least need or propriety, as between himself and an earthly punishing power alone, of his being made to suffer for what he had done, although, when third persons were introduced, he might, as a philosopher, admit the necessity of hurting him to frighten others. But when our neighbors do wrong, we sometimes feel the fitness of making them smart for it, whether they have repented or not. The feeling of fitness seems to me to be only vengeance in disguise, and I have already admitted that vengeance was an element, though not the chief element, of punishment.

But, again, the supposed intuition of fitness does not seem to me to be coexistensive with the thing to be accounted for. The lesser punishments are just as fit for the lesser crimes as the greater for the greater. The demand that crime should be followed by its punishment should therefore be equal and absolute in both. Again, a *malum prohibitum* is just as much a crime as a *malum in se*. If there is any general ground for punishment, it must apply to one case as much as to the other. But it will hardly be said that, if the wrong in the case just supposed consisted of a breach of the revenue laws, and the government had been indemnified for the loss, we should feel any internal necessity that a man who had thoroughly repented of his wrong should be punished for it, except on the ground that his act was known to others. If it was known, the law would have to verify its threats in order that others might believe and tremble. But if the fact was a secret between the sovereign and the subject, the sovereign, if wholly free from passion, would undoubtedly see that punishment in such a case was wholly without justification.

On the other hand, there can be no case in which the lawmaker makes certain conduct criminal without his thereby showing a wish and purpose to prevent that conduct. Prevention would accordingly seem to be the chief and only universal purpose of punishment. The law threatens certain pains if you do certain things, intending thereby to give you a new motive for not doing them. If you persist in doing them, it has to inflict the pains in order that its threats may continue to be believed.

If this is a true account of the law as it stands, the law does undoubtedly treat the individual as a means to an end, and uses him as a tool to increase the general welfare at his own expense. It has been suggested above, that this course is perfectly proper; but even if it is wrong, our criminal law follows it, and the theory of our criminal law must be shaped accordingly.

Further evidence that our law exceeds the limits of retribution, and subordinates consideration of the individual to that of the public well-being, will be found in some doctrines which cannot be satisfactorily explained on any other ground.

The first of these is, that even the deliberate taking of life will not be punished when it is the only way of saving one's own. This principle is not so clearly established as that next to be mentioned; but it has the support of very great authority.[8] If that is the law, it must go on one of two grounds, either that self-preference is proper in the case supposed, or that, even if it is improper, the law cannot prevent it by punishment, because a threat of death at some future time can never be a sufficiently powerful motive to make a man choose death now in order to avoid the threat. If the former ground is adopted, it admits that a single person may sacrifice another to himself, and *a fortiori* that a people may. If the latter view is taken, by abandoning punishment when it can no longer be expected to prevent an act, the law abandons the retributive and adopts the preventive theory.

The next doctrine leads to still clearer conclusions. Ignorance

[8] Cf. 1 East, P. C. 294; *United States* v. *Holmes*, 1 Wall. Jr. 1; 1 Bishop, Crim. Law, §§ 347–349, 845 (6th ed.); 4 Bl. Comm. 31.

of the law is no excuse for breaking it. This substantive principle is sometimes put in the form of a rule of evidence, that every one is presumed to know the law. It has accordingly been defended by Austin and others, on the ground of difficulty of proof. If justice requires the fact to be ascertained, the difficulty of doing so is no ground for refusing to try.[b] But every one must feel that ignorance of the law could never be admitted as an excuse, even if the fact could be proved by sight and hearing in every case. Furthermore, now that parties can testify, it may be doubted whether a man's knowledge of the law is any harder to investigate than many questions which are gone into. The difficulty, such as it is, would be met by throwing the burden of proving ignorance on the law-breaker.

The principle cannot be explained by saying that we are not only commanded to abstain from certain acts, but also to find out that we are commanded. For if there were such a second command, it is very clear that the guilt of failing to obey it would bear no proportion to that of disobeying the principal command if known, yet the failure to know would receive the same punishment as the failure to obey the principal law.

The true explanation of the rule is the same as that which accounts for the law's indifference to a man's particular temperament, faculties, and so forth. Public policy sacrifices the individual to the general good. It is desirable that the burden of all should be equal, but it is still more desirable to put an end to robbery and murder. It is no doubt true that there are many cases in which the criminal could not have known that he was breaking the law, but to admit the excuse at all would be to encourage ignorance where the law-maker has determined to make men know and obey, and justice to the individual is rightly outweighed by the larger interests on the other side of the scales.

If the foregoing arguments are sound, it is already manifest that liability to punishment cannot be finally and absolutely determined by considering the actual personal unworthiness of the criminal alone. That consideration will govern only so far as the public welfare permits or demands. And if we take into account the general result which the criminal law is intended to bring

[b] [unless we are justified in sacrificing individuals to public convenience.]

about, we shall see that the actual state of mind accompanying a criminal act plays a different part from what is commonly supposed.

For the most part, the purpose of the criminal law is only to induce external conformity to rule. All law is directed to conditions of things manifest to the senses. And whether it brings those conditions to pass immediately by the use of force, as when it protects a house from a mob by soldiers, or appropriates private property to public use, or hangs a man in pursuance of a judicial sentence, or whether it brings them about mediately through men's fears, its object is equally an external result. In directing itself against robbery or murder, for instance, its purpose is to put a stop to the actual physical taking and keeping of other men's goods, or the actual poisoning, shooting, stabbing, and otherwise putting to death of other men. If those things are not done, the law forbidding them is equally satisfied, whatever the motive.

Considering this purely external purpose of the law together with the fact that it is ready to sacrifice the individual so far as necessary in order to accomplish that purpose, we can see more readily than before that the actual degree of personal guilt involved in any particular transgression cannot be the only element, if it is an element at all, in the liability incurred. So far from its being true, as is often assumed, that the condition of a man's heart or conscience ought to be more considered in determining criminal than civil liability, it might almost be said that it is the very opposite of truth. For civil liability, in its immediate working, is simply a redistribution of an existing loss between two individuals; and it will be argued in the next Lecture that sound policy lets losses lie where they fall, except where a special reason can be shown for interference. The most frequent of such reasons is, that the party who is charged has been to blame.

It is not intended to deny that criminal liability, as well as civil, is founded on blameworthiness. Such a denial would shock the moral sense of any civilized community; or, to put it another way, a law which punished conduct which would not be blameworthy in the average member of the community would be too severe for that community to bear. It is only intended to point out that, when we are dealing with that part of the law which aims more directly than any other at establishing standards of conduct, we should expect there more than elsewhere to find that the tests of liability are external, and independent of the degree of evil in the particular person's motives or intentions. The conclusion follows directly from the nature of the standards to which conformity is required.[c] These are not only external, as was shown above, but they are of general application. They do not merely require that every man should get as near as he can to the best conduct possible for him. They require him at his own peril to come up to a certain height. They take no account of incapacities, unless the weakness is so marked as to fall into well-known exceptions, such as infancy or madness. They assume that every man is as able as every other to behave as they command. If they fall on any one class harder than on another, it is on the weakest. For it is precisely to those who are most likely to err by temperament, ignorance, or folly, that the threats of the law are the most dangerous.

The reconciliation of the doctrine that liability is founded on blameworthiness with the existence of liability where the party is not to blame, will be worked out more fully in the next Lecture. It is found in the conception of the average man, the man of ordinary intelligence and reasonable prudence. Liability is said to arise out of such conduct as would be blameworthy in him. But he is an ideal being, represented by the jury when they are appealed to, and his conduct is an external or objective standard when applied to any given individual. That individual may be morally without stain, because he has less than ordinary intelligence or prudence. But he is required to have those qualities at his peril. If he has them, he will not, as a general rule, incur liability without blameworthiness.

The next step is to take up some crimes in detail, and to discover what analysis will teach with regard to them.

I will begin with murder.[d] Murder is defined by Sir James

[c] [Pass here to nature of standards expressly instead of incidentally & say that evidence in detail will be subject of this & next 2 chapt.]

[d] [The law of murder will illustrate in detail this passage from the pure moral standard of blameworthiness to an objective one which though starting from it has left it out of sight—a transition wh. (ut sup. 33) is the

Stephen, in his Digest of Criminal Law,[9] as unlawful homicide with malice aforethought. In his earlier work,[10] he explained that malice meant wickedness, and that the law had determined what states of mind were wicked in the necessary degree. Without the same preliminary he continues in his Digest as follows:—

"Malice aforethought means any one or more of the following states of mind. . . .

"(*a.*) An intention to cause the death of, or grievous bodily harm to, any person, whether such person is the person actually killed or not;

"(*b.*) Knowledge that the act which causes death will probably cause the death of, or grievous bodily harm to, some person, whether such person is the person actually killed or not, although such knowledge is accompanied by indifference whether death or grievous bodily harm is caused or not, or by a wish that it may not be caused;

"(*c.*) An intent to commit any felony whatever;

"(*d.*) An intent to oppose by force any officer of justice on his way to, in, or returning from the execution of the duty of arresting, keeping in custody, or imprisoning any person whom he is lawfully entitled to arrest, keep in custody, or imprison, or the duty of keeping the peace or dispersing an unlawful assembly, provided that the offender has notice that the person killed is such an officer so employed."

Malice, as used in common speech, includes intent, and something more. When an act is said to be done with an intent to do harm, it is meant that a wish for the harm is the motive of the act. Intent, however, is perfectly consistent with the harm being regretted as such, and being wished only as a means to something else. But when an act is said to be done maliciously, it is meant, not only that a wish for the harmful effect is the motive, but also that the harm is wished for its own sake, or, as Austin would say with more accuracy, for the sake of the pleasurable feeling which knowledge of the suffering caused by the act would excite. Now it is apparent from Sir James Stephen's enumeration,

---

chief feature of the hist. of our law. The definition retains the ethical standard untouched in form.]

[9] Art. 223. [10] General View of the Criminal Law of England, p. 116.

that of these two elements of malice the intent alone is material to murder. It is just as much murder to shoot a sentry for the purpose of releasing a friend, as to shoot him because you hate him. Malice, in the definition of murder, has not the same meaning as in common speech, and, in view of the considerations just mentioned, it has been thought to mean criminal intention.[11]

But intent again will be found to resolve itself into two things; foresight that certain consequences will follow from an act, and the wish for those consequences working as a motive which induces the act.* The question then is, whether intent, in its turn, cannot be reduced to a lower term. Sir James Stephen's statement shows that it can be, and that knowledge that the act will probably cause death, that is, foresight of the consequences of the act, is enough in murder as in tort.

For instance, a newly born child is laid naked out of doors, where it must perish as a matter of course. This is none the less murder, that the guilty party would have been very glad to have a stranger find the child and save it.[12]

But again, What is foresight of consequences? It is a picture of a future state of things called up by knowledge of the present state of things, the future being viewed as standing to the present in the relation of effect to cause. Again, we must seek a reduction to lower terms. If the known present state of things is such that the act done will very certainly cause death, and the probability is a matter of common knowledge, one who does the act, knowing the present state of things, is guilty of murder, and the law will not inquire whether he did actually foresee the consequences or not. The test of foresight is not what this very criminal foresaw, but what a man of reasonable prudence would have foreseen.

On the other hand, there must be actual present knowledge of the present facts which make an act dangerous. The act is not enough by itself. An act, it is true, imports intention in a certain sense. It is a muscular contraction, and something more. A spasm

[11] Harris, Criminal Law, p. 13.

* [This wish and motive do not necessarily accompany the act. . . . And the intent now under analysis is an intent directed to the consequences of the act.]

[12] Steph. Dig. Crim. Law, Art. 223, Illustration (6), and n. 1.

is not an act. The contraction of the muscles must be willed. And as an adult who is master of himself foresees with mysterious accuracy the outward adjustment which will follow his inward effort, that adjustment may be said to be intended. But the intent necessarily accompanying the act ends there. Nothing would follow from the act except for the environment. All acts, taken apart from their surrounding circumstances, are indifferent to the law. For instance, to crook the forefinger with a certain force is the same act whether the trigger of a pistol is next it or not. It is only the surrounding circumstances of a pistol loaded and cocked, and of a human being in such relation to it as to be manifestly likely to be hit, that make the act a wrong. Hence, it is no sufficient foundation for liability, on any sound principle, that the proximate cause of loss was an act.

The reason for requiring an act is, that an act implies a choice, and that it is felt to be impolitic and unjust to make a man answerable for harm, unless he might have chosen otherwise. But the choice must be made with a chance of contemplating the consequence complained of, or else it has no bearing on responsibility for that consequence. If this were not true, a man might be held answerable for everything which would not have happened but for his choice at some past time. For instance, for having in a fit fallen on a man, which he would not have done had he not chosen to come to the city where he was taken ill.

All foresight of the future, all choice with regard to any possible consequence of action, depends on what is known at the moment of choosing. An act cannot be wrong, even when done under circumstances in which it will be hurtful, unless those circumstances are or ought to be known. A fear of punishment for causing harm cannot work as a motive, unless the possibility of harm may be foreseen. So far, then, as criminal liability is founded upon wrong-doing in any sense, and so far as the threats and punishments of the law are intended to deter men from bringing about various harmful results, they must be confined to cases where circumstances making the conduct dangerous were known.

Still, in a more limited way, the same principle applies to knowledge that applies to foresight. It is enough that such circumstances were actually known as would have led a man of common understanding to infer from them the rest of the group making up the present state of things. For instance, if a workman on a house-top at mid-day knows that the space below him is a street in a great city, he knows facts from which a man of common understanding would infer that there were people passing below. He is therefore bound to draw that inference, or, in other words, is chargeable with knowledge of that fact also, whether he draws the inference or not. If then, he throws down a heavy beam into the street, he does an act which a person of ordinary prudence would foresee is likely to cause death, or grievous bodily harm, and he is dealt with as if he foresaw it, whether he does so in fact or not. If a death is caused by the act, he is guilty of murder.[18] But if the workman has reasonable cause to believe that the space below is a private yard from which every one is excluded, and which is used as a rubbish-heap, his act is not blameworthy, and the homicide is a mere misadventure.

To make an act which causes death murder, then, the actor ought, on principle, to know, or have notice of the facts which make the act dangerous. There are certain exceptions to this principle which will be stated presently, but they have less application to murder than to some smaller statutory crimes. The general rule prevails for the most part in murder.

But furthermore, on the same principle, the danger which in fact exists under the known circumstances ought to be of a class which a man of reasonable prudence could foresee. Ignorance of a fact and inability to foresee a consequence have the same effect on blameworthiness. If a consequence cannot be foreseen, it cannot be avoided. But there is this practical difference, that whereas, in most cases, the question of knowledge is a question of the actual condition of the defendant's consciousness, the question of what he might have foreseen is determined by the standard of the prudent man, that is, by general experience. For it is to be remembered that the object of the law is to prevent human life being endangered or taken; and that, although it so far considers blameworthiness in punishing as not to hold a man responsible for consequences which no one, or only some exceptional specialist, could have foreseen, still the reason for this

[18] 4 Bl. Comm. 192.

limitation is simply to make a rule which is not too hard for the average member of the community. As the purpose is to compel men to abstain from dangerous conduct, and not merely to restrain them from evil inclinations, the law requires them at their peril to know the teachings of common experience, just as it requires them to know the law. Subject to these explanations, it may be said that the test of murder is the degree of danger to life attending the act under the known circumstances of the case.[14]

It needs no further explanation to show that, when the particular defendant does for any reason foresee what an ordinary man of reasonable prudence would not have foreseen, the ground of exemption no longer applies. A harmful act is only excused on the ground that the party neither did foresee, nor could with proper care have foreseen harm.

It would seem, at first sight, that the above analysis ought to exhaust the whole subject of murder. But it does not without some further explanation. If a man forcibly resists an officer lawfully making an arrest, and kills him, knowing him to be an officer, it may be murder, although no act is done which, but for his official function, would be criminal at all. So, if a man does an act with intent to commit a felony, and thereby accidentally kills another; for instance, if he fires at chickens, intending to steal them, and accidentally kills the owner, whom he does not see. Such a case as this last seems hardly to be reconcilable with the general principles which have been laid down. It has been argued somewhat as follows:—The only blameworthy act is firing at the chickens, knowing them to belong to another. It is neither more nor less so because an accident happens afterwards; and hitting a man, whose presence could not have been suspected, is an accident. The fact that the shooting is felonious does not make it any more likely to kill people. If the object of the rule is to prevent such accidents, it should make accidental killing with firearms murder, not accidental killing in the effort to steal; while, if its object is to prevent stealing, it would do better to hang one thief in every thousand by lot.

Still, the law is intelligible as it stands. The general test of murder is the degree of danger attending the acts under the

[14] Cf. 4 Bl. Comm. 197.

known state of facts. If certain acts are regarded as peculiarly dangerous under certain circumstances, a legislator may make them punishable if done under these circumstances, although the danger was not generally known. The law often takes this step, although it does not nowadays often inflict death in such cases. It sometimes goes even further, and requires a man to find out present facts, as well as to foresee future harm, at his peril, although they are not such as would necessarily be inferred from the facts known.

Thus it is a statutory offence in England to abduct a girl under sixteen from the possession of the person having lawful charge of her. If a man does acts which induce a girl under sixteen to leave her parents, he is not chargeable, if he had no reason to know that she was under the lawful charge of her parents,[15] and it may be presumed that he would not be, if he had reasonable cause to believe that she was a boy. But if he knowingly abducts a girl from her parents, he must find out her age at his peril. It is no defence that he had every reason to think her over sixteen.[16] So, under a prohibitory liquor law, it has been held that, if a man sells "Plantation Bitters," it is no defence that he does not know them to be intoxicating.[17] And there are other examples of the same kind.

Now, if experience shows, or is deemed by the law-maker to show, that somehow or other deaths which the evidence makes accidental happen disproportionately often in connection with other felonies, or with resistance to officers, or if on any other ground of policy it is deemed desirable to make special efforts for the prevention of such deaths, the law-maker may consistently treat acts which, under the known circumstances, are felonious, or constitute resistance to officers, as having a sufficiently dangerous tendency to be put under a special ban. The law may, therefore, throw on the actor the peril, not only of the consequences foreseen by him, but also of consequences which, although not predicted by common experience, the legislator apprehends. I do not, however, mean to argue that the rules under

[15] *Reg.* v. *Hibbert*, L. R. 1 C. C. 184.
[16] *Reg.* v. *Prince*, L. R. 2 C. C. 154.
[17] *Commonwealth* v. *Hallett*, 103 Mass. 452.

discussion arose on the above reasoning, any more than that they are right, or would be generally applied in this country.

Returning to the main line of thought it will be instructive to consider the relation of manslaughter to murder. One great difference between the two will be found to lie in the degree of danger attaching to the act in the given state of facts. If a man strikes another with a small stick which is not likely to kill, and which he has no reason to suppose will do more than slight bodily harm, but which does kill the other, he commits manslaughter, not murder.[18] But if the blow is struck as hard as possible with an iron bar an inch thick, it is murder.[19] So if, at the time of striking with a switch, the party knows an additional fact, by reason of which he foresees that death will be the consequence of a slight blow, as, for instance, that the other has heart disease, the offence is equally murder.[20] To explode a barrel of gunpowder in a crowded street, and kill people, is murder, although the actor hopes that no such harm will be done.[21] But to kill a man by careless riding in the same street would commonly be manslaughter.[22] Perhaps, however, a case could be put where the riding was so manifestly dangerous that it would be murder.

To recur to an example which has been used already for another purpose: "When a workman flings down a stone or piece of timber into the street, and kills a man; this may be either misadventure, manslaughter, or murder, according to the circumstances under which the original act was done: if it were in a country village, where few passengers are, and he calls out to all people to have a care, it is misadventure only; but if it were in London, or other populous town, where people are continually passing, it is manslaughter, though he gives loud warning; and murder, if he knows of their passing, and gives no warning at all." [23]

The law of manslaughter contains another doctrine which should be referred to in order to complete the understanding of

[18] Stephen, Dig. Cr. Law, Art. 223, Illustr. (5); Foster, 294, 295.
[19] Cf. *Gray's case*, cited 2 Strange, 774.
[20] Steph. Dig., Art. 223, Illustr. (1).
[21] Steph. Dig., Art. 223, Illustr. (8).
[22] *Rex* v. *Mastin*, 6 C. & P. 396. Cf. *Reg.* v. *Swindall*, 2 C. & K. 230.
[23] 4 Bl. Comm. 192.

the general principles of the criminal law. This doctrine is, that provocation may reduce an offence which would otherwise have been murder to manslaughter. According to current morality, a man is not so much to blame for an act done under the disturbance of great excitement, caused by a wrong done to himself, as when he is calm. The law is made to govern men through their motives, and it must, therefore, take their mental constitution into account.

It might be urged, on the other side, that, if the object of punishment is prevention, the heaviest punishment should be threatened where the strongest motive is needed to restrain; and primitive legislation seems sometimes to have gone on that principle. But if any threat will restrain a man in a passion, a threat of less than death will be sufficient, and therefore the extreme penalty has been thought excessive.

At the same time the objective nature of legal standards is shown even here. The mitigation does not come from the fact that the defendant was beside himself with rage. It is not enough that he had grounds which would have had the same effect on every man of his standing and education. The most insulting words are not provocation, although to this day, and still more when the law was established, many people would rather die than suffer them without action. There must be provocation sufficient to justify the passion, and the law decides on general considerations what provocations are sufficient.

It is said that even what the law admits to be "provocation does not extenuate the guilt of homicide, unless the person provoked is at the time when he does the deed deprived of the power of self-control by the provocation which he has received."[24] There are obvious reasons for taking the actual state of the defendant's consciousness into account to this extent. The only ground for not applying the general rule is, that the defendant was in such a state that he could not be expected to remember or be influenced by the fear of punishment; if he could be, the ground of exception disappears. Yet even here, rightly or wrongly, the law has gone far in the direction of adopting external tests. The courts seem to have decided between murder and manslaughter on such

[24] Steph. Dig. Cr. Law, Art. 225.

grounds as the nature of the weapon used,[25] or the length of time between the provocation and the act.[26] But in other cases the question whether the prisoner was deprived of self-control by passion has been left to the jury.[27]

As the object of this Lecture is not to give an outline of the criminal law, but to explain its general theory, I shall only consider such offences as throw some special light upon the subject, and shall treat of those in such order as seems best fitted for that purpose. It will now be useful to take up malicious mischief, and to compare the malice required to constitute that offence with the malice aforethought of murder.

The charge of malice aforethought in an indictment for murder has been shown not to mean a state of the defendant's mind, as is often thought, except in the sense that he knew circumstances which did in fact make his conduct dangerous. It is, in truth, an allegation like that of negligence, which asserts that the party accused did not come up to the legal standard of action under the circumstances in which he found himself, and also that there was no exceptional fact or excuse present which took the case out of the general rule. It is an averment of a conclusion of law which is permitted to abridge the facts (positive and negative) on which it is founded.

When a statute punishes the "wilfully and maliciously" injuring another's property, it is arguable, if not clear, that something more is meant. The presumption that the second word was not added without some meaning is seconded by the unreasonableness of making every wilful trespass criminal.[28] If this reasoning prevails, *maliciously* is here used in its popular sense, and imports that the motive for the defendant's act was a wish to harm the owner of the property, or the thing itself, if living, as an end, and for the sake of the harm. Malice in this sense has nothing in common with the malice of murder.

Statutory law need not profess to be consistent with itself, or with the theory adopted by judicial decisions. Hence there is strictly no need to reconcile such a statute with the principles

[25] *Rex* v. *Shaw*, 6 C. & P. 372. [26] *Rex* v. *Oneby*, 2 Strange, 766, 773.

[27] *Rex* v. *Hayward*, 6 C. & P. 157.

[28] *Commonwealth* v. *Walden*, 3 Cush. (Mass.) 558. Cf. Steph. Gen. View of the Crim. Law, 84.

which have been explained. But there is no inconsistency. Although punishment must be confined to compelling external conformity to a rule of conduct, so far that it can always be avoided by avoiding or doing certain acts as required, with whatever intent or for whatever motive, still the prohibited conduct may not be hurtful unless it is accompanied by a particular state of feeling.

Common disputes about property are satisfactorily settled by compensation. But every one knows that sometimes secret harm is done by neighbor to neighbor out of pure malice and spite. The damage can be paid for, but the malignity calls for revenge, and the difficulty of detecting the authors of such wrongs, which are always done secretly, affords a ground for punishment, even if revenge is thought insufficient.

How far the law will go in this direction it is hard to say. The crime of arson is defined to be the malicious and wilful burning of the house of another man, and is generally discussed in close connection with malicious mischief. It has been thought that the burning was not malicious where a prisoner set fire to his prison, not from a desire to consume the building, but solely to effect his escape. But it seems to be the better opinion that this is arson,[29] in which case an intentional burning is malicious within the meaning of the rule. When we remember that arson was the subject of one of the old appeals which take us far back into the early law,[30] we may readily understand that only intentional burnings were redressed in that way.[31] The appeal of arson was brother to the appeal *de pace et plagis*. As the latter was founded on a warlike assault, the former supposed a house-firing for robbery or revenge,[32] such as that by which Njal perished in the Icelandic Saga. But this crime seems to have had the same history as others. As soon as intent is admitted to be sufficient, the law is on the high-road to an external standard. A man who intentionally sets fire to his own house, which is so near to other houses that the fire will manifestly endanger them, is guilty of arson if one of the other houses is burned in consequence.[33] In this case, an act which would not have been arson, taking only its immedi-

[29] 2 Bishop Crim. Law, § 14 (6th ed.). [30] Glanv., Lib. XIV. c. 4.

[31] Bract., fol. 146 *b*. [32] Ibid.

[33] 2 East, P. C., c. 21, §§ 7, 8, pp. 1027, 1031.

ate consequences into account, becomes arson by reason of more remote consequences which were manifestly likely to follow, whether they were actually intended or not. If that may be the effect of setting fire to things which a man has a right to burn, so far as they alone are concerned, why, on principle, should it not be the effect of any other act which is equally likely under the surrounding circumstances to cause the same harm? Cases may easily be imagined where firing a gun, or making a chemical mixture, or piling up oiled rags, or twenty other things, might be manifestly dangerous in the highest degree and actually lead to a conflagration. If, in such cases, the crime is held to have been committed, an external standard is reached, and the analysis which has been made of murder applies here.

There is another class of cases in which intent plays an important part, for quite different reasons from those which have been offered to account for the law of malicious mischief. The most obvious examples of this class are criminal attempts. Attempt and intent, of course, are two distinct things. Intent to commit a crime is not itself criminal. There is no law against a man's intending to commit a murder the day after to-morrow. The law only deals with conduct. An attempt is an overt act. It differs from the attempted crime in this, that the act has failed to bring about the result which would have given it the character of the principal crime. If an attempt to murder results in death within a year and a day, it is murder. If an attempt to steal results in carrying off the owner's goods, it is larceny.

If an act is done of which the natural and probable effect under the circumstances is the accomplishment of a substantive crime, the criminal law, while it may properly enough moderate the severity of punishment if the act has not that effect in the particular case, can hardly abstain altogether from punishing it, on any theory. It has been argued that an actual intent is all that can give the act a criminal character in such instances.[34] But if the views which I have advanced as to murder and manslaughter are sound, the same principles ought logically to determine the criminality of acts in general. Acts should be judged by their tendency under the known circumstances, not by the actual intent which accompanies them.

[34] 1 Bishop, Crim. Law, § 735 (6th ed.).

It may be true that in the region of attempts, as elsewhere, the law began with cases of actual intent, as those cases are the most obvious ones. But it cannot stop with them, unless it attaches more importance to the etymological meaning of the word *attempt* than to the general principles of punishment. Accordingly there is at least color of authority for the proposition that an act is punishable as an attempt, if, supposing it to have produced its natural and probable effect, it would have amounted to a substantive crime.[35]

But such acts are not the only punishable attempts. There is another class in which actual intent is clearly necessary, and the existence of this class as well as the name (attempt) no doubt tends to affect the whole doctrine.

Some acts may be attempts or misdemeanors which could not have effected the crime unless followed by other acts on the part of the wrong-doer. For instance, lighting a match with intent to set fire to a haystack has been held to amount to a criminal attempt to burn it, although the defendant blew out the match on seeing that he was watched.[36] So the purchase of dies for making counterfeit coin is a misdemeanor, although of course the coin would not be counterfeited unless the dies were used.[37]

In such cases the law goes on a new principle, different from that governing most substantive crimes. The reason for punishing any act must generally be to prevent some harm which is foreseen as likely to follow that act under the circumstances in which it is done. In most substantive crimes the ground on which that likelihood stands is the common working of natural causes as shown by experience. But when an act is punished the natural effect of which is not harmful under the circumstances, that ground alone will not suffice. The probability does not exist unless there are grounds for expecting that the act done will be followed by other acts in connection with which its effect will be harmful, although not so otherwise. But as in fact no such acts have followed, it cannot, in general, be assumed, from the mere doing of what has been done, that they would have followed if

[35] *Reg.* v. *Dilworth*, 2 Moo. & Rob. 531; *Reg.* v. *Jones*, 9 C. & P. 258. The statement that a man is presumed to intend the natural consequences of his acts is a mere fiction disguising the true theory. See Lecture IV.

[36] *Reg.* v. *Taylor*, 1 F. & F. 511.

[37] *Reg.* v. *Roberts*, 25 L. J. M. C. 17; *s. c.* Dearsly, C. C. 539.

the actor had not been interrupted. They would not have followed it unless the actor had chosen, and the only way generally available to show that he would have chosen to do them is by showing that he intended to do them when he did what he did. The accompanying intent in that case renders the otherwise innocent act harmful, because it raises a probability that it will be followed by such other acts and events as will all together result in harm. The importance of the intent is not to show that the act was wicked, but to show that it was likely to be followed by hurtful consequences.

It will be readily seen that there are limits to this kind of liability. The law does not punish every act which is done with the intent to bring about a crime. If a man starts from Boston to Cambridge for the purpose of committing a murder when he gets there, but is stopped by the draw and goes home, he is no more punishable than if he had sat in his chair and resolved to shoot somebody, but on second thoughts had given up the notion. On the other hand, a slave who ran after a white woman, but desisted before he caught her, has been convicted of an attempt to commit rape.[38] We have seen what amounts to an attempt to burn a haystack; but it was said in the same case, that, if the defendant had gone no further than to buy a box of matches for the purpose, he would not have been liable.

Eminent judges have been puzzled where to draw the line, or even to state the principle on which it should be drawn, between the two sets of cases. But the principle is believed to be similar to that on which all other lines are drawn by the law. Public policy, that is to say, legislative considerations, are at the bottom of the matter; the considerations being, in this case, the nearness of the danger, the greatness of the harm, and the degree of apprehension felt. When a man buys matches to fire a haystack, or starts on a journey meaning to murder at the end of it, there is still a considerable chance that he will change his mind before he comes to the point. But when he has struck the match, or cocked and aimed the pistol, there is very little chance that he will not persist to the end, and the danger becomes so great that the law steps in. With an object which could not be used in-

[38] *Lewis* v. *The State*, 35 Ala. 380.

nocently, the point of intervention might be put further back, as in the case of the purchase of a die for coining.

The degree of apprehension may affect the decision, as well as the degree of probability that the crime will be accomplished. No doubt the fears peculiar to a slave-owning community had their share in the conviction which has just been mentioned.

There is one doubtful point which should not be passed over. It has been thought that to shoot at a block of wood thinking it to be a man is not an attempt to murder,[39] and that to put a hand into an empty pocket, intending to pick it, is not an attempt to commit larceny, although on the latter question there is a difference of opinion.[40] The reason given is, that an act which could not have effected the crime if the actor had been allowed to follow it up to all results to which in the nature of things it could have led, cannot be an attempt to commit that crime when interrupted. At some point or other, of course, the law must adopt this conclusion, unless it goes on the theory of retribution for guilt, and not of prevention of harm.

But even to prevent harm effectually it will not do to be too exact. I do not suppose that firing a pistol at a man with intent to kill him is any the less an attempt to murder because the bullet misses its aim. Yet there the act has produced the whole effect possible to it in the course of nature. It is just as impossible that that bullet under those circumstances should hit that man, as to pick an empty pocket. But there is no difficulty in saying that such an act under such circumstances is so dangerous, so far as the possibility of human foresight is concerned, that it should be punished. No one can absolutely know, though many would be pretty sure, exactly where the bullet will strike; and if the harm is done, it is a very great harm. If a man fires at a block, no harm can possibly ensue, and no theft can be committed in an empty pocket, besides that the harm of successful theft is less than that of murder. Yet it might be said that even such things as those should be punished, in order to make discouragement broad enough and easy to understand.

There remain to be considered certain substantive crimes,

[39] See *M'Pherson's case*, Dearsly & Bell, 197, 201, Bramwell, B.

[40] Cf. 1 Bishop, Crim. Law, §§ 741–745 (6th ed.).

which differ in very important ways from murder and the like, and for the explanation of which the foregoing analysis of intent in criminal attempts and analogous misdemeanors will be found of service.

The type of these is larceny. Under this name acts are punished which of themselves would not be sufficient to accomplish the evil which the law seeks to prevent, and which are treated as equally criminal, whether the evil has been accomplished or not. Murder, manslaughter, and arson, on the other hand, are not committed unless the evil is accomplished, and they all consist of acts the tendency of which under the surrounding circumstances is to hurt or destroy person or property by the mere working of natural laws.

In larceny the consequences immediately flowing from the act are generally exhausted with little or no harm to the owner. Goods are removed from his possession by trespass, and that is all, when the crime is complete. But they must be permanently kept from him before the harm is done which the law seeks to prevent. A momentary loss of possession is not what has been guarded against with such severe penalties. What the law means to prevent is the loss of it wholly and forever, as is shown by the fact that it is not larceny to take for a temporary use without intending to deprive the owner of his property. If then the law punishes the mere act of taking, it punishes an act which will not of itself produce the evil effect sought to be prevented, and punishes it before that effect has in any way come to pass.

The reason is plain enough. The law cannot wait until the property has been used up or destroyed in other hands than the owner's, or until the owner has died, in order to make sure that the harm which it seeks to prevent has been done. And for the same reason it cannot confine itself to acts likely to do that harm. For the harm of permanent loss of property will not follow from the act of taking, but only from the series of acts which constitute removing and keeping the property after it has been taken. After these preliminaries, the bearing of intent upon the crime is easily seen.

According to Mr. Bishop, larceny is "the taking and removing, by trespass, of personal property which the trespasser knows to belong either generally or specially to another, with the intent to deprive such owner of his ownership therein; and perhaps it should be added, for the sake of some advantage to the trespasser, —a proposition on which the decisions are not harmonious."[41]

There must be an intent to deprive such owner of his ownership therein, it is said. But why? Is it because the law is more anxious not to put a man in prison for stealing unless he is actually wicked, than it is not to hang him for killing another? That can hardly be. The true answer is, that the intent is an index to the external event which probably would have happened, and that, if the law is to punish at all, it must, in this case, go on probabilities, not on accomplished facts. The analogy to the manner of dealing with attempts is plain. Theft may be called an attempt to permanently deprive a man of his property, which is punished with the same severity whether successful or not. If theft can rightly be considered in this way, intent must play the same part as in other attempts. An act which does not fully accomplish the prohibited result may be made wrongful by evidence that but for some interference it would have been followed by other acts co-ordinated with it to produce that result. This can only be shown by showing intent. In theft the intent to deprive the owner of his property establishes that the thief would have retained, or would not have taken steps to restore, the stolen goods. Nor would it matter that the thief afterwards changed his mind and returned the goods. From the point of view of attempt, the crime was already complete when the property was carried off.

It may be objected to this view, that, if intent is only a makeshift which from a practical necessity takes the place of actual deprivation, it ought not to be required where the actual deprivation is wholly accomplished, provided the same criminal act produces the whole effect. Suppose, for instance, that by one and the same motion a man seizes and backs another's horse over a precipice. The whole evil which the law seeks to prevent is the natural and manifestly certain consequence of the act under the known circumstances. In such a case, if the law of larceny is consistent with the theories here maintained, the act should be passed upon according to its tendency, and the actual intent of the

[41] 2 Bishop, Crim. Law, § 758 (6th ed.).

wrong-doer not in any way considered. Yet it is possible, to say the least, that even in such a case the intent would make all the difference. I assume that the act was without excuse and wrongful, and that it would have amounted to larceny, if done for the purpose of depriving the owner of his horse. Nevertheless, if it was done for the sake of an experiment, and without actual foresight of the destruction, or evil design against the owner, the trespasser might not be held a thief.

The inconsistency, if there is one, seems to be explained by the way in which the law has grown. The distinctions of the common law as to theft are not those of a broad theory of legislation; they are highly technical, and very largely dependent upon history for explanation.[42]

The type of theft is taking to one's own use.[43] It used to be, and sometimes still is, thought that the taking must be *lucri causa*, for the sake of some advantage to the thief. In such cases the owner is deprived of his property by the thief's keeping it, not by its destruction, and the permanence of his loss can only be judged of beforehand by the intent to keep. The intent is therefore always necessary, and it is naturally stated in the form of a self-regarding intent. It was an advance on the old precedents when it was decided that the intent to deprive the owner of his property was sufficient. As late as 1815 the English judges stood only six to five in favor of the proposition that it was larceny to take a horse intending to kill it for no other purpose than to destroy evidence against a friend.[44] Even that case, however, did not do away with the universality of intent as a test, for the destruction followed the taking, and it is an ancient rule that the criminality of the act must be determined by the state of things at the time of the taking, and not afterwards. Whether the law of larceny would follow what seems to be the general principle of criminal law, or would be held back by tradition, could only be decided by a case like that supposed above, where the same act accomplishes both taking and destruction. As has been suggested already, tradition might very possibly prevail.

[42] Cf. Stephen, General View of Criminal Law of England, 49 *et seq.*
[43] Cf. Stephen, General View, 49–52; 2 East. P. C. 553.
[44] *Rex* v. *Cabbage*, Russ. & Ry. 292.

Another crime in which the peculiarities noticed in larceny are still more clearly marked, and at the same time more easily explained, is burglary. It is defined as breaking and entering any dwelling-house by night with intent to commit a felony therein.[45] The object of punishing such a breaking and entering is not to prevent trespasses, even when committed by night, but only such trespasses as are the first step to wrongs of a greater magnitude, like robbery or murder.[46] In this case the function of intent when proved appears more clearly than in theft, but it is precisely similar. It is an index to the probability of certain future acts which the law seeks to prevent. And here the law gives evidence that this is the true explanation. For if the apprehended act did follow, then it is no longer necessary to allege that the breaking and entering was with that intent. An indictment for burglary which charges that the defendant broke into a dwelling-house and stole certain property, is just as good as one which alleges that he broke in with intent to steal.[47]

It is believed that enough has now been said to explain the general theory of criminal liability, as it stands at common law. The result may be summed up as follows.

All acts are indifferent *per se*.

In the characteristic type of substantive crime acts are rendered criminal because they are done under circumstances in which they will probably cause some harm which the law seeks to prevent.

The test of criminality in such cases is the degree of danger shown by experience to attend that act under those circumstances.

In such cases the *mens rea*, or actual wickedness of the party, is wholly unnecessary, and all reference to the state of his consciousness is misleading if it means anything more than that the circumstances in connection with which the tendency of his act is judged are the circumstances known to him. Even the requirement of knowledge is subject to certain limitations. A man must

[45] Cf. 4 Bl. Comm. 224; Steph. Dig. Crim. Law, Arts. 316, 319.

[46] Cf. 4 Bl. Comm. 227, 228.

[47] 1 Starkie, Cr. Pl. 177. This doctrine goes further than my argument requires. For if burglary were dealt with only on the footing of an attempt, the whole crime would have to be complete at the moment of breaking into the house. Cf. *Rex* v. *Furnival*, Russ. & Ry. 445.

find out at his peril things which a reasonable and prudent man would have inferred from the things actually known. In some cases, especially of statutory crimes, he must go even further, and, when he knows certain facts, must find out at his peril whether the other facts are present which would make the act criminal. A man who abducts a girl from her parents in England must find out at his peril whether she is under sixteen.

In some cases it may be that the consequence of the act, under the circumstances, must be actually foreseen, if it is a consequence which a prudent man would not have foreseen. The reference to the prudent man, as a standard, is the only form in which blameworthiness as such is an element of crime, and what would be blameworthy in such a man is an element;—first, as a survival of true moral standards; second, because to punish what would not be blameworthy in an average member of the community would be to enforce a standard which was indefensible theoretically, and which practically was too high for that community.

In some cases, actual malice or intent, in the common meaning of those words, is an element in crime. But it will be found that, when it is so, it is because the act when done maliciously is followed by harm which would not have followed the act alone, or because the intent raises a strong probability that an act, innocent in itself, will be followed by other acts or events in connection with which it will accomplish the result sought to be prevented by the law.

LECTURE III

TORTS.—TRESPASS AND NEGLIGENCE

THE object of the next two Lectures is to discover whether there is any common ground at the bottom of all liability in tort, and if so, what that ground is. Supposing the attempt to succeed, it will reveal the general principle of civil liability at common law. The liabilities incurred by way of contract are more or less expressly fixed by the agreement of the parties concerned, but those arising from a tort are independent of any previous consent of the wrong-doer to bear the loss occasioned by his act. If A fails to pay a certain sum on a certain day, or to deliver a lecture on a certain night, after having made a binding promise to do so, the damages which he has to pay are recovered in accordance with his consent that some or all of the harms which may be caused by his failure shall fall upon him. But when A assaults or slanders his neighbor, or converts his neighbor's property, he does a harm which he has never consented to bear, and if the law makes him pay for it, the reason for doing so must be found in some general view of the conduct which every one may fairly expect and demand from every other, whether that other has agreed to it or not.

Such a general view is very hard to find. The law did not begin with a theory. It has never worked one out. The point from which it started and that at which I shall try to show that it has arrived, are on different planes. In the progress from one to the other, it is to be expected that its course should not be straight and its direction not always visible. All that can be done is to point out a tendency, and to justify it. The tendency, which is our main concern, is a matter of fact to be gathered from the cases. But the difficulty of showing it is much enhanced by the circumstance that, until lately, the substantive law has been approached only through the categories of the forms of action. Discussions of legislative principle have been darkened by arguments on the limits between trespass and case, or on the scope of a general issue. In place of a theory of tort, we have a theory of trespass. And even within that narrower limit, precedents of the time of the assize and *jurata* have been applied without a thought of their connection with a long forgotten procedure.

Since the ancient forms of action have disappeared, a broader treatment of the subject ought to be possible. Ignorance is the best of law reformers. People are glad to discuss a question on general principles, when they have forgotten the special knowledge necessary for technical reasoning. But the present willingness to generalize is founded on more than merely negative grounds. The philosophical habit of the day, the frequency of legislation, and the ease with which the law may be changed to meet the opinions and wishes of the public, all make it natural and unavoidable that judges as well as others should openly discuss the legislative principles upon which their decisions must always rest in the end, and should base their judgments upon broad considerations of policy to which the traditions of the bench would hardly have tolerated a reference fifty years ago.

The business of the law of torts is to fix the dividing lines between those cases in which a man is liable for harm which he has done, and those in which he is not. But it cannot enable him to predict with certainty whether a given act under given circumstances will make him liable, because an act will rarely have that effect unless followed by damage, and for the most part, if not always, the consequences of an act are not known, but only guessed at as more or less probable. All the rules that the law can lay down beforehand are rules for determining the conduct which will be followed by liability if it is followed by harm,—that is, the conduct which a man pursues at his peril. The only guide for the future to be drawn from a decision against a defendant in an action of tort is that similar acts, under circumstances which cannot be distinguished except by the result from those of the defendant, are done at the peril of the actor; that if he escapes liability, it is simply because by good fortune no harm comes of his conduct in the particular event.

If, therefore, there is any common ground for all liability in tort, we shall best find it by eliminating the event as it actually turns out, and by considering only the principles on which the peril of his conduct is thrown upon the actor. We are to ask what are the elements, on the defendant's side, which must all be present before liability is possible, and the presence of which will commonly make him liable if damage follows.

The law of torts abounds in moral phraseology. It has much to say of wrongs, of malice, fraud, intent, and negligence. Hence it may naturally be supposed that the risk of a man's conduct is thrown upon him as the result of some moral short-coming. But while this notion has been entertained, the extreme opposite will be found to have been a far more popular opinion;—I mean the notion that a man is answerable for all the consequences of his acts, or, in other words, that he acts at his peril always, and wholly irrespective of the state of his consciousness upon the matter.[a]

To test the former opinion it would be natural to take up successively the several words, such as *negligence* and *intent*, which in the language of morals designate various well-understood states of mind, and to show their significance in the law. To test the latter, it would perhaps be more convenient to consider it under the head of the several forms of action. So many of our authorities are decisions under one or another of these forms, that it will not be safe to neglect them, at least in the first instance; and a compromise between the two modes of approaching the subject may be reached by beginning with the action of trespass and the notion of negligence together, leaving wrongs which are defined as intentional for the next Lecture.

Trespass lies for unintentional, as well as for intended wrongs. Any wrongful and direct application of force is redressed by that action. It therefore affords a fair field for a discussion of the general principles of liability for unintentional wrongs at common law. For it can hardly be supposed that a man's responsi-

[a] [My own view has been stated at the end of the first lecture to be (state it), and I have considered the application of that view to crimes in the last lecture. I have now to consider whether it can be maintained as to torts.]

bility for the consequences of his acts varies as the remedy happens to fall on one side or the other of the penumbra which separates trespass from the action on the case. And the greater part of the law of torts will be found under one or the other of those two heads.

It might be hastily assumed that the action on the case is founded on the defendant's negligence. But if that be so, the same doctrine must prevail in trespass. It might be assumed that trespass is founded on the defendant's having caused damage by his act, without regard to negligence. But if that be true, the law must apply the same criterion to other wrongs differing from trespass only in some technical point; as, for instance, that the property damaged was in the defendant's possession. Neither of the above assumptions, however, can be hastily permitted. It might very well be argued that the action on the case adopts the severe rule just suggested for trespass, except when the action is founded on a contract. Negligence, it might be said, had nothing to do with the common-law liability for a nuisance, and it might be added that, where negligence was a ground of liability, a special duty had to be founded in the defendant's *super se assumpsit*, or public calling.[1] On the other hand, we shall see what can be said for the proposition, that even in trespass there must at least be negligence. But whichever argument prevails for the one form of action must prevail for the other. The discussion may therefore be shortened on its technical side, by confining it to trespass so far as may be practicable without excluding light to be got from other parts of the law.[b]

As has just been hinted, there are two theories of the common-law liability for unintentional harm. Both of them seem to receive the implied assent of popular textbooks, and neither of them is wanting in plausibility and the semblance of authority.

The first is that of Austin, which is essentially the theory of a criminalist. According to him, the characteristic feature of law, properly so called, is a sanction or detriment threatened and

[1] See Lecture VII. [Mem. Another possible view that force directly exerted is governed by stricter rules than remote conseq. of force prev. expended.]

[Trespass being the stronghold of the stricter doctrine here combatted.]

imposed by the sovereign for disobedience to the sovereign's commands. As the greater part of the law only makes a man civilly answerable for breaking it, Austin is compelled to regard the liability to an action as a sanction, or, in other words, as a penalty for disobedience. It follows from this, according to the prevailing views of penal law, that such liability ought only to be based upon personal fault; and Austin accepts that conclusion, with its corollaries, one of which is that negligence means a state of the party's mind.[3] These doctrines will be referred to later, so far as necessary.

The other theory is directly opposed to the foregoing. It seems to be adopted by some of the greatest common-law authorities, and requires serious discussion before it can be set aside in favor of any third opinion which may be maintained. According to this view, broadly stated, under the common law a man *acts* at his peril. It may be held as a sort of set-off, that he is never liable for omissions except in consequence of some duty voluntarily undertaken. But the whole and sufficient ground for such liabilities as he does incur outside the last class is supposed to be that he has voluntarily acted, and that damage has ensued. If the act was voluntary, it is totally immaterial that the detriment which followed from it was neither intended nor due to the negligence of the actor.

In order to do justice to this way of looking at the subject, we must remember that the abolition of the common-law forms of pleading has not changed the rules of substantive law. Hence, although pleaders now generally allege intent or negligence, anything which would formerly have been sufficient to charge a defendant in trespass is still sufficient, notwithstanding the fact that the ancient form of action and declaration has disappeared.

In the first place, it is said, consider generally the protection given by the law to property, both within and outside the limits of the last-named action. If a man crosses his neighbor's boundary by however innocent a mistake, or if his cattle escape into his neighbor's field, he is said to be liable in trespass *quare clausum fregit*. If an auctioneer in the most perfect good faith, and in the

[3] Austin, Jurisprudence (3d ed.), 440 *et seq.*, 474, 484, Lect. XX., XXIV., XXV.

regular course of his business, sells goods sent to his rooms for the purpose of being sold, he may be compelled to pay their full value if a third person turns out to be the owner, although he has paid over the proceeds, and has no means of obtaining indemnity.

Now suppose that, instead of a dealing with the plaintiff's property, the case is that force has proceeded directly from the defendant's body to the plaintiff's body, it is urged that, as the law cannot be less careful of the persons than of the property of its subjects, the only defences possible are similar to those which would have been open to an alleged trespass on land. You may show that there was no trespass by showing that the defendant did no act; as where he was thrown from his horse upon the plaintiff, or where a third person took his hand and struck the plaintiff with it. In such cases the defendant's body is the passive instrument of an external force, and the bodily motion relied on by the plaintiff is not his act at all. So you may show a justification or excuse in the conduct of the plaintiff himself. But if no such excuse is shown, and the defendant has voluntarily acted, he must answer for the consequences, however little intended and however unforeseen. If, for instance, being assaulted by a third person, the defendant lifted his stick and accidentally hit the plaintiff, who was standing behind him, according to this view he is liable, irrespective of any negligence toward the party injured.

The arguments for the doctrine under consideration are, for the most part, drawn from precedent, but it is sometimes supposed to be defensible as theoretically sound. Every man, it is said, has an absolute right to his person, and so forth, free from detriment at the hands of his neighbors. In the cases put, the plaintiff has done nothing; the defendant, on the other hand, has chosen to act. As between the two, the party whose voluntary conduct has caused the damage should suffer, rather than one who has had no share in producing it.

We have more difficult matter to deal with when we turn to the pleadings and precedents in trespass. The declaration says nothing of negligence, and it is clear that the damage need not have been intended. The words *vi et armis* and *contra pacem*, which might seem to imply intent, are supposed to have been inserted merely to give jurisdiction to the king's court. Glanvill says it belongs to the sheriff, in case of neglect on the part of lords of franchise, to take cognizance of mêlées, blows, and even wounds, unless the accuser add a charge of breach of the king's peace (*nisi accusator adjiciat de pace Domini Regis infracta*).[3] Reeves observes, "In this distinction between the sheriff's jurisdiction and that of the king, we see the reason of the allegation in modern indictments and writs, *vi et armis*, of 'the king's crown and dignity,' 'the king's peace,' and 'the peace,'—this last expression being sufficient, after the peace of the sheriff had ceased to be distinguished as a separate jurisdiction."[4]

Again, it might be said that, if the defendant's intent or neglect was essential to his liability, the absence of both would deprive his act of the character of a trespass, and ought therefore to be admissible under the general issue. But it is perfectly well settled at common law that "Not guilty" only denies the act.[5]

Next comes the argument from authority. I will begin with an early and important case.[6] It was trespass *quare clausum*. The defendant pleaded that he owned adjoining land, upon which was a thorn hedge; that he cut the thorns, and that they, against his will (*ipso invito*), fell on the plaintiff's land, and the defendant went quickly upon the same, and took them, which was the trespass complained of. And on demurrer judgment was given for the plaintiff. The plaintiff's counsel put cases which have been often repeated. One of them, Fairfax, said: "There is a diversity between an act resulting in a felony, and one resulting in a trespass. . . . If one is cutting trees, and the boughs fall on a man and wound him, in this case he shall have an action of trespass, &c., and also, sir, if one is shooting at butts, and his bow shakes in his hands, and kills a man, *ipso invito*, it is no

[3] Lib. I. c. 2, *ad fin.*

[4] Hist. English Law, I. 113 (bis), n. *a*; Id., ed. Finlason, I. 178, n. 1. Fitzherbert (N. B. 85, F.) says that in the vicontiel writ of trespass, which is not returnable into the king's court, it shall not be said *quare vi et armis*. Cf. Ib. 86, H.

[5] *Milman* v. *Dolwell*, 2 Camp. 378; *Knapp* v. *Salsbury*, 2 Camp. 500; *Pearcy* v. *Walter*, 6 C. & P. 232; *Hall* v. *Fearnley*, 3 Q. B. 919.

[6] Y. B. 6 Ed. IV. 7, pl. 18, A. D. 1466; cf. Ames, Cases in Tort, 69, for a translation, which has been followed for the most part.

felony, as has been said, &c.; but if he wounds one by shooting, he shall have a good action of trespass against him, and yet the shooting was lawful, &c., and the wrong which the other receives was against his will, &c.; and so here, &c." Brian, another counsel, states the whole doctrine, and uses equally familiar illustrations. "When one does a thing, he is bound to do it in such a way that by his act no prejudice or damage shall be done to &c. As if I am building a house, and when the timber is being put up a piece of timber falls on my neighbor's house and breaks his house, he shall have a good action, &c.; and yet the raising of the house was lawful, and the timber fell, *me invito*, &c. And so if one assaults me and I cannot escape, and I in self-defence lift my stick to strike him, and in lifting it hit a man who is behind me, in this case he shall have an action against me, yet my raising my stick was lawful in self-defence, and I hit him, *me invito*, &c.; and so here, &c."

"Littleton, J. to the same intent, and if a man is damaged he ought to be recompensed. . . . If your cattle come on my land and eat my grass, notwithstanding you come freshly and drive them out, you ought to make amends for what your cattle have done, be it more or less. . . . And, sir, if this should be law that he might enter and take the thorns, for the same reason, if he cut a large tree, he might come with his wagons and horses to carry the trees off, which is not reason, for perhaps he has corn or other crops growing, &c., and no more here, for the law is all one in great things and small. . . . Choke, C. J. to the same intent, for when the principal thing was not lawful, that which depends upon it was not lawful: for when he cut the thorns and they fell on my land, this falling was not lawful, and therefore his coming to take them out was not lawful. As to what was said about their falling in *ipso invito*, that is no plea, but he ought to show that he could not do it in any other way, or that he did all that was in his power to keep them out."

Forty years later,[7] the Year Books report Rede, J. as adopting the argument of Fairfax in the last case. In trespass, he says, "the intent cannot be construed; but in felony it shall be. As when a man shoots at butts and kills a man, it is not felony et il ser̃ come n'avoit l'entent de luy tuer; and so of a tiler on a house

[7] Y. B. 21 Hen. VII. 27, pl. 5, A. D. 1506.

who with a stone kills a man unwittingly, it is not felony.[8] But when a man shoots at the butts and wounds a man, though it is against his will, he shall be called a trespasser against his intent."

There is a series of later shooting cases, *Weaver* v. *Ward*,[9] *Dickenson* v. *Watson*,[10] and *Underwood* v. *Hewson*,[11] followed by the Court of Appeals of New York in *Castle* v. *Duryee*,[12] in which defences to the effect that the damage was done accidentally and by misfortune, and against the will of the defendant, were held insufficient.

In the reign of Queen Elizabeth it was held that where a man with a gun at the door of his house shot at a fowl, and thereby set fire to his own house and to the house of his neighbor, he was liable in an action on the case generally, the declaration not being on the custom of the realm, "viz. for negligently keeping his fire." "For the injury is the same, although this mischance was not by a common negligence, but by misadventure." [13]

The above-mentioned instances of the stick and shooting at butts became standard illustrations; they are repeated by Sir Thomas Raymond, in *Bessey* v. *Olliot*,[14] by Sir William Blackstone, in the famous squib case,[15] and by other judges, and have become familiar through the textbooks. Sir T. Raymond, in the above case, also repeats the thought and almost the words of Littleton, J., which have been quoted, and says further: "In all civil acts the law doth not so much regard the intent of the actor, as the loss and damage of the party suffering." Sir William Blackstone also adopts a phrase from *Dickenson* v. *Watson*, just cited: "Nothing but inevitable necessity" is a justification. So Lord Ellenborough, in *Leame* v. *Bray*: [16] "If the injury were received from the personal act of another, it was deemed sufficient to

[8] Cf. Bract, fol. 136 *b*. But cf. Stat. of Gloucester, 6 Ed. I. c. 9; Y. B. 2 Hen. IV. 18, pl. 8, by Thirning; Essays in Ang. Sax. Law, 276.

[9] Hobart, 134, A. D. 1616.

[10] Sir T. Jones, 205, A. D. 1682.

[11] 1 Strange, 596, A. D. 1723.

[12] 2 Keyes, 169, A. D. 1865.

[13] *Anonymous*, Cro. Eliz. 10, A. D. 1582.

[14] Sir T. Raym. 467, A. D. 1682.

[15] *Scott* v. *Shepherd*, 2 Wm. Bl. 892, A. D. 1773.

[16] 3 East, 593. See, further, Coleridge's note to 3 Bl. Comm. 123; Saunders, Negligence, ch. 1, § 1; argument in *Fletcher* v. *Rylands*, 3 H. & C. 774, 783; Lord Cranworth, in S. C., L. R. 3 H. L. 330, 341.

make it trespass"; or, according to the more frequently quoted language of Grose, J., in the same case: "Looking into all the cases from the Year Book in the 21 H. VII. down to the latest decision on the subject, I find the principle to be, that if the injury be done by the act of the party himself at the time, or he be the immediate cause of it, though it happen accidentally or by misfortune, yet he is answerable in trespass." Further citations are deemed unnecessary.

In spite, however, of all the arguments which may be urged for the rule that a man acts at his peril, it has been rejected by very eminent courts, even under the old forms of action. In view of this fact, and of the further circumstance that, since the old forms have been abolished, the allegation of negligence has spread from the action on the case to all ordinary declarations in tort which do not allege intent, probably many lawyers would be surprised that any one should think it worth while to go into the present discussion. Such is the natural impression to be derived from daily practice. But even if the doctrine under consideration had no longer any followers, which is not the case, it would be well to have something more than daily practice to sustain our views upon so fundamental a question; as it seems to me at least, the true principle is far from being articulately grasped by all who are interested in it, and can only be arrived at after a careful analysis of what has been thought hitherto. It might be thought enough to cite the decisions opposed to the rule of absolute responsibility, and to show that such a rule is inconsistent with admitted doctrines and sound policy. But we may go further with profit, and inquire whether there are not strong grounds for thinking that the common law has never known such a rule, unless in that period of dry precedent which is so often to be found midway between a creative epoch and a period of solvent philosophical reaction. Conciliating the attention of those who, contrary to most modern practitioners, still adhere to the strict doctrine, by reminding them once more that there are weighty decisions to be cited adverse to it, and that, if they have involved an innovation, the fact that it has been made by such magistrates as Chief Justice Shaw goes far to prove that the change was politic, I think I may assert that a little reflection will show that it was required not only by policy, but by consistency. I will begin with the latter.

The same reasoning which would make a man answerable in trespass for all damage to another by force directly resulting from his own act, irrespective of negligence or intent, would make him answerable in case for the like damage similarly resulting from the act of his servant, in the course of the latter's employment. The discussions of the company's negligence in many railway cases [17] would therefore be wholly out of place, for although, to be sure, there is a contract which would make the company liable for negligence, that contract cannot be taken to diminish any liability which would otherwise exist for a trespass on the part of its employees.

More than this, the same reasoning would make a defendant responsible for all damage, however remote, of which his act could be called the cause. So long, at least, as only physical or irresponsible agencies, however unforeseen, co-operated with the act complained of to produce the result, the argument which would resolve the case of accidentally striking the plaintiff, when lifting a stick in necessary self-defence, adversely to the defendant, would require a decision against him in every case where his act was a factor in the result complained of. The distinction between a direct application of force, and causing damage indirectly, or as a more remote consequence of one's act, although it may determine whether the form of action should be trespass or case, does not touch the theory of responsibility, if that theory be that a man acts at his peril. As was said at the outset, if the strict liability is to be maintained at all, it must be maintained throughout. A principle cannot be stated which would retain the strict liability in trespass while abandoning it in case. It cannot be said that trespass is for acts alone, and case for consequences of those acts. All actions of trespass are for consequences of acts, not for the acts themselves. And some actions of trespass are for consequences more remote from the defendant's act than in other instances where the remedy would be case.

An act is always a voluntary muscular contraction, and nothing

[17] Ex. gr. *Metropolitan Railway Co.* v. *Jackson*, 3 App. Cas. 193. See *M'Manus* v. *Crickett*, 1 East. 106, 108.

else. The chain of physical sequences which it sets in motion or directs to the plaintiff's harm is no part of it, and very generally a long train of such sequences intervenes. An example or two will make this extremely clear.

When a man commits an assault and battery with a pistol, his only act is to contract the muscles of his arm and forefinger in a certain way, but it is the delight of elementary writers to point out what a vast series of physical changes must take place before the harm is done. Suppose that, instead of firing a pistol, he takes up a hose which is discharging water on the sidewalk, and directs it at the plaintiff, he does not even set in motion the physical causes which must co-operate with his act to make a battery. Not only natural causes, but a living being, may intervene between the act and its effect. *Gibbons* v. *Pepper*,[18] which decided that there was no battery when a man's horse was frightened by accident or a third person and ran away with him, and ran over the plaintiff, takes the distinction that, if the rider by spurring is the cause of the accident, then he is guilty. In *Scott* v. *Shepherd*,[19] already mentioned, trespass was maintained against one who had thrown a squib into a crowd, where it was tossed from hand to hand in self-defence until it burst and injured the plaintiff. Here even human agencies were a part of the chain between the defendant's act and the result, although they were treated as more or less nearly automatic, in order to arrive at the decision.

Now I repeat, that, if principle requires us to charge a man in trespass when his act has brought force to bear on another through a comparatively short train of intervening causes, in spite of his having used all possible care, it requires the same liability, however numerous and unexpected the events between the act and the result. If running a man down is a trespass when the accident can be referred to the rider's act of spurring, why is it not a tort in every case, as was argued in *Vincent* v. *Stinehour*,[20] seeing that it can always be referred more remotely to his act of mounting and taking the horse out?

Why is a man not responsible for the consequences of an

[18] 1 Ld. Raym. 38; S. C. Salk. 637; 4 Mod. 404; A. D. 1695.
[19] 2 Wm. Bl. 892. Cf. *Clark* v. *Chambers*, 3 Q. B. D. 327, 330, 338.
[20] 7 Vt. 62.

act innocent in its direct and obvious effects, when those consequences would not have followed but for the intervention of a series of extraordinary, although natural, events? The reason is, that, if the intervening events are of such a kind that no foresight could have been expected to look out for them, the defendant is not to blame for having failed to do so. It seems to be admitted by the English judges that, even on the question whether the acts of leaving dry trimmings in hot weather by the side of a railroad, and then sending an engine over the track, are negligent, —that is, are a ground of liability,—the consequences which might reasonably be anticipated are material.[21] Yet these are acts which, under the circumstances, can hardly be called innocent in their natural and obvious effects. The same doctrine has been applied to acts in violation of statute which could not reasonably have been expected to lead to the result complained of.[22]

But there is no difference in principle between the case where a natural cause or physical factor intervenes after the act in some way not to be foreseen, and turns what seemed innocent to harm, and the case where such a cause or factor intervenes, unknown, at the time; as, for the matter of that, it did in the English cases cited. If a man is excused in the one case because he is not to blame, he must be in the other. The difference taken in *Gibbons* v. *Pepper*, cited above, is not between results which are and those which are not the consequences of the defendant's acts: it is between consequences which he was bound as a reasonable man to contemplate, and those which he was not. Hard spurring is just so much more likely to lead to harm than merely riding a horse in the street, that the court thought that the defendant would be bound to look out for the consequences of the one,

[21] *Smith* v. *London & South-Western Railway Co.*, L. R. 6 C. P. 14, 21. Cf. s. c., 5 id. 98, 103, 106.

[22] *Sharp* v. *Powell*, L. R. 7 C. P. 253. Cf. *Clark* v. *Chambers*, 3 Q. B. D. 327, 336–338. Many American cases could be cited which carry the doctrine further. But it is desired to lay down no proposition which admits of controversy, and it is enough for the present purposes that *Si home fait un loyal act, que apres devint illoyal, ceo est damnum sine injuria*. Latch, 13. I purposely omit any discussion of the true rule of damages where it is once settled that a wrong has been done. The text regards only the tests by which it is decided whether a wrong has been done.

while it would not hold him liable for those resulting merely from the other; because the possibility of being run away with when riding quietly, though familiar, is comparatively slight. If, however, the horse had been unruly, and had been taken into a frequented place for the purpose of being broken, the owner might have been liable, because "it was his fault to bring a wild horse into a place where mischief might probably be done." [23]

To return to the example of the accidental blow with a stick lifted in self-defence, there is no difference between hitting a person standing in one's rear and hitting one who was pushed by a horse within range of the stick just as it was lifted, provided that it was not possible, under the circumstances, in the one case to have known, in the other to have anticipated, the proximity. In either case there is wanting the only element which distinguishes voluntary acts from spasmodic muscular contractions as a ground of liability. In neither of them, that is to say, has there been an opportunity of choice with reference to the consequence complained of,—a chance to guard against the result which has come to pass. A choice which entails a concealed consequence is as to that consequence no choice.

The general principle of our law is that loss from accident must lie where it falls, and this principle is not affected by the fact that a human being is the instrument of misfortune. But relatively to a given human being anything is accident which he could not fairly have been expected to contemplate as possible, and therefore to avoid. In the language of the late Chief Justice Nelson of New York: "No case or principle can be found, or if found can be maintained, subjecting an individual to liability for an act done without fault on his part. . . . All the cases concede that an injury arising from inevitable accident, or, which in law or reason is the same thing, from an act that ordinary human care and foresight are unable to guard against, is but the misfortune of the sufferer, and lays no foundation for legal responsibility." [24] If this were not so, any act would be sufficient, however remote, which set in motion or opened the door for a

[23] *Mitchil* v. *Alestree*, 1 Ventris, 295; s. c., 3 Keb. 650; 2 Lev. 172. Compare *Hammack* v. *White*, 11 C. B. N. s. 588; *infra*, p. 125.

[24] *Harvey* v. *Dunlop*, Hill & Denio, (Lalor,) 193.

series of physical sequences ending in damage; such as riding the horse, in the case of the runaway, or even coming to a place where one is seized with a fit and strikes the plaintiff in an unconscious spasm. Nay, why need the defendant have acted at all, and why is it not enough that his existence has been at the expense of the plaintiff? The requirement of an act is the requirement that the defendant should have made a choice. But the only possible purpose of introducing this moral element is to make the power of avoiding the evil complained of a condition of liability. There is no such power where the evil cannot be foreseen.[25] Here we reach the argument from policy, and I shall accordingly postpone for a moment the discussion of trespasses upon land, and of conversions, and will take up the liability for cattle separately at a later stage.

A man need not, it is true, do this or that act,—the term *act* implies a choice,—but he must act somehow. Furthermore, the public generally profits by individual activity. As action cannot be avoided, and tends to the public good, there is obviously no policy in throwing the hazard of what is at once desirable and inevitable upon the actor.

The state might conceivably make itself a mutual insurance company against accidents, and distribute the burden of its citizens' mishaps among all its members. There might be a pension for paralytics, and state aid for those who suffered in person or estate from tempest or wild beasts. As between individuals it might adopt the mutual insurance principle *pro tanto*, and divide damages when both were in fault, as in the *rusticum judicium* of the admiralty, or it might throw all loss upon the actor irrespective of fault. The state does none of these things, however, and the prevailing view is that its cumbrous and expensive machinery ought not to be set in motion unless some clear benefit is to be derived from disturbing the *status quo*. State interference is an evil, where it cannot be shown to be a good. Universal insurance, if desired, can be better and more cheaply accomplished by private enterprise. The undertaking to redistribute losses simply on the ground that they resulted from the defendant's act would not only be open to these objections, but, as it is hoped

[25] See Lecture II. pp. 46, 47.

the preceding discussion has shown, to the still graver one of offending the sense of justice. Unless my act is of a nature to threaten others, unless under the circumstances a prudent man would have foreseen the possibility of harm, it is no more justifiable to make me indemnify my neighbor against the consequences, than to make me do the same thing if I had fallen upon him in a fit, or to compel me to insure him against lightning.

I must now recur to the conclusions drawn from innocent trespasses upon land, and conversions, and the supposed analogy of those cases to trespasses against the person, lest the law concerning the latter should be supposed to lie between two antinomies, each necessitating with equal cogency an opposite conclusion to the other.

Take first the case of trespass upon land attended by actual damage. When a man goes upon his neighbor's land, thinking it is his own, he intends the very act or consequence complained of. He means to intermeddle with a certain thing in a certain way, and it is just that intended intermeddling for which he is sued.[26] Whereas, if he accidentally hits a stranger as he lifts his staff in self-defence, the fact, which is the gist of the action,—namely, the contact between the staff and his neighbor's head,—was not intended, and could not have been foreseen. It might be answered, to be sure, that it is not for intermeddling with property, but for intermeddling with the plaintiff's property, that a man is sued; and that in the supposed cases, just as much as in that of the accidental blow, the defendant is ignorant of one of the facts making up the total environment, and which must be present to make his action wrong. He is ignorant, that is to say, that the true owner either has or claims any interest in the property in question, and therefore he does not intend a wrongful act, because he does not mean to deal with his neighbor's property. But the answer to this is, that he does intend to do the damage complained of. One who diminishes the value of property by intentional damage knows it belongs to somebody. If he thinks it belongs to himself, he expects whatever harm he may do to come out of his own pocket. It would be odd if he were to get rid of the burden by discovering that it belonged to his neighbor.

[26] Cf. *Hobart* v. *Hagget*, 3 Fairf. (Me.) 67.

It is a very different thing to say that he who intentionally does harm must bear the loss, from saying that one from whose acts harm follows accidentally, as a consequence which could not have been foreseen, must bear it.

Next, suppose the act complained of is an exercise of dominion over the plaintiff's property, such as a merely technical trespass or a conversion. If the defendant thought that the property belonged to himself, there seems to be no abstract injustice in requiring him to know the limits of his own titles, or, if he thought that it belonged to another, in holding him bound to get proof of title before acting. Consider, too, what the defendant's liability amounts to, if the act, whether an entry upon land or a conversion of chattels, has been unattended by damage to the property, and the thing has come back to the hands of the true owner. The sum recovered is merely nominal, and the payment is nothing more than a formal acknowledgment of the owner's title; which, considering the effect of prescription and statutes of limitation upon repeated acts of dominion, is no more than right.[27] All semblance of injustice disappears when the defendant is allowed to avoid the costs of an action by tender or otherwise.

But suppose the property has not come back to the hands of the true owner. If the thing remains in the hands of the defendant, it is clearly right that he should surrender it. And if instead of the thing itself he holds the proceeds of a sale, it is as reasonable to make him pay over its value in trover or assumpsit as it would have been to compel a surrender of the thing. But the question whether the defendant has subsequently paid over the proceeds of the sale of a chattel to a third person, cannot affect the rights of the true owner of the chattel. In the supposed case of an auctioneer, for instance, if he had paid the true owner, it would have been an answer to his bailor's claim. If he has paid his bailor instead, he has paid one whom he was not bound to pay, and no general principle requires that this should be held to divest the plaintiff's right.

Another consideration affecting the argument that the law as to trespasses upon property establishes a general principle, is that the defendant's knowledge or ignorance of the plaintiff's

[27] See *Bonomi* v. *Backhouse*, El. Bl. & El. 622, Coleridge, J., at p. 640.

title is likely to lie wholly in his own breast, and therefore hardly admits of satisfactory proof. Indeed, in many cases it cannot have been open to evidence at all at the time when the law was settled, before parties were permitted to testify. Accordingly, in *Basely v. Clarkson,*[28] where the defence set up to an action of trespass *quare clausum* was that the defendant in mowing his own land involuntarily and by mistake mowed down some of the plaintiff's grass, the plaintiff had judgment on demurrer. "For it appears the fact was voluntary, and his intention and knowledge are not traversable; they can't be known."

This language suggests that it would be sufficient to explain the law of trespass upon property historically, without attempting to justify it. For it seems to be admitted that if the defendant's mistake could be proved it might be material.[29] It will be noticed, further, that any general argument from the law of trespass upon land to that governing trespass against the person is shown to be misleading by the law as to cattle. The owner is bound at his peril to keep them off his neighbor's premises, but he is not bound at his peril in all cases to keep them from his neighbor's person.

The objections to such a decision as supposed in the case of an auctioneer do not rest on the general theory of liability, but spring altogether from the special exigencies of commerce. It does not become unjust to hold a person liable for unauthorized intermeddling with another's property, until there arises the practical necessity for rapid dealing. But where this practical necessity exists, it is not surprising to find, and we do find, a different tendency in the law. The absolute protection of property, however natural to a primitive community more occupied in production than in exchange, is hardly consistent with the requirements of modern business. Even when the rules which we have been considering were established, the traffic of the public markets was governed by more liberal principles. On the continent of Europe it was long ago decided that the policy of protecting titles must yield to the policy of protecting trade. Casaregis held that the general principle *nemo plus juris in alium transferre potest quam ipse habet* must give way in mercantile transactions

[28] 3 Levinz, 37, A. D. 1681.

[29] Compare the rule as to cattle in Y. B. 22 Edw. IV. 8, pl. 24, stated below, p. 94.

to *possession vaut titre.*[30] In later times, as markets overt have lost their importance, the Factors' Acts and their successive amendments have tended more and more in the direction of adopting the Continental doctrine.

I must preface the argument from precedent with a reference to what has been said already in the first Lecture about early forms of liability, and especially about the appeals. It was there shown that the appeals *de pace et plagis* and of mayhem became the action of trespass, and that those appeals and the early actions of trespass were always, so far as appears, for intentional wrongs.[31]

The *contra pacem* in the writ of trespass was no doubt inserted to lay a foundation for the king's writ; but there seems to be no reason to attribute a similar purpose to *vi et armis,* or *cum vi sua,* as it was often put. Glanvill says that wounds are within the sheriff's jurisdiction, unless the appellor adds a charge of breach of the king's peace.[32] Yet the wounds are given *vi et armis* as much in the one case as in the other. Bracton says that the lesser wrongs described by him belong to the king's jurisdiction, "because they are sometimes against the peace of our lord the king,"[33] while, as has been observed, they were supposed to be always committed intentionally. It might even perhaps be inferred that the allegation *contra pacem* was originally material, and it will be remembered that trespasses formerly involved the liability to pay a fine to the king.[34]

If it be true that trespass was originally confined to intentional wrongs, it is hardly necessary to consider the argument drawn from the scope of the general issue. In form it was a mitigation of the strict denial *de verbo in verbum* of the ancient procedure, to which the inquest given by the king's writ was unknown.[35] The strict form seems to have lasted in England some time after the trial of the issue by recognition was introduced.[36] When a recognition was granted, the inquest was, of course, only com-

[30] Disc. 123, pr.; 124, §§ 2, 3. As to the historical origin of the latter rule, compare Lecture V.

[31] Lecture I, pp. 6, 7. [32] Lib. I. c. 2, *ad fin.* [33] Fol. 155.

[34] Bro. *Trespass,* pl. 119; Finch, 198; 3 Bl. Comm. 118, 119.

[35] See Brunner, Schwurgerichte, p. 171.

[36] An example of the year 1195 will be found in Mr. Bigelow's very interesting and valuable Placita Anglo-Normannica, p. 285, citing Rot. Cur. Regis, 38; s. c.? Abbr. Plac., fol. 2, Ebor. rot. 5. The suit was by way of appeal; the cause of action, a felonious trespass. Cf. Bract., fol. 144 *a.*

petent to speak to the facts, as has been said above.[87] When the general issue was introduced, trespass was still confined to intentional wrongs.

We may now take up the authorities. It will be remembered that the earlier precedents are of a date when the assize and *jurata* had not given place to the modern jury. These bodies spoke from their own knowledge to an issue defined by the writ, or to certain familiar questions of fact arising in the trial of a cause, but did not hear the whole case upon evidence adduced. Their function was more limited than that which has been gained by the jury, and it naturally happened that, when they had declared what the defendant had done, the judges laid down the standard by which those acts were to be measured without their assistance. Hence the question in the Year Books is not a loose or general inquiry of the jury whether they think the alleged trespasser was negligent on such facts as they may find, but a well-defined issue of law, to be determined by the court, whether certain acts set forth upon the record are a ground of liability. It is possible that the judges may have dealt pretty strictly with defendants, and it is quite easy to pass from the premise that defendants have been held trespassers for a variety of acts, without mention of neglect, to the conclusion that any act by which another was damaged will make the actor chargeable. But a more exact scrutiny of the early books will show that liability in general, then as later, was founded on the opinion of the tribunal that the defendant ought to have acted otherwise, or, in other words, that he was to blame.

Returning first to the case of the thorns in the Year Book,[88] it will be seen that the falling of the thorns into the plaintiff's close, although a result not wished by the defendant, was in no other sense against his will. When he cut the thorns, he did an act which obviously and necessarily would have that consequence, and he must be taken to have foreseen and not to have prevented it. Choke, C. J. says, "As to what was said about their falling in, *ipso invito*, that is no plea, but he ought to show that he could

[87] An example may be seen in the Year Book, 30 & 31 Edward I. (Horwood), p. 106.

[88] 6 Ed. IV. 7, pl. 18.

not do it in any other way, or that he did all in his power to keep them out"; and both the judges put the unlawfulness of the entry upon the plaintiff's land as a consequence of the unlawfulness of dropping the thorns there. Choke admits that, if the thorns or a tree had been blown over upon the plaintiff's land, the defendant might have entered to get them. Chief Justice Crew says of this case, in *Millen* v. *Fawdry*,[39] that the opinion was that "trespass lies, because he did not plead that he did his best endeavor to hinder their falling there; yet this was a hard case." The statements of law by counsel in argument may be left on one side, although Brian is quoted and mistaken for one of the judges by Sir William Blackstone, in *Scott* v. *Shepherd*.

The principal authorities are the shooting cases, and, as shooting is an extra-hazardous act, it would not be surprising if it should be held that men do it at their peril in public places. The liability has been put on the general ground of fault, however, wherever the line of necessary precaution may be drawn. In *Weaver* v. *Ward*,[40] the defendant set up that the plaintiff and he were skirmishing in a trainband, and that when discharging his piece he wounded the plaintiff by accident and misfortune, and against his own will. On demurrer, the court says that "no man shall be excused of a trespass, . . . except it may be judged utterly without his fault. As if a man by force take my hand and strike you, or if here the defendant had said, that the plaintiff ran cross his piece when it was discharging, or had set forth the case with the circumstances so as it had appeared to the court that it had been inevitable, and that the defendant *had committed no negligence* to give occasion to the hurt." The later cases simply follow *Weaver* v. *Ward*.

The quotations which were made above in favor of the strict doctrine from Sir T. Raymond, in *Bessey* v. *Olliot*, and from Sir William Blackstone, in *Scott* v. *Shepherd*, are both taken from dissenting opinions. In the latter case it is pretty clear that the majority of the court considered that to repel personal danger by instantaneously tossing away a squib thrown by another upon one's stall was not a trespass, although a new motion was thereby imparted to the squib, and the plaintiff's eye was put out in

[39] Popham, 151; Latch, 13, 119, A. D. 1605. [40] Hobart, 134, A. D. 1616.

consequence. The last case cited above, in stating the arguments for absolute responsibility, was *Leame* v. *Bray*.[41] The question under discussion was whether the action (for running down the plaintiff) should not have been case rather than trespass, the defendant founding his objection to trespass on the ground that the injury happened through his neglect, but was not done wilfully. There was therefore no question of absolute responsibility for one's acts before the court, as negligence was admitted; and the language used is all directed simply to the proposition that the damage need not have been done intentionally.

In *Wakeman* v. *Robinson*,[42] another runaway case, there was evidence that the defendant pulled the wrong rein, and that he ought to have kept a straight course. The jury were instructed that, if the injury was occasioned by an immediate act of the defendant, it was immaterial whether the act was wilful or accidental. On motion for a new trial, Dallas, C. J. said, "If the accident happened entirely without default on the part of the defendant, or blame imputable to him, the action does not lie. . . . The accident was clearly occasioned by the default of the defendant. The weight of evidence was all that way. I am now called upon to grant a new trial, contrary to the justice of the case, upon the ground, that the jury were not called on to consider whether the accident was unavoidable, or occasioned by the fault of the defendant. There can be no doubt that the learned judge who presided would have taken the opinion of the jury on that ground, if he had been requested so to do." This language may have been inapposite under the defendant's plea (the general issue), but the pleadings were not adverted to, and the doctrine is believed to be sound.

In America there have been several decisions to the point. In *Brown* v. *Kendall*,[43] Chief Justice Shaw settled the question for Massachusetts. That was trespass for assault and battery, and it appeared that the defendant, while trying to separate two fighting dogs, had raised his stick over his shoulder in the act of striking, and had accidentally hit the plaintiff in the eye, inflicting upon him a severe injury. The case was stronger for the plaintiff than if the defendant had been acting in self-defence; but the

[41] 3 East, 593. [42] 1 Bing. 213, A. D. 1823. [43] 6 Cush. 292.

court held that, although the defendant was bound by no duty to separate the dogs, yet, if he was doing a lawful act, he was not liable unless he was wanting in the care which men of ordinary prudence would use under the circumstances, and that the burden was on the plaintiff to prove the want of such care.

In such a matter no authority is more deserving of respect than that of Chief Justice Shaw, for the strength of that great judge lay in an accurate appreciation of the requirements of the community whose officer he was. Some, indeed many, English judges could be named who have surpassed him in accurate technical knowledge, but few have lived who were his equals in their understanding of the grounds of public policy to which all laws must ultimately be referred. It was this which made him, in the language of the late Judge Curtis, the greatest *magistrate* which this country has produced.

Brown v. *Kendall* has been followed in Connecticut,[44] in a case where a man fired a pistol, in lawful self-defence as he alleged, and hit a bystander. The court was strongly of opinion that the defendant was not answerable on the general principles of trespass, unless there was a failure to use such care as was practicable under the circumstances. The foundation of liability in trespass as well as case was said to be negligence. The Supreme Court of the United States has given the sanction of its approval to the same doctrine.[45] The language of *Harvey* v. *Dunlop*[46] has been quoted, and there is a case in Vermont which tends in the same direction.[47]

Supposing it now to be conceded that the general notion upon which liability to an action is founded is fault or blameworthiness in some sense, the question arises, whether it is so in the sense of personal moral shortcoming, as would practically result from Austin's teaching. The language of Rede, J., which has been

[44] *Morris* v. *Platt*, 32 Conn. 75, 84 *et seq.*, A. D. 1864.

[45] *Nitro-glycerine Case* (*Parrot* v. *Wells*), 15 Wall. 524, 538.

[46] Hill & Denio, (Lalor,) 193; *Losee* v. *Buchanan*, 51 N. Y. 476, 489.

[47] *Vincent* v. *Stinehour*, 7 Vt. 62. See, further, Clayton, 22, pl. 38; Holt, C. J., in *Cole* v. *Turner*, 6 Mod. 149; Lord Hardwicke, in *Williams* v. *Jones*, Cas. temp. Hardw. 298; *Hall* v. *Fearnley*, 3 Q. B. 919; Martin, B., in *Coward* v. *Baddeley*, 4 H. & N. 478; *Holmes* v. *Mather*, L. R. 10 Ex. 261; *Bizzell* v. *Booker*, 16 Ark. 308; *Brown* v. *Collins*, 53 N. H. 442.

quoted from the Year Book, gives a sufficient answer. "In trespass the intent" (we may say more broadly, the defendant's state of mind) "cannot be construed." Suppose that a defendant were allowed to testify that, before acting, he considered carefully what would be the conduct of a prudent man under the circumstances, and, having formed the best judgment he could, acted accordingly. If the story was believed, it would be conclusive against the defendant's negligence judged by a moral standard which would take his personal characteristics into account. But supposing any such evidence to have got before the jury, it is very clear that the court would say, Gentlemen, the question is not whether the defendant thought his conduct was that of a prudent man, but whether you think it was.[48]

Some middle point must be found between the horns of this dilemma.[c]

The standards of the law are standards of general application. The law takes no account of the infinite varieties of temperament, intellect, and education which make the internal character of a given act so different in different men. It does not attempt to see men as God sees them, for more than one sufficient reason. In the first place, the impossibility of nicely measuring a man's powers and limitations is far clearer than that of ascertaining his knowledge of law, which has been thought to account for what is called the presumption that every man knows the law. But a more satisfactory explanation is, that, when men live in society, a certain average of conduct, a sacrifice of individual peculiarities going beyond a certan point, is necessary to the general welfare. If, for instance, a man is born hasty and awkward, is always having accidents and hurting himself or his neighbors, no doubt his congenital defects will be allowed for in the courts of Heaven, but his slips are no less troublesome to his neighbors than if they sprang from guilty neglect. His neighbors accordingly require

[48] *Blyth* v. *Birmingham Waterworks Co.*, 11 Exch. 781, 784; *Smith* v. *London & South-Western Ry. Co.*, L. R. 5 C. P. 98, 102. Compare Campbell, Negligence, § 1 (2d ed.), for Austin's point of view.

[c] [(State what it is)—that at the bottom of liability there is a notion of blameworthiness but yet that the deft's blameworthiness is not material.]

him, at his proper peril, to come up to their standard, and the courts which they establish decline to take his personal equation into account.

The rule that the law does, in general, determine liability by blameworthiness, is subject to the limitation that minute differences of character are not allowed for. The law considers, in other words, what would be blameworthy in the average man, the man of ordinary intelligence and prudence, and determines liability by that. If we fall below the level in those gifts, it is our misfortune; so much as that we must have at our peril, for the reasons just given. But he who is intelligent and prudent does not act at his peril, in theory of law. On the contrary, it is only when he fails to exercise the foresight of which he is capable, or exercises it with evil intent, that he is answerable for the consequences.

There are exceptions to the principle that every man is presumed to possess ordinary capacity to avoid harm to his neighbors, which illustrate the rule, and also the moral basis of liability in general. When a man has a distinct defect of such a nature that all can recognize it as making certain precautions impossible, he will not be held answerable for not taking them. A blind man is not required to see at his peril; and although he is, no doubt, bound to consider his infirmity in regulating his actions, yet if he properly finds himself in a certain situation, the neglect of precautions requiring eyesight would not prevent his recovering for an injury to himself, and, it may be presumed, would not make him liable for injuring another. So it is held that, in cases where he is the plaintiff, an infant of very tender years is only bound to take the precautions of which an infant is capable; the same principle may be cautiously applied where he is defendant.[49] Insanity is a more difficult matter to deal with, and no general rule can be laid down about it. There is no doubt that in many cases a man may be insane, and yet perfectly capable of taking the precautions, and of being influenced by the motives, which the circumstances demand. But if insanity of a pronounced type

[49] Cf. Bro. *Corone*, pl. 6; *Neal* v. *Gillett*, 23 Conn. 437, 442; D. 9. 2. 5, § 2; D. 48. 8. 12.

exists, manifestly incapacitating the sufferer from complying with the rule which he has broken, good sense would require it to be admitted as an excuse.

Taking the qualification last established in connection with the general proposition previously laid down, it will now be assumed that, on the one hand, the law presumes or requires a man to possess ordinary capacity to avoid harming his neighbors, unless a clear and manifest incapacity be shown; but that, on the other, it does not in general hold him liable for unintentional injury, unless, possessing such capacity, he might and ought to have foreseen the danger, or, in other words, unless a man of ordinary intelligence and forethought would have been to blame for acting as he did. The next question is, whether this vague test is all that the law has to say upon the matter, and the same question in another form, by whom this test is to be applied.

Notwithstanding the fact that the grounds of legal liability are moral to the extent above explained, it must be borne in mind that law only works within the sphere of the senses. If the external phenomena, the manifest acts and omissions, are such as it requires, it is wholly indifferent to the internal phenomena of conscience. A man may have as bad a heart as he chooses, if his conduct is within the rules. In other words, the standards of the law are external standards, and, however much it may take moral considerations into account, it does so only for the purpose of drawing a line between such bodily motions and rests as it permits, and such as it does not. What the law really forbids, and the only thing it forbids, is the act on the wrong side of the line, be that act blameworthy or otherwise.

Again, any legal standard must, in theory, be one which would apply to all men, not specially excepted, under the same circumstances. It is not intended that the public force should fall upon an individual accidentally, or at the whim of any body of men. The standard, that is, must be fixed. In practice, no doubt, one man may have to pay and another may escape, according to the different feelings of different juries. But this merely shows that the law does not perfectly accomplish its ends. The theory or intention of the law is not that the feeling of approbation or blame which a particular twelve may entertain should be the criterion. They are supposed to leave their idiosyncrasies on one side, and to represent the feeling of the community. The ideal average prudent man, whose equivalent the jury is taken to be in many cases, and whose culpability or innocence is the supposed test, is a constant, and his conduct under given circumstances is theoretically always the same.

Finally, any legal standard must, in theory, be capable of being known. When a man has to pay damages, he is supposed to have broken the law, and he is further supposed to have known what the law was.

If, now, the ordinary liabilities in tort arise from failure to comply with fixed and uniform standards of external conduct, which every man is presumed and required to know, it is obvious that it ought to be possible, sooner or later, to formulate these standards at least to some extent, and that to do so must at last be the business of the court. It is equally clear that the featureless generality, that the defendant was bound to use such care as a prudent man would do under the circumstances, ought to be continually giving place to the specific one, that he was bound to use this or that precaution under these or those circumstances. The standard which the defendant was bound to come up to was a standard of specific acts or omissions, with reference to the specific circumstances in which he found himself. If in the whole department of unintentional wrongs the courts arrived at no further utterance than the question of negligence, and left every case, without rudder or compass, to the jury, they would simply confess their inability to state a very large part of the law which they required the defendant to know, and would assert, by implication, that nothing could be learned by experience. But neither courts nor legislatures have ever stopped at that point.

From the time of Alfred to the present day, statutes and decisions have busied themselves with defining the precautions to be taken in certain familiar cases; that is, with substituting for the vague test of the care exercised by a prudent man, a precise one of specific acts or omissions. The fundamental thought is still the same, that the way prescribed is that in which prudent men are in the habit of acting, or else is one laid down for cases where prudent men might otherwise be in doubt.

It will be observed that the existence of the external tests of liability which will be mentioned, while it illustrates the tendency of the law of tort to become more and more concrete by judicial decision and by statute, does not interfere with the general doctrine maintained as to the grounds of liability. The argument of this Lecture, although opposed to the doctrine that a man acts or exerts force at his peril, is by no means opposed to the doctrine that he does certain particular acts at his peril. It is the coarseness, not the nature, of the standard which is objected to. If, when the question of the defendant's negligence is left to a jury, negligence does not mean the actual state of the defendant's mind, but a failure to act as a prudent man of average intelligence would have done, he is required to conform to an objective standard at his peril, even in that case. When a more exact and specific rule has been arrived at, he must obey that rule at his peril to the same extent. But, further, if the law is wholly a standard of external conduct, a man must always comply with that standard at his peril.

Some examples of the process of specification will be useful. In LL. Alfred, 36,[50] providing for the case of a man's staking himself on a spear carried by another, we read, "Let this (liability) be if the point be three fingers higher than the hindmost part of the shaft; if they be both on a level, . . . be that without danger."

The rule of the road and the sailing rules adopted by Congress from England are modern examples of such statutes. By the former rule, the question has been narrowed from the vague one, Was the party negligent? to the precise one, Was he on the right or left of the road? To avoid a possible misconception, it may be observed that, of course, this question does not necessarily and under all circumstances decide that of liability; a plaintiff may have been on the wrong side of the road, as he may have been negligent, and yet the conduct of the defendant may have been unjustifiable, and a ground of liability.[51] So, no doubt,

[50] 1 Thorpe, p. 85; cf. LL. Hen. I., c. 88, § 3.
[51] *Spofford* v. *Harlow*, 3 Allen, 176.

a defendant could justify or excuse being on the wrong side, under some circumstances. The difference between alleging that a defendant was on the wrong side of the road, and that he was negligent, is the difference between an allegation of facts requiring to be excused by a counter allegation of further facts to prevent their being a ground of liability, and an allegation which involves a conclusion of law, and denies in advance the existence of an excuse. Whether the former allegation ought not to be enough, and whether the establishment of the fact ought not to shift the burden of proof, are questions which belong to the theory of pleading and evidence, and could be answered either way consistently with analogy. I should have no difficulty in saying that the allegation of facts which are ordinarily a ground of liability, and which would be so unless excused, ought to be sufficient. But the forms of the law, especially the forms of pleading, do not change with every change of its substance, and a prudent lawyer would use the broader and safer phrase.

The same course of specification which has been illustrated from the statute-book ought also to be taking place in the growth of judicial decisions. That this should happen is in accordance with the past history of the law. It has been suggested already that in the days of the assize and *jurata* the court decided whether the facts constituted a ground of liability in all ordinary cases. A question of negligence might, no doubt, have gone to the jury. Common sense and common knowledge are as often sufficient to determine whether proper care has been taken of an animal, as they are to say whether A or B owns it. The cases which first arose were not of a kind to suggest analysis, and negligence was used as a proximately simple element for a long time before the need or possibility of analysis was felt. Still, when an issue of this sort is found, the dispute is rather what the acts or omissions of the defendant were than on the standard of conduct.[52] The distinction between the functions of court and jury does not come in question until the parties differ as to the

[52] See 27 Ass., pl. 56, fol. 141; Y. B. 43 Edw. III. 33, pl. 38. The plea in the latter case was that the defendant performed the cure as well as he knew how, without this that the horse died for default of his care. The inducement, at least, of this plea seems to deal with negligence as meaning the actual state of the party's mind.

standard of conduct. Negligence, like ownership, is a complex conception. Just as the latter imports the existence of certain facts, and also the consequence (protection against all the world) which the law attaches to those facts, the former imports the existence of certain facts (conduct), and also the consequence (liability) which the law attaches to those facts. In most cases the question is upon the facts, and it is only occasionally that one arises on the consequence.

It will have been noticed how the judges pass on the defendant's acts (on grounds of fault and public policy) in the case of the thorns, and that in *Weaver* v. *Ward*[53] it is said that the facts constituting an excuse, and showing that the defendant was free from negligence, should have been spread upon the record, in order that the court might judge. A similar requirement was laid down with regard to the defence of probable cause in an action for malicious prosecution.[54] And to this day the question of probable cause is always passed on by the court. Later evidence will be found in what follows.

There is, however, an important consideration, which has not yet been adverted to. It is undoubtedly possible that those who have the making of the law should deem it wise to put the mark higher in some cases than the point established by common practice at which blameworthiness begins. For instance, in *Morris* v. *Platt*,[55] the court, while declaring in the strongest terms that, in general, negligence is the foundation of liability for accidental trespasses, nevertheless hints that, if a decision of the point were necessary, it might hold a defendant to a stricter rule where the damage was caused by a pistol, in view of the danger to the public of the growing habit of carrying deadly weapons. Again, it might well seem that to enter a man's house for the purpose of carrying a present, or inquiring after his health when he was ill, was a harmless and rather praiseworthy act, although crossing the owner's boundary was intentional. It is not supposed that an action would lie at the present day for such a cause, unless

[53] Hobart, 134.

[54] See *Knight* v. *Jermin*, Cro. Eliz. 134; *Chambers* v. *Taylor*, Cro. Eliz. 900.

[55] 32 Conn. 75, 89, 90.

the defendant had been forbidden the house. Yet in the time of Henry VIII. it was said to be actionable if without license, "for then under that color my enemy might be in my house and kill me."[56] There is a clear case where public policy establishes a standard of overt acts without regard to fault in any sense. In like manner, policy established exceptions to the general prohibition against entering another's premises, as in the instance put by Chief Justice Choke in the Year Book, of a tree being blown over upon them, or when the highway became impassable, or for the purpose of keeping the peace.[57]

Another example may perhaps be found in the shape which has been given in modern times to the liability for animals, and in the derivative principle of *Rylands* v. *Fletcher*,[58] that when a person brings on his lands, and collects and keeps there, anything likely to do mischief if it escapes, he must keep it in at his peril; and, if he does not do so, is *prima facie* answerable for all the damage which is the natural consequence of its escape. Cases of this sort do not stand on the notion that it is wrong to keep cattle, or to have a reservoir of water, as might have been thought with more plausibility when fierce and useless animals only were in question.[59] It may even be very much for the public good that the dangerous accumulation should be made (a consideration which might influence the decision in some instances, and differently in different jurisdictions); but as there is a limit to the nicety of inquiry which is possible in a trial, it may be considered that the safest way to secure care is to throw the risk upon the person who decides what precautions shall be taken. The liability for trespasses of cattle seems to lie on the boundary line between rules based on policy irrespective of fault, and requirements intended to formulate the conduct of a prudent man.

It has been shown in the first Lecture how this liability for cattle arose in the early law, and how far the influence of early notions might be traced in the law of to-day. Subject to what is

[56] Y. B. 12 Hen. VIII. 2 *b*, pl. 2.

[57] Keilway, 46 *b*.

[58] L. R. 3 H. L. 330, 339; L. R. 1 Ex. 265, 279–282; 4 H. & C. 263; 3 id. 774.

[59] See *Card* v. *Case*, 5 C. B. 622, 633, 634.

there said, it is evident that the early discussions turn on the general consideration whether the owner is or is not to blame.[60] But they do not stop there: they go on to take practical distinctions, based on common experience. Thus, when the defendant chased sheep out of his land with a dog, and as soon as the sheep were out called in his dog, but the dog pursued them into adjoining land, the chasing of the sheep beyond the defendant's line was held no trespass, because "the nature of a dog is such that he cannot be ruled suddenly."[61]

It was lawful in ploughing to turn the horses on adjoining land, and if while so turning the beasts took a mouthful of grass, or subverted the soil with the plough, against the will of the driver, he had a good justification, because the law will recognize that a man cannot at every instant govern his cattle as he will.[62] So it was said that, if a man be driving cattle through a town, and one of them goes into another man's house, and he follows him, trespass does not lie for this.[63] So it was said by Doderidge, J., in the same case, that if deer come into my land out of the forest, and I chase them with dogs, it is excuse enough for me to wind my horn to recall the dogs, because by this the warden of the forest has notice that a deer is being chased.[64]

The very case of *Mason* v. *Keeling*,[65] which is referred to in the first Lecture for its echo of primitive notions, shows that the working rules of the law had long been founded on good sense. With regard to animals not then treated as property, which in the main were the wilder animals, the law was settled that, "if they are of a tame nature, there must be notice of the ill quality; and

[60] See Lecture I. p. 22 and n. 64.

[61] *Mitten* v. *Fandrye*, Popham, 161; s. c., 1 Sir W. Jones, 136; s. c., nom. *Millen* v. *Hawery*, Latch, 13; id. 119. In the latter report, at p. 120, after reciting the opinion of the court in accordance with the text, it is said that judgment was given *non obstant* for the plaintiff; contrary to the earlier statement in the same book, and to Popham and Jones; but the principle was at all events admitted. For the limit, see *Read* v. *Edwards*, 17 C. B. N. S. 245.

[62] Y. B. 22 Edw. IV. 8, pl. 24.

[63] Popham, at p. 162; s. c., Latch, at p. 120; cf. *Mason* v. *Keeling*, 1 Ld. Raym. 606, 608. But cf. Y. B. 20 Edw. IV. 10, 11, pl. 10.

[64] Latch, at p. 120. This is a further illustration of the very practical grounds on which the law of trespass was settled.

[65] 12 Mod. 332, 335; s. c., 1 Ld. Raym. 606, 608.

the law takes notice, that a dog is not of a fierce nature, but rather the contrary."[66] If the animals "are such as are naturally mischievous in their kind, he shall answer for hurt done by them, without any notice."[67] The latter principle has been applied to the case of a bear,[68] and amply accounts for the liability of the owner of such animals as horses and oxen in respect of trespasses upon land, although, as has been seen, it was at one time thought to stand upon his ownership. It is said to be the universal nature of cattle to stray, and, when straying in cultivated land, to do damage by trampling down and eating the crops, whereas a dog does no harm. It is also said to be usual and easy to restrain them.[69] If, as has been suggested, the historical origin of the rule was different, it does not matter.

Following the same line of thought, the owner of cattle is not held absolutely answerable for all damage which they may do the person. According to Lord Holt in the above opinion, these animals, "which are not so familiar to mankind" as dogs, "the owner ought to confine, and take all reasonable caution that they do no mischief. . . . But . . . if the owner puts a horse or an ox to grass in his field, which is adjoining to the highway, and the horse or the ox breaks the hedge and runs into the highway, and kicks or gores some passenger, an action will not lie against the owner; otherwise, if he had notice that they had done such a thing before."

Perhaps the most striking authority for the position that the judge's duties are not at an end when the question of negligence is reached, is shown by the discussions concerning the law of bailment. Consider the judgment in *Coggs* v. *Bernard*,[70] the

[66] 12 Mod. 335; Dyer, 25 *b*, pl. 162, and cas. in marg.; 4 Co. Rep. 18 *b*; *Buxendin* v. *Sharp*, 2 Salk. 662; s. c., 3 Salk. 169; s. c., nom. *Bayntine* v. *Sharp*, 1 Lutw. 90; *Smith* v. *Pelah*, 2 Strange, 264; *May* v. *Burdett*, 9 Q. B. 101; *Card* v. *Case*, 5 C. B. 622.

[67] 12 Mod. 335. See *Andrew Baker's case*, 1 Hale, P. C. 430.

[68] *Besozzi* v. *Harris*, 1 F. & F. 92.

[69] See *Fletcher* v. *Rylands*, L. R. 1 Ex. 265, 281, 282; *Cox* v. *Burbridge*, 13 C. B. N. S. 430, 441; *Read* v. *Edwards*, 17 C. B. N. S. 245, 260; *Lee* v. *Riley*, 18 C. B. N. S. 722; *Ellis* v. *Loftus Iron Co.*, L. R. 10 C. P. 10; 27 Ass., pl. 56, fol. 141; Y. B. 20 Ed. IV. 11, pl. 10; 13 Hen. VII. 15, pl. 10; Keilway, 3 *b*, pl. 7. Cf. 4 Kent (12th ed.), 110, n. 1, *ad fin.*

[70] 2 Ld. Raym. 909; 13 Am. L. R. 609.

treatises of Sir William Jones and Story, and the chapter of Kent upon the subject. They are so many attempts to state the duty of the bailee specifically, according to the nature of the bailment and of the object bailed. Those attempts, to be sure, were not successful, partly because they were attempts to engraft upon the native stock a branch of the Roman law which was too large to survive the process, but more especially because the distinctions attempted were purely qualitative, and were therefore useless when dealing with a jury.[71] To instruct a jury that they must find the defendant guilty of gross negligence before he can be charged, is open to the reproach that for such a body the word "gross" is only a vituperative epithet. But it would not be so with a judge sitting in admiralty without a jury. The Roman law and the Supreme Court of the United States agree that the word means something.[72] Successful or not, it is enough for the present argument that the attempt has been made.

The principles of substantive law which have been established by the courts are believed to have been somewhat obscured by having presented themselves oftenest in the form of rulings upon the sufficiency of evidence. When a judge rules that there is no evidence of negligence, he does something more than is embraced in an ordinary ruling that there is no evidence of a fact. He rules that the acts or omissions proved or in question do not constitute a ground of legal liability, and in this way the law is gradually enriching itself from daily life, as it should. Thus, in *Crafton* v. *Metropolitan Railway Co.*,[73] the plaintiff slipped on the defendant's stairs and was severely hurt. The cause of his slipping was that the brass nosing of the stairs had been worn smooth by travel over it, and a builder testified that in his opinion the staircase was unsafe by reason of this circumstance and the absence of a hand-rail. There was nothing to contradict this except that great numbers of persons had passed over the stairs and that no accident had happened there, and the plaintiff had a verdict. The court set the verdict aside, and ordered a nonsuit. The ruling was in form that there was no evidence of negligence to go to the jury; but this was obviously equivalent to saying, and did in

[71] See *Grill* v. *General Iron Screw Collier Co.*, L. R. 1 C. P. 600, 612, 614.
[72] *Railroad Co.* v. *Lockwood*, 17 Wall. 357, 383. [73] L. R. 1 C. P. 300.

fact mean, that the railroad company had done all that it was bound to do in maintaining such a staircase as was proved by the plaintiff. A hundred other equally concrete instances will be found in the text-books.

On the other hand, if the court should rule that certain acts or omissions coupled with damage were conclusive evidence of negligence unless explained, it would, in substance and in truth, rule that such acts or omissions were a ground of liability,[74] or prevented a recovery, as the case might be. Thus it is said to be actionable negligence to let a house for a dwelling knowing it to be so infected with small-pox as to be dangerous to health, and concealing the knowledge.[75] To explain the acts or omissions in such a case would be to prove different conduct from that ruled upon, or to show that they were not, juridically speaking, the cause of the damage complained of. The ruling assumes, for the purposes of the ruling, that the facts in evidence are all the facts.

The cases which have raised difficulties needing explanation are those in which the court has ruled that there was *prima facie* evidence of negligence, or some evidence of negligence to go to the jury.

Many have noticed the confusion of thought implied in speaking of such cases as presenting mixed questions of law and fact. No doubt, as has been said above, the averment that the defendant has been guilty of negligence is a complex one: first, that he has done or omitted certain things; second, that his alleged conduct does not come up to the legal standard. And so long as the controversy is simply on the first half, the whole complex averment is plain matter for the jury without special instructions, just as a question of ownership would be where the only dispute was as to the fact upon which the legal conclusion was founded.[76] But when a controversy arises on the second half, the question whether the court or the jury ought to judge of the defendant's conduct is wholly unaffected by the accident, whether

[74] See *Gorham* v. *Gross*, 125 Mass. 232, 239, bottom.

[75] *Minor* v. *Sharon*, 112 Mass. 477, 487.

[76] See *Winsmore* v. *Greenbank*, Willes, 577, 583; *Rex* v. *Oneby*, 2 Strange, 766, 773; *Lampleigh* v. *Brathwait*, Hobart, 105, 107; Wigram, Disc., pl. 249; Evans on Pleading, 49, 138, 139, 143 *et seq.*; Id., Miller's ed., pp. 147, 149.

there is or is not also a dispute as to what that conduct was. If there is such a dispute, it is entirely possible to give a series of hypothetical instructions adapted to every state of facts which it is open to the jury to find. If there is no such dispute, the court may still take their opinion as to the standard. The problem is to explain the relative functions of court and jury with regard to the latter.

When a case arises in which the standard of conduct, pure and simple, is submitted to the jury, the explanation is plain. It is that the court, not entertaining any clear views of public policy applicable to the matter, derives the rule to be applied from daily experience, as it has been agreed that the great body of the law of tort has been derived. But the court further feels that it is not itself possessed of sufficient practical experience to lay down the rule intelligently. It conceives that twelve men taken from the practical part of the community can aid its judgment.[77] Therefore it aids its conscience by taking the opinion of the jury.

But supposing a state of facts often repeated in practice, is it to be imagined that the court is to go on leaving the standard to the jury forever? Is it not manifest, on the contrary, that if the jury is, on the whole, as fair a tribunal as it is represented to be, the lesson which can be got from that source will be learned? Either the court will find that the fair teaching of experience is that the conduct complained of usually is or is not blameworthy, and therefore, unless explained, is or is not a ground of liability; or it will find the jury oscillating to and fro, and will see the necessity of making up its mind for itself. There is no reason why any other such question should not be settled, as well as that of liability for stairs with smooth strips of brass upon their edges. The exceptions would mainly be found where the standard was rapidly changing, as, for instance, in some questions of medical treatment.[78]

If this be the proper conclusion in plain cases, further conse-

[77] See *Detroit & Milwaukee R. R. Co.* v. *Van Steinburg*, 17 Mich. 99, 120.

[78] In the small-pox case, *Minor* v. *Sharon*, 112 Mass. 477, while the court ruled with regard to the defendant's conduct as has been mentioned, it held that whether the plaintiff was guilty of contributory negligence in not having vaccinated his children was "a question of fact, and was properly left to the jury," p. 488.

quences ensue. Facts do not often exactly repeat themselves in practice; but cases with comparatively small variations from each other do. A judge who has long sat at *nisi prius* ought gradually to acquire a fund of experience which enables him to represent the common sense of the community in ordinary instances far better than an average jury. He should be able to lead and to instruct them in detail, even where he thinks it desirable, on the whole, to take their opinion. Furthermore, the sphere in which he is able to rule without taking their opinion at all should be continually growing.

It has often been said, that negligence is pure matter of fact, or that, after the court has declared the evidence to be such that negligence *may* be inferred from it, the jury are always to decide whether the inference shall be drawn.[79] But it is believed that the courts, when they lay down this broad proposition, are thinking of cases where the conduct to be passed upon is not proved directly, and the main or only question is what that conduct was, not what standard shall be applied to it after it is established.

Most cases which go to the jury on a ruling that there is evidence from which they may find negligence, do not go to them principally on account of a doubt as to the standard, but of a doubt as to the conduct. Take the case where the fact in proof is an event such as the dropping of a brick from a railway bridge over a highway upon the plaintiff, the fact must be inferred that the dropping was due, not to a sudden operation of weather, but to a gradual falling out of repair which it was physically possible for the defendant to have prevented, before there can be any question as to the standard of conduct.[80]

So, in the case of a barrel falling from a warehouse window, it must be found that the defendant or his servants were in charge of it, before any question of standard can arise.[81] It will be seen that in each of these well-known cases the court assumed a rule which would make the defendant liable if his conduct was such as the evidence tended to prove. When there is no question as

[79] *Metropolitan Railway Co.* v. *Jackson*, 3 App. Cas. 193, 197.

[80] See *Kearney* v. *London, Brighton, & S. Coast Ry. Co.*, L. R. 5 Q. B. 411, 414, 417; s. c., 6 id. 759.

[81] *Byrne* v. *Boadle*, 2 H. & C. 722.

to the conduct established by the evidence, as in the case of a collision between two trains belonging to the same company, the jury have, sometimes at least, been told in effect that, if they believed the evidence, the defendant was liable.[82]

The principal argument that is urged in favor of the view that a more extended function belongs to the jury as matter of right, is the necessity of continually conforming our standards to experience. No doubt the general foundation of legal liability in blameworthiness, as determined by the existing average standards of the community, should always be kept in mind, for the purpose of keeping such concrete rules as from time to time may be laid down conformable to daily life. No doubt this conformity is the practical justification for requiring a man to know the civil law, as the fact that crimes are also generally sins is one of the practical justifications for requiring a man to know the criminal law. But these considerations only lead to the conclusion that precedents should be overruled when they become inconsistent with present conditions; and this has generally happened, except with regard to the construction of deeds and wills. On the other hand, it is very desirable to know as nearly as we can the standard by which we shall be judged at a given moment, and, moreover, the standards for a very large part of human conduct do not vary from century to century.

The considerations urged in this Lecture are of peculiar importance in this country, or at least in States where the law is as it stands in Massachusetts. In England, the judges at *nisi prius* express their opinions freely on the value and weight of the evidence, and the judges *in banc*, by consent of parties, constantly draw inferences of fact. Hence nice distinctions as to the province of court and jury are not of the first necessity. But when judges are forbidden by statute to charge the jury with respect to matters of fact, and when the court *in banc* will never hear a case calling for inferences of fact, it becomes of vital importance to understand that, when standards of conduct are left to the jury, it is a temporary surrender of a judicial function which may be resumed at any moment in any case when the court feels com-

[82] See *Skinner* v. *London, Brighton, & S. Coast Ry. Co.*, 5 Exch. 787. But cf. *Hammack* v. *White*, 11 C. B. N. S. 588, 594.

petent to do so. Were this not so, the almost universal acceptance of the first proposition in this Lecture, that the general foundation of liability for unintentional wrongs is conduct different from that of a prudent man under the circumstances, would leave all our rights and duties throughout a great part of the law to the necessarily more or less accidental feelings of a jury.

It is perfectly consistent with the views maintained in this Lecture that the courts have been very slow to withdraw questions of negligence from the jury, without distinguishing nicely whether the doubt concerned the facts or the standard to be applied. Legal, like natural divisions, however clear in their general outline, will be found on exact scrutiny to end in a penumbra or debatable land. This is the region of the jury, and only cases falling on this doubtful border are likely to be carried far in court. Still, the tendency of the law must always be to narrow the field of uncertainty. That is what analogy, as well as the decisions on this very subject, would lead us to expect.

The growth of the law is very apt to take place in this way. Two widely different cases suggest a general distinction, which is a clear one when stated broadly. But as new cases cluster around the opposite poles, and begin to approach each other, the distinction becomes more difficult to trace; the determinations are made one way or the other on a very slight preponderance of feeling, rather than of articulate reason; and at last a mathematical line is arrived at by the contact of contrary decisions, which is so far arbitrary that it might equally well have been drawn a little farther to the one side or to the other, but which must have been drawn somewhere in the neighborhood of where it falls.[83]

In this way exact distinctions have been worked out upon questions in which the elements to be considered are few. For instance, what is a reasonable time for presenting negotiable paper, or what is a difference in kind and what a difference only in quality, or the rule against perpetuities.

An example of the approach of decisions towards each other from the opposite poles, and of the function of the jury midway, is to be found in the Massachusetts adjudications, that, if a child

[83] American Law Review, 654 *et seq.*, July, 1873.

of two years and four months is unnnecessarily sent unattended across and down a street in a large city, he cannot recover for a negligent injury; [84] that to allow a boy of eight to be abroad alone is not necessarily negligent; [85] and that the effect of permitting a boy of ten to be abroad after dark is for the jury; [86] coupled with the statement, which may be ventured on without authority, that such a permission to a young man of twenty possessed of common intelligence has no effect whatever.

Take again the law of ancient lights in England. An obstruction to be actionable must be substantial. Under ordinary circumstances the erection of a structure a hundred yards off, and one foot above the ground, would not be actionable. One within a foot of the window, and covering it, would be, without any finding of a jury beyond these facts. In doubtful cases midway, the question whether the interference was substantial has been left to the jury.[87] But as the elements are few and permanent, an inclination has been shown to lay down a definite rule, that, in ordinary cases, the building complained of must not be higher than the distance of its base from the dominant windows. And although this attempt to work out an exact line requires much caution, it is entirely philosophical in spirit.[88]

The same principle applies to negligence. If the whole evidence in the case was that a party, in full command of his senses and intellect, stood on a railway track, looking at an approaching engine until it ran him down, no judge would leave it to the jury to say whether the conduct was prudent. If the whole evidence was that he attempted to cross a level track, which was visible for half a mile each way, and on which no engine was in sight, no court would allow a jury to find negligence. Between these extremes are cases which would go to the jury. But it is obvious that the limit of safety in such cases, supposing no further elements present, could be determined almost to a foot by mathematical calculation.

[84] *Callahan* v. *Bean*, 9 Allen, 401. [85] *Carter* v. *Towne*, 98 Mass. 567.

[86] *Lovett* v. *Salem & South Danvers R. R. Co.*, 9 Allen, 557.

[87] *Back* v. *Stacey*, 2 C. & P. 465.

[88] Cf. *Beadel* v. *Perry*, L. R. 3 Eq. 465; *City of London Brewery Co.* v. *Tennant*, L. R. 9 Ch. 212, 220; *Hackett* v. *Baiss*, L. R. 20 Eq. 494; *Theed* v. *Debenham*, 2 Ch. D. 165.

The trouble with many cases of negligence is, that they are of a kind not frequently recurring, so as to enable any given judge to profit by long experience with juries to lay down rules, and that the elements are so complex that courts are glad to leave the whole matter in a lump for the jury's determination.

I reserve the relation between negligent and other torts for the next Lecture.

LECTURE IV

FRAUD, MALICE, AND INTENT.—THE THEORY OF TORTS

THE next subjects to be considered are fraud, malice, and intent. In the discussion of unintentional wrongs, the greatest difficulty to be overcome was found to be the doctrine that a man acts always at his peril. In what follows, on the other hand, the difficulty will be to prove that actual wickedness of the kind described by the several words just mentioned is not an element in the civil wrongs to which those words are applied.

It has been shown, in dealing with the criminal law, that, when we call an act malicious in common speech, we mean that harm to another person was intended to come of it, and that such harm was desired for its own sake as an end in itself. For the purposes of the criminal law, however, intent alone was found to be important, and to have the same consequences as intent with malevolence superadded. Pursuing the analysis, intent was found to be made up of foresight of the harm as a consequence, coupled with a desire to bring it about, the latter being conceived as the motive for the act in question. Of these, again, foresight only seemed material. As a last step, foresight was reduced to its lowest term, and it was concluded that, subject to exceptions which were explained, the general basis of criminal liability was knowledge, at the time of action, of facts from which common experience showed that certain harmful results were likely to follow.

It remains to be seen whether a similar reduction is possible on the civil side of the law, and whether thus fraudulent, malicious, intentional, and negligent wrongs can be brought into a philosophically continuous series.

A word of preliminary explanation will be useful. It has been shown in the Lecture just referred to that an act, although always importing intent, is *per se* indifferent to the law. It is a willed, and therefore an intended co-ordination of muscular contractions. But the intent necessarily imported by the act ends there. And all muscular motions or co-ordinations of them are harmless apart from concomitant circumstances, the presence of which is not necessarily implied by the act itself. To strike out with the fist is the same act, whether done in a desert or in a crowd.

The same considerations which have been urged to show that an act alone, by itself, does not and ought not to impose either civil or criminal liability, apply, at least frequently, to a series of acts, or to conduct, although the series shows a further co-ordination and a further intent. For instance, it is the same series of acts to utter a sentence falsely stating that a certain barrel contains No. 1 Mackerel, whether the sentence is uttered in the secrecy of the closet, or to another man in the course of a bargain. There is, to be sure, in either case, the further intent, beyond the co-ordination of muscles for a single sound, to allege that a certain barrel has certain contents,—an intent necessarily shown by the ordering of the words. But both the series of acts and the intent are *per se* indifferent. They are innocent when spoken in solitude, and are only a ground of liability when certain concomitant circumstances are shown.

The intent which is meant when spoken of as an element of legal liability is an intent directed toward the harm complained of, or at least toward harm. It is not necessary in every case to carry the analysis back to the simple muscular contractions out of which a course of conduct is made up. On the same principle that requires something more than an act followed by damage to make a man liable, we constantly find ourselves at liberty to assume a co-ordinated series of acts as a proximately simple element, *per se* indifferent, in considering what further circumstances or facts must be present before the conduct in question is at the actor's peril. It will save confusion and the need of repetition if this is borne in mind in the following discussion.

The chief forms of liability in which fraud, malice, and intent are said to be necessary elements, are deceit, slander and libel, malicious prosecution, and conspiracy, to which, perhaps, may be added trover.

Deceit is a notion drawn from the moral world, and in its popular sense distinctly imports wickedness. The doctrine of the common law with regard to it is generally stated in terms which are only consistent with actual guilt, and an actual guilty intent. It is said that a man is liable to an action for deceit if he makes a false representation to another, knowing it to be false, but intending that the other should believe and act upon it, if the person addressed believes it, and is thereby persuaded to act to his own harm. This is no doubt the typical case, and it is a case of intentional moral wrong. Now, what is the party's conduct here. It consists in uttering certain words, so ordered that the utterance of them imports a knowledge of the meaning which they would convey if heard. But that conduct with only that knowledge is neither moral nor immoral. Go one step further, and add the knowledge of another's presence within hearing, still the act has no determinate character. The elements which make it immoral are the knowledge that the statement is false, and the intent that it shall be acted on.

The principal question then is, whether this intent can be reduced to the same terms as it has been in other cases. There is no difficulty in the answer. It is perfectly clear that the intent that a false representation should be acted on would be conclusively established by proof that the defendant knew that the other party intended to act upon it. If the defendant foresaw the consequence of his acts, he is chargeable, whether his motive was a desire to induce the other party to act, or simply an unwillingness for private reasons to state the truth. If the defendant knew a present fact (the other party's intent), which, according to common experience, made it likely that his act would have the harmful consequence, he is chargeable, whether he in fact foresaw the consequence or not.

In this matter the general conclusion follows from a single instance. For the moment it is admitted that in one case knowledge of a present fact, such as the other party's intent to act on the false statement, dispenses with proof of an intent to induce him to act upon it, it is admitted that the lesser element is all that is necessary in the larger compound. For intent embraces knowledge sufficing for foresight, as has been shown. Hence, when you prove intent you prove knowledge, and intent may often be the easier to prove of the two. But when you prove knowledge you do not prove intent.

It may be said, however, that intent is implied or presumed in such a case as has been supposed. But this is only helping out a false theory by a fiction. It is very much like saying that a consideration is presumed for an instrument under seal; which is merely a way of reconciling the formal theory that all contracts must have a consideration with the manifest fact that sealed instruments do not require one. Whenever it is said that a certain thing is essential to liability, but that it is conclusively presumed from something else, there is always ground for suspicion that the essential element is to be found in that something else, and not in what is said to be presumed from it.

With regard to the intent necessary to deceit, we need not stop with the single instance which has been given. The law goes no farther than to require proof either of the intent, or that the other party was justified in inferring such intention. So that the whole meaning of the requirement is, that the natural and manifest tendency of the representation, under the known circumstances, must have been to induce the opinion that it was made with a view to action, and so to induce action on the faith of it. The standard of what is called intent is thus really an external standard of conduct under the known circumstances, and the analysis of the criminal law holds good here.

Nor is this all. The law pursuing its course of specification, as explained in the last Lecture, decides what is the tendency of representations in certain cases,—as, for instance, that a horse is sound at the time of making a sale; or, in general, of any statement of fact which it is known the other party intends to rely on. Beyond these specific rules lies the vague realm of the jury.

The other moral element in deceit is knowledge that the statement was false. With this I am not strictly concerned, because all that is necessary is accomplished when the elements of risk are reduced to action and knowledge. But it will aid in the general object of showing that the tendency of the law everywhere is to transcend moral and reach external standards, if this knowledge of falsehood can be transmuted into a formula not necessarily importing guilt, although, of course, generally accompanied by it in fact. The moment we look critically at it, we find the moral side shade away.

The question is, what known circumstances are enough to throw the risk of a statement upon him who makes it, if it induces another man to act, and it turns out untrue. Now, it is evident that a man may take the risk of his statement by express agreement, or by an implied one which the law reads into his bargain. He may in legal language warrant the truth of it, and if it is not true, the law treats it as a fraud, just as much when he makes it fully believing it, as when he knows that it is untrue, and means to deceive. If, in selling a horse, the seller warranted him to be only five years old, and in fact he was thirteen, the seller could be sued for a deceit at common law, although he thought the horse was only five.[1] The common-law liability for the truth of statements is, therefore, more extensive than the sphere of actual moral fraud.

But, again, it is enough in general if a representation is made recklessly, without knowing whether it is true or false. Now what does "recklessly" mean. It does not mean actual personal indifference to the truth of the statement. It means only that the data for the statement were so far insufficient that a prudent man could not have made it without leading to the inference that he was indifferent. That is to say, repeating an analysis which has been gone through with before, it means that the law, applying a general objective standard, determines that, if a man makes his statement on those data, he is liable, whatever was the state of his mind, and although he individually may have been perfectly free from wickedness in making it.

Hence similar reasoning to that which has been applied already to intent may be applied to knowledge of falsity. Actual knowledge may often be easier to prove than that the evidence was insufficient to warrant the statement, and when proved it contains the lesser element. But as soon as the lesser element is

[1] *Williamson* v. *Allison*, 2 East, 446.

shown to be enough, it is shown that the law is ready to apply an external or objective standard here also.

Courts of equity have laid down the doctrine in terms which are so wholly irrespective of the actual moral condition of the defendant as to go to an opposite extreme. It is said that "when a representation in a matter of business is made by one man to another calculated to induce him to adapt his conduct to it, it is perfectly immaterial whether the representation is made knowing it to be untrue, or whether it is made believing it to be true, if, in fact, it was untrue."[2]

Perhaps the actual decisions could be reconciled on a narrower principle, but the rule just stated goes the length of saying that in business matters a man makes every statement (of a kind likely to be acted on) at his peril. This seems hardly justifiable in policy. The moral starting-point of liability in general should never be forgotten, and the law cannot without disregarding it hold a man answerable for statements based on facts which would have convinced a wise and prudent man of their truth. The public advantage and necessity of freedom in imparting information, which privileges even the slander of a third person, ought *a fortiori*, it seems to me, to privilege statements made at the request of the party who complains of them.

The common law, at any rate, preserves the reference to morality by making fraud the ground on which it goes. It does not hold that a man always speaks at his peril. But starting from the moral ground, it works out an external standard of what would be fraudulent in the average prudent member of the community, and requires every member at his peril to avoid that. As in other cases, it is gradually accumulating precedents which decide that certain statements under certain circumstances are at the peril of the party who makes them.

The elements of deceit which throw the risk of his conduct upon a party are these. First, making a statement of facts purporting to be serious. Second, the known presence of another within hearing. Third, known facts sufficient to warrant the ex-

[2] *Leather* v. *Simpson*, L. R. 11 Eq. 398, 406. On the other hand, the extreme moral view is stated in *Weir* v. *Bell*, 3 Ex. D. 238, 243.

pectation or suggest the probability that the other party will act on the statement. (What facts are sufficient has been specifically determined by the courts in some instances; in others, no doubt, the question would go to the jury on the principles heretofore explained.) Fourth, the falsehood of the statement. This must be known, or else the known evidence concerning the matter of the statement must be such as would not warrant belief according to the ordinary course of human experience. (On this point also the court may be found to lay down specific rules in some cases.[8])

I next take up the law of slander. It has often been said that malice is one of the elements of liability, and the doctrine is commonly stated in this way: that malice must exist, but that it is presumed by law from the mere speaking of the words; that again you may rebut this presumption of malice by showing that the words were spoken under circumstances which made the communication privileged,—as, for instance, by a lawyer in the necessary course of his argument, or by a person answering in good faith to inquiries as to the character of a former servant,—and then, it is said, the plaintiff may meet this defence in some cases by showing that the words were spoken with actual malice.

All this sounds as if at least actual intent to cause the damage complained of, if not malevolence, were at the bottom of this class of wrongs. Yet it is not so. For although the use of the phrase "malice" points as usual to an original moral standard, the rule that it is presumed upon proof of speaking certain words is equivalent to saying that the overt conduct of speaking those words may be actionable whether the consequence of damage to the plaintiff was intended or not. And this falls in with the general theory, because the manifest tendency of slanderous words is to harm the person of whom they are spoken. Again, the real substance of the defence is not that the damage was not intended,—that would be no defence at all; but that, whether it was intended or not,—that is, even if the defendant foresaw it and foresaw it with pleasure,—the manifest facts and circumstances under which he said it were such that the law considered

[8] As to actual knowledge and intent, see Lecture II, p. 48.

the damage to the plaintiff of less importance than the benefit of free speaking.

It is more difficult to apply the same analysis to the last stage of the process, but perhaps it is not impossible. It is said that the plaintiff may meet a case of privilege thus made out on the part of the defendant, by proving actual malice, that is, actual intent to cause the damage complained of. But how is this actual malice made out? It is by showing that the defendant knew the statement which he made was false, or that his untrue statements were grossly in excess of what the occasion required. Now is it not very evident that the law is looking to a wholly different matter from the defendant's intent? The fact that the defendant foresaw and foresaw with pleasure the damage to the plaintiff, is of no more importance in this case than it would be where the communication was privileged. The question again is wholly a question of knowledge, or other external standard. And what makes even knowledge important? It is that the reason for which a man is allowed in the other instances to make false charges against his neighbors is wanting. It is for the public interest that people should be free to give the best information they can under certain circumstances without fear, but there is no public benefit in having lies told at any time; and when a charge is known to be false, or is in excess of what is required by the occasion, it is not necessary to make that charge in order to speak freely, and therefore it falls under the ordinary rule, that certain charges are made at the party's peril in case they turn out to be false, whether evil consequences were intended or not. The defendant is liable, not because his intent was evil, but because he made false charges without excuse.

It will be seen that the peril of conduct here begins farther back than with deceit, as the tendency of slander is more universally harmful. There must be some concomitant circumstances. There must at least be a human being in existence whom the statement designates. There must be another human being within hearing who understands the statement, and the statement must be false. But it is arguable that the latter of these facts need not be known, as certainly the falsity of the charge need not be, and that a man must take the risk of even an idle statement being heard, unless he made it under known circumstances of privilege. It would be no great curtailment of freedom to deny a man immunity in attaching a charge of crime to the name of his neighbor, even when he supposes himself alone. But it does not seem clear that the law would go quite so far as that.

The next form of liability is comparatively insignificant. I mean the action for malicious prosecution. A man may recover damages against another for maliciously and without probable cause instituting a criminal, or, in some cases, a civil prosecution against him upon a false charge. The want of probable cause refers, of course, only to the state of the defendant's knowledge, not to his intent. It means the absence of probable cause in the facts known to the defendant when he instituted the suit. But the standard applied to the defendant's consciousness is external to it. The question is not whether he thought the facts to constitute probable cause, but whether the court thinks they did.

Then as to malice. The conduct of the defendant consists in instituting proceedings on a charge which is in fact false, and which has not prevailed. That is the root of the whole matter. If the charge was true, or if the plaintiff has been convicted, even though he may be able now to prove that he was wrongly convicted, the defendant is safe, however great his malice, and however little ground he had for his charge.

Suppose, however, that the charge is false, and does not prevail. It may readily be admitted that malice did originally mean a malevolent motive, an actual intent to harm the plaintiff by making a false charge. The legal remedy here, again, started from the moral basis, the occasion for it, no doubt, being similar to that which gave rise to the old law of conspiracy, that a man's enemies would sometimes seek his destruction by setting the criminal law in motion against him. As it was punishable to combine for such a purpose, it was concluded, with some hesitation, that, when a single individual wickedly attempted the same thing, he should be liable on similar grounds.[4] I must fully admit that there is weighty authority to the effect that malice in its ordinary

[4] Cf. *Knight* v. *German*, Cro. Eliz. 70; s. c., ib. 134.

sense is to this day a distinct fact to be proved and to be found by the jury.

But this view cannot be accepted without hesitation. It is admitted that, on the one side, the existence of probable cause, believed in, is a justification notwithstanding malice;[5] that, on the other, "it is not enough to show that the case appeared sufficient to this particular party, but it must be sufficient to induce a sober, sensible and discreet person to act upon it, or it must fail as a justification for the proceeding upon general grounds."[6] On the one side, malice alone will not make a man liable for instituting a groundless prosecution; on the other, his justification will depend, not on his opinion of the facts, but on that of the court. When his actual moral condition is disregarded to this extent, it is a little hard to believe that the existence of an improper motive should be material. Yet that is what malice must mean in this case, if it means anything.[7] For the evil effects of a successful indictment are of course intended by one who procures another to be indicted. I cannot but think that a jury would be told that knowledge or belief that the charge was false at the time of making it was conclusive evidence of malice. And if so, on grounds which need not be repeated, malice is not the important thing, but the facts known to the defendant.

Nevertheless, as it is obviously treading on delicate ground to make it actionable to set the regular processes of the law in motion, it is, of course, entirely possible to say that the action shall be limited to those cases where the charge was preferred from improper motives, at least if the defendant thought that there was probable cause. Such a limitation would stand almost alone in the law of civil liability. But the nature of the wrong is peculiar, and, moreover, it is quite consistent with the theory of liability here advanced that it should be confined in any given instance to actual wrong-doing in a moral sense.

The only other cause of action in which the moral condition of the defendant's consciousness might seem to be important is

[5] *Mitchell* v. *Jenkins*, 5 B. & Ad. 588, 594; *Turner* v. *Ambler*, 10 Q. B. 252, 257, 261.

[6] Redfield, C. J. in *Barron* v. *Mason*, 31 Vt. 189, 197.

[7] *Mitchell* v. *Jenkins*, 5 B. & Ad. 588, 595.

conspiracy. The old action going by that name was much like malicious prosecution, and no doubt was originally confined to cases where several persons had conspired to indict another from malevolent motives. But in the modern action on the case, where conspiracy is charged, the allegation as a rule only means that two or more persons were so far co-operating in their acts that the act of any one was the act of all. Generally speaking, the liability depends not on the co-operation or conspiring, but on the character of the acts done, supposing them all to be done by one man, or irrespective of the question whether they were done by one or several. There may be cases, to be sure, in which the result could not be accomplished, or the offence could not ordinarily be proved, without a combination of several; as, for instance, the removal of a teacher by a school board. The conspiracy would not affect the case except in a practical way, but the question would be raised whether, notwithstanding the right of the board to remove, proof that they were actuated by malevolence would not make a removal actionable. Policy, it might be said, forbids going behind their judgment, but actual evil motives coupled with the absence of grounds withdraw this protection, because policy, although it does not require them to take the risk of being right, does require that they should judge honestly on the merits.[8]

Other isolated instances like the last might, perhaps, be found in different parts of the law, in which actual malevolence would affect a man's liability for his conduct. Again, in trover for the conversion of another's chattel, where the dominion exercised over it was of a slight and ambiguous nature, it has been said that the taking must be "with the intent of exercising an ownership over the chattel inconsistent with the real owner's right of possession."[9] But this seems to be no more than a faint shadow of the doctrine explained with regard to larceny, and does not require any further or special discussion. Trover is commonly understood to go, like larceny, on the plaintiff's being deprived of his property, although in practice every possessor has the action, and,

[8] See *Burton* v. *Fulton*, 49 Penn. St. 151.
[9] Rolfe, B. in *Fouldes* v. *Willoughby*, 8 Meeson & Welsby, 540.

generally speaking, the shortest wrongful withholding of possession is a conversion.

Be the exceptions more or less numerous, the general purpose of the law of torts is to secure a man indemnity against certain forms of harm to person, reputation, or estate, at the hands of his neighbors, not because they are wrong, but because they are harms. The true explanation of the reference of liability to a moral standard, in the sense which has been explained, is not that it is for the purpose of improving men's hearts, but that it is to give a man a fair chance to avoid doing the harm before he is held responsible for it. It is intended to reconcile the policy of letting accidents lie where they fall, and the reasonable freedom of others with the protection of the individual from injury.

But the law does not even seek to indemnify a man from all harms. An unrestricted enjoyment of all his possibilities would interfere with other equally important enjoyments on the part of his neighbors. There are certain things which the law allows a man to do, notwithstanding the fact that he foresees that harm to another will follow from them. He may charge a man with crime if the charge is true. He may establish himself in business where he foresees that the effect of his competition will be to diminish the custom of another shopkeeper, perhaps to ruin him. He may erect a building which cuts another off from a beautiful prospect, or he may drain subterranean waters and thereby drain another's well; and many other cases might be put.

As any of these things may be done with foresight of their evil consequences, it would seem that they might be done with intent, and even with malevolent intent, to produce them. The whole argument of this Lecture and the preceding tends to this conclusion. If the aim of liability is simply to prevent or indemnify from harm so far as is consistent with avoiding the extreme of making a man answer for accident, when the law permits the harm to be knowingly inflicted it would be a strong thing if the presence of malice made any difference in its decisions.[a] That might happen, to be sure, without affecting the general views maintained

[a] [more especially if my argument be accepted that malice in general means only knowledge sufficient to show the danger of the act.]

here, but it is not to be expected, and the weight of authority is against it.

As the law, on the one hand, allows certain harms to be inflicted irrespective of the moral condition of him who inflicts them, so, at the other extreme, it may on grounds of policy throw the absolute risk of certain transactions on the person engaging in them, irrespective of blameworthiness in any sense. Instances of this sort have been mentioned in the last Lecture,[10] and will be referred to again.

Most liabilities in tort lie between these two extremes, and are founded on the infliction of harm which the defendant had a reasonable opportunity to avoid at the time of the acts or omissions which were its proximate cause. But as fast as specific rules are worked out in place of the vague reference to the conduct of the average man, they range themselves alongside of other specific rules based on public policy, and the grounds from which they spring cease to be manifest. So that, as will be seen directly, rules which seem to lie outside of culpability in any sense have sometimes been referred to remote fault, while others which started from the general notion of negligence may with equal ease be referred to some extrinsic ground of policy.

Apart from the extremes just mentioned, it is now easy to see how the point at which a man's conduct begins to be at his own peril is generally fixed. When the principle is understood on which that point is determined by the law of torts, we possess a common ground of classification, and a key to the whole subject, so far as tradition has not swerved the law from a consistent theory. It has been made pretty clear from what precedes, that I find that ground in knowledge of circumstances accompanying an act or conduct indifferent but for those circumstances.

But it is worth remarking, before that criterion is discussed, that a possible common ground is reached at the preceding step in the descent from malice through intent and foresight. Foresight is a possible common denominator of wrongs at the two extremes of malice and negligence. The purpose of the law is to prevent or secure a man indemnity from harm at the hands of his neighbors, so far as consistent with other considerations which have

[10] *Supra*, pp. 92 *et seq.*

been mentioned, and excepting, of course, such harm as it permits to be intentionally inflicted. When a man foresees that harm will result from his conduct, the principle which exonerates him from accident no longer applies, and he is liable. But, as has been shown, he is bound to foresee whatever a prudent and intelligent man would have foreseen, and therefore he is liable for conduct from which such a man would have foreseen that harm was liable to follow.

Accordingly, it would be possible to state all cases of negligence in terms of imputed or presumed foresight. It would be possible even to press the presumption further, applying the very inaccurate maxim, that every man is presumed to intend the natural consequences of his own acts; and this mode of expression will, in fact, be found to have been occasionally used,[11] more especially in the criminal law, where the notion of intent has a stronger foothold.[12] The latter fiction is more remote and less philosophical than the former; but, after all, both are equally fictions. Negligence is not foresight, but precisely the want of it; and if foresight were presumed, the ground of the presumption, and therefore the essential element, would be the knowledge of facts which made foresight possible.

Taking knowledge, then, as the true starting-point, the next question is how to determine the circumstances necessary to be known in any given case in order to make a man liable for the consequences of his act. They must be such as would have led a prudent man to perceive danger, although necessarily to foresee the specific harm. But this is a vague test. How is it decided what those circumstances are? The answer must be, by experience.

But there is one point which has been left ambiguous in the preceding Lecture and here, and which must be touched upon. It has been assumed that conduct which the man of ordinary intelligence would perceive to be dangerous under the circumstances, would be blameworthy if pursued by him. It might not be so, however. Suppose that, acting under the threats of twelve

[11] See, e. g., Cooley, Torts, 164.

[12] *Rex* v. *Dixon*, 3 Maule & Selwyn, 11, 15; *Reg.* v. *Hicklin*, L. R. 3 Q. B. 360; 5 C. & P. 266, n.

armed men, which put him in fear of his life, a man enters another's close and takes a horse. In such a case, he actually contemplates and chooses harm to another as the consequence of his act. Yet the act is neither blameworthy nor punishable. But it might be actionable, and Rolle, C. J. ruled that it was so in *Gilbert* v. *Stone.*[13] If this be law, it goes the full length of deciding that it is enough if the defendant has had a chance to avoid inflicting the harm complained of. And it may well be argued that, although he does wisely to ransom his life as he best may, there is no reason why he should be allowed to intentionally and permanently transfer his misfortunes to the shoulders of his neighbors.

It cannot be inferred, from the mere circumstance that certain conduct is made actionable, that therefore the law regards it as wrong, or seeks to prevent it. Under our mill acts a man has to pay for flowing his neighbor's lands, in the same way that he has to pay in trover for converting his neighbor's goods. Yet the law approves and encourages the flowing of lands for the erection of mills.

Moral predilections must not be allowed to influence our minds in settling legal distinctions. If we accept the test of the liability alone, how do we distinguish between trover and the mill acts? or between conduct which is prohibited, and that which is merely taxed? The only distinction which I can see is in the difference of the collateral consequences attached to the two classes of conduct. In the one, the maxim *in pari delicto potior est conditio defendentis,* and the invalidity of contracts contemplating it, show that the conduct is outside the protection of the law. In the other, it is otherwise.[14] This opinion is confirmed by the fact, that almost the only cases in which the distinction between prohibition and taxation come up concern the application of these maxims.

But if this be true, liability to an action does not necessarily import wrong-doing. And this may be admitted without at all impairing the force of the argument in the foregoing Lecture, which only requires that people should not be made to pay for accidents which they could not have avoided.

It is doubtful, however, whether the ruling of Chief Justice

[13] Aleyn, 35; Style, 72; A. D. 1648.

[14] 1 Kent (12th ed.), 467, n. 1; 6 Am. Law Rev. 723–725; 7 id. 652.

Rolle would now be followed. The squib case, *Scott* v. *Shepherd*, and the language of some text-books, are more or less opposed to it.[15] If the latter view is law, then an act must in general not only be dangerous, but on which would be blameworthy on the part of the average man, in order to make the actor liable. But, aside from such exceptional cases as *Gilbert* v. *Stone*, the two tests agree, and the difference need not be considered in what follows.

I therefore repeat, that experience is the test by which it is decided whether the degree of danger attending given conduct under certain known circumstances is sufficient to throw the risk upon the party pursuing it.

For instance, experience shows that a good many guns supposed to be unloaded go off and hurt people. The ordinarily intelligent and prudent member of the community would foresee the possibility of danger from pointing a gun which he had not inspected into a crowd, and pulling the trigger, although it was said to be unloaded. Hence, it may very properly be held that a man who does such a thing does it at his peril, and that, if damage ensues, he is answerable for it. The co-ordinated acts necessary to point a gun and pull a trigger, and the intent and knowledge shown by the co-ordination of those acts, are all consistent with entire blamelessness. They threaten harm to no one without further facts. But the one additional circumstance of a man in the line and within range of the piece makes the conduct manifestly dangerous to any one who knows the fact. There is no longer any need to refer to the prudent man, or general experience. The facts have taught their lesson, and have generated a concrete and external rule of liability. He who snaps a cap upon a gun pointed in the direction of another person, known by him to be present, is answerable for the consequences.

The question what a prudent man would do under given circumstances is then equivalent to the question what are the teachings of experience as to the dangerous character of this or that conduct under these or those circumstances; and as the teach-

[15] 2 Wm. Bl. 892, A. D. 1773; *supra*, p. 74; Addison on Torts (4th ed.), 264, citing Y. B. 37 Hen. VI. 37, pl. 26, which hardly sustains the broad language of the text.

ings of experience are matters of fact, it is easy to see why the jury should be consulted with regard to them. They are, however, facts of a special and peculiar function. Their only bearing is on the question, what ought to have been done or omitted under the circumstances of the case, not on what was done. Their function is to suggest a rule of conduct.

Sometimes courts are induced to lay down rules by facts of a more specific nature; as that the legislature passed a certain statute, and that the case at bar is within the fair meaning of its words; or that the practice of a specially interested class, or of the public at large, has generated a rule of conduct outside the law which it is desirable that the courts should recognize and enforce. These are matters of fact, and have sometimes been pleaded as such. But as their only importance is, that, if believed, they will induce the judges to lay down a rule of conduct, or in other words a rule of law, suggested by them, their tendency in most instances is to disappear as fast as the rules suggested by them become settled.[16] While the facts are uncertain, as they are still only motives for decision upon the law,—grounds for legislation, so to speak,—the judges may ascertain them in any way which satisfies their conscience. Thus, courts recognize the statutes of the jurisdiction judicially, although the laws of other jurisdictions, with doubtful wisdom, are left to the jury.[17] They may take judicial cognizance of a custom of merchants.[18] In former days, at least, they might inquire about it *in pais* after a demurrer.[19] They may act on the statement of a special jury, as in the time of Lord Mansfield and his successors, or upon the finding of a common jury based on the testimony of witnesses, as is the practice to-day in this country. But many instances will be found in the text-books which show that, when the facts are ascertained, they soon cease to be referred to, and give place to a rule of law.

[16] Compare *Crouch* v. *London & N. W. R. Co.*, 14 C. B. 255, 283; *Calye's Case*, 8 Co. Rep. 32; Co. Lit. 89 *a*, n. 7; 1 Ch. Pl. (1st ed.), 219, (6th ed.), 216, 217; 7 Am. Law Rev. 656 *et seq.*

[17] But cf. *The Pawashick*, 2 Lowell, 142.

[18] *Gibson* v. *Stevens*, 8 How. 384, 398, 399; *Barnett* v. *Brandão*, 6 Man. & Gr. 630, 665; *Hawkins* v. *Cardy*, 1 Ld. Raym. 360.

[19] *Pickering* v. *Barkley*, Style, 132; *Wegerstoffe* v. *Keene*, 1 Strange, 214, 216, 223; *Smith* v. *Kendall*, 6 T. R. 123, 124.

The same transition is noticeable with regard to the teachings of experience. There are many cases, no doubt, in which the court would lean for aid upon a jury; but there are also many in which the teaching has been formulated in specific rules. These rules will be found to vary considerably with regard to the number of concomitant circumstances necessary to throw the peril of conduct otherwise indifferent on the actor. As the circumstances become more numerous and complex, the tendency to cut the knot with the jury becomes greater. It will be useful to follow a line of cases up from the simple to the more complicated, by way of illustration. The difficulty of distinguishing rules based on other grounds of policy from those which have been worked out in the field of negligence, will be particularly noticed.

In all these cases it will be found that there has been a voluntary act on the part of the person to be charged. The reason for this requirement was shown in the foregoing Lecture. Unnecessary though it is for the defendant to have intended or foreseen the evil which he has caused, it is necessary that he should have chosen the conduct which led to it. But it has also been shown that a voluntary act is not enough, and that even a co-ordinated series of acts or conduct is often not enough by itself. But the co-ordination of a series of acts shows a further intent than is necessarily manifested by any single act, and sometimes proves with almost equal certainty the knowledge of one or more concomitant circumstances. And there are cases where conduct with only the intent and knowledge thus necessarily implied is sufficient to throw the risk of it on the actor.

For instance, when a man does the series of acts called walking, it is assumed for all purposes of responsibility that he knows the earth is under his feet. The conduct *per se* is indifferent, to be sure. A man may go through the motions of walking without legal peril, if he chooses to practise on a private treadmill; but if he goes through the same motions on the surface of the earth, it cannot be doubted that he knows that the earth is there. With that knowledge, he acts at his peril in certain respects. If he crosses his neighbor's boundary, he is a trespasser. The reasons for this strict rule have been partially discussed in the last Lecture. Possibly there is more of history or of past or present notions of policy in its explanation than is there suggested, and at any rate I do not care to justify the rule. But it is intelligible. A man who walks knows that he is moving over the surface of the earth, he knows that he is surrounded by private estates which he has no right to enter, and he knows that his motion, unless properly guided, will carry him into those estates. He is thus warned, and the burden of his conduct is thrown upon himself.

But the act of walking does not throw the peril of all possible consequences upon him. He may run a man down in the street, but he is not liable for that unless he does it negligently. Confused as the law is with cross-lights of tradition, and hard as we may find it to arrive at any perfectly satisfactory general theory, it does distinguish in a pretty sensible way, according to the nature and degree of the different perils incident to a given situation.

From the simple case of walking we may proceed to the more complex cases of dealings with tangible objects of property. It may be said that, generally speaking, a man meddles with such things at his own risk. It does not matter how honestly he may believe that they belong to himself, or are free to the public, or that he has a license from the owner, or that the case is one in which the law has limited the rights of ownership; he takes the chance of how the fact may turn out, and if the fact is otherwise than as he supposes, he must answer for his conduct. As has been already suggested, he knows that he is exercising more or less dominion over property, or that he is injuring it; he must make good his right if it is challenged.

Whether this strict rule is based on the common grounds of liability, or upon some special consideration of past or present policy, policy has set some limits to it, as was mentioned in the foregoing Lecture.

Another case of conduct which is at the risk of the party without further knowledge than it necessarily imports, is the keeping of a tiger or bear, or other animal of a species commonly known to be ferocious. If such an animal escapes and does damage, the owner is liable simply on proof that he kept it. In this instance the comparative remoteness of the moment of choice in the line of causation from the effect complained of, will be particularly noticed. Ordinary cases of liability arise out of a choice which was the proximate cause of the harm upon which the action is founded. But here there is usually no question of negligence in guarding the beast. It is enough in most, if not in all cases, that the owner has chosen to keep it. Experience has shown that tigers and bears are alert to find means of escape, and that, if they escape, they are very certain to do harm of a serious nature. The possibility of a great danger has the same effect as the probability of a less one, and the law throws the risk of the venture on the person who introduces the peril into the community.

This remoteness of the opportunity of choice goes far to show that this risk in thrown upon the owner for other reasons than the ordinary one of imprudent conduct. It has been suggested that the liability stood upon remote inadvertence.[20] But the law does not forbid a man to keep a menagerie, or deem it in any way blameworthy. It has applied nearly as strict a rule to dealings which are even more clearly beneficial to the community than a show of wild beasts.

This seems to be one of those cases where the ground of liability is to be sought in policy coupled with tradition, rather than in any form of blameworthiness, or the existence of such a chance to avoid doing the harm as a man is usually allowed. But the fact that remote inadvertence has been suggested for an explanation illustrates what has been said about the difficulty of deciding whether a given rule is founded on special grounds, or has been worked out within the sphere of negligence, when once a special rule has been laid down.

It is further to be noticed that there is no question of the defendant's knowledge of the nature of tigers, although without that knowledge he cannot be said to have intelligently chosen to subject the community to danger. Here again even in the domain of knowledge the law applies its principle of averages. The fact that tigers and bears are dangerous is so generally known, that a man who keeps them is presumed to know their peculiarities. In other words, he does actually know that he has an animal with

[20] *Card* v. *Case*, 5 C. B. 622, 634. Cf. Austin (3d ed.), 513.

certain teeth, claws, and so forth, and he must find out the rest of what an average member of the community would know, at his peril.

What is true as to damages in general done by ferocious wild beasts is true as to a particular class of damages done by domestic cattle, namely, trespasses upon another's land. This has been dealt with in former Lectures, and it is therefore needless to do more than to recall it here, and to call attention to the distinction based on experience and policy between damage which is and that which is not of a kind to be expected. Cattle generally stray and damage cultivated land when they get upon it. They only exceptionally hurt human beings.

I need not recur to the possible historical connection of either of these last forms of liability with the *noxæ deditio*, because, whether that origin is made out or not, the policy of the rule has been accepted as sound, and carried further in England within the last few years by the doctrine that a man who brings upon his land and keeps there anything likely to do mischief if it escape, must keep it in at his peril.[21] The strictness of this principle will vary in different jurisdictions, as the balance varies between the advantages to the public and the dangers to individuals from the conduct in question. Danger of harm to others is not the only thing to be considered, as has been said already. The law allows some harms to be intentionally inflicted, and *a fortiori* some risks to be intentionally run. In some Western States a man is not required to keep his cattle fenced in. Some courts have refused to follow *Rylands* v. *Fletcher*.[22] On the other hand, the principle has been applied to artificial reservoirs of water, to cesspools, to accumulations of snow and ice upon a building by reason of the form of its roof, and to party walls.[23]

In these cases, as in that of ferocious animals, it is no excuse that the defendant did not know, and could not have found out, the weak point from which the dangerous object escaped. The period of choice was further back, and, although he was not to

[21] *Rylands* v. *Fletcher*, L. R. 3 H. L. 330; *supra*, p. 93.

[22] See *Marshall* v. *Welwood*, 38 N. J. (9 Vroom), 339; 2 Thompson, Negligence, 1234, n. 3.

[23] *Gorham* v. *Gross*, 125 Mass. 232; *supra*, p. 93.

blame, he was bound at his peril to know that the object was a continual threat to his neighbors, and that is enough to throw the risk of the business on him.

I now pass to cases one degree more complex than those thus far considered. In these there must be another concomitant circumstance known to the party in addition to those of which the knowledge is necessarily or practically proved by his conduct. The cases which naturally suggest themselves again concern animals. Experience as interpreted by the English law has shown that dogs, rams, and bulls are in general of a tame and mild nature, and that, if any one of them does by chance exhibit a tendency to bite, butt, or gore, it is an exceptional phenomenon. Hence it is not the law that a man keeps dogs, rams, bulls, and other like tame animals at his peril as to the personal damages which they may inflict, unless he knows or has notice that the particular animal kept by him has the abnormal tendency which they do sometimes show. The law has, however, been brought a little nearer to actual experience by statute in many jurisdictions.

Now let us go one step farther still. A man keeps an unbroken and unruly horse, knowing it to be so. That is not enough to throw the risk of its behavior on him. The tendency of the known wildness is not dangerous generally, but only under particular circumstances. Add to keeping, the attempt to break the horse; still no danger to the public is disclosed. But if the place where the owner tries to break it is a crowded thoroughfare, the owner knows an additional circumstance which, according to common experience, makes this conduct dangerous, and therefore must take the risk of what harm may be done.[24] On the other hand, if a man who was a good rider bought a horse with no appearance of vice and mounted it to ride home, there would be no such apparent danger as to make him answerable if the horse became unruly and did damage.[25] Experience has measured the probabilities and draws the line between the two cases.

Whatever may be the true explanation of the rule applied to keeping tigers, or the principle of *Rylands* v. *Fletcher,* in the last

[24] *Mitchil* v. *Alestree,* 1 Vent. 295; s. c., 3 Keb. 650; 2 Lev. 172; *supra,* p. 76.

[25] *Hammack* v. *White,* 11 C. B. n. s. 588.

cases we have entered the sphere of negligence, and, if we take a case lying somewhere between the two just stated, and add somewhat to the complexity of the circumstances, we shall find that both conduct and standard would probably be left without much discrimination to the jury, on the broad issue whether the defendant had acted as a prudent man would have done under the circumstances.

As to wrongs called malicious or intentional it is not necessary to mention the different classes a second time, and to find them a place in this series. As has been seen, they vary in the number of circumstances which must be known. Slander is conduct which is very generally at the risk of the speaker, because, as charges of the kind with which it deals are manifestly detrimental, the questions which practically arise for the most part concern the defence of truth or privilege. Deceit requires more, but still simple facts. Statements do not threaten the harm in question unless they are made under such circumstances as to naturally lead to action, and are made on insufficient grounds.

It is not, however, without significance, that certain wrongs are described in language importing intent. The harm in such cases is most frequently done intentionally, and, if intent to cause a certain harm is shown, there is no need to prove knowledge of facts which made it likely that harm would follow. Moreover, it is often much easier to prove intent directly, than to prove the knowledge which would make it unnecessary.

The cases in which a man is treated as the responsible cause of a given harm, on the one hand, extend beyond those in which his conduct was chosen in actual contemplation of that result, and in which, therefore, he may be said to have chosen to cause that harm; and, on the other hand, they do not extend to all instances where the damages would not have happened but for some remote election on his part. Generally speaking, the choice will be found to have extended further than a simple act, and to have co-ordinated acts into conduct. Very commonly it will have extended further still, to some external consequence. But generally, also, it will be found to have stopped short of the consequence complained of.

The question in each case is whether the actual choice, or, in other words, the actually contemplated result, was near enough to the remoter result complained of to throw the peril of it upon the actor.

Many of the cases which have been put thus far are cases where the proximate cause of the loss was intended to be produced by the defendant. But it will be seen that the same result may be caused by a choice at different points. For instance, a man is sued for having caused his neighbor's house to burn down. The simplest case is, that he actually intended to burn it down. If so, the length of the chain of physical causes intervening is of no importance, and has no bearing on the case.

But the choice may have stopped one step farther back. The defendant may have intended to light a fire on his own land, and may not have intended to burn the house. Then the nature of the intervening and concomitant physical causes becomes of the highest importance. The question will be the degree of danger attending the contemplated (and therefore chosen) effect of the defendant's conduct under the circumstances known to him. If this was very plain and very great, as, for instance, if his conduct consisted in lighting stubble near a haystack close to the house, and if the manifest circumstances were that the house was of wood, the stubble very dry, and the wind in a dangerous quarter, the court would probably rule that he was liable. If the defendant lighted an ordinary fire in a fireplace in an adjoining house, having no knowledge that the fireplace was unsafely constructed, the court would probably rule that he was not liable. Midway, complicated and doubtful cases would go to the jury.

But the defendant may not even have intended to set the fire, and his conduct and intent may have been simply to fire a gun, or, remoter still, to walk across a room, in doing which he involuntarily upset a bottle of acid. So that cases may go to the jury by reason of the remoteness of the choice in the series of events, as well as because of the complexity of the circumstances attending the act or conduct. The difference is, perhaps, rather dramatic than substantial.

But the philosophical analysis of every wrong begins by determining what the defendant has actually chosen, that is to say, what his voluntary act or conduct has been, and what consequences he has actually contemplated as flowing from them, and then goes on to determine what dangers attended either the conduct under the known circumstances, or its contemplated consequence under the contemplated circumstances.

Take a case like the glancing of Sir Walter Tyrrel's arrow. If an expert marksman contemplated that the arrow would hit a certain person, *cadit quæstio*. If he contemplated that it would glance in the direction of another person, but contemplated no more than that, in order to judge of his liability we must go to the end of his foresight, and, assuming the foreseen event to happen, consider what the manifest danger was then. But if no such event was foreseen, the marksman must be judged by the circumstances known to him at the time of shooting.

The theory of torts may be summed up very simply. At the two extremes of the law are rules determined by policy without reference of any kind to morality. Certain harms a man may inflict even wickedly; for certain others he must answer, although his conduct has been prudent and beneficial to the community.

But in the main the law started from those intentional wrongs which are the simplest and most pronounced cases, as well as the nearest to the feeling of revenge which leads to self-redress. It thus naturally adopted the vocabulary, and in some degree the tests, of morals. But as the law has grown, even when its standards have continued to model themselves upon those of morality, they have necessarily become external, because they have considered, not the actual condition of the particular defendant, but whether his conduct would have been wrong in the fair average member of the community, whom he is expected to equal at his peril.

In general, this question will be determined by considering the degree of danger attending the act or conduct under the known circumstances. If there is danger that harm to another will follow, the act is generally wrong in the sense of the law.

But in some cases the defendant's conduct may not have been morally wrong, and yet he may have chosen to inflict the harm, as he has acted in fear of his life. In such cases he will be liable, or not, according as the law makes moral blameworthiness, within the limits explained above, the ground of liability, or deems it sufficient if the defendant has had reasonable warning of danger before acting. This distinction, however, is generally unimportant, and the known tendency of the act under the known circumstances to do harm may be accepted as the general test of conduct.

The tendency of a given act to cause harm under given circumstances must be determined by experience. And experience either at first hand or through the voice of the jury is continually working out concrete rules, which in form are still more external and still more remote from a reference to the moral condition of the defendant, than even the test of the prudent man which makes the first stage of the division between law and morals. It does this in the domain of wrongs described as intentional, as systematically as in those styled unintentional or negligent.

But while the law is thus continually adding to its specific rules, it does not adopt the coarse and impolitic principle that a man acts always at his peril. On the contrary, its concrete rules, as well as the general questions addressed to the jury, show that the defendant must have had at least a fair chance of avoiding the infliction of harm before he becomes answerable for such a consequence of his conduct. And it is certainly arguable that even a fair chance to avoid bringing harm to pass is not sufficient to throw upon a person the peril of his conduct, unless, judged by average standards, he is also to blame for what he does.

LECTURE V

THE BAILEE AT COMMON LAW

So far the discussion has been confined to the general principles of liability, and to the mode of ascertaining the point at which a man begins to act at his own peril. But it does not matter to a man whether he acts at his own peril or not, unless harm comes of it, and there must always be some one within reach of the consequences of the act before any harm can be done. Furthermore, and more to the point, there are certain forms of harm which are not likely to be suffered, and which can never be complained of by any one except a person who stands in a particular relation to the actor or to some other person or thing. Thus it is neither a harm nor a wrong to take fish from a pond unless the pond is possessed or owned by some one, and then only to the possessor or owner. It is neither a harm nor a wrong to abstain from delivering a bale of wool at a certain time and place, unless a binding promise has been made so to deliver it, and then it is a wrong only to the promisee.

The next thing to be done is to analyze those special relations out of which special rights and duties arise. The chief of them—and I mean by the word "relations" relations of fact simply—are possession and contract, and I shall take up those subjects successively.

The test of the theory of possession which prevails in any system of law is to be found in its mode of dealing with persons who have a thing within their power, but who do not own it, or assert the position of an owner for themselves with regard to it,—bailees, in a word. It is necessary, therefore, as a preliminary to understanding the common-law theory of possession, to study the common law with regard to bailees.

The state of things which prevailed on the border between

England and Scotland within recent times, and which is brought back in the flesh by the ballad of the Fray o' Suport, is very like that which in an earlier century left its skeleton in the folk-laws of Germany and England. Cattle were the principal property known, and cattle-stealing the principal form of wrongful taking of property. Of law there was very little, and what there was depended almost wholly upon the party himself to enforce. The Salic Law of the fifth century and the Anglo-Saxon laws of Alfred are very full in their directions about following the trail. If the cattle were come up with before three days were gone, the pursuer had the right to take and keep them, subject only to swearing that he lost them against his will. If more than three days went by before the cattle were found, the defendant might swear, if he could, to facts which would disprove the claimant's loss.

This procedure was in truth a legal procedure; but it depended for its beginning and for its execution on the party making the claim. From its "executive" nature, it could hardly have been started by any other than the person on the spot, in whose keeping the cattle were. The oath was to the effect that the party had lost possession against his will. But if all that a man had to swear was that he had lost possession against his will, it is a natural conclusion that the right to take the oath and make use of the procedure depended on possession, and not on ownership. Possession was not merely sufficient, but it was essential. Only he who was in possession could say that he had lost the property against his will, just as only he who was on the spot could follow the cattle.[1]

[1] Laband, Vermögensrechtlichen Klagen, § 16, pp. 108 *et seq.*; Heusler, Gewere, 487, 492. These authors correct the earlier opinion of Bruns, R. d. Besitzes, § 37, pp. 313 *et seq.*, adopted by Sohm in his Proc. d. Lex Salica, § 9. Cf. the discussion of *sua* in writs of trespass, &c. in the English law, at the end of Lecture VI. Those who wish short accounts in English may consult North Amer. Rev., CX. 210, and see Id., CXVIII. 416; Essays in Anglo-Saxon Law, pp. 212 *et seq.* Our knowledge as to the primitive form of action is somewhat meagre and dependent on inference. Some of the earliest texts are Ed. Liutpr. 131; Lex Baiw., XV. 4; L. Frision. Add. X.; L. Visig., V. 5. 1; L. Burg., XLIX. 1, 2. The edict of Liutprand, dealing with housebreaking followed by theft of property left in charge of the householder, lays down that the owner shall look to the bailee alone, and the bailee shall hold the thief both for the housebreaking and for the stolen goods. Because, as it says, we cannot raise two claims out of one *causa;* somewhat as our law

This, so far as known, was the one means afforded by the early law of our race for the recovery of property lost against one's will. So that, in a word, this procedure, modelled on the self-redress natural to the case which gave rise to it, was the only remedy, was confined to the man in possession, and was not open to the owner unless he was that man.

To this primitive condition of society has been traced a rule which maintained itself to later times and a more civilized procedure, that, if chattels were intrusted by their owner to another person, the bailee, and not the bailor, was the proper party to sue for their wrongful appropriation by a third. It followed that if the bailee, or person so intrusted, sold or gave the goods in his charge to another, the owner could only look to the bailee, and could not sue the stranger; not from any principle in favor of trade, intended to protect those who bought in good faith from parties in possession, but because there was no form of action known which was open to him. But as the remedies were all in the bailee's hands, it also followed that he was bound to hold his bailor harmless. If the goods were lost, it was no excuse that they were stolen without his fault. He alone could recover the lost property, and therefore he was bound to do so.

In the course of time this reason ceased to exist. An owner out of possession could sue the wrongful taker of his property, as well as one who had possession. But the strict liability of the bailee remained, as such rules do remain in the law, long after the causes which gave rise to it had disappeared, and at length we find cause and effect inverted. We read in Beaumanoir (A. D. 1283) that, if a hired thing is stolen, the suit belongs to the bailee, because he is answerable to the person from whom he hired.[2] At first the bailee was answerable to the owner, because he was the only person who could sue. Now it was said he could sue because he was answerable to the owner.

All the above peculiarities reappear in the Anglo-Norman law,

was unable to divide the severing a thing from the realty, and the conversion of it, into two different wrongs. Compare, further, Jones, Bailm. 112; Exodus xxii. 10–12; LL. Alfred, 28; 1 Thorpe, Anc. L., p. 51; Gaii Inst., III. §§ 202–207.

[2] XXXI. 16.

and from that day to this all kinds of bailees have been treated as having possession in a legal sense, as I shall presently show.

It is desirable to prove the native origin of our law of bailment, in order that, when theory comes to be considered, modern German opinion may not be valued at more than its true worth. The only existing theories on the subject come from Germany. The German philosophers who have written upon law have known no other system than the Roman, and the German lawyers who have philosophized have been professors of Roman law. Some rules which we think clear are against what the German civilians would regard as first principles. To test the value of those principles, or at least to prevent the hasty assumption that they are universal, toward which there is a slight tendency among English writers, it is well to realize that we are dealing with a new system, of which philosophy has not yet taken account.

In the first place, we find an action to recover stolen property, which, like the Salic procedure, was based on possession, not on title. Bracton says that one may sue for his chattel as stolen, by the testimony of good men, and that it does not matter whether the thing thus taken was his own property or another's, provided it was in his custody.[3]

The point of especial importance, it will be remembered, was the oath. The oath of the *probi homines* would seem from the letter of Bracton to have been that the thing was lost (*adirata*), and this we are expressly told was the fact in a report of the year 1294. "Note that where a man's chattel is lost (ou la chosse de un home est endire), he may count that he [the finder] tortiously detains it, &c., and tortiously for this that whereas he lost the said thing on such a day, &c., he [the loser] came on such a day, &c. (la vynt yl e en jour), and found it in the house of such an one, and told him, &c., and prayed him to restore the thing, but that he would not restore it, &c., to his damage, &c.; and if he, &c. In

[3] "Poterit enim rem suam petere [civiliter] ut adiratam per testimonium proborum hominum, et sic consequi rem suam quamvis furatam. . . . Et non refert utrum res quæ ita subtracta fuit extiterit illius appellantis propria vel alterius, dum tamen de custodia sua." Bract., fol. 150 *b*, 151; Britton (Nich. ed.), I. 59, 60 [23 *b*], *De Larcyns;* cf. ib. 67 [26 *b*]; Fleta, fol. 54, L. I. c. 38, § 1.

this case, the demandant must prove (his own hand the twelfth) *that he lost the thing.*"[4]

Assuming that as the first step we find a procedure kindred to that of the early German folk-laws, the more important question is whether we find any principles similar to those which have just been explained. One of these, it will be remembered, concerned wrongful transfer by the bailee. We find it laid down in the Year Books that, if I deliver goods to a bailee to keep for me, and he sells or gives them to a stranger, the property is vested in the stranger by the gift, and I cannot maintain trespass against him; but that I have a good remedy against the bailee by writ of detinue (for his failure to return the goods).[5] These cases have been understood, and it would seem on the whole rightly, not merely to deny trespass to the bailor, but any action whatever. Modern writers have added, however, the characteristically modern qualification, that the purchase must be *bona fide,* and without notice.[6] It may be answered, that the proposition extends to gifts as well as to sales by the bailee, that there is no such condition in the old books, and that it is contrary to the spirit of the strict doctrines of the common law to read it in. No lawyer needs to be told that, even so qualified, this is no longer the law.[7] The doctrine of the Year Books must be regarded as a survival from the primitive times when we have seen the same rule in force, unless we are prepared to believe that in the fifteenth century they had a nicer feeling for the rights of *bona fide* purchasers than at present.

The next point in logical order would be the degree of responsibility to which the bailee was held as towards his bailor who intrusted him. But for convenience I will consider first the explanation which was given of the bailee's right of action against third

[4] Y. B. 21 & 22 Ed. I. 466–468, noticed in North Amer. Rev., CXVIII. 421, n. (So Britton [26 *b*], "Si il puse averreer la perte.") This is not trover. The declaration in detinue *per inventionem* was called "un newfound Haliday" in Y. B. 33 Hen. VI. 26, 27; cf. 7 Hen. VI. 22, pl. 3; *Isack* v. *Clarke,* 1 Rolle, R. 126, 128.

[5] Y. B. 2 Ed. IV. 4, 5, pl. 9; 21 Hen. VII. 39, pl. 49; Bro. *Trespass,* pl. 216, 295.

[6] 2 Wms. Saund. 47, n. 1. See above, p. 132.

[7] Notes to Saunders, *Wilbraham* v. *Snow,* note (*h*).

persons wrongfully taking the goods from his possession. The inverted explanation of Beaumanoir will be remembered, that the bailee could sue because he was answerable over, in place of the original rule, that he was answerable over so strictly because only he could sue. We find the same reasoning often repeated in the Year Books, and, indeed, from that day to this it has always been one of the commonplaces of the law. Thus Hankford, then a judge of the Common Bench, says (*circa* A. D. 1410),[8] "If a stranger takes beasts in my custody, I shall have a writ of trespass against him, and shall recover the value of the beasts, because I am chargeable for the beasts to my bailor, who has the property." There are cases in which this reasoning was pushed to the conclusion, that if, by the terms of the trust, the bailee was not answerable for the goods if stolen, he would not have an action against the thief.[9] The same explanation is repeated to this day. Thus we read in a well-known textbook, "For the bailee being responsible to the bailor, if the goods be lost or damaged by negligence, or if he do not deliver them up on lawful demand, it is therefore reasonable that he should have a right of action," &c.[10] In general, nowadays, a borrower or hirer of property is not answerable if it is taken from him against his will, and if the reason offered were a true one, it would follow that, as he was not answerable over, he could not sue the wrong-doer. It would only be necessary for the wrong-doer to commit a wrong so gross as to free the bailee from responsibility, in order to deprive him of his right of action. The truth is, that any person in possession, whether intrusted and answerable over or not, a finder of property

[8] Y. B. 11 Hen. IV. 23, 24. See, further, Y. B. 8 Ed. IV. 6, pl. 5; 9 Ed. IV. 34, pl. 9; 3 Hen. VII. 4, pl. 16; 20 Hen. VII. 1, pl. 1; 21 Hen. VII. 14 *b*, pl. 23; 13 Co. Rep. 69; 1 Roll. Abr. 4 (I), pl. 1; F. N. B. 86, n. *a*; *supra*, p. 132.

[9] Fitz. Abr. *Barre*, pl. 130; Y. B. 9 Ed. IV. 34, pl. 9; 12 Am. Law Rev. 694.

[10] 2 Steph. Comm. (6th ed.), 83, cited Dicey, Parties, 353; 2 Bl. Comm. 453; 2 Kent, 585. As the bailee recovered the whole value of the goods, the old reason, that he was answerable over, has in some cases become a new rule, (seemingly based on a misunderstanding,) that the bailee is a trustee for the bailor as to the excess over his own damage. Cf. *Lyle* v. *Barker*, 5 Binn. 457, 460; 7 Cowen, 681, n.; *White* v. *Webb*, 15 Conn. 302, 305; in the order cited. (Thence the new rule has been extended to insurance recovered by a bailee. 1 Hall, N. Y. 84, 91; 3 Kent's Comm. (12th ed.), 371, 376, n. 1 (*a*).) In this form it ceases to be a reason for allowing the action.

as well as a bailee, can sue any one except the true owner for interfering with his possession, as will be shown more particularly at the end of the next Lecture.

The bailor also obtained a right of action against the wrong-doer at a pretty early date. It is laid down by counsel in 48 Edward III.,[11] in an action of trespass by an agister of cattle, that, "in this case, he who has the property may have a writ of trespass, and he who has the custody another writ of trespass. Persay: Sir, it is true. But he who recovers first shall oust the other of the action, and so it shall be in many cases, as if tenant by *elegit* is ousted, each shall have the assize, and, if the one recover first, the writ of the other is abated, and so here."

It would seem from other books that this was spoken of bailments generally, and was not limited to those which are terminable at the pleasure of the bailor. Thus in 22 Edward IV., counsel say, "If I bail to you my goods, and another takes them out of your possession, I shall have good action of trespass *quare vi et armis*."[12] And this seems to have been Rolle's understanding in the passage usually relied on by modern courts.[13]

It was to be expected that some action should be given to the bailor as soon as the law had got machinery which could be worked without help from the fresh pursuit and armed hands of the possessor and his friends. To allow the bailor to sue, and to give him trespass, were pretty nearly the same thing before the action on the case was heard of. Many early writs will be found which show that trespass had not always the clear outline which it developed later. The point which seems to be insisted on in the Year Books is, as Brooke sums it up in the margin of his Abrigment, that two shall have an *action* for a single act,—not that both shall have trespass rather than case.[14] It should be added that the Year Books quoted do not go beyond the case of a wrongful taking out of the custody of the bailee, the old case of the folk-

[11] Y. B. 48 Ed. III. 20, pl. 8; Bro. *Trespass*, pl. 67. Cf. 1 Britton (Nich. ed.), 67 [26 *b*]; Y. B. 6 Hen. VII. 12, pl. 9; 12 Ed. IV. 13, pl. 9; 12 Am. Law Rev. 694.

[12] Y. B. 22 Ed. IV. 5, pl. 16.

[13] 2 Rolle, Abr. 569, *Trespass*, 5. Cf. Y. B. 20 Hen. VII. 5, pl. 15; 21 Hen. VII. 39, pl. 49; Clayton, 135, pl. 243; 2 Wms. Saund. 47 *e* (3d ed.).

[14] Bro. *Trespass*, pl. 67 in marg.; cf. Ed. Liutpr. 131, cited *supra*, p. 131, n.

laws.[15] Even thus limited, the right to maintain trespass is now denied where the bailee has the exclusive right to the goods by lease or lien; [16] although the doctrine has been repeated with reference to bailments terminable at the pleasure of the bailor.[17] But the modified rule does not concern the present discussion, any more than the earlier form, because it still leaves open the possessory remedies to all bailees without exception. This appears from the relation of the modified rule to the ancient law; from the fact that Baron Parke, in the just cited case of *Manders* v. *Williams*, hints that he would have been prepared to apply the old rule to its full extent but for *Gordon* v. *Harper*, and still more obviously from the fact, that the bailee's right to trespass and trover is asserted in the same breath with that of the bailor, as well as proved by express decisions to be cited.

It is true that in *Lotan* v. *Cross*,[18] Lord Ellenborough ruled at nisi prius that a lender could maintain trespass for damage done to a chattel in the hands of a borrower, and that the case is often cited as authority without remark. Indeed, it is sometimes laid down generally, in reputable text-books, that a gratuitous bailment does not change the possession, but leaves it in the bailor; [19] that a gratuitous bailee is quasi a servant of the bailor, and the possession of one is the possession of the other; and that it is for this reason that, although the bailee may sue on his possession, the bailor has the same actions.[20] A part of this confusion has already been explained, and the rest will be when I come to speak of servants, between whom and all bailees there is a broad and well-known distinction. But on whatever ground *Lotan* v. *Cross* may stand, if on any, it cannot for a moment be admitted that

[15] In one instance, where, against the opinion of Brian, the bailor was allowed to sue for damage to the chattel by a stranger, the action seems to have been case. Y. B. 12 Ed. IV. 13, pl. 9; cf. the margin of the report.

[16] *Gordon* v. *Harper*, 7 T. R. 9; *Lord* v. *Price*, L. R. 9 Ex. 54; *Muggridge* v. *Eveleth*, 9 Met. 233. Cf. Clayton, 135, pl. 243.

[17] *Nicolls* v. *Bastard*, 2 C. M. & R. 659, 660; *Manders* v. *Williams*, 4 Exch. 339, 343, 344; *Morgan* v. *Ide*, 8 Cush. 420; *Strong* v. *Adams*, 30 Vt. 221, 223; *Little* v. *Fossett*, 34 Me. 545.

[18] 2 Camp. 464; cf. *Mears* v. *London & South-Western Railway Co.*, 11 C. B. N. S. 849, 854.

[19] Addison, Torts (4th ed.), 364.

[20] Wms. Pers. Prop., 26 (5th ed.), 27 (7th ed.).

borrowers in general have not trespass and trover. A gratuitous deposit for the sole benefit of the depositor is a much stronger case for the denial of these remedies to the depositary; yet we have a decision by the full court, in which Lord Ellenborough also took part, that a depositary has case, the reasoning implying that *a fortiori* a borrower would have trespass. And this has always been the law.[21] It has been seen that a similar doctrine necessarily resulted from the nature of the early German procedure; and the cases cited in the note show that, in this as in other respects, the English followed the traditions of their race.

The meaning of the rule that all bailees have the possessory remedies is, that in the theory of the common law every bailee has a true possession, and that a bailee recovers on the strength of his possession, just as a finder does, and as even a wrongful possessor may have full damages or a return of the specific thing from a stranger to the title. On the other hand, so far as the possessory actions are still allowed to bailors, it is not on the ground that they also have possession, but is probably by a survival, which has been explained, and which in the modern form of the rule is an anomaly.[22] The reason usually given is, that a right of immediate possession is sufficient,—a reason which excludes the notion that the bailor is actually possessed.

The point which is essential to understanding the common-law theory of possession is now established: that all bailees from time immemorial have been regarded by the English law as possessors, and entitled to the possessory remedies. It is not strictly necessary to go on and complete the proof that our law of bailment is of pure German descent. But, apart from curiosity, the doctrine remaining to be discussed has had such important influence upon the law of the present day, that I shall follow it out with some

[21] *Rooth* v. *Wilson*, 1 B. & Ald. 59; Y. B. 48 Ed. III. 20, pl. 8; 11 Hen. IV. 17, pl. 39; 11 Hen. IV. 23, 24, pl. 46 (Tre. "ou d'apprompter"); 21 Hen. VII. 14 *b*, pl. 23; Godbolt, 173, pl. 239; *Sutton* v. *Buck*, 2 Taunt. 302, 309; *Burton* v. *Hughes*, 2 Bing. 173; *Nicolls* v. *Bastard*, 2 C. M. & R. 659, 660; *Manders* v. *Williams*, 4 Exch. 339, 343, 344; 2 Wms. Saund., note to *Wilbraham* v. *Snow;* 2 Kent, 585, 568, 574; *Moran* v. *Portland* S. P. Co., 35 Me. 55. See, further, Lecture VI. *ad fin.*

[22] Cf. *Lord* v. *Price*, L. R. 9 Ex. 54, 56, *supra*, p. 136.

care. That doctrine was the absolute responsibility of the bailee to the bailor, if the goods were wrongfully taken from him.[23]

The early text-writers are not as instructive as might be hoped, owing to the influence of the Roman law. Glanvill, however, says in terms that, if a borrowed thing be destroyed or lost in any way while in the borrower's custody, he is absolutely bound to return a reasonable price.[24] So does Bracton, who partially repeats but modifies the language of Justinian as to *commodatum*, *depositum*, and *pignus*;[25] and as to the duty of the hirer to use the care of a *diligentissimus paterfamilias*.[26]

The language and decisions of the courts are perfectly clear; and there we find the German tradition kept alive for several centuries. I begin with the time of Edward II., about 1315. In detinue the plea was that the plaintiff delivered the defendant a chest locked with his key, that the chattels were in the chest, and that they were taken from the defendant together with his own goods by robbery. The replication was that the goods were delivered to the defendant out of enclosure, and Fitzherbert says the party was driven to that issue;[27] which implies that, if not in the chest, but in the defendant's custody, he was liable. Lord Holt, in *Coggs* v. *Bernard*,[28] denies that the chest would make any difference; but the old books agree that there is no delivery if the goods are under lock and key; and this is the origin of the distinction as to carriers breaking bulk in modern criminal law.[29] In the reign of Edward III.,[30] the case of a pledge came up, which seems always to have been regarded as a special bailment to keep as one's own goods. The defence was, that the goods were stolen with the defendant's own. The plaintiff was driven to reply

[23] *Supra*, p. 132.

[24] Lib. X. c. 13; cf. ib., c. 8.

[25] "Is qui rem commodatam accepit, ad ipsam restituendam tenetur, vel ejus precium, si forte incendio, ruina, naufragio, aut latronum, vel hostium incursu, consumpta fuerit vel deperdita, substracta, vel ablata." Fol. 99, *a*, *b*. This has been thought a corrupt text (Güterbock, Bracton, by Coxe, p. 175; 2 Twiss, Bract. Int. xxviii.), but agrees with Glanvill, *supra*, and with Fleta, L. II, c. 56, § 5.

[26] Bract., fol. 62 *b*, c. 28, § 2; Fleta, L. II. c. 59, § 4, fol. 128. Cf. Just. Inst. 3. 24, § 5; ib. 15, § 2.

[27] Y. B. 8 Ed. II. 275; Fitz. *Detinue*, pl. 59.

[28] 2 Ld. Raym. 909.

[29] Y. B. 13 Ed. IV. 9, pl. 5. See Lecture VI.

[30] 29 Ass. 163, pl. 28.

a tender before the theft, which would have put an end to the pledge, and left the defendant a general bailee.[81] Issue was taken thereon, which confirms the other cases, by implying that in that event the defendant would be liable.

Next I take a case of the time of Henry VI., A. D. 1455.[82] This was an action of debt against the Marshal of the Marshalsea, or jailer of the King's Bench prison, for an escape of a prisoner. Jailers in charge of prisoners were governed by the same law as bailees in charge of cattle. The body of the prisoner was delivered to the jailer to keep under the same liabilities that cows or goods might have been.[83] He set up in defence that enemies of the king broke into the prison and carried off the prisoner, against the will of the defendant. The question was whether this was a good defence. The court said that, if alien enemies of the king, for instance the French, released the prisoner, or perhaps if the burning of the prison gave him a chance to escape, the excuse would be good, "because then [the defendant] has remedy against no one." But if subjects of the king broke the prison, the defendant would be liable, for they are not enemies, but traitors, and then, it is implied, the defendant would have a right of action against them, and therefore would himself be answerable. In this case the court got very near to the original ground of liability, and distinguished accordingly. The person intrusted was liable in those cases where he had a remedy over against the wrongdoer (and in which, originally, he was the only person who had such a remedy); and, on the other hand, his liability, being founded on that circumstance, ceased where the remedy ceased. The jailer could not sue the soldiers of an invading army of Frenchmen; but in theory he could sue any British subject who carried off the prisoner, however little it was likely that he would get much satisfaction in that way.

A few years later the law is stated the same way by the famous Littleton. He says that, if goods are delivered to a man, he shall

[81] Cf. *Ratcliff* v. *Davis*, Yelv. 178; Cro. Jac. 244; Noy, 137; 1 Bulstr. 29.

[82] Y. B. 33 Hen. VI. 1, pl. 3. This case is cited and largely relied on in *Woodlife's Case, infra; Southcote* v. *Bennett, infra; Pickering* v. *Barkley*, Style, 132 (24 Car. I., covenant on a charter-party); and *Morse* v. *Slue, infra;* in short, in all the leading cases on bailment.

[83] Cf. Abbreviatio Placitorum, p. 343, col. 2, rot. 37, 17 Ed. II.

have an action of trespass if they are carried off, for he is chargeable over.[34] That is, he is bound to make the loss good to the party who intrusted him.

In 9 Edward IV.,[35] Danby says if a bailee received goods to keep as his proper goods, then robbery shall excuse him, otherwise not. Again, in a later case,[36] robbery is said not to be an excuse. There may have been some hesitation as to robbery when the robber was unknown, and so the bailee had no remedy over,[37] or even as to robbery generally, on the ground that by reason of the felony the bailee could not go against either the robber's body or his estate; for the one was hanged and the other forfeited.[38] But there is not a shadow of doubt that the bailee was not excused by an ordinary wrongful taking. "If the goods are taken by a trespasser, of whom the bailee has conusance, he shall be chargeable to his bailor, and shall have his action over against his trespasser." [39] The same point was touched in other passages of the Year Books,[40] and the rule of law is clearly implied by the reason which was given for the bailee's right to sue in the cases cited above.

The principle was directly decided in accordance with the ancient law in the famous case of *Southcote* v. *Bennet*.[41] This was detinue of goods delivered to the defendant to keep safely. The defendant confessed the delivery, and set up that he was robbed of the goods by J. S. "And, after argument at the bar, Gawdy and Clench, *ceteris absentibus*, held that the plaintiff ought to recover, *because it was not a special bailment;* that the defendant accepted them to keep as his proper goods, and not otherwise; *but it is a delivery*, which chargeth him to keep them at his peril. And it is not any plea in a *detinue* to say that he was robbed by one such; for he hath his remedy over by trespass, or appeal,

[34] Y. B. 9 Ed. IV. 34, pl. 9; 2 Ed. IV. 15, pl. 7. It is proper to add, that in the latter case Littleton does not seem to distinguish between servants and bailees.

[35] Y. B. 9 Ed. IV. 40, pl. 22. So Brian, in 20 Ed. IV. 11, pl. 10, *ad fin.*

[36] Y. B. 10 Hen. VII. 25, 26, pl. 3.

[37] Cf. L. Baiw., XV. 5; Y. B. 33 Hen. VI. 1, pl. 3.

[38] Y. B. 6 Hen. VII. 12, pl. 9; Bro. *Detinue*, pl. 37; 10 Hen. VI. 21, pl. 69.

[39] Y. B. 3 Hen. VII. 4, pl. 16. Cf. 10 Hen. VI. 21, pl. 69.

[40] Y. B. 11 Hen. IV. 23, 24; 6 Hen. VII. 12, pl. 9.

[41] Cro. Eliz. 815; 4 Co. Rep. 83 *b;* Co. Lit. 89; 2 Bl. Comm. 452.

to have them again." The above from Croke's report implies, what Lord Coke expressly says, that "to be kept, and to be kept safe, is all one," and both reports agree that the obligation was founded on the delivery alone. Croke's report confirms the caution which Lord Coke adds to his report: "Note, reader, it is good policy for him who takes any goods to keep, to take them in special manner, scil. to keep them as he keeps his own goods, . . . or if they happen to be stolen or purloined, that he shall not be answerable for them; for he who accepted them ought to take them in such or the like manner, or otherwise he may be charged by his general acceptance."

Down to this time, at least, it was clear law that, if a person accepted the possession of goods to keep for another even as a favor, and lost them by wrongful taking, wholly without his fault, he was bound to make good the loss, unless when he took possession he expressly stipulated against such a responsibility. The attempts of Lord Holt in *Coggs* v. *Bernard,* and of Sir William Jones in his book on Bailments, to show that *Southcote* v. *Bennet* was not sustained by authority, were futile, as any one who will study the Year Books for himself may see. The same principle was laid down seven years before by Peryam, C. B., in *Drake* v. *Royman,*[42] and *Southcote's Case* was followed as a leading precedent without question for a hundred years.

Thus the circle of analogies between the English and the early German law is complete. There is the same procedure for lost property, turning on the single question whether the plaintiff had lost possession against his will; the same principle that, if the person intrusted with the property parted with it to another, the owner could not recover it, but must get his indemnity from his bailee; the same inverted explanation, that the bailee could sue because he was answerable over, but the substance of the true doctrine in the rule that when he had no remedy he was not answerable; and, finally, the same absolute responsibility for loss, even when happening without fault on the part of the person intrusted. The last and most important of these principles is seen in force as late as the reign of Queen Elizabeth. We have now to follow its later fortunes.

[42] Savile, 133, 134. Cf. Bro. *Accion sur le Case,* pl. 103; Dyer, 161 *a, b.*

A common carrier is liable for goods which are stolen from him, or otherwise lost from his charge except by the act of God or the public enemy. Two notions have been entertained with regard to the source of this rule: one, that it was borrowed from the Roman law; [43] the other, that it was introduced by custom, as an exception to the general law of bailment, in the reigns of Elizabeth and James I.[44]

I shall try to show that both these notions are wrong, that this strict responsibility is a fragmentary survival from the general law of bailment which I have just explained; and that the modifications which the old law has undergone were due in part to a confusion of ideas which came in with the displacement of detinue by the action on the case, in part to conceptions of public policy which were read into the precedents by Lord Holt, and in part to still later conceptions of policy which have been read into the reasonings of Lord Holt by later judges.

Southcote's Case was decided in the forty-third year of Queen Elizabeth (A. D. 1601). I think the first mention of a carrier, pertinent to the question, occurs in *Woodlife's Case*,[45] decided four or five years earlier (38 or 39 Eliz., A. D. 1596 or 1597). It was an action of account for merchandise delivered to the defendant, it would seem as a factor (*"pur merchandizer"*),—clearly not as a carrier. Plea, robbery at sea with defendant's own goods. Gawdy, one of the judges who decided *Southcote's Case*, thought the plea bad; but Popham, C. J. said that, though it would not be a good plea for a carrier because he is paid for his carriage, there was a difference in this respect between carriers and other servants and factors.

This is repeated in *Southcote's Case*, and appears to involve a double distinction,—first between paid and unpaid bailees, next between bailees and servants. If the defendant was a servant not having control over the goods, he might not fall within the law of bailment, and factors are treated on the footing of servants in the early law.

The other diversity marked the entrance of the doctrine of con-

[43] *Nugent* v. *Smith*, 1 C. P. D. 19, Brett, J., at p. 28.
[44] *Nugent* v. *Smith*, 1 C. P. D. 423, Cockburn, C. J., at p. 428.
[45] Moore, 462; Owen, 57.

sideration into the law of bailment. Consideration originally meant *quid pro quo*, as will be explained hereafter. It was thus dealt with in Doctor and Student [46] when the principle was still young. Chief Justice Popham probably borrowed his distinction between paid and unpaid bailees from that work, where common carriers are mentioned as an example of the former class. A little earlier, reward made no difference.[47]

But in *Woodlife's Case*, in reply to what the Chief Justice had said, Gawdy cited the case of the Marshal of the King's Bench,[48] stated above, whereupon Popham fell back on the old distinction that the jailer had a remedy over against the rebels, but that there was no remedy over in the case at bar.

The other cases relied on were some of those on general bailment collected above; the same authorities, in short, on which *Southcote's Case* was founded. The principle adopted was the same as in *Southcote's Case*, subject only to the question whether the defendant fell within it. Nothing was said of any custom of the realm, or ever had been in any reported case before this time; and I believe this to be the first instance in which carriers are in any way distinguished from any other class of persons intrusted with goods. There is no hint of any special obligation peculiar to them in the old books; and it certainly is not true, that this case introduced one. It will be noticed, with reference to what follows, that Popham does not speak of common carriers, but of carriers.

Next came *Southcote's Case* [49] (43 Eliz., A. D. 1601), which presented the old law pure and simple, irrespective of reward or any modern innovation. In this and the earlier instances of loss by theft, the action was detinue, counting, we may presume, simply on a delivery and wrongful detainer.

But about this time important changes took place in the procedure usually adopted, which must be explained. If the chattel could be returned *in specie*, detinue afforded no satisfaction for damage which it might have suffered through the bailee's neglect.[50] The natural remedy for such damage was the action on the case. But before this could be made entirely satisfactory, there

[46] Dial. 2, ch. 38, A. D. 1530.
[47] Keilway, 160, pl. 2 (2 Hen. VIII.); cf. ib. 77 *b* (21 Hen. VII.).
[48] Y. B. 33 Hen. VI. 1, pl. 3.
[49] 4 Co. Rep. 83 *b;* Cro. Eliz. 815.
[50] Keilway, 160, pl. 2.

were certain difficulties to be overcome. The neglect which occasioned the damage might be a mere omission, and what was there akin to trespass in a nonfeasance to sustain the analogy upon which trespass on the case was founded? Moreover, to charge a man for not acting, you must show that it was his duty to act. As pleadings were formerly construed, it would not have been enough to allege that the plaintiff's goods were damaged by the defendant's negligence.[51] These troubles had been got over by the well-known words, *super se assumpsit*, which will be explained later. Assumpsit did not for a long time become an independent action of contract, and the allegation was simply the inducement to an action of tort. The ground of liability was that the defendant had started upon the undertaking, so that his negligent omission, which let in the damage, could be connected with his acts as a part of his dealing with the thing.[52] We shall find Lord Holt recognizing this original purport of assumpsit when we come to *Coggs* v. *Bernard*. Of course it was not confined to cases of bailment.

But there was another way besides this by which the defendant could be charged with a duty and made liable in case, and which, although less familiar to lawyers, has a special bearing on the law of carriers in later times. If damage had been done or occasioned by the act or omission of the defendant in the pursuit of some of the more common callings, such as that of a farrier, it seems that the action could be maintained, without laying an assumpsit, on the allegation that he was a "common" farrier.[53] The latter principle was also wholly independent of bailment. It expressed the general obligation of those exercising a public or "common" business to practise their art on demand, and show skill in it. "For," as Fitzherbert says, "it is the duty of every artificer to exercise his art rightly and truly as he ought." [54]

[51] Y. B. 19 Hen. VI. 49, *ad fin.* Cf. *Mulgrave* v. *Ogden*, Cro. Eliz. 219; s. c., Owen, 141, 1 Leon. 224; with *Isaack* v. *Clark*, 2 Bulstr. 306, at p. 312, Coke, J.

[52] See Lecture VII.

[53] Paston, J., in Y. B. 19 Hen. VI. 49. See, also, *Rogers* v. *Head*, Cro. Jac. 262; *Rich* v. *Kneeland*, Cro. Jac. 330, which will be mentioned again. An innkeeper must be a common innkeeper, Y. B. 11 Hen. IV. 45. See further, 3 Bl. Comm. 165, where "the transition from status to contract" will be found to have taken place.

[54] F. N. B. 94 D; *infra*. p. 160.

When it had thus been established that case would lie for damage when occasioned by the omission, as well as when caused by the act, of the defendant, there was no reason for denying it, even if the negligent custody had resulted in the destruction of the property.[55] From this it was but a step to extend the same form of action to all cases of loss by a bailee, and so avoid the defendant's right to wage his law. Detinue, the primitive remedy, retained that mark of primitive procedure. The last extension was made about the time of *Southcote's Case*.[56] But when the same form of action thus came to be used alike for damage or destruction by the bailee's neglect and for loss by a wrong-doer against whom the bailee had a remedy over, a source was opened for confusion with regard to the foundation and nature of the defendant's duty.

In truth, there were two sets of duties,—one not peculiar to bailees, arising from the assumpsit or public calling of the defendant, as just explained; the other, the ancient obligation, peculiar to them as such, of which *Southcote's Case* was an example. But any obligation of a bailee might be conceived of as part of a contract of bailment, and after assumpsit had become appropriated to contract, and the doctrine of consideration had been developed (both of which had happened in Lord Coke's time), it seemed unnecessary to distinguish nicely between the two sets of duties just mentioned, provided a consideration and special promise could be alleged. Furthermore, as formerly the defendant's public calling had the same effect as an assumpsit for the purpose of charging him in tort, it seems now to have been thought an equally good substitute for a special promise, in order to charge him in assumpsit. In *Rogers* v. *Head*,[57] the

[55] Y. B. 7 Hen. IV. 14; 12 Ed. IV. 13, pl. 9, 10; Dyer, 22 *b*.

[56] The process may be traced by reading, in the following order, Y. B. 2 Hen. VII. 11; Keilway, 77 *b*, *ad fin.* (21 Hen. VII.); ib. 160, pl. 2 (2 Hen. VIII.); *Drake* v. *Royman*, Savile, 133, 134 (36 Eliz.); *Mosley* v. *Fosset*, Moore, 543 (40 Eliz.); 1 Roll. Abr. 4, F, pl. 5; *Rich* v. *Kneeland*, Cro. Jac. 330 (11 Jac. I.).

[57] Cro. Jac. 262 (8 Jac. I.). Compare Maynard's argument in *Williams* v. *Hide*, Palmer, 548; *Symons* v. *Darknoll*, ib. 523, and other cases below; 1 Roll. Abr. 4, F, pl. 3. *Mosley* v. *Fosset*, Moore, 543 (40 Eliz.), an obscurely reported case, seems to have been assumpsit against an agistor, for a horse stolen while in his charge, and asserts *obiter* that "without such special assumpsit the action does not lie." This must have reference to the form of

argument was, that to charge one in assumpsit you must show either his public calling at the time of the delivery, or a special promise on sufficient consideration. This argument assumes that a bailee who received goods in the course of a public employment, for instance as a common carrier, could be charged in this form of action for a breach of either of the above sets of duties, by alleging either his public calling or his reward and a special promise. It seems to have been admitted, as was repeatedly decided before and since that case, that one who was not a common carrier could have been charged for non-delivery in a special action; that is, in case as distinguished from assumpsit.

Suppose, next, that the plaintiff sued in case for a tort. As before, the breach of duty complained of might be such damage to property as had always been sued for in that form of action, or it might be a loss by theft for which detinue would formerly have been brought, and which fell on the bailee only by reason of the bailment. If the goods had been stolen, the bailee's liability rested neither on his common calling nor on his assumpsit and his neglect, but arose from the naked facts that he had accepted a delivery and that the goods were gone, and in such cases it ought to have been enough to allege those facts in the declaration.[58] But it was very natural that the time-honored foundations for the action on the case in its more limited application should still be laid in the pleadings, even after the scope of the action had been enlarged. We shall have to inquire, later, whether the principles of *Southcote's Case* were not also extended in the opposite direction to cases not falling within it. The reasons for the rule which it laid down had lost their meaning centuries before Gawdy and Clench were born, when owners had acquired the right to sue for the wrongful taking of property in the hands of bailees, and the rule itself was a dry precedent likely to be followed according to the letter because the spirit had departed. It had begun to totter when the reporter cautioned bailees to accept in such terms as to get rid of it.[59]

---

the action, as the judges who decided *Southcote's Case* took part in the decision. See, further, *Evans* v. *Yeoman*, Clayton, 33.

[58] See *Symons* v. *Darknoll*, and the second count in *Morse* v. *Slue infra.* (The latter case shows the averment of negligence to have been mere form.) Cf. 1 Salk. 18, top.

[59] *Supra*, p. 142.

Accordingly, although that decision was the main authority relied on for the hundred years between it and *Coggs* v. *Bernard* whenever a peculiar responsibility was imposed upon bailees, we find that sometimes an assumpsit was laid as in the early precedents,[60] or more frequently that the bailee was alleged to be a common bargeman, or common carrier, or the like, without much reference to the special nature of the tort in question; and that the true bearing of the allegation was sometimes lost sight of. At first, however, there were only some slight signs of confusion in the language of one or two cases, and if the duty was conceived to fall within the principle of *Southcote's Case*, pleaders did not always allege the common or public calling, which was held unnecessary.[61] But they also adopted other devices from the precedents in case, or to strengthen an obligation which they did not well understand. Chief Justice Popham had sanctioned a distinction between paid and unpaid bailees, hence it was deemed prudent to lay a reward. Negligence was of course averred; and finally it became frequent to allege an obligation by the law and custom of the realm. This last deserves a little further attention.

There is no writ in the Register alleging any special obligation of common carriers by the custom of the realm. But the writ against innkeepers did lay a duty "by the law and custom of England," and it was easy to adopt the phrase. The allegation did not so much imply the existence of a special principle, as state a proposition of law in the form which was then usual. There are other writs of trespass which allege a common-law duty in the same way, and others again setting forth a statutory obligation.[62] So "the judges were sworn to execute justice according to law and the custom of England." [63]

The duties of a common carrier, so far as the earlier evidence goes, were simply those of bailees in general, coupled with the

[60] *Boson* v. *Sandford*, Shower, 101; *Coggs* v. *Bernard*, *infra*.

[61] *Symons* v. *Darknoll*, *infra*.

[62] Reg. Brev. 92 *b*, 95 *a*, 98 *a*, 100 *b*, 104 *a*; cf. Y. B. 19 Ed. II. 624; 30 Ed. III. 25, 26; 2 Hen. IV. 18, pl. 6; 22 Hen. VI. 21, pl. 38; 32 & 33 Ed. I., Int., xxxiii.; Brunner, Schwurgerichte, 177; id. Französische, Inhaberpapier, 9, n. 1.

[63] 12 Co. Rep. 64.

liabilities generally attached to the exercise of a public calling. The word "common" addressed itself only to the latter point, as has been shown above. This is further illustrated by the fact that, when the duty was thus set forth, it was not alleged as an obligation peculiar to common carriers as such, but was laid as the custom of law of common hoymen, or lightermen, &c., according to the business of the party concerned. It will be noticed that Chief Justice Holt in *Coggs* v. *Bernard* states the liability as applicable to all bailees for reward, exercising a public employment, and mentions common hoymen and masters of ships alongside of, not as embraced under, common carriers. It will also be noticed in the cases before that time, that there is no settled formula for the obligation in question, but that it is set forth in each case that the defendant was answerable for what he was said to have done or omitted in the particular instance.[64]

Returning now to the succession of the cases, *Rich* v. *Kneeland*[65] is the next in order (11 Jac. I., A. D. 1613). It was an action on the case (tort), against a common hoyman. In Croke's report nothing is said of custom; but the declaration avers that the defendant was a common bargeman, that the plaintiff delivered him a portmanteau, &c. to carry, and paid him for it, and that the defendant *tam negligenter custodivit,* that it was taken from him by persons unknown,—like the second count in *Morse* v. *Slue,* below. The plea was demurred to, and adjudged for the plaintiff. A writ of error being brought, it was assigned that "this action lies not against a common bargeman without special promise. But all the Justices and Barons held, that it well lies as against a common carrier upon the land." If we follow this report, it seems at the first glance that importance was attributed to the common calling. But as the loss was clearly within the principle of *Southcote's Case,* which required neither special promise nor common calling for its application, and which remained unquestioned law for three quarters of a century later, the court must have referred to the form of action employed (case), and not to

[64] See, besides the following cases, the declaration in *Chamberlain* v. *Cooke,* 2 Ventris, 75 (1 W. & M.), and note especially the variations of statement in *Morse* v. *Slue,* set forth below, in the text.

[65] Hobart, 17; Cro. Jac. 330. See also *George* v. *Wilburn,* 1 Roll. Abr. 6, pl. 4 (A. D. 1638).

the liability of the defendant in some form of action (detinue). The objection was that "this action lies not," not that the defendant was not liable, "without special promise." Even thus narrowed, it rather countenances the notion that allegations which were necessary to charge a man for damage happening through his neglect, in the more ancient and familiar use of this action, were also necessary in this new extension of it to a different class of wrongs. As it was now pretty clear that case would lie for a nonfeasance, the notion was mistaken, and we shall see that it was denied in subsequent decisions.[66]

According to Hobart's report, it was alleged that the defendant was a common hoyman, to carry goods by water, for hire, &c., that by the custom of England such carriers ought to keep the goods, &c., so as they should not be lost by the default of them or their servants, &c. "And it was resolved that, though it was laid as a custom of the realm, yet indeed it is common law." This last resolution may only mean that the custom of the realm and the common law are the same thing, as had been said concerning innkeepers long before.[67] But the law as to innkeepers, which was called the custom of the realm in the writ, had somewhat the air of a special principle extending beyond the law of bailment, inasmuch as their liability extended to goods within the inn, of which they had not the custody, and the court may have meant to make an antithesis between such a special principle and the common law or general law of bailment governing the present case.

Whatever doubts some of Croke's language might raise, standing alone, the fact remains indisputable, that for nearly a century from *Woodlife's Case* the liability of carriers for loss of goods, whether the custom of the realm or the defendant's common calling was alleged or not, was placed upon the authority and was intended to be decided on the principle of *Southcote's Case.*

Symons v. *Darknoll*[68] (4 Car. I., A. D. 1628) is precisely in point. The declaration was, that, by the common law, every

[66] The use which has been made of this case in later times shows the extreme difficulty in distinguishing between principles of substantive law and rules relating only to procedure, in the older books.

[67] Y. B. 22 Hen. VI. 21, pl. 38; *supra*, p. 148, n. 62.

[68] Palmer, 523.

lighterman ought so to manage his lighter that the goods carried therein should not perish. "And although no promise laid, it seemed to the court that the plaintiff should recover; and not alleging that defendant was common lighterman was no harm. Hyde, C. J., delivery makes the contract." This did not mean that delivery was a good consideration for a promise; but, as was laid down in *Southcote's Case*, that delivery, without a special acceptance to keep only as one's own goods, bound the bailee to keep safely, and therefore made it unnecessary to allege either an assumpsit or the defendant's common calling. Whitlock, J. called attention to the fact that the action was tort, not contract. "*Et en cest case . . . Southcote's Case fuit cite.*"

The same rule is stated as to bailments in general, the same year, by Sergeant Maynard *arguendo* in *Williams* v. *Hide*,[69] again citing *Southcote's Case*.

In *Kenrig* v. *Eggleston*[70] (24 Car. I., A. D. 1648), "case against a country carrier for not delivering a box," &c., of which he was robbed, nothing was said about custom, nor of defendant's being a common carrier, unless the above words imply that he was; but it was laid down, as in *Southcote's Case*, that "it must come on the carrier's part to make special acceptance" if he would lessen his liability as bailee.

Nicholls v. *Moore*[71] (13 Car. II., A. D. 1661) was case against a "water carrier," between Hull and London, laying a delivery to him at York. It was moved in arrest of judgment, that the defendant did not undertake to carry the goods from York to Hull. "But notwithstanding this *per totam curiam*, the defendant shall be charged on his general receipt at York, according to *Southcote's Case*."

It is fair to mention that in *Matthews* v. *Hopkins*[72] (17 Car. II.) the declaration was on the custom of the realm against a common carrier, and there was a motion in arrest of judgment, because there was a misrecital of the custom of the realm, and the defendant was not alleged to have been a carrier at the time of the receipt, and also because counts in trover, and in case on the custom, were joined. Judgment was arrested, it would seem on

[69] Palmer, 548. [70] Aleyn, 93. [71] 1 Sid. 36.
[72] 1 Sid. 244. Cf. *Dalston* v. *Janson*, 1 Ld. Raym. 58.

the latter ground, but the court continued: "And, athough the declaration may be good without recital of the custom of the realm, as Hobart says, still it is the better way to recite it."

We now come to the great case of *Morse* v. *Slue* [73] (23 & 24 Car. II., A. D. 1671, 1672). This was an action against the master of a ship lying in the river Thames, for the loss of goods intrusted to him. The goods in question were taken away by robbers, and it was found that the ship had the usual guard at the time. There seem to have been two counts, one on the law and custom of England (1 Vent. 190), for masters of ships "carefully to govern, preserve, and defend goods shipped, so long as said ship should remain in the river Thames" (2 Keb. 866); "to keep safely [goods shipped to be carried from London beyond sea] without loss or subtraction, *ita quod pro defectu* of them they may not come to any damage" (1 Vent. 190); "to keep safely goods delivered to them to carry, dangers of the sea excepted" (2 Levinz, 69; the exception last stated was perhaps drawn by the reporter from the usual form of bills of lading referred to in argument). The second count, which is usually overlooked, was a special count in case, "on delivery and being stolen by his neglect." [74]

The case was twice argued, and all the reports agree, as far as they go, in their statements of the points insisted on.

Holt, for the plaintiff, maintained: [75] 1. That the master receives goods generally, citing *Southcote's Case*, and that "only guardian in socage who hath the custody by law, and factor who is servant at the master's dispose, and so cannot take care, are exempt." 2. That the master has a reward for his keeping, and is therefore a proper person to be sued. 3. That the master has a remedy over, citing the case of the Marshal of the King's Bench.[76] That the mischief would be great if the master were not liable, as merchants put their trust in him, and no particular default need be shown, as appears by the bill of lading, and, finally, that neglect appeared.

On the other side, it was urged that no neglect was found, and

[73] 2 Keb. 866; 3 id. 72, 112, 135; 2 Lev. 69; 1 Vent. 190, 238; 1 Mod. 85; Sir T. Raym. 220.

[74] 2 Keb. 866. See 3 Keb. 74; 1 Mod. 85; Sir T. Raym. 220.

[75] 3 Keb. 72.

[76] Y. B. 33 Hen. VI. 1; *supra*, p. 140.

that the master was only a servant; so that, if any one was liable, the owners were.[77] It was also suggested that, as there would have been no liability if the goods had been taken at sea, when the case would have fallen within the admiralty law, it was absurd that a different rule should govern the beginning of the voyage from that which would have governed the rest of it.[78]

On the second argument, it was again maintained for the plaintiff that the defendant was liable "at the common law on the general bailment," citing *Southcote's Case,* and also that, by the Roman and maritime law, he was liable as a public carrier and master of a ship.

The opinion of the court was delivered by Chief Justice Hale. It was held that, the ship being within the body of the county, the admiralty law did not apply; or, according to 1 Mod. 85, note *a*, "the master could not avail himself of the rules of the civil law, by which masters are not chargeable *pro damno fatali*"; that the master was liable to an action because he took a reward; that "he might have made a caution for himself, which he omitting and taking in the goods generally, he shall answer for what happens." [79] The case of *Kenrig* v. *Eggleston* [80] seems also to have been referred to. It was further said that the master was rather an officer than a servant, and in effect received his wages from the merchant who paid freight. Finally, on the question of negligence, that it was not sufficient to have the usual number of men to guard the ship, but that it was neglect not to have enough to guard the goods, unless in case of the common enemies, citing the case of the Marshal, which it will be remembered was merely the principle of *Southcote's Case* and the common law of bailment in another form.[81]

It will be observed that this case did not go on any special custom, either as to common carriers or shipmasters, but that all the arguments and the opinion of the court assumed that, if the case was to be governed by the common law, and not by the milder provisions of the civil law relied on for the defence, and

[77] 3 Keble, 73. This is the main point mentioned by Sir T. Raymond and Levinz.

[78] Cf. 1 Mod. 85.

[79] 1 Ventris, 238, citing *Southcote's Case* in the margin. Cf. 3 Keble, 135.

[80] Aleyn, 93; *supra*, p. 151.

[81] See also 1 Hale, P. C. 512, 513.

if the defendant could be regarded as a bailee, and not merely a servant of the owners, then the general law of bailment would apply, and the defendant would be charged, as in *Southcote's Case*, "by his general acceptance."

It can hardly be supposed, however, that so enlightened a judge as Sir Matthew Hale would not have broken away from the Year Books, if a case had arisen before him where property had been received as a pure favor to the plaintiff, without consideration or reward, and was taken from the defendant by robbery. Such a case was tried before Chief Justice Pemberton, and he very sensibly ruled that no action lay, declining to follow the law of Lord Coke's time to such extreme results[82] (33 Car. II., A. D. 1681).

About the same time, the defendant's common calling began to assume a new importance. The more important alternative allegation, the assumpsit, had the effect in the end of introducing the not intrinsically objectionable doctrine that all duties arising from a bailment are founded on contract.[83] But this allegation, having now a special action to which it had given rise, was not much used where the action was tort, while the other averment occurs with increasing frequency. The notion was evidently gaining ground that the liability of common carriers for loss of goods, whatever the cause of the loss might be, arose from a special principle peculiar to them, and not applicable to bailees in general. The confusion of independent duties which has been explained, and of which the first trace was seen in *Rich* v. *Kneeland*, was soon to become complete.[84] Holt became Chief Justice. Three

[82] *King* v. *Viscount Hertford*, 2 Shower, 172, pl. 164; cf. *Woodlife's Case*, *supra*.

[83] *Boson* v. *Sandford*, 1 Shower, 101 (2 W. & M.). See above, pp. 144–145, 146; below, p. 155. Modern illustrations of the doctrine will be found in *Fleming* v. *Manchester, Sheffield, & Lincolnshire Railway Co.*, 4 Q. B. D. 81, and cases cited. In *Boorman* v. *Brown*, 3 Q. B. 511, 526, the reader will find the primitive assumpsit, which was the inducement to a declaration in tort, interpreted as meaning contract in the modern sense. It will be seen directly that Lord Holt took a different view. Note the mode of dealing with the Marshal's case, 33 Hen. VI. 1, in Aleyn, 27.

[84] See *Lovett* v. *Hobbs*, 2 Shower, 127 (32 Car. II.); *Chamberlain* v. *Cooke*, 2 Ventris, 75 (1 W. & M.); *Boson* v. *Sandford*, 1 Shower, 101, citing *Southcote's Case* (2 W. & M.); *Upshare* v. *Aidee*, 1 Comyns, 25 (8 W. III.); *Middleton* v. *Fowler*, 1 Salk. 288 (10 W. III.).

of the cases in the last note were rulings of his. In *Lane* v. *Cotton*[85] (13 Will. III., A. D. 1701), he showed his disapproval of *Southcote's Case,* and his impression that the common law of bailment was borrowed from Rome. The overthrow of *Southcote's Case* and the old common law may be said to date from *Coggs* v. *Bernard*[86] (2 Anne, A. D. 1703). Lord Holt's famous opinion in the latter case quotes largely from the Roman law as it filtered to him through Bracton; but, whatever influence that may have had upon his general views, the point decided and the distinctions touching common carriers were of English growth.

The action did not sound in contract. The cause was for damage to the goods, and the plaintiff sued for a tort, laying an assumpsit by way of inducement to a charge of negligence, as in the days of Henry VI. The plea was not guilty. But after verdict for the plaintiff, there was a motion in arrest of judgment, "for that it was not alleged in the declaration that the defendant was a common porter, nor averred that he had anything for his pains." Consideration was never alleged or thought of in the primitive assumpsit, but in the modern action of contract in that form it was required. Hence, it was inferred that, wherever an assumpsit was laid, even in an action of tort for damage to property, it was the allegation of a contract, and that a consideration must be shown for the undertaking, although the contrary had been decided in the reign of Queen Elizabeth.[87] But the motion did not prevail, and judgment was given for the plaintiff. Lord Holt was well aware that the use of an assumpsit was not confined to contract. It is true that he said, "The owner's trusting [the defendant] with the goods is a sufficient consideration to oblige him to a careful management," or to return them; but this means as distinguished from a consideration sufficient to oblige him to carry them, which he thought the defendant would not have been bound to do. He then expressly says, "This is a different case, for assumpsit does not only signify a future agreement, but, in such cases as this, it signifies an actual entry upon the thing and taking the trust upon himself"; following the earlier cases in

[85] 12 Mod. 472. [86] 2 Ld. Raym. 909.
[87] *Powtuary* v. *Walton*, 1 Roll. Abr. 10, pl. 5 (39 Eliz.). Cf. Keilway, 160.

the Year Books.[88] This was enough for the decision, and the rule in *Southcote's Case* had nothing to do with the matter. But as the duty of common carriers by reason of their calling was now supposed to extend to all kinds of losses, and the doctrine of *Southcote's Case* was probably supposed to extend to many kinds of damage, it became necessary, in a general discussion, to reconcile or elect between the two principles.

The Chief Justice therefore proceeded to distinguish between bailees for reward exercising a public employment, such as common carriers, common hoymen, masters of ships, &c., and other bailees; denied the rule in *Southcote's Case* as to the latter; said that the principle of strict responsibility was confined to the former class, and was applied to them on grounds of public policy, and that factors were exonerated, not because they were mere servants, as had always been laid down (among others, by himself in arguing *Morse* v. *Slue*), but because they were not within the reason of the rule.

The reader who has followed the argument so far, will hardly need to be convinced that this did not mean the adoption of the Prætor's Edict. There is further evidence at hand if required.

In the first place, as we have seen, there was a century of precedents ending with *Morse* v. *Slue*, argued by Holt himself, in which the liability of masters of ships, hoymen, carriers, &c. had been adjudicated. *Morse* v. *Slue* is cited and relied on, and there is no hint of dissatisfaction with the other cases. On the contrary, they furnished the examples of bailees for reward exercising a public calling. The distinction between bailees for reward and others is Chief Justice Popham's; the latter qualification (exercising a public calling) was also English, as has partly appeared already, and as will be explained further on.

In the next place, the strict rule is not confined to *nautæ*, *caupones*, and *stabularii*, nor even to common carriers; but is applied to all bailees for reward, exercising a public calling.

In the next place, the degree of responsibility is precisely that

[88] 2 Ld. Raym. 919. See Lecture VII. How little Lord Holt meant to adopt the modern view, that delivery, being a detriment to the owner, was a consideration, may be further seen by examining the cases put and agreed to by him from the Year Books.

of bailees in general, as worked out by the previous decisions; but quite unlike and much more severe than that imposed by the Roman law, as others have observed.[89]

And, finally, the exemption from liability for acts of God or the public enemy is characteristically English, as will be proved further on.

But it has been partially shown in this Lecture that the law of to-day has made the carrier's burden heavier than it was in the time of the Year Books. *Southcote's Case,* and the earlier authorities which have been cited, all refer to a loss by robbery, theft, or trespass, and hold the bailee liable, where, in theory at least, he has a remedy over. It was with reference to such cases, as has been seen, that the rule arose, although it is not improbable that it would have been applied to an unexplained loss; the writ against innkeepers reads *absque subtractione seu amissione custodire.* In later times, the principle may have been extended from loss by theft to loss by destruction. In *Symons* v. *Darknoll*[90] (4 Car. I.), already cited as decided on the authority of *Southcote's Case,* the goods were spoiled, not stolen, and probably had not even perished *in specie.* Before this time, the old rule had become an arbitrary precedent, followed according to its form with little thought of its true intent.

The language of *Coggs* v. *Bernard* is, that "the law charges the person thus intrusted to carry goods as against all events but acts of God and the enemies of the king." This was adopted by solemn decision in Lord Mansfield's time, and it is now settled that the common carrier "is liable for all losses which do not fall within the excepted cases."[91] That is to say, he has become an insurer to that extent, not only against the disappearance or destruction, but against all forms of damage to the goods except as excepted above.

The process by which this came to pass has been traced above, but a few words may be added here. The Year Books, even in dealing with the destruction (as distinguished from the con-

[89] 2 Kent, 598; 1 C. P. D. 429.

[90] Palmer, 523. See too Keilway, 77 *b*, and 160, pl. 2, where the encroachment of case on detinue, and the corresponding confusion in principle, may be pretty clearly seen taking place. But see p. 138, *supra*.

[91] 2 Kent, 597; *Forward* v. *Pittard*, 1 T. R. 27.

version) of chattels in the hands of a bailee, always state his liability as based upon his fault, although it must be admitted that the language is used *alio intuitu.*[92] A jettison, in tempest, seems to have been a good plea for a factor in the time of Edward III.,[93] but that cannot be relied on for an analogy. The argument from the Marshal's case[94] is stronger. There it appears to have been thought that burning of the prison was as good an excuse for an escape as a release by alien enemies. This must refer to an accidental fire, and would seem to imply that he was not liable in that event, if not in fault. The writs in the Register against bailees to keep or carry goods, all have the general allegation of negligence, and so do the older precedents of declarations, so far as I have observed, whether stating the custom of the realm or not.[95] But a bailee was answerable for goods wrongfully taken from him, as an innkeeper was for goods stolen from his inn, irrespective of negligence.[96]

It is true that the Marshal's case speaks of his negligent keeping when the prisoners were released by rebels, (although that was far less likely to result from negligence, one would think, than a fire in the prison,) and that after Lord Coke's time negligence was alleged, although the goods had been lost by wrongful taking. So the writ against innkeepers is *pro defectu hujusmodi hospitatorum.* In these instances, neglect only means a failure *de facto* to keep safely. As was said at a much later date, "everything is a negligence in a carrier or hoyman that the law does not excuse."[97] The allegation is simply the usual allegation of actions on the case, and seems to have extended itself from the earlier declarations for damage, when case supplanted detinue and the use of the former action became universal. It can hardly have been immaterial to the case for which it was first introduced. But the short reason for disbelieving that there was any warrant in

[92] Cf. Y. B. 7 Hen. IV. 14; 2 Hen. VII. 11; Keilway, 77 *b*, 160, pl. 2, and other cases already cited.

[93] Y. B. 41 Ed. III. 3, pl. 8.

[94] Y. B. 33 Hen. VI. 1, pl. 3.

[95] Reg. Brev. 107 *a*, 108 *a*, 110 *a*, *b*; entries cited 1 T. R. 29.

[96] See above, pp. 167, 175 *et seq.*; 12 Am. Law Rev. 692, 693; Y. B. 42 Ed. III. 11, pl. 13; 42 Ass., pl. 17.

[97] 1 Wilson, 282; cf. 2 Kent (12th ed.), 596, n. 1, *b*.

the old law for making the carrier an insurer against damage is, that there seem to be no early cases in which bailees were held to such a responsibility, and that it was not within the principle on which they were made answerable for a loss by theft.

Having traced the process by which a common carrier has been made an insurer, it only remains to say a word upon the origin of the admitted exceptions from the risk assumed. It has been seen already how loss by the public enemy came to be mentioned by Chief Justice Holt. It is the old distinction taken in the Marshal's case,[98] that there the bailee has no remedy over.

With regard to the act of God, it was a general principle, not peculiar to carriers nor to bailees, that a duty was discharged if an act of God made it impossible of performance. Lord Coke mentions the case of jettison from a Gravesend barge,[99] and another of a party bound to keep and maintain sea-walls from overflowing, as subject to the same limitation,[100] and a similar statement as to contracts in general will be found in the Year Books.[101] It is another form of the principle which has been laboriously reargued in our own day, that parties are excused from the performance of a contract which has become impossible before breach from the perishing of the thing, or from change of circumstances the continued existence of which was the foundation of the contract, provided there was no warranty and no fault on the part of the contractor. Whether the act of God has now acquired a special meaning with regard to common carriers may be left for others to consider.

It appears, from the foregoing evidence, that we cannot determine what classes of bailees are subject to the strict responsibility imposed on common carriers by referring to the Prætor's Edict and then consulting the lexicons under *Nautæ*, *Caupones*, or *Stabularii*. The question of precedent is simply to what extent the old common law of bailment still survives. We can only answer it by enumerating the decisions in which the old law is

[98] Y. B. 33 Hen. VI. 1, pl. 3. [99] *Mouse's Case*, 12 Co. Rep. 63.

[100] *Bird* v. *Astcock*, 2 Bulstr. 280; cf. Dyer, 33 *a*, pl. 10; *Keighley's Case*, 10 Co. Rep. 139 *b*, 140.

[101] Y. B. 40 Ed. III. 5, 6, pl. 11; see also *Williams* v. *Hide*, Palmer, 548: Shep. Touchst. 173.

applied; and we shall find it hard to bring them together under a general principle. The rule in *Southcote's Case* has been done away with for bailees in general: that is clear. But it is equally clear that it has not maintained itself, even within the limits of the public policy invented by Chief Justice Holt. It is not true to-day that all bailees for reward exercising a public calling are insurers. No such doctrine is applied to grain-elevators or deposit-vaults.[102]

How Lord Holt came to distinguish between bailees for reward and others has been shown above. It is more pertinent here to notice that his further qualification, exercising a public calling, was part of a protective system which has passed away. One adversely inclined might say that it was one of many signs that the law was administered in the interest of the upper classes. It has been shown above that if a man was a common farrier he could be charged for negligence without an assumpsit. The same judge who threw out that intimation established in another case that he could be sued if he refused to shoe a horse on reasonable request.[103] Common carriers and common innkeepers were liable in like case, and Lord Holt stated the principle: "If a man takes upon him a public employment, he is bound to serve the public as far as the employment extends, and for refusal an action lies." [104] An attempt to apply this doctrine generally at the present day would be thought monstrous. But it formed part of a consistent scheme for holding those who followed useful callings up to the mark. Another part was the liability of persons exercising a public employment for loss or damage, enhanced in cases of bailment by what remained of the rule in *Southcote's Case*. The scheme has given way to more liberal notions; but the *disjecta membra* still move.

Lord Mansfield stated his views of public policy in terms not unlike those used by Chief Justice Holt in *Coggs* v. *Bernard*, but distinctly confines their application to common carriers. "But there is a further degree of responsibility by the custom of the

[102] See *Safe Deposit Company of Pittsburgh* v. *Pollock*, 85 Penn. 391.
[103] Paston, J., in Y. B. 21 Hen. VI. 55; Keilway, 50 *a*, pl. 4; Hardres, 163.
[104] *Lane* v. *Cotton*, 1 Ld. Raym. 646, 654; 1 Salk. 18; 12 Mod. 484.

realm, that is, by the common law; a carrier is in the nature of an insurer. . . . To prevent litigation, collusion, and the necessity of going into circumstances impossible to be unravelled, the law presumes against the carrier, unless," &c.[105]

At the present day it is assumed that the principle is thus confined, and the discussion is transferred to the question who are common carriers. It is thus conceded, by implication, that Lord Holt's rule has been abandoned. But the trouble is, that with it disappear not only the general system which we have seen that Lord Holt entertained, but the special reasons repeated by Lord Mansfield. Those reasons apply to other bailees as well as to common carriers. Besides, hoymen and masters of ships were not originally held because they were common carriers, and they were all three treated as co-ordinate species, even in *Coggs* v. *Bernard*, where they were mentioned only as so many instances of bailees exercising a public calling. We do not get a new and single principle by simply giving a single name to all the cases to be accounted for. If there is a sound rule of public policy which ought to impose a special responsibility upon common carriers, as those words are now understood, and upon no others, it has never yet been stated. If, on the other hand, there are considerations which apply to a particular class among those so designated, —for instance, to railroads, who may have a private individual at their mercy, or exercise a power too vast for the common welfare,—we do not prove that the reasoning extends to a general ship or a public cab by calling all three common carriers.

If there is no common rule of policy, and common carriers remain a merely empirical exception from general doctrine, courts may well hesitate to extend the significance of those words. Furthermore, notions of public policy which would not leave parties free to make their own bargains are somewhat discredited in most departments of the law.[106] Hence it may perhaps be concluded that, if any new case should arise, the degree of responsibility, and the validity and interpretation of any contract

[105] *Forward* v. *Pittard*, 1 T. R. 27, 33.

[106] *Printing and Numerical Registering Co.* v. *Sampson*, L. R. 19 Eq. 462, 465.

of bailment that there may be, should stand open to argument on general principles, and that the matter has been set at large so far as early precedent is concerned.

I have treated of the law of carriers at greater length than is proportionate, because it seems to me an interesting example of the way in which the common law has grown up, and, especially, because it is an excellent illustration of the principles laid down at the end of the first Lecture. I now proceed to the discussion for the sake of which an account of the law of bailment was introduced, and to which an understanding of that part of the law is a necessary preliminary.

LECTURE VI

POSSESSION

Possession is a conception which is only less important than contract. But the interest attaching to the theory of possession does not stop with its practical importance in the body of English law. The theory has fallen into the hands of the philosophers, and with them has become a corner-stone of more than one elaborate structure. It will be a service to sound thinking to show that a far more civilized system than the Roman is framed upon a plan which is irreconcilable with the *a priori* doctrines of Kant and Hegel. Those doctrines are worked out in careful correspondence with German views of Roman law. And most of the speculative jurists of Germany, from Savigny to Ihering, have been at once professors of Roman law, and profoundly influenced if not controlled by some form of Kantian or post-Kantian philosophy. Thus everything has combined to give a special bent to German speculation, which deprives it of its claim to universal authority.

Why is possession protected by the law, when the possessor is not also an owner? That is the general problem which has much exercised the German mind. Kant, it is well known, was deeply influenced in his opinions upon ethics and law by the speculations of Rousseau. Kant, Rousseau, and the Massachusetts Bill of Rights agree that all men are born *free* and *equal*, and one or the other branch of that declaration has afforded the answer to the question why possession should be protected from that day to this. Kant and Hegel start from freedom. The freedom of the will, Kant said, is the essence of man. It is an end in itself; it is that which needs no further explanation, which is absolutely to be respected, and which it is the very end and object of all government to realize and affirm. Possession is to be protected because a man by taking possession of an object has brought it within the sphere of his will. He has extended his personality into or over that object. As Hegel would have said, possession is the objective realization of free will. And by Kant's postulate, the will of any individual thus manifested is entitled to absolute respect from every other individual, and can only be overcome or set aside by the universal will, that is, by the state, acting through its organs, the courts.

Savigny did not follow Kant on this point. He said that every act of violence is unlawful, and seemed to consider protection of possession a branch of protection to the person.[1] But to this it was answered that possession was protected against disturbance by fraud as well as by force, and his view is discredited. Those who have been contented with humble grounds of expediency seem to have been few in number, and have recanted or are out of favor.

The majority have followed in the direction pointed out by Kant. Bruns, an admirable writer, expresses a characteristic yearning of the German mind, when he demands an internal juristic necessity drawn from the nature of possession itself, and therefore rejects empirical reasons.[2] He finds the necessity he seeks in the freedom of the human will, which the whole legal system does but recognize and carry out. Constraint of it is a wrong, which must be righted without regard to conformity of the will to law, and so on in a Kantian vein.[3] So Gans, a favorite disciple of Hegel, "The will is of itself a substantial thing to be protected, and this individual will has only to yield to the higher common will."[4] So Puchta, a great master, "The will which wills itself, that is, the recognition of its own personality, is to be protected."[5]

The chief variation from this view is that of Windscheid, a writer now in vogue. He prefers the other branch of the declaration in the Bill of Rights. He thinks that the protection to possession stands on the same grounds as protection against *injuria*,

[1] Possession, § 6, Eng. tr., pp. 27, 28.
[2] R. d. Besitzes, 487.
[3] R. d. Besitzes, 490, 491.
[4] Bruns, R. d. Besitzes, 415; Windscheid, Pand. § 148, n. 6. Further Hegelian discourse may be found in Dr. J. Hutchison Sterling's Lectures on the Philosophy of Law.
[5] Institutionen, §§ 224, 226; Windscheid, Pand. § 148, n. 6.

that every one is the equal of every other in the state, and that no one shall raise himself over the other.[6] Ihering, to be sure, a man of genius, took an independent start, and said that possession is ownership on the defensive; and that, in favor of the owner, he who is exercising ownership in fact (i. e. the possessor) is freed from the necessity of proving title against one who is in an unlawful position. But to this it was well answered by Bruns, in his later work, that it assumes the title of disseisors to be generally worse than that of disseisees, which cannot be taken for granted, and which probably is not true in fact.[7]

It follows from the Kantian doctrine, that a man in possession is to be confirmed and maintained in it until he is put out by an action brought for the purpose. Perhaps another fact besides those which have been mentioned has influenced this reasoning, and that is the accurate division between possessory and petitory actions or defences in Continental procedure.[8] When a defendant in a possessory action is not allowed to set up title in himself, a theorist readily finds a mystical importance in possession.

But when does a man become entitled to this absolute protection? On the principle of Kant, it is not enough that he has the custody of a thing. A protection based on the sacredness of man's personality requires that the object should have been brought within the sphere of that personality, that the free will should have unrestrainedly set itself into that object. There must be then an intent to appropriate it, that is, to make it part of one's self, or one's own.

Here the prevailing view of the Roman law comes in to fortify principle with precedent. We are told that, of the many who might have the actual charge or custody of a thing, the Roman law recognized as possessor only the owner, or one holding as owner and on his way to become one by lapse of time. In later days it made a few exceptions on practical grounds. But beyond the pledgee and the sequester (a receiver appointed by the court) these exceptions are unimportant and disputed.[9] Some of the

[6] Windscheid, Pand. § 148, n. 6.

[7] Besitzklagen, 276, 279.

[8] Bruns, R. d. Besitzes, 499.

[9] Bruns, R. d. Besitzes, § 2, pp. 5 *et seq.*; Puchta, *Besitz*, in Weiske, Rechtslex.; Windscheid, Pand. § 154, pp. 461 *et seq.* (4th ed.).

Roman jurists state in terms that depositaries and borrowers have not possession of the things intrusted to them.[10] Whether the German interpretation of the sources goes too far or not, it must be taken account of in the examination of German theories.

Philosophy by denying possession to bailees in general cunningly adjusted itself to the Roman law, and thus put itself in a position to claim the authority of that law for the theory of which the mode of dealing with bailees was merely a corollary. Hence I say that it is important to show that a far more developed, more rational, and mightier body of law than the Roman, gives no sanction to either premise or conclusion as held by Kant and his successors.

In the first place, the English law has always had the good sense [11] to allow title to be set up in defence to a possessory action. In the assize of novel disseisin, which was a true possessory action, the defendant could always rely on his title.[12] Even when possession is taken or kept in a way which is punished by the criminal law, as in case of forcible entry and detainer, proof of title allows the defendant to retain it, and in many cases has been held an answer to an action of trespass. So in trespass for taking goods the defendant may set up title in himself. There might seem to be a trace of the distinction in the general rule, that the title cannot be tried in trespass *quare clausum*. But this is an exception commonly put on the ground that the judgment cannot change the property, as trespass for chattels or trover can.[13] The rule that you cannot go into title in a possessory action presupposes great difficulty in the proof, the *probatio diabolica* of the Canon law, delays in the process, and importance of possession *ad interim*,—all of which mark a stage of society which has long been passed. In ninety-nine cases out of a hundred, it is about as easy and cheap to prove at least a *prima facie* title as it is to prove possession.

[10] D. 41. 2. 3, § 20; 13. 6. 8 & 9. Cf. D. 41. 1. 9, § 5.

[11] But see Ihering, Geist d. Röm. R., § 62, French tr., IV. p. 51.

[12] Heusler thinks this merely a result of the English formalism and narrowness in their interpretation of the word *suo* in the writ (*disseisivit de tenemento suo*). Gewere, 429–432. But there was no such narrowness in dealing with *catalla sua* in trepass. See below, pp. 190–191.

[13] See, further, Bracton, fol. 413; Y. B. 6 Hen. VII. 9, pl. 4.

In the next place, and this was the importance of the last Lecture to this subject, the common law has always given the possessory remedies to all bailees without exception. The right to these remedies extends not only to pledgees, lessees, and those having a lien, who exclude their bailor, but to simple bailees, as they have been called, who have no interest in the chattels, no right of detention as against the owner, and neither give nor receive a reward.[14]

Modern German statutes have followed in the same path so far as to give the possessory remedies to tenants and some others. Bruns says, as the spirit of the Kantian theory required him to say, that this is a sacrifice of principle to convenience.[15] But I cannot see what is left of a principle which avows itself inconsistent with convenience and the actual course of legislation. The first call of a theory of law is that it should fit the facts. It must explain the observed course of legislation. And as it is pretty certain that men will make laws which seem to them convenient without troubling themselves very much what principles are encountered by their legislation, a principle which defies convenience is likely to wait some time before it finds itself permanently realized.

It remains, then, to seek for some ground for the protection of possession outside the Bill of Rights or the Declaration of Independence, which shall be consistent with the larger scope given to the conception in modern law.

The courts have said but little on the subject. It was laid down in one case that it was an extension of the protection which the law throws around the person, and on that ground held that trespass *quare clausum* did not pass to an assignee in bankruptcy.[16] So it has been said, that to deny a bankrupt trover against strangers for goods coming to his possession after his bankruptcy would be "an invitation to all the world to scramble for the possession of them"; and reference was made to "grounds of policy and convenience." [17] I may also refer to the cases of capture, some of which will be cited again. In the Greenland

[14] *Infra*, p. 191.

[15] R. d. Besitzes, 494.

[16] *Rogers* v. *Spence*, 13 M. & W. 579, 581.

[17] *Webb* v. *Fox*, 7 T. R. 391, 397.

whale-fishery, by the English custom, if the first striker lost his hold on the fish, and it was then killed by another, the first had no claim; but he had the whole if he kept fast to the whale until it was struck by the other, although it then broke from the first harpoon. By the custom in the Gallipagos, on the other hand, the first striker had half the whale, although control of the line was lost.[18] Each of these customs has been sustained and acted on by the English courts, and Judge Lowell has decided in accordance with still a third, which gives the whale to the vessel whose iron first remains in it, provided claim be made before cutting in.[19] The ground as put by Lord Mansfield is simply that, were it not for such customs, there must be a sort of warfare perpetually subsisting between the adventurers.[20] If courts adopt different rules on similar facts, according to the point at which men will fight in the several cases, it tends, so far as it goes, to shake an *a priori* theory of the matter.

Those who see in the history of law the formal expression of the development of society will be apt to think that the proximate ground of law must be empirical, even when that ground is the fact that a certain ideal or theory of government is generally entertained. Law, being a practical thing, must found itself on actual forces. It is quite enough, therefore, for the law, that man, by an instinct which he shares with the domestic dog, and of which the seal gives a most striking example, will not allow himself to be dispossessed, either by force or fraud, of what he holds, without trying to get it back again.[21] Philosophy may find a hundred reasons to justify the instinct, but it would be totally immaterial if it should condemn it and bid us surrender without a murmur. As long as the instinct remains, it will be more comfortable for the law to satisfy it in an orderly manner, than to leave people to themselves. If it should do otherwise, it would become a matter for pedagogues, wholly devoid of reality.

I think we are now in a position to begin the analysis of possession. It will be instructive to say a word in the first place upon

[18] *Fennings* v. *Lord Grenville*, 1 Taunt. 241; *Littledale* v. *Scaith*, ib. 243, n. (*a*); cf. *Hogarth* v. *Jackson*, M. & M. 58; *Skinner* v. *Chapman*, ib. 59, n.

[19] *Swift* v. *Gifford*, 2 Lowell, 110.

[20] 1 Taunt. 248.

[21] Cf. Wake, Evolution of Morality, Part I. ch. 4, pp. 296 *et seq.*

a preliminary question which has been debated with much zeal in Germany. Is possession a fact or a right? This question must be taken to mean, by possession and right, what the law means by those words, and not something else which philosophers or moralists may mean by them; for as lawyers we have nothing to do with either, except in a legal sense. If this had always been borne steadily in mind, the question would hardly have been asked.

A legal right is nothing but a permission to exercise certain natural powers, and upon certain conditions to obtain protection, restitution, or compensation by the aid of the public force. Just so far as the aid of the public force is given a man, he has a legal right, and this right is the same whether his claim is founded in righteousness or iniquity. Just so far as possession is protected, it is as much a source of legal rights as ownership is when it secures the same protection.

Every right is a consequence attached by the law to one or more facts which the law defines, and wherever the law gives any one special rights not shared by the body of the people, it does so on the ground that certain special facts, not true of the rest of the world, are true of him. When a group of facts thus singled out by the law exists in the case of a given person, he is said to be entitled to the corresponding rights; meaning, thereby, that the law helps him to constrain his neighbors, or some of them, in a way in which it would not, if all the facts in question were not true of him. Hence, any word which denotes such a group of facts connotes the rights attached to it by way of legal consequences, and any word which denotes the rights attached to a group of facts connotes the group of facts in like manner.

The word "possession" denotes such a group of facts. Hence, when we say of a man that he has possession, we affirm directly that all the facts of a certain group are true of him, and we convey indirectly or by implication that the law will give him the advantage of the situation. Contract, or property, or any other substantive notion of the law, may be analyzed in the same way, and should be treated in the same order. The only difference is, that, while possession denotes the facts and connotes the consequence, property always, and contract with more uncertainty and oscillation, denote the consequence and connote the facts. When we say that a man owns a thing, we affirm directly that he has the benefit of the consequences attached to a certain group of facts, and, by implication, that the facts are true of him. The important thing to grasp is, that each of these legal compounds, possession, property, and contract, is to be analyzed into fact and right, antecedent and consequent, in like manner as every other. It is wholly immaterial that one element is accented by one word, and the other by the other two. We are not studying etymology, but law. There are always two things to be asked: first, what are the facts which make up the group in question; and then, what are the consequences attached by the law to that group. The former generally offers the only difficulties.

Hence, it is almost tautologous to say that the protection which the law attaches by way of consequence to possession, is as truly a right in a legal sense as those consequences which are attached to adverse holding for the period of prescription, or to a promise for value or under seal. If the statement is aided by dramatic reinforcement, I may add that possessory rights pass by descent or devise, as well as by conveyance,[22] and that they are taxed as property in some of the States.[23]

We are now ready to analyze possession as understood by the common law. In order to discover the facts which constitute it, it will be found best to study them at the moment when possession is first gained. For then they must all be present in the same way that both consideration and promise must be present at the moment of making a contract. But when we turn to the continuance of possessory rights, or, as is commonly said, the continuance of possession, it will be agreed by all schools that less than all the facts required to call those rights into being need continue presently true in order to keep them alive.

To gain possession, then, a man must stand in a certain physical relation to the object and to the rest of the world, and must have a certain intent. These relations and this intent are the facts of which we are in search.

The physical relation to others is simply a relation of manifested

[22] *Asher* v. *Whitlock*, L. R. 1 Q. B. 1.
[23] *People* v. *Shearer*, 30 Cal. 645.

power coextensive with the intent, and will need to have but little said about it when the nature of the intent is settled. When I come to the latter, I shall not attempt a similar analysis to that which has been pursued with regard to intent as an element of liability. For the principles developed as to intent in that connection have no relation to the present subject, and any such analysis so far as it did not fail would be little more than a discussion of evidence. The intent inquired into here must be overtly manifested, perhaps, but all theories of the grounds on which possession is protected would seem to agree in leading to the requirement that it should be actual, subject, of course, to the necessary limits of legal investigation.

But, besides our power and intent as towards our fellow-men, there must be a certain degree of power over the object. If there were only one other man in the world, and he was safe under lock and key in jail, the person having the key would not possess the swallows that flew over the prison. This element is illustrated by cases of capture, although no doubt the point at which the line is drawn is affected by consideration of the degree of power obtained as against other people, as well as by that which has been gained over the object. The Roman and the common law agree that, in general, fresh pursuit of wild animals does not give the pursuer the rights of possession. Until escape has been made impossible by some means, another may step in and kill or catch and carry off the game if he can. Thus it has been held that an action does not lie against a person for killing and taking a fox which had been pursued by another, and was then actually in the view of the person who had originally found, started, and chased it.[24] The Court of Queen's Bench even went so far as to decide, notwithstanding a verdict the other way, that when fish were nearly surrounded by a seine, with an opening of seven fathoms between the ends, at which point boats were stationed to frighten them from escaping, they were not reduced to possession as against a stranger who rowed in through the opening and helped himself.[25] But the difference between the power over the

[24] 2 Kent's Comm. 349, citing *Pierson* v. *Post*, 3 Caines (N. Y.) 175; *Buster* v. *Newkirk*, 20 Johnson (N. Y.) 75.
[25] *Young* v. *Hichens*, 6 Q. B. 606.

object which is sufficient for possession, and that which is not, is clearly one of degree only, and the line may be drawn at different places at different times on grounds just referred to. Thus we are told that the legislature of New York enacted, in 1844, that any one who started and pursued deer in certain counties of that State should be deemed in possession of the game so long as he continued in fresh pursuit of it,[26] and to that extent modified the New York decisions just cited. So, while Justinian decided that a wild beast so badly wounded that it might easily be taken must be actually taken before it belongs to the captors,[27] Judge Lowell, with equal reason, has upheld the contrary custom of the American whalemen in the Arctic Ocean, mentioned above, which gives a whale to the vessel whose iron first remains in it, provided claim be made before cutting in.[28]

We may pass from the physical relation to the object with these few examples, because it cannot often come into consideration except in the case of living and wild things. And so we come to the intent, which is the really troublesome matter. It is just here that we find the German jurists unsatisfactory, for reasons which I have already explained. The best known theories have been framed as theories of the German interpretation of the Roman law, under the influence of some form of Kantian or post-Kantian philosophy. The type of Roman possession, according to German opinion, was that of an owner, or of one on his way to become owner. Following this out, it was said by Savigny, the only writer on the subject with whom English readers are generally acquainted, that the *animus domini,* or intent to deal with the thing as owner, is in general necessary to turn a mere physical detention into juridical possession.[29] We need not stop to inquire whether this modern form or the ψυχὴ δεσπόζοντος (*animus dominantis, animus dominandi*) of Theophilus [30] and the Greek sources is more exact; for either excludes, as the

[26] 2 Kent's Comm. 349, n. (*d*).

[27] Inst. 2. 1, § 13.

[28] *Swift* v. *Gifford,* 2 Lowell, 110.

[29] Savigny, R. d. Besitzes, § 21.

[30] II. 9, § 4; III. 29, § 2. *Animus domini* will be used here as shortly indicating the general nature of the intent required even by those who deny the fitness of the expression, and especially because Savigny's opinion is that which has been adopted by English writers.

civilians and canonists do, and as the German theories must, most bailees and termors from the list of possessors.[81]

The effect of this exclusion as interpreted by the Kantian philosophy of law, has been to lead the German lawyers to consider the intent necessary to possession as primarily self-regarding. Their philosophy teaches them that a man's physical power over an object is protected because he has the will to make it his, and it has thus become a part of his very self, the external manifestation of his freedom.[82] The will of the possessor being thus conceived as self-regarding, the intent with which he must hold is pretty clear: he must hold for his own benefit. Furthermore, the self-regarding intent must go to the height of an intent to appropriate; for otherwise, it seems to be implied, the object would not truly be brought under the personality of the possessor.

The grounds for rejecting the criteria of the Roman law have been shown above. Let us begin afresh. Legal duties are logically antecedent to legal rights. What may be their relation to moral rights if there are any, and whether moral rights are not in like manner logically the offspring of moral duties, are questions which do not concern us here. These are for the philosopher, who approaches the law from without as part of a larger series of human manifestations. The business of the jurist is to make known the content of the law; that is, to work upon it from within, or logically, arranging and distributing it, in order, from its *summum genus* to its *infima species,* so far as practicable. Legal duties then come before legal rights. To put it more broadly, and avoid the word duty, which is open to objection, the direct working of the law is to limit freedom of action or choice on the part of a greater or less number of persons in certain specified ways; while the power of removing or enforcing this limitation which is generally confided to certain other private persons, or, in other words, a right corresponding to the burden, is not a necessary or universal correlative. Again, a large part of the advantages enjoyed by one

[81] Cf. Bruns, R. d. Besitzes, 413, and ib. 469, 474, 493, 494, 505; Windscheid, Pand. § 149, n. 5 (p. 447, 4th ed.); Puchta, Inst. § 226.

[82] *Supra,* pp. 163–164; 2 Puchta, Inst. § 226 (5th ed.), pp. 545, 546.

who has a right are not created by the law. The law does not enable me to use or abuse this book which lies before me. That is a physical power which I have without the aid of the law. What the law does is simply to prevent other men to a greater or less extent from interfering with my use or abuse. And this analysis and example apply to the case of possession, as well as to ownership.

Such being the direct working of the law in the case of possession, one would think that the *animus* or intent most nearly parallel to its movement would be the intent of which we are in search. If what the law does is to exclude others from interfering with the object, it would seem that the intent which the law should require is an intent to exclude others. I believe that such an intent is all that the common law deems needful, and that on principle no more should be required.

It may be asked whether this is not simply the *animus domini* looked at from the other side. If it were, it would nevertheless be better to look at the front of the shield than at the reverse. But it is not the same if we give to the *animus domini* the meaning which the Germans give it, and which denies possession to bailees in general. The intent to appropriate or deal with a thing as owner can hardly exist without an intent to exclude others, and something more; but the latter may very well be where there is no intent to hold as owner. A tenant for years intends to exclude all persons, including the owner, until the end of his term; yet he has not the *animus domini* in the sense explained. Still less has a bailee with a lien, who does not even mean to use, but only to detain the thing for payment. But, further, the common law protects a bailee against strangers, when it would not protect him against the owner, as in the case of a deposit or other bailment terminable at pleasure; and we may therefore say that the intent even to exclude need not be so extensive as would be implied in the *animus domini*. If a bailee intends to exclude strangers to the title, it is enough for possession under our law, although he is perfectly ready to give the thing up to its owner at any moment; while it is of the essence of the German view that the intent must not be relative, but an absolute, self-regarding intent to take the benefit of the thing. Again, if the motives or wishes, and even the intentions, most present to the mind of a possessor, were all self-regarding, it would not follow that the intent toward others was not the important thing in the analysis of the law. But, as we have seen, a depositary is a true possessor under the common-law theory, although his intent is not self-regarding, and he holds solely for the benefit of the owner.

There is a class of cases besides those of bailees and tenants, which will probably, although not necessarily, be decided one way or the other, as we adopt the test of an intent to exclude, or of the *animus domini*. *Bridges* v. *Hawkesworth* [83] will serve as a starting-point. There, a pocket-book was dropped on the floor of a shop by a customer, and picked up by another customer before the shopkeeper knew of it. Common-law judges and civilians would agree that the finder got possession first, and so could keep it as against the shopkeeper. For the shopkeeper, not knowing of the thing, could not have the intent to appropriate it, and, having invited the public to his shop, he could not have the intent to exclude them from it. But suppose the pocket-book had been dropped in a private room, how should the case be decided? There can be no *animus domini* unless the thing is known of; but an intent to exclude others from it may be contained in the larger intent to exclude others from the place where it is, without any knowledge of the object's existence.

In *McAvoy* v. *Medina*,[84] a pocket-book had been left upon a barber's table, and it was held that the barber had a better right than the finder. The opinion is rather obscure. It takes a distinction between things voluntarily placed on a table and things dropped on the floor, and may possibly go on the ground that, when the owner leaves a thing in that way, there is an implied request to the shopkeeper to guard it, which will give him a better right than one who actually finds it before him. This is rather strained, however, and the court perhaps thought that the barber had possession as soon as the customer left the shop. A little later, in a suit for a reward offered to the finder of a pocket-book, brought by one who discovered it where the owner had left it, on a desk for the use of customers in a bank outside

[83] 15 Jur. 1079; 21 L. J. Q. B. 75; 7 Eng. L. & Eq. 424. [84] 11 Allen, 548.

the teller's counter, the same court said that this was not the finding of a lost article, and that "the occupants of the banking house, and not the plaintiff, were the proper depositaries of an article so left."[35] This language might seem to imply that the plaintiff was not the person who got possession first after the defendant, and that, although the floor of a shop may be likened to a street, the public are to be deemed excluded from the shop's desks, counters, and tables except for the specific use permitted. Perhaps, however, the case only decides that the pocket-book was not lost within the condition of the offer.

I should not have thought it safe to draw any conclusion from wreck cases in England, which are mixed up with questions of prescription and other rights. But the precise point seems to have been adjudicated here. For it has been held that, if a stick of timber comes ashore on a man's land, he thereby acquires a "right of possession" as against an actual finder who enters for the purpose of removing it.[36] A right of possession is said to be enough for trespass; but the court seems to have meant possession by the phrase, inasmuch as Chief Justice Shaw states the question to be which of the parties had "the preferable claim, by mere naked possession, without other title," and as there does not seem to have been any right of possession in the case unless there was actual possession.

In a criminal case, the property in iron taken from the bottom of a canal by a stranger was held well laid in the canal company, although it does not appear that the company knew of it, or had any lien upon it.[37]

The only intent concerning the thing discoverable in such instances is the general intent which the occupant of land has to exclude the public from the land, and thus, as a consequence, to exclude them from what is upon it.

The Roman lawyers would probably have decided all these cases differently, although they cannot be supposed to have

[35] *Kincaid* v. *Eaton*, 98 Mass. 139.

[36] *Barker* v. *Bates*, 13 Pick. 255, 257, 261; *Proctor* v. *Adams*, 113 Mass. 376, 377; 1 Bl. Comm. 297, Sharsw. ed., n. 14. Cf. *Blades* v. *Higgs*, 13 C. B. N. S. 844, 847, 848, 850, 851; 11 H. L. C. 621; *Smith* v. *Smith*, Strange, 955.

[37] *Reg.* v. *Rowe*, Bell, C. C. 93.

worked out the refined theories which have been built upon their remains.[38]

I may here return to the case of goods in a chest delivered under lock and key, or in a bale, and the like. It is a rule of the criminal law, that, if a bailee of such a chest or bale wrongfully sells the entire chest or bale, he does not commit larceny, but if he breaks bulk he does, because in the former case he does not, and in the latter he does, commit a trespass.[39] The reason sometimes offered is, that, by breaking bulk, the bailee determines the bailment, and that the goods at once revest in the possession of the bailor. This is, perhaps, an unnecessary, as well as inadequate fiction.[40] The rule comes from the Year Books, and the theory of the Year Books was, that, although the chest was delivered to the bailee, the goods inside of it were not, and this theory was applied to civil as well as criminal cases. The bailor has the power and intent to exclude the bailee from the goods, and therefore may be said to be in possession of them as against the bailee.[41]

On the other hand, a case in Rhode Island [42] is against the view here taken. A man bought a safe, and then, wishing to sell it again, sent it to the defendant, and gave him leave to keep his books in it until sold. The defendant found some bank-notes stuck in a crevice of the safe, which coming to the plaintiff's ears he demanded the safe and the money. The defendant sent back the safe, but refused to give up the money, and the court sustained him in his refusal. I venture to think this decision wrong. Nor would my opinion be changed by assuming, what the report does not make perfectly clear, that the defendant received the safe as bailee, and not as servant or agent, and that his permis-

[38] See, as to treasure hidden in another's land, D. 41. 2. 44, pr.; D. 10. 4. 15. Note the different opinions in D. 41. 2. 3, § 3.

[39] 3 Inst. 107; 1 Hale, P. C. 504, 505; 2 Bishop, Crim. Law, §§ 834, 860 (6th ed.).

[40] *Reg.* v. *Middleton*, L. R. 2 C. C. 38, 55. Cf. *Halliday* v. *Holgate*, L. R. 3 Ex. 299, 302.

[41] Cf. Y. B. 8 Ed. II. 275; Fitzh. Abr. *Detinue*, pl. 59; Y. B. 13 Ed. IV. 9, pl. 5; Keilway, 160, pl. 2; *Merry* v. *Green*, 7 M. & W. 623, 630. It may not be necessary to go quite so far, however, and these cases are not relied on as establishing the theory. For wrong explanations, see 2 East, P. C. 696.

[42] *Durfee* v. *Jones*, 11 R. I. 588.

sion to use the safe was general. The argument of the court goes on the plaintiff's not being a finder. The question is whether he need be. It is hard to believe that, if the defendant had stolen the bills from the safe while it was in the owner's hands, the property could not have been laid in the safe-owner,[43] or that the latter could not have maintained trover for them if converted under those circumstances. Sir James Stephen seems to have drawn a similar conclusion from *Cartwright* v. *Green* and *Merry* v. *Green;* [44] but I believe that no warrant for it can be found in the cases, and still less for the reason suggested.

It will be understood, however, that *Durfee* v. *Jones* is perfectly consistent with the view here maintained of the general nature of the necessary intent, and that it only touches the subordinate question, whether the intent to exclude must be directed to the specific thing, or may be even unconsciously included in a larger intent, as I am inclined to believe.

Thus far, nothing has been said with regard to the custody of servants. It is a well-known doctrine of the criminal law, that a servant who criminally converts property of his master intrusted to him and in his custody as servant, is guilty of theft, because he is deemed to have taken the property from his master's possession. This is equivalent to saying that a servant, having the custody of his master's property as servant, has not possession of that property, and it is so stated in the Year Books.[45]

The anomalous distinction according to which, if the servant receives the thing from another person for his master, the servant has the possession, and so cannot commit theft,[46] is made more rational by the old cases. For the distinction taken in them is, that, while the servant is in the house or with his master, the latter retains possession, but if he delivers his horse to his servant

[43] *Reg.* v. *Rowe*, Bell, C. C. 93, stated above.

[44] 8 Ves. 405; 7 M. & W. 623; Stephen, Crim. Law, Art. 281, Ill. (4). p. 197. He says, "because [the owner of the safe] cannot be presumed to intend to act as the owner of it when he discovers it,"—a reason drawn from Savigny, but not fitted to the English law, as has been shown.

[45] Y. B. 13 Ed. IV. 9, 10, pl. 5; 21 Hen. VII. 14, pl. 21. Cf. 3 Hen. VII. 12, pl. 9; Steph. Crim. Law, Art. 297, and App., note xvii.

[46] Steph. Crim. Law, Art. 297, and App., note xvii. p. 382. It may be doubted whether the old law would have sanctioned the rule in this form. F. N. B. 91 E; Y. B. 2 Ed. IV. 15, pl. 7.

to ride to market, or gives him a bag to carry to London, then the thing is out of the master's possession and in the servant's.[47] In this more intelligible form, the rule would not now prevail. But one half of it, that a guest at a tavern has not possession of the plate with which he is served, is no doubt still law, for guests in general are likened to servants in their legal position.[48]

There are few English decisions, outside the criminal law, on the question whether a servant has possession. But the Year Books do not suggest any difference between civil and criminal cases, and there is an almost unbroken tradition of courts and approved writers that he has not, in any case. A master has maintained trespass against a servant for converting cloth which he was employed to sell,[49] and the American cases go the full length of the old doctrine. It has often been remarked that a servant must be distinguished from a bailee.

But it may be asked how the denial of possession to servants can be made to agree with the test proposed, and it will be said with truth that the servant has as much the intent to exclude the world at large as a borrower. The law of servants is unquestionably at variance with that test; and there can be no doubt that those who have built their theories upon the Roman law have been led by this fact, coupled with the Roman doctrine as to bailees in general, to seek the formula of reconciliation where they have. But, in truth, the exception with regard to servants stands on purely historical grounds. A servant is denied possession, not from any peculiarity of intent with regard to the things in his custody, either towards his master or other people, by which he is distinguished from a depositary, but simply as one of the incidents of his status. It is familiar that the status of a servant maintains many marks of the time when he was a slave. The liability of the master for his torts is one instance. The

[47] Y. B. 21 Hen. VII. 14, pl. 21; 13 Co. Rep. 69.

[48] They have been said to be a part of the family *pro hac vice*. *Southcote* v. *Stanley*, 1 H. & N. 247, 250. Cf. Y. B. 2 Hen. IV. 18, pl. 6.

[49] Moore, 248, pl. 392; s. c., Owen, 52; F. N. B. 91 E; 2 Bl. Comm. 396; 1 H. Bl. 81, 84; 1 Chitty, Pl. 170 (1st ed.); Dicey, Parties, 358; 9 Mass. 104; 7 Cowen, 294; 3 S. & R. 20; 13 Iredell, 18; 6 Barb. 362, and cases cited. Some of the American cases have been denied, on the ground that the custodian was not a servant. Cf. *Holiday* v. *Hicks*, Cro. Eliz. 638, 661, 746; *Drope* v. *Theyar*, Popham, 178, 179.

present is another. A slave's possession was his owner's possession on the practical ground of the owner's power over him,[50] and from the fact that the slave had no standing before the law. The notion that his personality was merged in that of his family head survived the era of emancipation.

I have shown in the first Lecture[51] that agency arose out of the earlier relation in the Roman law, through the extension *pro hac vice* to a freeman of conceptions derived from that source. The same is true, I think, of our own law, the later development of which seems to have been largely under Roman influence. As late as Blackstone, agents appear under the general head of servants, and the first precedents cited for the peculiar law of agents were cases of master and servant. Blackstone's language is worth quoting: "There is yet a fourth species of servants, if they may be so called, being rather in a superior, a ministerial capacity; such as *stewards, factors,* and *bailiffs:* whom, however, the law considers as servants *pro tempore,* with regard to such of their acts as affect their master's or employer's property."[52]

It is very true that in modern times many of the effects of either relation—master and servant or principal and agent—may be accounted for as the result of acts done by the master himself. If a man tells another to make a contract in his name, or commands him to commit a tort, no special conception is needed to explain why he is held; although even in such cases, where the intermediate party was a freeman, the conclusion was not reached until the law had become somewhat mature. But, if the title Agency deserves to stand in the law at all, it must be because some peculiar consequences are attached to the fact of the relation. If the mere power to bind a principal to an authorized contract were all, we might as well have a chapter on ink and paper

[50] Bracton, fol. 6 *a*, § 3, 12 *a*, 17 *a*, Cap. V. *ad fin.*, 25 *a*, *b*, etc; Puchta, Inst. § 228.

[51] See also 7 Am. Law Rev. 62 *et seq.*; 10 Am. Law Rev. 431; 2 Kent, Comm. (12th ed.), 260, n. 1.

[52] 1 Comm. 427. Cf. Preface to Paley on Agency. Factors are always called servants in the old books, see, e. g., *Woodlife's Case*, Owen, 57; *Holiday* v. *Hicks*, Cro. Eliz. 638; *Southcote's Case*, 4 Co. Rep. 83 *b*, 84 *a*; *Southern* v. *How*, Cro. Jac. 468; St. 21 Jac. I., c. 16, § 3; *Morse* v. *Slue*, 3 Keble, 72. As to bailiffs, see Bract. 26 *b*, "*Restituat domino, vel servienti,*" etc.; Y. B. 7 Hen. IV. 14, pl. 18.

as on agents. But it is not all. Even in the domain of contract, we find the striking doctrine that an undisclosed principal has the rights as well as the obligations of a known contractor, —that he can be sued, and, more remarkable, can sue on his agent's contract. The first precedent cited for the position that a promise to an agent may be laid as a promise to the principal, is a case of master and servants.[53]

As my present object is only to show the meaning of the doctrine of identification in its bearing upon the theory of possession, it would be out of place to consider at any length how far that doctrine must be invoked to explain the liability of principals for their agents' torts, or whether a more reasonable rule governs other cases than that applied where the actor has a tolerably defined status as a servant. I allow myself a few words, because I shall not be able to return to the subject.

If the liability of a master for the torts of his servant had hitherto been recognized by the courts as the decaying remnant of an obsolete institution, it would not be surprising to find it confined to the cases settled by ancient precedent. But such has not been the fact. It has been extended to new relations by analogy.[54] It exists where the principal does not stand in the relation of *paterfamilias* to the actual wrong-doer.[55] A man may be held for another where the relation was of such a transitory nature as to exclude the conception of status, as for the negligence of another person's servant momentarily acting for the defendant, or of a

[53] Paley, Agency, c. 4, § 1, citing Godbolt, 360. See, further, F. N. B. 120, G; Fitzh. Abr. *Dette*, pl. 3; Y. B. 8 Ed. IV. 11, pl. 9. These rules seem to be somewhat modern even as to servants. The liability of a master for debts contracted by his servant is very narrowly limited in the earlier Year Books.

[54] I am inclined to think that this extension has been largely due to the influence of the Roman law. See Lecture I. p. 20, n. 54, and observe the part which the precedents as to fire (e. g., Y. B. 2 Hen. IV. 18, pl. 6) have played in shaping the modern doctrine of master and servant. *Tuberville* v. *Stampe*, 1 Ld. Raym. 264 (where Lord Holt's examples are from the Roman law); *Brucker* v. *Fromont*, 6 T. R. 659; *M'Manus* v. *Crickett*, 1 East, 106; *Patten* v. *Rea*, 2 C. B. N. S. 606. In *Southern* v. *How*, Popham, 143, Doctor and Student is referred to for the general principles of liability. Doctor and Student states Roman law. See, further, *Boson* v. *Sandford*, 1 Shower, 101, 102.

[55] Bac. Abr. *Master and Servant*, K; Smith, Master and Servant (3d ed.), 260, n. (*t*).

neighbor helping him as a volunteer;[56] and, so far as known, no principal has ever escaped on the ground of the dignity of his agent's employment.[57] The courts habitually speak as if the same rules applied to brokers and other agents, as to servants properly so called.[58] Indeed, it has been laid down in terms, that the liability of employers is not confined to the case of servants,[59] although the usual cases are, of course, those of menial servants, and the like, who could not pay a large verdict.

On the other hand, if the peculiar doctrines of agency are anomalous, and form, as I believe, the vanishing point of the servile status, it may well happen that common sense will refuse to carry them out to their furthest applications. Such conflicts between tradition and the instinct of justice we may see upon the question of identifying a principal who knows the truth with an agent who makes a false representation, in order to make out a fraud, as in *Cornfoot* v. *Fowke*,[60] or upon that as to the liability of a principal for the frauds of his agent discussed in many English cases.[61] But, so long as the fiction which makes the root of a master's liability is left alive, it is as hopeless to reconcile the differences by logic as to square the circle.

[56] *Clapp* v. *Kemp*, 122 Mass. 481; *Murray* v. *Currie*, L. R. 6 C. P. 24, 28; *Hill* v. *Morey*, 26 Vt. 178.

[57] See, e. g., *Patten* v. *Rea*, 2 C. B. N. S. 606; *Bolingbroke* v. *Swindon Local Board*, L. R. 9 C. P. 575.

[58] *Freeman* v. *Rosher*, 13 Q. B. 780, 785; *Gauntlett* v. *King*, 3 C. B. N. S. 59; *Haseler* v. *Lemoyne*, 28 L. J. C. P. 103; *Collett* v. *Foster*, 2 H. & N. 356; *Barwick* v. *English Joint Stock Bank*, L. R. 2 Ex. 259, 265, 266; *Lucas* v. *Mason*, L. R. 10 Ex. 251, 253, last paragraph; *Mackay* v. *Commercial Bank of New Brunswick*, L. R. 5 P. C. 394, 411, 412. So as to partners, 3 Kent's Comm. (12th ed.), 46, notes (*d*) & 1.

[59] *Bush* v. *Steinman*, 1 B. & P. 404, 409.

[60] 6 M. & W. 358. Cf. *Udell* v. *Atherton*, 7 H. & N. 172, 184, for a comment like that in the text. Other grounds for the decision are immaterial here.

[61] *Mackay* v. *Commercial Bank of New Brunswick*, L. R. 5 P. C. 394; *Barwick* v. *English Joint Stock Bank*, L. R. 2 Ex. 259; *Western Bank of Scotland* v. *Addie*. L. R. 1 H. L. Sc. 145; 2 Kent (12th ed.), 616, n. 1; *Swift* v. *Jewsbury*, L. R. 9 Q. B. 301, overruling s. c. *sub nom. Swift* v. *Winterbotham*, L. R. 8 Q. B. 244; *Weir* v. *Bell*, 3 Ex. D. 238, 244. The objections which Baron Bramwell mentions (L. R. 9 Q. B. 315) to holding one man liable for the frauds of another, are objections to the peculiar consequences attaching to the relation of master and servant in general, and have been urged in that more general form by the same learned judge. 12 Am. Law Rev. 197, 200; 2 H. & N. 356, 361. See 7 Am. Law Rev. 61, 62.

In an article in the American Law Review [62] I referred to an expression of Godefroi with regard to agents; *eadem est persona domini et procuratoris.*[63] This notion of a fictitious unity of person has been pronounced a darkening of counsel in a recent useful work.[64] But it receives the sanction of Sir Henry Maine,[65] and I believe that it must stand as expressing an important aspect of the law, if, as I have tried to show, there is no adequate and complete explanation of the modern law, except by the survival in practice of rules which lost their true meaning when the objects of them ceased to be slaves. There is no trouble in understanding what is meant by saying that a slave has no legal standing, but is absorbed in the family which his master represents before the law. The meaning seems equally clear when we say that a free servant, in his relations as such, is in many respects likened by the law to a slave (not, of course, to his own detriment as a freeman). The next step is simply that others not servants in a general sense may be treated as if servants in a particular connection. This is the progress of ideas as shown us by history; and this is what is meant by saying that the characteristic feature which justifies agency as a title of the law is the absorption *pro hac vice* of the agent's legal individuality in that of his principal.

If this were carried out logically, it would follow that an agent constituted to hold possession in his principal's name would not be regarded as having the legal possession, or as entitled to trespass. But, after what has been said, no opinion can be expressed whether the law would go so far, unless it is shown by precedent.[66] The nature of the case put will be observed. It is that of an agent constituted for the very point and purpose of possession. A bailee may be an agent for some other purpose. A free servant may be made a bailee. But the bailee holds in his own name, as we say, following the Roman idiom, and the servant or agent holding as such does not.

It would hardly be worth while, if space allowed, to search

[62] 7 Am. Law Rev. 63 (Oct. 1872).

[63] D. 44. 2. 4, note 17, Elzevir ed.

[64] Hunter's Roman Law, 431.

[65] Ancient Hist. of Inst. 235.

[66] Cf. *Gillett* v. *Ball*, 9 Penn. St. 13; *Craig* v. *Gilbreth*, 47 Me. 416; *Nickolson* v. *Knowles*, 5 Maddock, 47; *Williams* v. *Pott*, L. R. 12 Eq. 149; *Adams* v. *Jones*, 12 Ad. & El. 455; Bracton, fol. 28 *b*, 42 *b*, 43. And compare with the passage cited above from Blackstone: "Possidet, cujus nomine possidetur, procurator alienæ possessioni præstat *ministerium*." D. 41. 2. 18, pr.

the books on this subject, because of the great confusion of language to be found in them. It has been said, for instance, in this connection, that a carrier is a servant; [67] while nothing can be clearer than that, while goods are in his custody, they are in his possession.[68] So where goods remain in the custody of a vendor, appropriation to the contract and acceptance have been confounded with delivery.[69] Our law has adopted the Roman doctrine,[70] that there may be a delivery, that is, a change of possession, by a change in the character in which the vendor holds, but has not always imitated the caution of the civilians with regard to what amounts to such a change.[71] Bailees are constantly spoken of as if they were agents to possess,—a confusion made easier by the fact that they generally are agents for other purposes. Those cases which attribute possession to a transferee of goods in the hands of a middleman,[72] without distinguishing whether the middleman holds in his own name or the buyer's, are generally right in the result, no doubt, but have added to the confusion of thought upon the subject.

German writers are a little apt to value a theory of possession somewhat in proportion to the breadth of the distinction which it draws between juridical possession and actual detention; but, from the point of view taken here, it will be seen that the grounds for denying possession and the possessory remedies to servants and agents holding as such—if, indeed, the latter have not those remedies—are merely historical, and that the general theory can only take account of the denial as an anomaly. It will also be perceived that the ground on which servants and depositaries have been often likened to each other, namely, that they both hold

[67] *Ward* v. *Macaulay*, 4 T. R. 489, 490. Cf. as to factors *supra*, p. 180.

[68] *Berndtson* v. *Strang*, L. R. 3 Ch. 588, 590.

[69] Blackburn, Sale, 33; *Marvin* v. *Wallis*, 6 El. & Bl. 726.

[70] D. 41. 2. 18, pr. "Quod meo nomine possideo, possum alieno nomine possidere: nec enim muto mihi causam possessionis, sed desino possidere et alium possessorem ministerio meo facio. Nec idem est possidere et alieno nomine possidere: nam possidet, cujus nomine possidetur, procurator alienæ possessioni præstat ministerium." Thus showing that the vendor changed possession by holding *in the name* of the purchaser, as his agent to possess. Cf. Bracton, fol. 28 *b*.

[71] Windscheid, Pand. § 155, n. 8 *a*; 2 Kent (12th ed.), 492, n. 1 (*a*). It should be kept in mind also that the Roman law denied possession to bailees.

[72] See, e. g., *Farina* v. *Home*, 16 M. & W. 119, 123.

for the benefit of another and not for themselves, is wholly without influence on our law, which has always treated depositaries as having possession; and is not the true explanation of the Roman doctrine, which did not decide either case upon that ground, and which decided each for reasons different from those on which it decided the other.

It will now be easy to deal with the question of power as to third persons. This is naturally a power coextensive with the intent. But we must bear in mind that the law deals only or mainly with manifested facts; and hence, when we speak of a power to exclude others, we mean no more than a power which so appears in its manifestation. A powerful ruffian may be within equal reach and sight when a child picks up a pocket-book; but if he does nothing, the child has manifested the needful power as well as if it had been backed by a hundred policemen. Thus narrowed, it might be suggested that the manifestation of power is only important as a manifestation of intent. But the two things are distinct, and the former becomes decisive when there are two contemporaneous and conflicting intents. Thus, where two parties, neither having title, claimed a crop of corn adversely to each other, and cultivated it alternately, and the plaintiff gathered and threw it in small piles in the same field, where it lay for a week, and then each party simultaneously began to carry it away, it was held the plaintiff had not gained possession.[73] But if the first interference of the defendant had been after the gathering into piles, the plaintiff would probably have recovered.[74] So where trustees possessed of a schoolroom put in a schoolmaster, and he was afterwards dismissed, but the next day (June 30) re-entered by force; on the fourth of July he was required by notice to depart, and was not ejected until the eleventh; it was considered that the schoolmaster never got possession as against the trustees.[75]

We are led, in this connection, to the subject of the continuance of the rights acquired by gaining possession. To gain pos-

[73] *McGahey* v. *Moore*, 3 Ired. (N. C.) 35.

[74] *Reader* v. *Moody*, 3 Jones (N. C.) 372. Cf. *Basset* v. *Maynard*, Cro. Eliz. 819, 820.

[75] *Browne* v. *Dawson*, 12 A. & E. 624. Cf. D. 43. 16. 17; ib. 3, § 9; D. 41. 2. 18, § 3; Clayton, 147, pl. 268.

session, it has been seen, there must be certain physical relations, as explained, and a certain intent. It remains to be inquired, how far these facts must continue to be presently true of a person in order that he may keep the rights which follow from their presence. The prevailing view is that of Savigny. He thinks that there must be always the same *animus* as at the moment of acquisition, and a constant power to reproduce at will the original physical relations to the object. Every one agrees that it is not necessary to have always a present power over the thing, otherwise one could only possess what was under his hand. But it is a question whether we cannot dispense with even more. The facts which constitute possession are in their nature capable of continuing presently true for a lifetime. Hence there has arisen an ambiguity of language which has led to much confusion of thought. We use the word "possession," indifferently, to signify the presence of all the facts needful to gain it, and also the condition of him who, although some of them no longer exist, is still protected as if they did. Consequently it has been only too easy to treat the cessation of the facts as the loss of the right, as some German writers very nearly do.[76]

But it no more follows, from the single circumstance that certain facts must concur in order to create the rights incident to possession, that they must continue in order to keep those rights alive, than it does, from the necessity of a consideration and a promise to create a right *ex contractu,* that the consideration and promise must continue moving between the parties until the moment of performance. When certain facts have once been made manifest which confer a right, there is no general ground on which the law need hold the right at an end except the manifestation of some fact inconsistent with its continuance, although the reasons for conferring the particular right may have great weight in determining what facts shall be deemed to be so. Cessation of the original physical relations to the object might be treated as such a fact; but it never has been, unless in times of more ungoverned violence than the present. On the same principle, it is only a question of tradition or policy whether a cessation of the power to reproduce the original physical relations

[76] Cf. Bruns, R. d. Besitzes, 503.

shall affect the continuance of the rights. It does not stand on the same ground as a new possession adversely taken by another. We have adopted the Roman law as to animals *feræ naturæ*, but the general tendency of our law is to favor appropriation. It abhors the absence of proprietary or possessory rights as a kind of vacuum. Accordingly, it has been expressly decided, where a man found logs afloat and moored them, but they again broke loose and floated away, and were found by another, that the first finder retained the rights which sprung from his having taken possession, and that he could maintain trover against the second finder, who refused to give them up.[77]

Suppose that a finder of a purse of gold has left it in his country-house, which is lonely and slightly barred, and he is a hundred miles away, in prison. The only person within twenty miles is a thoroughly equipped burglar at his front door, who has seen the purse through a window, and who intends forthwith to enter and take it. The finder's power to reproduce his former physical relation to the gold is rather limited, yet I believe that no one would say that his possession was at an end until the burglar, by an overt act, had manifested his power and intent to exclude others from the purse. The reason for this is the same which has been put with regard to the power to exclude at the moment of gaining possession. The law deals, for the most part, with overt acts and facts which can be known by the senses. So long as the burglar has not taken the purse, he has not manifested his intent; and until he breaks through the barrier which measures the present possessor's power of excluding him, he has not manifested his power. It may be observed further, that, according to the tests adopted in this Lecture, the owner of the house has a present possession in the strictest sense, because, although he has not the power which Savigny says is necessary, he has the present intent and power to exclude others.

It is conceivable that the common law should go so far as to deal with possession in the same way as a title, and should hold

[77] *Clark* v. *Maloney*, 3 Harrington (Del.), 68. Bruns (R. d. Besitzes, 503, 507) comes to the same conclusion on practical grounds of convenience, although he utterly repudiates it on theory. I must refer to what I said above touching these conflicts between theory and convenience.

that, when it has once been acquired, rights are acquired which continue to prevail against all the world but one, until something has happened sufficient to divest ownership.

The possession of rights, as it is called, has been a fighting-ground for centuries on the Continent. It is not uncommon for German writers to go so far as to maintain that there may be a true possession of obligations; this seeming to accord with a general view that possession and right are in theory coextensive terms; that the mastery of the will over an external object in general (be that object a thing or another will), when in accord with the general will, and consequently lawful, is called right, when merely *de facto* is possession.[78] Bearing in mind what was said on the question whether possession was a fact or right, it will be seen that such an antithesis between possession and right cannot be admitted as a *legal* distinction. The facts constituting possession generate rights as truly as do the facts which constitute ownership, although the rights of a mere possessor are less extensive than those of an owner.

Conversely, rights spring from certain facts supposed to be true of the person entitled to such rights. Where these facts are of such a nature that they can be made successively true of different persons, as in the case of the occupation of land, the corresponding rights may be successively enjoyed. But when the facts are past and gone, such as the giving of a consideration and the receiving of a promise, there can be no claim to the resulting rights set up by any one except the party of whom the facts were originally true,—in the case supposed, the original contractee,—because no one but the original contractee can fill the situation from which they spring.

It will probably be granted by English readers, that one of the essential constituent facts consists in a certain relation to a material object. But this object may be a slave, as well as a horse;[79] and conceptions originated in this way may be extended by a

[78] Bruns, R. d. Besitzes, § 57, p. 486. A learned writer of more ancient date asks why a doctor has not a possessory action if you cease to employ him, and answers "Sentio actionem non tenere, sed sentio tantum, nec si vel morte mineris, possum dicere quare. Tu lector, si sapis, rationes decidendi suggere." Hommel, Rhaps., qu. 489, cited, Bruns, 407.

[79] *Gardiner* v. *Thibodeau*, 14 La. An. 732.

survival to free services. It is noticeable that even Bruns, in the application of his theory, does not seem to go beyond cases of status and those where, in common language, land is bound for the services in question, as it is for rent.[80] Free services being so far treated like servile, even by our law, that the master has a right of property in them against all the world, it is only a question of degree where the line shall be drawn. It would be possible to hold that, as one might be in possession of a slave without title, so one might have all the rights of an owner in free services rendered without contract. Perhaps there is something of that sort to be seen when a parent recovers for the seduction of a daughter over twenty-one, although there is no actual contract of service.[81] So, throughout the whole course of the canon law and in the early law of England, rents were regarded as so far a part of the realty as to be capable of possession and disseisin, and they could be recovered like land by an assize.[82]

But the most important case of the so-called possession of rights in our law, as in the Roman, occurs with regard to easements. An easement is capable of possession in a certain sense. A man may use land in a certain way, with the intent to exclude all others from using it in any way inconsistent with his own use, but no further. If this be true possession, however, it is a limited possession of land, not of a right, as others have shown. But where an easement has been actually created, whether by deed or prescription, although it is undoubtedly true that any possessor of the dominant estate would be protected in its enjoyment, it has not been so protected in the past on the ground that the easement was in itself an object of possession, but by the survival of precedents explained in a later Lecture.[83] Hence, to test the existence of a mere possession of this sort which the law will protect, we will take the case of a way used *de facto* for four years, but in which no easement has yet been acquired,

[80] Bruns, 483.

[81] 2 Kent (12th ed.), 205, n. 1. Cf. Y. B. 21 Hen. VI. 8, 9, pl. 19; American note to *Scott* v. *Shepherd*, in 1 Sm. L. C. (Am. ed.).

[82] Britton (Nich. ed.), I. 277 (cf. Bract., fol. 164 *b;* Fleta, fol. 214; Glanv., Lib. XIII, c. 37); Littleton, §§ 237–240, 588, 589; 3 Bl. Comm. 170; 3 Cruise, Dig., tit. xxviii., *Rents*, ch. 2, § 34.

[83] See Lecture XI.

and ask whether the possessor of the *quasi* dominant tenement would be protected in his use as against third persons. It is conceivable that he should be, but I believe that he would not.[84]

The chief objection to the doctrine seems to be, that there is almost a contradiction between the assertions that one man has a general power and intent to exclude the world from dealing with the land, and that another has the power to use it in a particular way, and to exclude the owner from interfering with that. The reconciliation of the two needs somewhat artificial reasoning. However, it should be borne in mind that the question in every case is not what was the actual power of the parties concerned, but what was their manifested power. If the latter stood thus balanced, the law might recognize a kind of split possession. But if it does not recognize it until a right is acquired, then the protection of a disseisor in the use of an easement must still be explained by a reference to the facts mentioned in the Lecture referred to.

The consequences attached to possession are substantially those attached to ownership, subject to the question of the continuance of possessory rights which I have touched upon above. Even a wrongful possessor of a chattel may have full damages for its conversion by a stranger to the title, or a return of the specific thing.[85]

It has been supposed, to be sure, that a "special property" was necessary in order to maintain replevin[86] or trover.[87] But modern cases establish that possession is sufficient, and an examination of the sources of our law proves that special property did not mean anything more. It has been shown that the procedure for the recovery of chattels lost against one's will, described by Bracton, like its predecessor on the Continent, was based upon possession. Yet Bracton, in the very passage in which he expressly

[84] Cf. *Stockport Water Works* v. *Potter*, 3 H. & C. 300, 318. The language in the seventh English edition of 1 Sm. L. C., 300, is rather too broad. If the law should protect a possessor of land in the enjoyment of water coming to it, it would do so because the use of the water was regarded as a part of the enjoyment of that land, and would by no means imply that it would do the same in the case just put of a way over land of another.

[85] *Jeffries* v. *Great Western Railway Co.*, 5 El. & Bl. 802. Cf. *Armory* v. *Delamirie*, 1 Strange, 505, 1 Sm. L. C.

[86] Co. Lit. 145 *b*. [87] 2 Wms. Saund. 47 *b*, note 1, to *Wilbraham* v. *Snow*.

makes that statement, uses a phrase which, but for the explanation, would seem to import ownership,—"Poterit rem *suam* petere." [88] The writs of later days used the same language, and when it was objected, as it frequently was, to a suit by a bailee for a taking of *bona et catalla sua*, that it should have been for *bona in custodia sua existentia*, it was always answered that those in the Chancery would not frame a writ in that form.[89]

The substance of the matter was, that goods in a man's possession were his (*sua*), within the meaning of the writ. But it was very natural to attempt a formal reconciliation between that formal word and the fact by saying that, although the plaintiff had not the general property in the chattels, yet he had a property as against strangers,[90] or a special property. This took place, and, curiously enough, two of the earliest instances in which I have found the latter phrase used are cases of a depositary,[91] and a borrower.[92] Brooke says that a wrongful taker "has title against all but the true owner." [93] In this sense the special property was better described as a "possessory property," as it was, in deciding that, in an indictment for larceny, the property could be laid in the bailee who suffered the trespass.[94]

I have explained the inversion by which a bailee's right of action against third persons was supposed to stand on his responsibility over, although in truth it was the foundation of that responsibility, and arose simply from his possession. The step was short, from saying that bailees could sue because they were answerable over,[95] to saying that they had the property as against strangers, or a special property, because they were answerable over,[96] and next that they could sue because they had a special

[88] Bract., fol. 150 *b*, 151; *supra*, p. 133; Y. B. 22 Ed. I. 466–468.

[89] Y. B. 48 Ed. III. 20; 11 Hen. IV. 17; 11 Hen. IV. 23, 24; 21 Hen. VII. 14. The meaning of *sua* is discussed in Y. B. 10 Ed. IV. 1, B, by Catesby. Compare Laband, Vermögensrechtlichen Klagen, 111; Heusler, Gewere, 492 *et seq.*, correcting Bruns, R. d. Besitzes, 300 *et seq.*; Sohm, Proc. d. L. Sal., § 6.

[90] Y. B. 11 Hen. IV. 17, pl. 39.

[91] Y. B. 21 Hen. VII. 14 *b*, pl. 23.

[92] Godbolt, 173, pl. 239. Cf. 11 Hen. IV. 17, pl. 39.

[93] Bro. Abr. *Trespass*, pl. 433, cit. Y. B. 13 Hen. VII. 10.

[94] Kelyng, 39. See, further, Buller, N. P. 33.

[95] Lecture V.; Y. B. 20 Hen. VII. 1, pl. 11.

[96] Y. B. 21 Hen. VII. 14 *b*, pl. 23.

property and were answerable over.[97] And thus the notion that special property meant something more than possession, and was a requisite to maintaining an action, got into the law.

The error was made easier by a different use of the phrase in a different connection. A bailee was in general answerable for goods stolen from his custody, whether he had a lien or not. But the law was otherwise as to a pledgee, if he had kept the pledge with his own goods, and the two were stolen together.[98] This distinction was accounted for, at least in Lord Coke's time, by saying that the pledge was, in a sense, the pledgee's own, that he had a special property in it, and thus that the ordinary relation of bailment did not exist, or that the undertaking was only to keep as his own goods.[99] The same expression was used in discussing the pledgee's right to assign the pledge.[100] In this sense the term applied only to pledges, but its significance in a particular connection was easily carried over into the others in which it was used, with the result that the special property which was requisite to maintain the possessory actions was supposed to mean a qualified interest in the goods.

With regard to the legal consequences of possession, it only remains to mention that the rules which have been laid down with regard to chattels also prevail with regard to land. For although the plaintiff in ejectment must recover on the strength of his own title as against a defendant in possession, it is now settled that prior possession is enough if the defendant stands on his possession alone.[101] Possession is of course sufficient for trespass.[102] And although the early remedy by assize was restricted to those who had a technical seisin, this was for reasons which do not affect the general theory.

Before closing I must say a word concerning ownership and kindred conceptions. Following the order of analysis which has been pursued with regard to possession, the first question must be, What are the facts to which the rights called ownership are

[97] 1 Roll. Abr. 4, 5 (I), pl. 1. Cf. *Arnold* v. *Jefferson*, 1 Ld. Raym. 275.

[98] 29 Ass., fol. 163, pl. 28. [99] *Southcote's Case*, 4 Co. Rep. 83 *b*.

[100] *Mores* v. *Conham*, Owen, 123. Cf. *Ratcliff* v. *Davis*, 1 Bulstr. 29.

[101] *Doe* v. *Dyball*, Mood. & M. 346 and note; 2 Wms. Saund. 111, and later notes; 1 Ad. & El. 119; *Asher* v. *Whitlock*, L. R. I Q. B. 1.

[102] *Graham* v. *Peat*, 1 East, 244.

attached as a legal consequence? The most familiar mode of gaining ownership is by conveyance from a previous owner. But that presupposes ownership already existing, and the problem is to discover what calls it into being.

One fact which has this effect is first possession. The captor of wild animals, or the taker of fish from the ocean, has not merely possession, but a title good against all the world. But the most common mode of getting an original and independent title is by certain proceedings, in court or out of it, adverse to all the world. At one extreme of these is the proceeding *in rem* of the admiralty, which conclusively disposes of the property in its power, and, when it sells or condemns it, does not deal with this or that man's title, but gives a new title paramount to all previous interests, whatsoever they may be. The other and more familiar case is prescription, where a public adverse holding continued for a certain time has a similar effect. A title by prescription is not a presumed conveyance from this or that owner alone, it extinguishes all previous and inconsistent claims. The two coalesce in the ancient fine with proclamations where the combined effect of the judgment and the lapse of a year and a day was to bar all claims.[103]

So rights analogous to those of ownership may be given by the legislature to persons of whom some other set of facts is true. For instance, a patentee, or one to whom the government has issued a certain instrument, and who in fact has made a patentable invention.[a]

But what are the rights of ownership? They are substantially the same as those incident to possession. Within the limits prescribed by policy, the owner is allowed to exercise his natural powers over the subject-matter uninterfered with, and is more or less protected in excluding other people from such interference. The owner is allowed to exclude all, and is accountable to no one. The possessor is allowed to exclude all but one, and is accountable to no one but him. The great body of questions which

[103] As to this period see Heusler, Gewere. Cf. Laveleye, Propriété, 166.

[a] [The only importance of the difference in the facts to wh. similar conseq. are attached lies in the greater diff. attending the theory of conveyances, when the facts are anything but a relation to a physical object.]

have made the subject of property so large and important are questions of conveyancing, not necessarily or generally dependent on ownership as distinguished from possession. They are questions of the effect of not having an independent and original title, but of coming in under a title already in existence, or of the modes in which an original title can be cut up among those who come in under it. These questions will be dealt with and explained where they belong, in the Lectures on Successions.

LECTURE VII

CONTRACT.—I. HISTORY [a]

THE doctrine of contract has been so thoroughly remodelled to meet the needs of modern times, that there is less necessity here than elsewhere for historical research. It has been so ably discussed that there is less room here than elsewhere for essentially new analysis. But a short account of the growth of modern doctrines, whether necessary or not, will at least be interesting, while an analysis of their main characteristics cannot be omitted, and may present some new features.

It is popularly supposed that the oldest forms of contract known to our law are covenant and debt, and they are of early date, no doubt. But there are other contracts still in use which, although they have in some degree put on modern forms, at least suggest the question whether they were not of equally early appearance.

One of these, the promissory oath, is no longer the foundation of any rights in private law. It is used, but mainly as a solemnity connected with entering upon a public office. The judge swears that he will execute justice according to law, the juryman that he will find his verdict according to law and the evidence, the newly adopted citizen that he will bear true faith and allegiance to the government of his choice.

But there is another contract which plays a more important part. It may, perhaps, sound paradoxical to mention the contract of suretyship. Suretyship, nowadays, is only an accessory obligation, which presupposes a principal undertaking, and which, so far as the nature of the contract goes, is just like any other. But,

[a] [The forms of early contract are not sufficiently distinguished from the substance on this page. The forms were the oath, (infra) the fides facta, & writing . . . Writing & record seem to have begun as evidence and to have become distinct form—]

as has been pointed out by Laferrière,[1] and very likely by earlier writers, the surety of ancient law was the hostage, and the giving of hostages was by no means confined to international dealings.

In the old metrical romance of Huon of Bordeaux, Huon, having killed the son of Charlemagne, is required by the Emperor to perform various seeming impossibilities as the price of forgiveness. Huon starts upon the task, leaving twelve of his knights as hostages.[2] He returns successful, but at first the Emperor is made to believe that his orders have been disobeyed. Thereupon Charlemagne cries out, "I summon hither the pledges for Huon. I will hang them, and they shall have no ransom."[3] So, when Huon is to fight a duel, by way of establishing the truth or falsehood of a charge against him, each party begins by producing some of his friends as hostages.

When hostages are given for a duel which is to determine the truth or falsehood of an accusation, the transaction is very near to the giving of similar security in the trial of a cause in court. This was in fact the usual course of the Germanic procedure. It will be remembered that the earliest appearance of law was as a substitute for the private feuds between families or clans. But while a defendant who did not peaceably submit to the jurisdiction of the court might be put outside the protection of the law, so that any man might kill him at sight, there was at first no way of securing the indemnity to which the plaintiff was entitled unless the defendant chose to give such security.[4]

The English customs which have been preserved to us are somewhat more advanced, but one of the noticeable features in their procedure is the giving of security at every step. All lawyers will remember a trace of this in the fiction of John Doe and Richard Roe, the plaintiff's pledges to prosecute his action. But a more significant example is found in the rule repeated in many of the early laws, that a defendant accused of a wrong must either find security or go to prison.[5] This security was the hostage of earlier

[1] 2 Hist. du Droit Franç., pp. 146 *et seq.*, 152.

[2] Anciens Poètes de la France, (Guessard,) p. 71.

[3] Page 283; cf. 284, cxviii. *et seq.*, 44, lxix.

[4] Sohm, Proc. d. Lex. Sal., §§ 15, 23–25, tr. Thévenin, pp. 80, 105, 106, 122.

[5] Essays in A. S. Law, p. 292.

days, and later, when the actions for punishment and for redress were separated from each other, became the bail of the criminal law. The liability was still conceived in the same way as when the bail actually put his own body into the power of the party secured.

One of Charlemagne's additions to the Lex Salica speaks of a freeman who has committed himself to the power of another by way of surety.[6] The very phrase is copied in the English laws of Henry I.[7] We have seen what this meant in the story of Huon of Bordeaux. The Mirror of Justices [8] says that King Canute used to judge the mainprisors according as the principals when their principals appeared not in judgment, but that King Henry I. confined Canute's rule to mainprisors who were consenting to the fact.

As late as the reign of Edward III., Shard, an English judge, after stating the law as it still is, that bail are a prisoner's keepers, and shall be charged if he escapes, observes, that some say that the bail shall be hanged in his place.[9] This was the law in the analogous case of a jailer.[10] The old notion is to be traced in the form still given by modern writers for the undertaking of bail for felony. They are bound "body for body," [11] and modern law-books find it necessary to state that this does not make them liable to the punishment of the principal offender if he does not appear, but only to a fine.[12] The contract also differed from our modern ideas in the mode of execution. It was simply a solemn admission of liability in the presence of the officer authorized to take it. The signature of the bail was not necessary,[13] and it was not requisite that the person bailed should bind himself as a party.[14]

But these peculiarities have been modified or done away with by statute, and I have dwelt upon the case, not so much as a

[6] Cap. VIII., Merkel, p. 48.

[7] Cap. LXXXIX. § 3, Essays in A. S. Law, p. 291.

[8] Chap. IV. § 16.

[9] Fitzh. Abr. *Mainprise*, pl. 12 (H. 33 Ed. III.); Staundforde, P. C. 65.

[10] Abbr. Plac., p. 343, col. 2, rot. 37, 17 Ed. II.

[11] Jacob, L. D., "Bail." Cf. 1 Bulstr. 45; Hawkins, P. C., II. ch. 15, § 83; Abbr. Plac., p. 343, col. 2, rot. 37, 17 Ed. II.

[12] Highmore, Bail, p. 199; Jacob, L. D., "Bail." Cf. 2 Laferrière, Hist. du Droit Franç., p. 148.

[13] Highmore, p. 195.

[14] Ibid., p. 200.

special form of contract differing from all others as because the history of its origin shows one of the first appearances of contract in our law. It is to be traced to the gradual increase of faith in the honor of a hostage if the case calling for his surrender should arrive, and to the consequent relaxation of actual imprisonment. An illustration may be found in the parallel mode of dealing with the prisoner himself. His bail, to whom his body is supposed to be delivered, have a right to seize him at any time and anywhere, but he is allowed to go at large until surrendered. It will be noticed that this form of contract, like debt as dealt with by the Roman law of the Twelve Tables, and for the same motive, although by a different process, looked to the body of the contracting party as the ultimate satisfaction.

Debt is another and more popular candidate for the honors of priority. Since the time of Savigny, the first appearance of contract both in Roman and German law has often been attributed to the case of a sale by some accident remaining incomplete. The question does not seem to be of great philosophical significance. For to explain how mankind first learned to promise, we must go to metaphysics, and find out how it ever came to frame a future tense. The nature of the particular promise which was first enforced in a given system can hardly lead to any truth of general importance. But the history of the action of debt is instructive, although in a humbler way. It is necessary to know something about it in order to understand the enlightened rules which make up the law of contract at the present time.

In Glanvill's treatise the action of debt is found already to be one of the well-known remedies. But the law of those days was still in a somewhat primitive state, and it will easily be imagined that a form of action which goes back as far as that was not founded on any very delicate discriminations. It was, as I shall try to show directly, simply the general form in which any money claim was collected, except unliquidated claims for damages by force, for which there was established the equally general remedy of trespass.

It has been thought that the action was adopted from the then more civilized procedure of the Roman law. A natural opinion, seeing that all the early English law-writers adopt their phraseology and classification from Rome. Still it seems much more probable that the action is of pure German descent. It has the features of the primitive procedure which is found upon the Continent, as described by Laband.[15]

The substance of the plaintiff's claim as set forth in the writ of debt is that the defendant owes him so much and wrongfully withholds it. It does not matter, for a claim framed like that, how the defendant's duty arises. It is not confined to contract. It is satisfied if there is a duty to pay on any ground. It states a mere conclusion of law, not the facts upon which that conclusion is based, and from which the liability arises. The old German complaint was, in like manner, "A owes me so much."

It was characteristic of the German procedure that the defendant could meet that complaint by answering, in an equally general form, that he did not owe the plaintiff. The plaintiff had to do more than simply allege a debt, if he would prevent the defendant from escaping in that way. In England, if the plaintiff had not something to show for his debt, the defendant's denial turned him out of court; and even if he had, he was liable to be defeated by the defendant's swearing with some of his friends to back him that he owed nothing. The chief reason why debt was supplanted for centuries by a later remedy, assumpsit, was the survival of this relic of early days.

Finally, in England as in Germany, debt for the detention of money was the twin brother of the action brought for wrongfully withholding any other kind of chattel. The gist of the complaint in either case was the same.

It seems strange that this crude product of the infancy of law should have any importance for us at the present time. Yet whenever we trace a leading doctrine of substantive law far enough back, we are very likely to find some forgotten circumstance of procedure at its source. Illustrations of this truth have been given already. The action of debt and the other actions of contract will furnish others. Debt throws most light upon the doctrine of consideration.

Our law does not enforce every promise which a man may make. Promises made as ninety-nine promises out of a hundred

[15] Vermögensrechtlichen Klagen.

are, by word of mouth or simple writing, are not binding unless there is a consideration for them. That is, as it is commonly explained, unless the promisee has either conferred a benefit on the promisor, or incurred a detriment, as the inducement to the promise.

It has been thought that this rule was borrowed from the Roman law by the Chancery, and, after undergoing some modification there, passed into the common law.

But this account of the matter is at least questionable. So far as the use of words goes, I am not aware that consideration is distinctly called *cause* before the reign of Elizabeth; in the earlier reports it always appears as *quid pro quo*. Its first appearance, so far as I know, is in Fleta's account of the action of debt,[16] and although I am inclined to believe that Fleta's statement is not to be trusted, a careful consideration of the chronological order of the cases in the Year Books will show, I think, that the doctrine was fully developed in debt before any mention of it in equity can be found. One of the earliest references to what a promisor was to have for his undertaking was in the action of assumpsit.[17] But the doctrine certainly did not originate there. The first mention of consideration in connection with equity which I have seen is in the form of *quid pro quo*,[18] and occurs after the requirement had been thoroughly established in debt.[19]

The single fact that a consideration was never required for contracts under seal, unless Fleta is to be trusted against the great weight of nearly contemporaneous evidence, goes far to show that the rule cannot have originated on grounds of policy as a rule of substantive law. And conversely, the coincidence of the doctrine with a peculiar mode of procedure points very strongly to the probability that the peculiar requirement and the peculiar procedure were connected. It will throw light on the question to put together a few undisputed facts, and to consider what consequences naturally followed. It will therefore be desirable to examine the action of debt a little further. But it is only fair

[16] II. c. 60, § 25. Glanvill's *"justa debendi causa"* (Lib. X. c. 4) seems remote from consideration.

[17] Y. B. 3 Hen. VI. 36.

[18] Y. B. 37 Hen. VI. 13, pl. 3.

[19] Y. B. 37 Hen. VI. 8, pl. 33.

to admit, at the outset, that I offer the explanation which follows with great hesitation, and, I think, with a full appreciation of the objections which might be urged.

It was observed a moment ago, that, in order to recover against a defendant who denied his debt, the plaintiff had to show something for it; otherwise he was turned over to the limited jurisdiction of the spiritual tribunals.[20] This requirement did not mean evidence in the modern sense. It meant simply that he must maintain his cause in one of the ways then recognized by law. These were three, the duel, a writing, and witnesses. The duel need not be discussed, as it soon ceased to be used in debt, and has no bearing on what I have to say. Trial by writing and by witnesses, on the other hand, must both be carefully studied. It will be convenient to consider the latter first and to find out what these witnesses were.

One thing we know at the start; they were not witnesses as we understand the term. They were not produced before a jury for examination and cross-examination, nor did their testimony depend for its effect on being believed by the court that heard it. Nowadays, a case is not decided by the evidence, but by a verdict, or a finding of facts, followed by a judgment. The oath of a witness has no effect unless it is believed. But in the time of Henry II. our trial by jury did not exist. When an oath was allowed to be sworn it had the same effect, whether it was believed or not. There was no provision for sifting it by a second body. In those cases where a trial by witnesses was possible, if the party called on to go forward could find a certain number of men who were willing to swear in a certain form, there was an end of the matter.

Now this seems like a more primitive way of establishing a debt than the production of the defendant's written acknowledgment, and it is material to discover its origin.

The cases in which this mode of trial was used appear from the early books and reports to have been almost wholly confined to claims arising out of a sale or loan. And the question at once occurs, whether we are not upon the traces of an institution which was already ancient when Glanvill wrote. For centuries before

[20] Glanv., Lib. X. c. 12; Bract., fol. 400 *b*, § 10; 22 Ass., pl. 70, fol. 101.

the Conquest the Anglo-Saxon law[21] had required the election of a certain number of official witnesses, two or three of whom were to be called in to every bargain of sale. The object for which these witnesses were established is not commonly supposed to have been the proof of debts. They go back to a time when theft and similar offences were the chief ground of litigation, and the purpose for which they were appointed was to afford a means of deciding whether a person charged with having stolen property had come by it rightfully or not. A defendant could clear himself of the felony by their oath that he had bought or received the thing openly in the way appointed by law.

Having been present at the bargain, the witnesses were able to swear to what they had seen and heard, if any question arose between the parties. Accordingly, their use was not confined to disposing of a charge of felony. But that particular service identifies the transaction witnesses of the Saxon period. Now we know that the use of these witnesses did not at once disappear under Norman influence. They are found with their old function in the laws of William the Conqueror.[22] The language of Glanvill seems to prove that they were still known under Henry II. He says that, if a purchaser cannot summon in the man from whom he bought, to warrant the property to him and defend the suit, (for if he does, the peril is shifted to the seller,) then if the purchaser has sufficient proof of his having lawfully bought the thing, *de legittimo marcatu suo*, it will clear him of felony. But if he have not sufficient suit, he will be in danger.[23] This is the law of William over again. It follows that purchasers still used the transaction witnesses.

But Glanvill also seems to admit the use of witness to establish debts.[24] As the transaction witnesses were formerly available for

[21] Essays in A. S. Law, 187.

[22] I. 45; III. 10.

[23] Lib. X. c. 17. Suit, *secta*, was the term applied to the persons whose oath the party tendered.

[24] Lib. X. c. 12 (Beames, p. 262); c. 8 & c. 5 (Beames, pp. 256, 251); cf. Lib. IV. c. 6, where witnesses are tendered *de visu et auditu*. Cf. Bract., fol. 315 *b*, § 6; Fleta, II. c. 63, § 10, p. 137. It was no doubt true, as Glanvill says, Lib. X. c. 17, that the usual mode of proof was by a writing or by duel, and that the King's Court did not generally give protection to private agreements made anywhere except in the Court of the King (Lib. X. c. 8). But it can hardly be that debts were never established by witness in his time, in view of the continuous evidence from Bracton onwards.

this purpose, I see no reason to doubt that they still were, and that he is speaking of them here also.[25] Moreover, for a long time after Henry II., whenever an action was brought for a debt of which there was no written evidence, the plaintiff, when asked what he had to show for it, always answered "good suit," and tendered his witnesses, who were sometimes examined by the court.[26] I think it is not straining the evidence to infer that the "good suit" of the later reports was the descendant of the Saxon transaction witnesses, as it has been shown that Glanvill's *secta* was.[27]

Assuming this step in the argument to have been taken, it will be well to recall again for a moment the original nature of the witness oath. It was confined to facts within the witnesses' knowledge by sight and hearing. But as the purposes for which witnesses were provided only required their presence when property changed hands, the principal case in which they could be of service between the parties to a bargain was when a debt was claimed by reason of the delivery of property. The purpose did not extend to agreements which were executory on both sides, because there no question of theft could arise. And Glanvill shows that in his time the King's Court did not enforce such agreements.[28] Now, if the oath of the *secta* could only be used to establish a debt where the transaction witnesses could have sworn, it will be seen, readily enough, how an accident of procedure may have led to a most important rule of substantive law.

The rule that witnesses could only swear to facts within their knowledge, coupled with the accident that these witnesses were

[25] But cf. Brunner, Schwurgerichte, 399. I do not go so far as to say that they were still a living institution. However that may be, tradition must at least have modelled itself on what had been the function of the former official body.

[26] Bract., fol. 315 *b*, § 6; Britt. (Nich.) I. p. 162; Magna Charta, c. 38; Y. B. 21 Ed. I. 456; 7 Ed. II. 242; 18 Ed. II. 582; 3 Bl. Comm. 295, 344. Cf. 17 Ed. III, 48 *b*.

[27] Cf. Glanv., Lib. IV. c. 6.

[28] Lib. X. c. 18. It is possible that this means no more than Glanvill's often repeated statement, that the King's Court did not, generally speaking, take cognizance of private agreements. The substantive law was, perhaps, still limited by traditions from the infancy of contract. See pp. 248, 251, 259, 260. The proposition in its broadest form may have been based on the inability to try such agreements in any way but those which have been specified. Cf. the requirement of *aliam diracionationem* and *aliis probationibus*, in Lib. X. c. 12. But cf. Ibid. with Essays in A. S. Law, pp. 189, 190.

not used in transactions which might create a debt, except for a particular fact, namely, the delivery of property, together with the further accident that this delivery was *quid pro quo,* was equivalent to the rule that, when a debt was proved by witnesses there must be *quid pro quo.* But these debts proved by witnesses, instead of by deed are what we call simple contract debts, and thus beginning with debt, and subsequently extending itself to other contracts, is established our peculiar and most important doctrine that every simple contract must have a consideration. This was never the law as to debts or contracts proved in the usual way by the defendant's seal, and the fact that it applied only to obligations which were formerly established by a procedure of limited use, goes far to show that the connection with procedure was not accidental.

The mode of proof soon changed, but as late as the reign of Queen Elizabeth we find a trace of this original connection. It is said, "But the common law requires that there should be a new cause (i. e. consideration), whereof the country may have intelligence or knowledge for the trial of it, if need be, so that it is necessary for the Public-weal."[29] Lord Mansfield showed his intuition of the historical grounds of our law when he said, "I take it that the ancient notion about the want of consideration was for the sake of *evidence* only; for when it is reduced into *writing,* as in covenants, specialties, bonds, etc., there was no objection to the want of consideration."[30]

If it should be objected that the preceding argument is necessarily confined to debt, whereas the requirement of consideration applies equally to all simple contracts, the answer is, that in all probability the rule originated with debt, and spread from debt to other contracts.

But, again, it may be asked whether there were no other contracts proved by witness except those which have been mentioned. Were there no contracts proved in that way to which the accidental consideration was wanting? To this also there is an easy answer. The contracts enforced by the civil courts, even as late as Henry II., were few and simple. The witness procedure

[29] *Sharington* v. *Strotton,* Plowden, 298, at p. 302, M. 7 & 8 Eliz.
[30] *Pillans* v. *Mierop,* 3 Burrow, 1663, 1669.

was no doubt broad enough for all the contracts which were made in early times. Besides those of sale, loan, and the like, which have been mentioned, I find but two contractual obligations. These were the warranties accompanying a sale and suretyship which was referred to at the beginning of the Lecture. Of the former, warranty of title was rather regarded as an obligation raised by the law out of the relation of buyer and seller than as a contract. Other express warranties were matters within the knowledge of the transaction witnesses, and were sworn to by them in Saxon times.[31]

But in the Norman period warranty is very little heard of, except with regard to land, and then it was decided by the duel. It so wholly disappeared, except where it was embodied in a deed, that it can have had no influence upon the law of consideration. I shall therefore assume, without more detail, that it does not bear upon the case.

Then as to the pledge or surety. He no longer paid with his body, unless in very exceptional cases, but his liability was translated into money, and enforced in an action of debt. This time-honored contract, like the other debts of Glanvill's time, could be established by witness without a writing,[32] and in this case there was not such a consideration, such a benefit to the promisor, as the law required when the doctrine was first enunciated. But this also is unimportant, because his liability on the oath of witness came to an end, as well as that of the warrantor, before the foundations were laid for the rule which I am seeking to explain. A writing soon came to be required, as will be seen in a moment.

The result so far is, that the only action of contract in Glanvill's time was debt, that the only debts recovered without writing were those which have been described, and that the only one of these for which there was not *quid pro quo* ceased to be recoverable in that way by the reign of Edward III.

But great changes were beginning in the reign of Henry II. More various and complex contracts soon came to be enforced. It may be asked, Why was not the scope of the witness oath en-

[31] 1 Thorpe, Anc. Laws, 181, Oaths, 7, 8.

[32] Glanv., Lib. X. c. 5 (Beames, p. 251); Y. B. 7 Ed. II. 242; Novæ Narr. *Dette-Vers plege*, Rastell's Law Tracts, p. 253, D, 2 Finl. Reeves, 376.

larged, or, if any better proof were forthcoming, why was not the *secta* done away with, and other oral testimony admitted? In any event, what can the law of Henry II.'s time have to do with consideration, which was not heard of until centuries later?

It is manifest that a witness oath, which disposes of a case by the simple fact that it is sworn, is not a satisfactory mode of proof. A written admission of debt produced in court, and sufficiently identified as issuing from the defendant, is obviously much better. The only weak point about a writing is the means of identifying it as the defendant's, and this difficuty disappeared as soon as the use of seals became common. This had more or less taken place in Glanvill's time, and then all that a party had to do was to produce the writing and satisfy the court by inspection that the impression on the wax fitted his opponent's seal.[33] The oath of the *secta* could always be successfully met by wager of law,[34] that is, by a counter oath on the part of the defendant, with the same or double the number of fellow-swearers produced by the plaintiff. But a writing proved to be the defendant's could not be contradicted.[35] For if a man said he was bound, he was bound. There was no question of consideration, because there was as yet no such doctrine. He was equally bound if he acknowledged an obligation in any place having a record, such as the superior courts, by which his acknowledgment could be proved. Indeed, to this day some securities are taken simply by an oral admission before the clerk of a court noted by him in his papers. The advantage of the writing was not only that it furnished better proof in the old cases, but also that it made it possible to enforce obligations for which there would otherwise have been no proof at all.

What has been said sufficiently explains the preference of proof by writing to proof by the old-fashioned witness oath. But there were other equally good reasons why the latter should not be extended beyond its ancient limits. The transaction witnesses

[33] Glanv., Lib. X. c. 12 (Beames, p. 263); Bract., fol. 398 *b*, § 1. The favorite proof by duel was also allowed, but this disappeared. When the inquest became general, the execution of the deed was tried, like any other fact, by that means.

[34] Bract., fol. 315 *b*, § 6, 400 *b*; Coke, 2d Inst., 44, 45.

[35] Glanv., Lib. X. c. 12 (Beames, p. 263); Bract., fol. 100 *b*, § 9.

were losing their statutory and official character. Already in Glanvill's time the usual modes of proving a debt were by the duel or by writing.[36] A hundred years later Bracton shows that the *secta* had degenerated to the retainers and household of the party, and he says that their oath raises but a slight presumption.[37]

Moreover, a new mode of trial was growing up, which, although it was not made use of in these cases[38] for a good while, must have tended to diminish the estimate set on the witness oath by contrast. This was the beginning of our trial by jury. It was at first an inquest of the neighbors most likely to know about a disputed matter of fact. They spoke from their own knowledge, but they were selected by an officer of the court instead of by the interested party, and were intended to be impartial.[39] Soon witnesses were summoned before them, not, as of old, to settle the case by their oath, but to aid the inquest to find a verdict by their testimony. With the advent of this enlightened procedure, the *secta* soon ceased to decide the case, and it may well be asked why it did not disappear altogether, and leave no traces.

Taking into account the conservatism of the English law, and the fact that, before deeds came in, the only debts for which there had been a remedy were debts proved by the transaction witnesses, it would not have been a surprise to find the tender of suit persisting in those cases. But there was another reason still more imperative. The defence in debt where there was no deed was by wager of law.[40] A section of Magna Charta was interpreted to prohibit a man's being put to his law on the plaintiff's own statement without good witness.[41] Hence, the statute required witness—that is, the *secta*—in every case of debt where the plaintiff did not rely upon a writing. Thus it happened that suit continued to be tendered in those cases where it had been of old,[42] and as the defendant, if he did not admit the debt in such

[36] Glanv., Lib. X. c. 17 (Beames, p. 272).

[37] Bract., fol. 400 *b*, § 9.

[38] Cf. Y. B. 20 Ed. I. 304, and 34 Ed. I., 150, 152; ib. 330, 332; 35 Ed. I. 546.

[39] Bract., fol. 400 *b*, § 8.

[40] Cf. Y. B. 20 Ed. I. 304.

[41] Cap. 28; 32 & 33 Ed. I. 516; 18 Ed. II. 582; Fleta, II. c. 63, § 9; Coke, 2d Inst., 44; 3 Bl. Comm. 344.

[42] Y. B. 18 Ed. II. 582; 17 Ed. III. 48 *b*, pl. 14.

cases, always waged his law, it was long before the inquest got much foothold.

To establish a debt which arose merely by way of promise or acknowledgment, and for which there had formerly been no mode of trial provided, you must have a writing, the new form of proof which introduced it into the law. The rule was laid down, "by parol the party is not obliged." [43] But the old debts were not conceived of as raised by a promise.[44] They were a "duty" springing from the defendant's receipt of property, a fact which could be seen and sworn to. In these cases the old law maintained and even extended itself a little by strict analogy.

But the undertaking of a surety, in whatever form it was clothed, did not really arise out of any such fact. It had become of the same nature as other promises, and it was soon doubted whether it should not be proved by the same evidence.[45] By the reign of Edward III., it was settled that a deed was necessary,[46] except where the customs of particular cities had kept the old law in force.[47]

This reign may be taken as representing the time when the divisions and rules of procedure were established which have lasted until the present day. It is therefore worth while to repeat and sum up the condition of the law at that time.

It was still necessary that the *secta* should be tendered in every action of debt for which no writing was produced. For this, as well as for the other reasons which have been mentioned, the sphere of such actions was not materially enlarged beyond those cases which had formerly been established by the witness-oath. As suretyship was no longer one of these, they became strictly limited to cases in which the debt arose from the receipt of a *quid pro quo*. Moreover there was no other action of contract which could be maintained without a writing. New species of contracts were now enforced by an action of covenant, but there a deed was always necessary. At the same time the *secta* had

[43] Y. B. 29 Ed. III. 25, 26; cf. 48 Ed. III. 6, pl. 11; Fleta, II. c. 60, § 25; Glanvill, Lib. X. c. 12.

[44] Cf. Bro. *Acc. sur le Case*, pl. 5; s. c., 27 Hen. VIII. 24, 25, pl. 3.

[45] Y. B. 18 Ed. III. 13, pl. 7.

[46] Y B. 44 Ed. III. 21, pl. 23.

[47] F. N. B. 122, I, in margin. Cf. F. N. B. 122 K; Y. B. 43 Ed. III. 11, pl. 1; s. c., Bro. *Pledges*, pl. 3; 9 Hen. V. 14, pl. 23.

shrunk to a form, although it was still argued that its function was more important in contract than elsewhere. It could no longer be examined before the court.[48] It was a mere survival, and the transaction witness had ceased to be an institution. Hence, the necessity of tendering the witness oath did not fix the limit of debt upon simple contract except by tradition, and it is not surprising to find that the action was slightly extended by analogy from its scope in Glanvill's time.

But debt remained substantially at the point which I have indicated, and no new action available for simple contracts was introduced for a century. In the mean time the inversion which I have explained took place, and what was an accident of procedure had become a doctrine of substantive law. The change was easy when the debts which could be enforced without deed all sprung from a benefit to the debtor.

The influence of the Roman law, no doubt, aided in bringing about this result. It will be remembered that in the reign of Henry II. most simple contracts and debts for which there was not the evidence of deed or witness were left to be enforced by the ecclesiastical courts, so far as their jurisdiction extended.[49] Perhaps it was this circumstance which led Glanvill and his successors to apply the terminology of the civilians to common-law debts. But whether he borrowed it from the ecclesiastical courts, or went directly to the fountain-head, certain it is that Glanvill makes use of the classification and technical language of the Corpus Juris throughout his tenth book.

There were certain special contracts in the Roman system called real, which bound the contractor either to return a certain thing put into his hands by the contractee, as in a case of lease or loan, or to deliver other articles of the same kind, as when grain, oil, or money was lent. This class did not correspond, except in the most superficial way, with the common-law debts. But Glanvill adopted the nomenclature, and later writers began to draw con-

[48] Y. B. 17 Ed. III. 48 *b*, pl. 14. Cf. Fortescue (Amos), 67, n.; 3 Bl. Comm. 295.

[49] For limit, see Constit. of Clarendon, c. 15; Glanv., Lib. X. c. 8, 12; Y. B. 22 Ass., pl. 70, fol. 101; 45 Ed. III. 24, pl. 30; 19 R. II., Fitzh. Abr. *Dett*, pl. 166; 37 Hen. VI. 8, pl. 18; 14 Ed. IV. 6, pl. 3; 15 Ed. IV. 32, pl. 14; 19 Ed. IV. 10, pl. 18; 20 Ed. IV. 3, pl. 17.

clusions from it. The author of Fleta, a writer by no means always intelligent in following and adopting his predecessors' use of the Roman law,[50] says that to raise a debt there must be not only a certain thing promised, but a certain thing promised in return.[51]

If Fleta had confined his statement to debts by simple contract, it might well have been suggested by the existing state of the law. But as he also required a writing and a seal, in addition to the matter given or promised in return, the doctrine laid down by him can hardly have prevailed at any time. It was probably nothing more than a slight vagary of reasoning based upon the Roman elements which he borrowed from Bracton.

It only remains to trace the gradual appearance of consideration in the decisions. A case of the reign of Edward III.[52] seems to distinguish between a parol obligation founded on voluntary payments by the obligee and one founded on a payment at the obligor's request. It also speaks of the debt or "duty" in that case as arising by cause of payments. Somewhat similar language is used in the next reign.[53] So, in the twelfth year of Henry IV.,[54] there is an approach to the thought: "If money is promised to a man for making a release, and he makes the release, he will have a good action of debt in the matter." In the next reign[55] it was decided that, in such a case, the plaintiff could not recover without having executed the release, which is explained by the editor on the ground that *ex nudo pacto non oritur actio*. But the most important fact is, that from Edward I. to Henry VI. we find no case where a debt was recovered, unless a consideration had in fact been received.

Another fact to be noticed is, that since Edward III. debts arising from a transaction without writing are said to arise from contract, as distinguished from debts arising from an obligation.[56] Hence, when consideration was required as such, it was required in contracts not under seal, whether debts or not. Under Henry

[50] See for an illustration 2 Kent's Comm. (12th ed.), 451, n. 1 (*b*).

[51] *Repromittatur*, but cf. *pro servitio tuo vel pro homagio*, Fleta, II. c. 60, § 25.

[52] Y. B. 29 Ed. III. 25, 26. But cf. 48 Ed. III. 3, pl. 6.

[53] 19 R. II., Fitzh. Abr. *Dett*, pl. 166.

[54] Y. B. 12 Hen. IV. 17, pl. 13, *ad fin.*

[55] Y. B. 9 Hen. V. 14, pl. 23.

[56] (Cf. 13 Ed. II. 403; 17 Ed. III. 48, pl. 14; 29 Ed. III. 25, 26.) 41 Ed. III. 7, pl. 15; 46 Ed. III. 6, pl. 16; Fitzh. Abr. *Dett*, pl. 166.

VI. *quid pro quo* became a necessity in all such contracts. In the third year of that reign[57] it was objected to an action upon an assumpsit for not building a mill, that it was not shown what the defendant was to have for doing it. In the thirty-sixth year of the same reign (A. D. 1459), the doctrine appears full grown, and is assumed to be familiar.[58]

The case turned upon a question which was debated for centuries before it was settled, whether debt would lie for a sum of money promised by the defendant to the plaintiff if he would marry the defendant's daughter. But whereas formerly the debate had been whether the promise was not so far incident to the marriage that it belonged exclusively to the jurisdiction of the spiritual courts, it now touched the purely mundane doubt whether the defendant had had *quid pro quo.*

It will be remembered that the fact formerly sworn to by the transaction witnesses was a benefit to the defendant, namely, a delivery of the things sold or the money lent to him. Such cases, also, offer the most obvious form of consideration. The natural question is, what the promisor was to have for his promise.[59] It is only by analysis that the supposed policy of the law is seen to be equally satisfied by a detriment incurred by the promisee. It therefore not unnaturally happened that the judges, when they first laid down the law that there must be *quid pro quo,* were slow to recognize a detriment to the contractee as satisfying the requirement which had been laid down. In the case which I have mentioned some of the judges were inclined to hold that getting rid of his daughter was a sufficient benefit to the defendant to make him a debtor for the money which he promised; and there was even some hint of the opinion, that marrying the lady was a consideration, because it was a detriment to the promisee.[60] But the other opinion prevailed, at least for a time, because the defendant had had nothing from the plaintiff sufficient to raise a debt.[61]

So it was held that a service rendered to a third person upon the

[57] Y. B. 3 Hen. VI. 36, pl. 33. [58] Y. B. 37 Hen. VI. 8, pl. 18.

[59] E. g., Rolfe in Y. B. 3 Hen. VI. 36, pl. 23.

[60] Y. B. 37 Hen. VI. 8, pl. 18. Cf. Bro. *Feoffements al Uses,* pl. 54; Plowden, 301.

[61] Y. B. 15 Ed. IV. 32, pl. 14; (s. c., 14 Ed. IV. 6, pl. 3;) 17 Ed. IV. 4, pl. 4.

defendant's request and promise of a reward, would not be enough,[62] although not without strong opinions to the contrary, and for a time the precedents were settled. It became established law that an action of debt would only lie upon a consideration actually received by and enuring to the benefit of the debtor.

It was, however, no peculiarity of either the action or the contract of debt which led to this view, but the imperfectly developed theory of consideration prevailing between the reigns of Henry VI. and Elizabeth. The theory was the same in assumpsit,[63] and in equity.[64] Wherever consideration was mentioned, it was as *quid pro quo*, as what the contractor was to have for his contract.

Moreover, before consideration was ever heard of, debt was the time-honored remedy on every obligation to pay money enforced by law, except the liability to damages for a wrong.[65] It has been shown already that a surety could be sued in debt until the time of Edward III. without a writing, yet a surety receives no benefit from the dealing with his principal. For instance, if a man sells corn to A, and B says, "I will pay if A does not," the sale does B no good so far as appears by the terms of the bargain. For this reason, debt cannot now be maintained against a surety in such a case.

It was not always so. It is not so to this day if there is an obligation under seal. In that case, it does not matter how the obligation arose, or whether there was any consideration for it or not. But a writing was a more general way of establishing a debt in Glanvill's time than witness, and it is absurd to determine the scope of the action by considering only a single class of debts enforced by it. Moreover, a writing for a long time was only another, although more conclusive, mode of proof. The foundation of the action was the same, however it was proved. This was a duty or "duity"[66] to the plaintiff, in other words, the money was due him, no matter how, as any one may see by reading the earlier Year Books. Hence it was, that debt lay equally upon a judgment,[67] which established such a duty by matter of record,

[62] Cf. Y. B. 37 Hen. VI. 8, pl. 18; 17 Ed. IV. 4, 5; Plowden, 305, 306.

[63] Y. B. 3 Hen. VI. 36, pl. 33.

[64] Y. B. 37 Hen. VI. 13.

[65] As to requirement of certain sum, cf. Y. B. 12 Ed. II. 375; Fleta, II. c. 60, § 24.

[66] Y. B. 29 Ed. III. 25, 26; 40 Ed. III. 24, pl. 27; 43 Ed. III. 2, pl. 5.

[67] Y. B. 43 Ed. III. 2, pl. 5; 46 Ed. III. 25, pl. 10; 50 Ed. III. 5, pl. 11.

or upon the defendant's admission recorded in like manner.[68]

To sum up, the action of debt has passed through three stages. At first, it was the only remedy to recover money due, except when the liability was simply to pay damages for a wrongful act. It was closely akin to—indeed it was but a branch of—the action for any form of personal property which the defendant was bound by contract or otherwise to hand over to the plaintiff.[69] If there was a contract to pay money, the only question was how you could prove it. Any such contract, which could be proved by any of the means known to early law, constituted a debt. There was no theory of consideration, and therefore, of course, no limit to either the action or the contract based upon the nature of the consideration received.

The second stage was when the doctrine of consideration was introduced in its earlier form of a benefit to the promisor. This applied to all contracts not under seal while it prevailed, but it was established while debt was the only action for money payable by such contracts. The precedents are, for the most part, precedents in debt.

The third stage was reached when a larger view was taken of consideration, and it was expressed in terms of detriment to the promisee. This change was a change in the substantive law, and logically it should have been applied throughout. But it arose in another and later form of action, under circumstances peculiarly connected with that action, as will be explained hereafter. The result was that the new doctrine prevailed in the new action, and the old in the old, and that what was really the anomaly of inconsistent theories carried out side by side disguised itself in the form of a limitation upon the action of debt. That action did not remain, as formerly, the remedy for all binding contracts to pay money, but, so far as parol contracts were concerned, could only be used where the consideration was a benefit actually received by the promisor. With regard to obligations arising in any other way, it has remained unchanged.

I must now devote a few words to the effect upon our law of the other mode of proof which I have mentioned. I mean charters. A charter was simply a writing. As few could write, most people

[68] Cf. Glanv., Lib. X. c. 8; Fleta, II. c. 60, § 25.

[69] Y. B. 35 Ed. I. 454; 12 Ed. II. 375.

had to authenticate a document in some other way, for instance, by making their mark. This was, in fact, the universal practice in England until the introduction of Norman customs.[70] With them seals came in. But as late as Henry II. they were said by the Chief Justice of England to belong properly only to kings and to very great men.[71] I know no ground for thinking that an authentic charter had any less effect at that time when not under seal than when it was sealed.[72] It was only evidence either way, and is called so in many of the early cases.[73] It could be waived, and suit tendered in its place.[74] Its conclusive effect was due to the satisfactory nature of the evidence, not to the seal.[75]

But when seals came into use they obviously made the evidence of the charter better, in so far as the seal was more difficult to forge than a stroke of the pen. Seals acquired such importance, that, for a time, a man was bound by his seal, although it was affixed without his consent.[76] At last a seal came to be required, in order that a charter should have its ancient effect.[77]

A covenant or contract under seal was no longer a promise well proved; it was a promise of a distinct nature, for which a distinct form of action came to be provided.[78] I have shown how the requirement of consideration became a rule of substantive law, and also why it never had any foothold in the domain of covenants. The exception of covenants from the requirement became a rule of substantive law also. The man who had set his hand to a charter, from being bound because he had consented to be, and because there was a writing to prove it,[79] was now held by force of the seal and by deed alone as distinguished from all other writings. And to maintain the integrity of an inadequate theory, a seal was said to import a consideration.

[70] Ducange, "Sigillum"; Ingulph. 901.

[71] Big. Pl. Ang. Norm. 177.

[72] Big. Pl. Ang. Norm. 177; Bract., fol. 100 *b*, § 9, "scriptura." But cf. Y. B. 30 Ed. I. 158; Fleta, II. c. 60, § 25.

[73] Y. B. 33 Ed. I. 354, 356; 35 Ed. I. 455, top, 41 Ed. III. 7, pl. 15; 44 Ed. III. 21, pl. 23. Cf. 39 Hen. VI. 34, pl. 46.

[74] Y. B. 7 Ed. II. 242. Cf. 35 Ed. I. 452.

[75] Cf. Bract., fol. 100 *b*, § 9.

[76] Cf. Glanv., Lib. X. c. 12; Dugdale, Antiq. Warwic. 673, cited Ducange, "Sigillum"; Bract., fol. 396 *b*, § 3; 1 Britt. (Nich.) 163, § 17; Abbrev. Plac. 8 Joh., Berk. rot. 4, pp. 55, 56; ib. 19 Ed. I., Norf. & Suff. rot. 7, p. 284; ib. Index "Sigillum."

[77] Y. B. 30 Ed. I. 158; Fleta, II. c. 60, § 25, p. 130.

[78] 45 Ed. III. 24, pl. 30.

[79] Bract., fol. 100 *b*, § 9.

Nowadays, it is sometimes thought more philosophical to say that a covenant is a formal contract, which survives alongside of the ordinary consensual contract, just as happened in the Roman law. But this is not a very instructive way of putting it either. In one sense, everything is form which the law requires in order to make a promise binding over and above the mere expression of the promisor's will. Consideration is a form as much as a seal. The only difference is, that one form is of modern introduction, and has a foundation in good sense, or at least falls in with our common habits of thought, so that we do not notice it, whereas the other is a survival from an older condition of the law, and is less manifestly sensible, or less familiar. I may add, that, under the influence of the latter consideration, the law of covenants is breaking down. In many States it is held that a mere scroll or flourish of the pen is a sufficient seal. From this it is a short step to abolish the distinction between sealed and unsealed instruments altogether, and this has been done in some of the Western States.

While covenants survive in a somewhat weak old age, and debt has disappeared, leaving a vaguely disturbing influence behind it, the whole modern law of contract has grown up through the medium of the action of Assumpsit, which must now be explained.

After the Norman conquest all ordinary actions were begun by a writ issuing from the king, and ordering the defendant to be summoned before the court to answer the plaintiff. These writs were issued as a matter of course, in the various well-known actions from which they took their names. There were writs of debt and of covenant; there were writs of trespass for forcible injuries to the plaintiff's person, or to property in his possession, and so on. But these writs were only issued for the actions which were known to the law, and without a writ the court had no authority to try a case. In the time of Edward I. there were but few of such actions. The cases in which you could recover money of another fell into a small number of groups, for each of which there was a particular form of suing and stating your claim.

These forms had ceased to be adequate. Thus there were many cases which did not exactly fall within the definition of a trespass, but for which it was proper that a remedy should be furnished. In order to furnish a remedy, the first thing to be done was to furnish a writ. Accordingly, the famous statute of 13 Edward I., c. 24, authorized the office from which the old writs issued to frame new ones in cases similar in principle to those for which writs were found, and requiring like remedy, but not exactly falling within the scope of the writs already in use.

Thus writs of trespass on the case began to make their appearance; that is, writs stating a ground of complaint analogous to a trespass, but not quite amounting to a trespass as it had been sued for in the older precedents. To take an instance which is substantially one of the earliest cases, suppose that a man left a horse with a blacksmith to be shod, and he negligently drove a nail into the horse's foot. It might be that the owner of the horse could not have one of the old writs, because the horse was not in his possession when the damage was done. A strict trespass upon property could only be committed against the person in possession of it. It could not be committed by one who was in possession himself.[80] But as laming the horse was equally a wrong, whether the owner held the horse by the bridle or left it with the smith, and as the wrong was closely analogous to a trespass, although not one, the law gave the owner a writ of trespass on the case.[81]

An example like this raises no difficulty; it is as much an action of tort for a wrong as trespass itself. No contract was stated, and none was necessary on principle. But this does not belong to the class of cases to be considered, for the problem before us is to trace the origin of assumpsit, which is an action of contract. Assumpsit, however, began as an action of trespass on the case, and the thing to be discovered is how trespass on the case ever became available for a mere breach of agreement.

It will be well to examine some of the earliest cases in which an undertaking (assumpsit) was alleged. The first reported in the books is of the reign of Edward III.[82] The plaintiff alleged that the defendant undertook to carry the plaintiff's horse safely across the Humber, but surcharged the boat, by reason of which the

[80] Cf. 5 Co. Rep. 13 *b*, 14 *a*, with 1 Roll. Rep. 126, 128; Y. B. 43 Ed. III. 30, pl. 15.

[81] Y. B. 46 Ed. III. 19, pl. 19; s. c. Bro. *Acc. sur le Case*, pl. 22.

[82] Y. B. 22 Ass., pl. 41, fol. 94.

horse perished. It was objected that the action should have been either covenant for breach of the agreement, or else trespass. But it was answered that the defendant committed a wrongful act when he surcharged the boat, and the objection was overruled. This case again, although an undertaking was stated, hardly introduced a new principle. The force did not proceed directly from the defendant, to be sure, but it was brought to bear by the combination of his overloading and then pushing into the stream.

The next case is of the same reign, and goes further.[88] The writ set forth that the defendant undertook to cure the plaintiff's horse of sickness (*manucepit equum prædicti W. de infirmitate*), and did his work so negligently that the horse died. This differs from the case of laming the horse with a nail in two respects. It does not charge any forcible act, nor indeed any act at all, but a mere omission. On the other hand, it states an undertaking, which the other did not. The defendant at once objected that this was an action for a breach of an undertaking, and that the plaintiff should have brought covenant. The plaintiff replied, that he could not do that without a deed, and that the action was for negligently causing the death of the horse; that is, for a tort, not for a breach of contract. Then, said the defendant, you might have had trespass. But the plaintiff answered that by saying that the horse was not killed by force, but died *per def. de sa cure;* and upon this argument the writ was adjudged good, Thorpe, J. saying that he had seen a man indicted for killing a patient by want of care (default in curing), whom he had undertaken to cure.

Both these cases, it will be seen, were dealt with by the court as pure actions of tort, notwithstanding the allegation of an undertaking on the part of the defendant. But it will also be seen that they are successively more remote from an ordinary case of trespass. In the case last stated, especially, the destroying force did not proceed from the defendant in any sense. And thus we are confronted with the question, What possible analogy could have been found between a wrongful act producing harm, and a failure to act at all?

Before I attempt to answer it, let me illustrate a little further

[88] Y. B. 43 Ed. III. 33, pl. 38.

by examples of somewhat later date. Suppose a man undertook to work upon another's house, and by his unskilfulness spoiled his employer's timbers; it would be like a trespass, although not one, and the employer would sue in trespass on the case. This was stated as clear law by one of the judges in the reign of Henry IV.[84] But suppose that, instead of directly spoiling the materials, the carpenter had simply left a hole in the roof through which the rain had come in and done the damage. The analogy to the previous case is marked, but we are a step farther away from trespass, because the force does not come from the defendant. Yet in this instance also the judges thought that trespass on the case would lie.[85] In the time of Henry IV. the action could not have been maintained for a simple refusal to build according to agreement; but it was suggested by the court, that, if the writ had mentioned "that the thing had been commenced and then by negligence not done, it would have been otherwise."[86]

I now recur to the question, What likeness could there have been between an omission and a trespass sufficient to warrant a writ of trespass on the case? In order to find an answer it is essential to notice that in all the earlier cases the omission occurred in the course of dealing with the plaintiff's person or property, and occasioned damage to the one or the other. In view of this fact, Thorpe's reference to indictments for killing a patient by want of care, and the later distinction between neglect before and after the task is commenced, are most pregnant. The former becomes still more suggestive when it is remembered that this is the first argument or analogy to be found upon the subject.

The meaning of that analogy is plain. Although a man has a perfect right to stand by and see his neighbor's property destroyed, or, for the matter of that, to watch his neighbor perish for want of his help, yet if he once intermeddles he has no longer the same freedom. He cannot withdraw at will. To give a more specific example, if a surgeon from benevolence cuts the umbilical cord of a newly-born child, he cannot stop there and watch the patient bleed to death. It would be murder wilfully to allow

[84] Y. B. 11 Hen. IV. 33, pl. 60.

[85] Y. B. 3 Hen. VI. 36, pl. 33.

[86] Y. B. 2 Hen. IV. 3, pl. 9; 11 Hen. IV. 33, pl. 60. Cf. 3 Hen. VI. 36, pl. 33.

death to come to pass in that way, as much as if the intention had been entertained at the time of cutting the cord. It would not matter whether the wickedness began with the act, or with the subsequent omission.

The same reasoning applies to civil liability. A carpenter need not go to work upon another man's house at all, but if he accepts the other's confidence and intermeddles, he cannot stop at will and leave the roof open to the weather. So in the case of the farrier, when he had taken charge of the horse, he could not stop at the critical moment and leave the consequences to fortune. So, still more clearly, when the ferryman undertook to carry a horse across the Humber, although the water drowned the horse, his remote acts of overloading his boat and pushing it into the stream in that condition occasioned the loss, and he was answerable for it.

In the foregoing cases the duty was independent of contract, or at least was so regarded by the judges who decided them, and stood on the general rules applied to human conduct even by the criminal law. The immediate occasion of the damage complained of may have been a mere omission letting in the operation of natural forces. But if you connect it, as it was connected in fact, with the previous dealings, you have a course of action and conduct which, taken as a whole, has caused or occasioned the harm.

The objection may be urged, to be sure, that there is a considerable step from holding a man liable for the consequences of his acts which he might have prevented, to making him answerable for not having interfered with the course of nature when he neither set it in motion nor opened the door for it to do harm, and that there is just that difference between making a hole in a roof and leaving it open, or cutting the cord and letting it bleed, on the one side, and the case of a farrier who receives a sick horse and omits proper precautions, on the other.[87]

There seem to be two answers to this. First, it is not clear that such a distinction was adverted to by the court which decided the case which I have mentioned. It was alleged that the defendant performed his cure so negligently that the horse died. It might

[87] Cf. 19 Hen. VI. 49, pl. 5 *ad fin.*, Newton, C. J.

not have occurred to the judges that the defendant's conduct possibly went no further than the omission of a series of beneficial measures. It was probably assumed to have consisted of a combination of acts and neglects, which taken as a whole amounted to an improper dealing with the thing.

In the next place, it is doubtful whether the distinction is a sound one on practical grounds. It may well be that, so long as one allows a trust to be reposed in him, he is bound to use such precautions as are known to him, although he has made no contract, and is at liberty to renounce the trust in any reasonable manner. This view derives some support from the issue on which the parties went to trial, which was that the defendant performed the cure as well as he knew how, without this, that the horse died for default of his care (cure?).[88]

But it cannot be denied that the allegation of an undertaking conveyed the idea of a promise, as well as that of an entering upon the business in hand. Indeed, the latter element is sufficiently conveyed, perhaps, without it. It may be asked, therefore, whether the promise did not count for something in raising a duty to act. So far as this involves the consequence that the action was in fact for the breach of a contract, the answer has been given already, and is sustained by too great a weight of authority to be doubted.[89] To bind the defendant by a contract, an instrument under seal was essential. As has been shown, already, even the ancient sphere of debt had been limited by this requirement, and in the time of Edward III. a deed was necessary even to bind a surety. It was so *a fortiori* to introduce a liability upon promises not enforced by the ancient law. Nevertheless, the suggestion was made at an early date, that an action on the case for damage by negligence, that is, by an omission of proper precautions, alleging an undertaking by way of inducement, was in fact an action of contract.

Five years after the action for negligence in curing a horse, which has been stated, an action was brought[90] in similar form

[88] Cf. Y. B. 48 Ed. III. 6, pl. 11.

[89] Cases *supra;* Y. B. 2 Hen. IV. 3, pl. 9; 11 Hen. IV. 33. Cf. 3 Hen. VI. 36, pl. 33; 20 Hen. VI. 34, pl. 4; 2 Hen. VII. 11, pl. 9.

[90] Y. B. 48 Ed. III. 6, pl. 11. Cf. Fitzh. Abr. *Acc. sur le Case,* pl. 37, 11 R. II: 14 Hen. VI. 18. But cf. 43 Ed. III. 33, pl. 38.

against a surgeon, alleging that he undertook to cure the plaintiff's hand, and that by his negligence the plaintiff's hand was maimed. There was, however, this difference, that it was set forth that the plaintiff's hand had been wounded by one T. B. And hence it appeared that, however much the bad treatment may have aggravated matters, the maiming was properly attributable to T. B., and that the plaintiff had an action against him. This may have led the defendant to adopt the course he did, because he felt uncertain whether any action of tort would lie. He took issue on the undertaking, assuming that to be essential to the plaintiff's case, and then objected that the writ did not show the place of the undertaking, and hence was bad, because it did not show whence the inquest should be summoned to speak to that point. The writ was adjudged bad on that ground, which seems as if the court sanctioned the defendant's view. Indeed, one of the judges called it an action of covenant, and said that "of necessity it was maintainable without specialty, because for so small a matter a man cannot always have a clerk at hand to write a deed" (*pur faire especialty*). At the same time the earlier cases which have been mentioned were cited and relied on, and it is evident that the court was not prepared to go beyond them, or to hold that the action could be maintained on its merits apart from the technical objection. In another connection it seems to have considered the action from the point of view of trespass.[91]

Whatever questions this case may suggest, the class of actions which alleged an undertaking on the part of the defendant continued to be dealt with as actions or tort for a long time after Edward III. The liability was limited to damage to person or property arising after the defendant had entered upon the employment. And it was mainly through reasoning drawn from the law of tort that it was afterwards extended, as will be seen.

At the beginning of the reign of Henry VI. it was probably still the law that the action would not lie for a simple failure to keep a promise.[92] But it had been several times suggested, as has been

[91] Cf. Candish's reasons for allowing wager of law with Y. B. 32 & 33 Ed. I., Preface, p. xxxvi., citing the old rules of pleading printed at the end of the tract entitled, Modus tenendi unum Hundredum sive Curiam de Recordo, in Rastell's Law Tracts, p. 410, E, F, G.

[92] Y. B. 3 Hen. VI. 36, pl. 33.

shown, that it would be otherwise if the omission or neglect occurred in the course of performance, and the defendant's conduct had been followed by physical damage.[93] This suggestion took its most striking form in the early years of Henry VI., when the case of the carpenter leaving a hole in the roof was put.[94] When the courts had got as far as this, it was easy to go one step farther, and to allow the same effect to an omission at any stage, followed by similar damage.

What is the difference in principle, it was asked, a few years later,[95] between the cases where it is admitted that the action will lie, and that of a smith who undertakes to shoe a horse and does not, by reason of which the horse goes lame,—or that of a lawyer, who undertakes to argue your case, and, after thus inducing you to rely upon him, neglects to be present, so that you lose it? It was said that in the earlier instances the duty was dependent on or accessory to the covenant, and that, if the action would lie on the accessory matter, it would lie on the principal.[96] It was held on demurrer that an action would lie for not procuring certain releases which the defendant had undertaken to get.

Five years later another case [97] came up, which was very like that of the farrier in the reign of Edward III. It was alleged that the defendant undertook to cure the plaintiff's horse, and applied medicine so negligently that the horse died. In this, as in the earlier case, the issue was taken on the assumpsit. And now the difference between an omission and an act was clearly stated, the declaration was held not to mean necessarily anything more than an omission, and it was said that but for the undertaking the defendant would have owed no duty to act. Hence the allegation of the defendant's promise was material, and an issue could properly be taken on it.

This decision distinctly separated from the mass of actions on the case a special class arising out of a promise as the source of the defendant's obligation, and it was only a matter of time for that class to become a new and distinct action of contract. Had

[93] Y. B. 2 Hen. IV. 3, pl. 9; 11 Hen. IV. 33, pl. 60; 3 Hen. VI. 36, pl. 33.
[94] 3 Hen. VI. 36, pl. 33.
[95] Y. B. 14 Hen. VI. 18, pl. 58.
[96] Ibid. Cf. 48 Ed. III. 6, pl. 11.
[97] Y. B. 19 Hen. VI. 49, pl. 5. See, further, Y. B. 20 Hen. VI. 25 pl. 11.

this change taken place at once, the doctrine of consideration, which was first definitely enunciated about the same time, would no doubt have been applied, and a *quid pro quo* would have been required for the undertaking.[98] But the notion of tort was not at once abandoned. The law was laid down at the beginning of the reign of Henry VII., in accordance with the earlier decisions, and it was said that the action would not lie for a failure to keep a promise, but only for negligence after the defendant had entered upon his undertaking.[99]

So far as the action did not exceed the true limits of tort, it was immaterial whether there was a consideration for the undertaking or not. But when the mistake was made of supposing that all cases, whether proper torts or not, in which an assumpsit was alleged, were equally founded on the promise, one of two erroneous conclusions was naturally thought to follow. Either no assumpsit needed any *quid pro quo*,[100] as there was clearly none in the older precedents, (they being cases of pure tort,) or else those precedents were wrong, and a *quid pro quo* should be alleged in every case. It was long recognized with more or less understanding of the true limit, that, in cases where the gist of the action was negligent damage to property, a consideration was not necessary.[101] And there are some traces of the notion that it was always superfluous, as late as Charles I.

In a case of that reign, the defendant retained an attorney to act in a suit for a third person, and promised to pay him all his fees and expenses. The attorney rendered the service, and then brought debt. It was objected that debt did not lie, because there was no contract between the parties, and the defendant had not any *quid pro quo*. The court adopted the argument, and said that there was no contract or consideration to ground this action, but that the plaintiff might have sued in assumpsit.[102]

It was, perhaps, the lingering of this idea, and the often re-

[98] Cf. Y. B. 3 Hen. VI. 36, pl. 33.

[99] Y. B. 2 Hen. VII. 11, pl. 9. Cf. 20 Hen. VI. 34, pl. 4.

[100] Cf. Y. B. 14 Hen. VI. 18, pl. 58; 21 Hen. VII. 41, pl. 66, Fineux, C. J.

[101] Keilway, 160, pl. 2 (2 Hen. VIII.); *Powtuary* v. *Walton*, 1 Roll. Abr. 10, pl. 5 (39 Eliz.); *Coggs* v. *Bernard*, 2 Ld. Raym. 909 (2 Anne, A. D. 1703). *Supra*, p. 154.

[102] *Sands* v. *Trevilian*, Cro. Car. 193, 194 (Mich. 4 Car. I., A. D. 1629).

peated notion that an assumpsit was not a contract,[103] to which was attributable a more enlarged theory of consideration than prevailed in debt. It was settled that assumpsit would lie for a mere omission or nonfeasance. The cases which have been mentioned of the reign of Henry VI. were followed by others in the latter years of Henry VII.,[104] and it was never again doubted. An action for such a cause was clearly for a breach of promise, as had been recognized from the time of Edward III. If so, a consideration was necessary.[105] Notwithstanding occasional vagaries, that also had been settled or taken for granted in many cases of Queen Elizabeth's time. But the bastard origin of the action which gave rise to the doubt how far any consideration at all was necessary, made it possible to hold considerations sufficient which had been rejected in debt.

Another circumstance may not have been without its influence. It would seem that, in the period when assumpsit was just growing into its full proportions, there was some little inclination to identify consideration with the Roman *causa*, taken in its broadest sense. The word "cause" was used for consideration in the early years of Elizabeth, with reference to a covenant to stand seized to uses.[106] It was used in the same sense in the action of assumpsit.[107] In the last cited report, although the principal case only laid down a doctrine that would be followed to-day, there was also stated an anonymous case which was interpreted to mean that an executed consideration furnished upon request, but without any promise of any kind, would support a subsequent promise to pay for it.[108] Starting from this authority and the word

[103] Bro. *Acc. sur le Case*, pl. 5; s. c., Y. B. 27 Hen. VIII. 24, 25, pl. 3; *Sidenham* v. *Worlington*, 2 Leon. 224, A. D. 1585.

[104] Y. B. 21 Hen. VII. 30, pl. 5; ib. 41, pl. 66.

[105] Y. B. 3 Hen. VI. 36, pl. 33.

[106] *Sharington* v. *Strotton*, Plowden, 298 (Mich. 7 & 8 Eliz.); ib. 309, note on "the civil law."

[107] *Hunt* v. *Bate*, 3 Dyer, 272 *a* (10 Eliz., A. D. 1568).

[108] See Lecture VIII. Mr. Langdell, Contracts, §§ 92, 94, suggests the ingenious explanation for this doctrine, that it was then held that no promise could be implied in fact from the request. There may be evidence which I do not know, but the case cited (*Bosden* v. *Thinne*, Yelv. 40) for this statement was not decided until A. D. 1603, while the implication of *Hunt* v. *Bate*, *supra*, which was the authority followed by the cases to be explained, is all the other way.

"cause," the conclusion was soon reached that there was a great difference between a contract and an assumpsit; and that, whereas in contracts "everything which is requisite ought to concur and meet together, viz. the consideration of the one side, and the sale or the promise on the other side, . . . to maintain an action upon an assumpsit, the same is not requisite, for it is sufficient if there be a moving cause or consideration precedent; for which cause or consideration the promise was made." [109]

Thus, where the defendant retained the plaintiff to be miller to his aunt at ten shillings a week, it was held that assumpsit would lie, because the service, though not beneficial to the defendant, was a charge or detriment to the plaintiff.[110] The old questions were reargued, and views which were very near prevailing in debt under Henry VI., prevailed in assumpsit under Elizabeth and James.

A surety could be sued in assumpsit, although he had ceased to be liable in debt.[111] There was the same remedy on a promise in consideration that the plaintiff would marry the defendant's daughter.[112] The illusion that assumpsit thus extended did not mean contract, could not be kept up. In view of this admission and of the ancient precedents, the law oscillated for a time in the direction of reward as the true essence of consideration.[113] But the other view prevailed, and thus, in fact, made a change in the substantive law. A simple contract, to be recognized as binding by the courts of Henry VI., must have been based upon a benefit to the debtor; now a promise might be enforced in consideration of a detriment to the promisee. But in the true archaic spirit the doctrine was not separated or distinguished from the remedy which introduced it, and thus debt in modern times has presented the altered appearance of a duty limited to cases where the consideration was of a special sort.

[109] *Sidenham* v. *Worlington*, 2 Leon. 224, A. D. 1585.

[110] *Read* v. *Baxter*, 3 Dyer, 272 *b*, n. (26 & 27 Eliz.). Cf. *Richards and Bartlet's Case*, 1 Leon. 19 (26 Eliz.).

[111] Bro. *Acc. sur le Case*, pl. 5; S. C., Y. B. 27 Hen. VIII. 24, 25, pl. 3; 3 Dyer, 272, n.

[112] *Marsh* v. *Rainsford*, 3 Dyer, 272 *b*, n.; S. C., 2 Leon. 111, and Cro. Eliz. 59, *sub. nom. Marsh* v. *Kavenford*.

[113] *Smith and Smith's Case*, 3 Leon. 88, A. D. 1583; *Riches and Briggs*, Yelv. 4, A. D. 1601; *Pickas* v. *Guile*, Yelv. 128, A. D. 1608.

The later fortunes of assumpsit can be briefly told. It introduced bilateral contracts, because a promise was a detriment, and therefore a sufficient consideration for another promise. It supplanted debt, because the existence of the duty to pay was sufficient consideration for a promise to pay, or rather because, before a consideration was required, and as soon as assumpsit would lie for a nonfeasance, this action was used to avoid the defendant's wager of law. It vastly extended the number of actionable contracts, which had formerly been confined to debts and covenants, whereas nearly any promise could be sued in assumpsit; and it introduced a theory which has had great influence on modern law,—that all the liabilities of a bailee are founded on contract.[114] Whether the prominence which was thus given to contract as the foundation of legal rights and duties had anything to do with the similar prominence which it soon acquired in political speculation, it is beyond my province to inquire.

[114] *Supra*, p. 154. Lord Coke's caution not to rely on the abridgments is very necessary to the proper study of the history of consideration. The abridgments apply the doctrine to cases which make no mention of it, and which were decided before it was ever heard of.

LECTURE VIII

CONTRACT.—II. ELEMENTS

THE general method to be pursued in the analysis of contract is the same as that already explained with regard to possession. Wherever the law gives special rights to one, or imposes special burdens on another, it does so on the ground that certain special facts are true of those individuals. In all such cases, therefore, there is a twofold task. First, to determine what are the facts to which the special consequences are attached; second, to ascertain the consequences. The first is the main field of legal argument. With regard to contracts the facts are not always the same. They may be that a certain person has signed, sealed, and delivered a writing of a certain purport. They may be that he has made an oral promise, and that the promisee has furnished him a consideration.

The common element of all contracts might be said to be a promise, although even a promise was not necessary to a liability in debt as formerly understood. But as it will not be possible to discuss covenants further, and as consideration formed the main topic of the last Lecture, I will take up that first. Furthermore, as there is an historical difference between consideration in debt and in assumpsit, I shall confine myself to the latter, which is the later and more philosophical form.

It is said that any benefit conferred by the promisee on the promisor, or any detriment incurred by the promisee, may be a consideration. It is also thought that every consideration may be reduced to a case of the latter sort, using the word "detriment" in a somewhat broad sense.

To illustrate the general doctrine, suppose that a man is desirous of having a cask of brandy carried from Boston to Cambridge, and that a truckman, either out of kindness or from some other motive, says that he will carry it, and it is delivered to him accordingly. If he carelessly staves in the cask, there would perhaps be no need to allege that he undertook to carry it, and on principle, and according to the older cases, if an undertaking was alleged, no consideration for the assumpsit need be stated.[1] The ground of complaint in that case would be a wrong, irrespective of contract. But if the complaint was that he did not carry it as agreed, the plaintiff's difficulty would be that the truckman was not bound to do so unless there was a consideration for his promise. Suppose, therefore, that it was alleged that he promised to do so in consideration of the delivery to him. Would this be a sufficient consideration? The oldest cases, going on the notion of benefit to the promisor, said that it could not be, for it was a trouble, not a benefit.[2] Then take it from the side of detriment. The delivery is a necessary condition to the promisor's doing the kindness, and if he does it, the delivery, so far from being a detriment to the promisee, is a clear benefit to him.

But this argument is a fallacy. Clearly the delivery would be sufficient consideration to enable the owner to declare in assumpsit for the breach of those duties which arose, irrespective of contract, from the defendant's having undertaken to deal with the thing.[3] It would be a sufficient consideration for any promise not involving a dealing with the thing for its performance, for instance, to pay a thousand dollars.[4] And the law has not pronounced the consideration good or bad according to the nature of the promise founded upon it. The delivery is a sufficient consideration for any promise.[5]

The argument on the other side leaves out of sight the point of time at which the sufficiency of the consideration is to be determined. This is the moment when the consideration is furnished. At that moment the delivery of the cask is a detriment in

[1] Y. B. 46 Ed. III. 19, pl. 19; 19 Hen. VI. 49, pl. 5; Keilway, 160, pl. 2; *Powtuary* v. *Walton*, 1 Roll. Abr. 10, pl. 5; *Coggs* v. *Bernard*, 2 Ld. Raym. 909.

[2] *Riches and Briggs*, Yelv. 4, A. D. 1601; *Pickas* v. *Guile*, Yelv. 128.

[3] *Bainbridge* v. *Firmstone*, 8 Ad. & El. 743, A. D. 1838.

[4] *Wilkinson* v. *Oliveira*, 1 Bing. N. C. 490, A. D. 1835; *Haigh* v. *Brooks*, 10 Ad. & El. 309; ib. 323; *Hart* v. *Miles*, 4 C. B. N. S. 371, A. D. 1858.

[5] *Wheatley* v. *Low*, Cro. Jac. 668, A. D. 1623. Cf. *Byne and Playne's Case*, 1 Leon. 220, 221 (32 & 33 Eliz.).

the strictest sense. The owner of the cask has given up a present control over it, which he has a right to keep, and he has got in return, not a performance for which a delivery was necessary, but a mere promise of performance. The performance is still future.[6]

But it will be seen that, although the delivery may be a consideration, it will not necessarily be one. A promise to carry might be made and accepted on the understanding that it was mere matter of favor, without consideration, and not legally binding. In that case the detriment of delivery would be incurred by the promisee as before, but obviously it would be incurred for the sole purpose of enabling the promisor to carry as agreed.

It appears to me that it has not always been sufficiently borne in mind that the same thing may be a consideration or not, as it is dealt with by the parties. The popular explanation of *Coggs* v. *Bernard* is, that the delivery was a consideration for a promise to carry the casks safely. I have given what I believe to be the true explanation, and that which I think Lord Holt had in view, in the fifth Lecture.[7] But whether that which I have offered be true or not, a serious objection to the one which is commonly accepted is that the declaration does not allege that the delivery was the consideration.

The same caution should be observed in construing the terms of an agreement. It is hard to see the propriety of erecting any detriment which an instrument may disclose or provide for, into a consideration, unless the parties have dealt with it on that footing. In many cases a promisee may incur a detriment without thereby furnishing a consideration. The detriment may be nothing but a condition precedent to performance of the promise, as where a man promises another to pay him five hundred dollars if he breaks his leg.[8]

The courts, however, have gone far towards obliterating this distinction. Acts which by a fair interpretation of language would seem to have been contemplated as only the compliance with a

[6] *Wilkinson* v. *Oliveira*, 1 Bing. N. C. 490; *Haigh* v. *Brooks*, 10 Ad. & El. 309; *Hart* v. *Miles*, 4 C. B. N. S. 371; 6 Am. Law Rev. 47, Oct. 1871.

[7] *Supra*, pp. 155, 156. See also Lecture VII.

[8] Byles, J., in *Shadwell* v. *Shadwell*, 30 L. J. C. P. 145, 149.

condition, have been treated as the consideration of the promise.[9] And so have counter promises in an agreement which expressly stated other matters as the consideration.[10] So it should be mentioned, subject to the question whether there may not be a special explanation for the doctrine, that it is said that an assignment of a leasehold cannot be voluntary under the statute of 27 Elizabeth, c. 4, because the assignee comes into the obligations of the tenant.[11] Yet the assignee's incurring this detriment may not be contemplated as the inducement of the assignment, and in many cases only amounts to a deduction from the benefit conferred, as a right of way would be, especially if the only obligation is to pay rent, which issues out of the land in theory of law.

But although the courts may have sometimes gone a little far in their anxiety to sustain agreements, there can be no doubt of the principle which I have laid down, that the same thing may be a consideration or not, as it is dealt with by the parties. This raises the question how a thing must be dealt with, in order to make it a consideration.

It is said that consideration must not be confounded with motive. It is true that it must not be confounded with what may be the prevailing or chief motive in actual fact.[a] A man may promise to paint a picture for five hundred dollars, while his chief motive may be a desire for fame. A consideration may be given and accepted, in fact, solely for the purpose of making a promise binding. But, nevertheless, it is the essence of a consideration, that, by the terms of the agreement, it is given and accepted as the motive or inducement of the promise. Conversely, the promise must be made and accepted as the conventional motive or inducement for furnishing the consideration. The root of the whole matter is the relation of reciprocal conventional inducement, each for the other, between consideration and promise.

A good example of the former branch of the proposition is to be found in a Massachusetts case. The plaintiff refused to let certain

[9] *Shadwell* v. *Shadwell*, *ubi supra*; *Burr* v. *Wilcox*, 13 Allen, 269, 272, 273.

[10] *Thomas* v. *Thomas*, 2 Q. B. 851.

[11] *Price* v. *Jenkins*, 5 Ch. D. 619. Cf. *Crabbe* v. *Moxey*, 1 W. R. 226; *Thomas* v. *Thomas*, 2 Q. B. 851; Monahan, Method of Law, 141 *et seq*.

[a] [The whole doctrine of contract is formal & external.]

wood be removed from his land by one who had made an oral bargain and given his note for it, unless he received additional security. The purchaser and the plaintiff accordingly went to the defendant, and the defendant put his name upon the note. The plaintiff thereupon let the purchaser carry off the wood. But, according to the testimony, the defendant signed without knowing that the plaintiff was to alter his position in any way on the faith of the signature, and it was held that, if that story was believed, there was no consideration.[12]

An illustration of the other half of the rule is to be found in those cases where a reward is offered for doing something, which is afterwards done by a person acting in ignorance of the offer. In such a case the reward cannot be claimed, because the alleged consideration has not been furnished on the faith of the offer. The tendered promise has not induced the furnishing of the consideration. The promise cannot be set up as a conventional motive when it was not known until after the alleged consideration was performed.[13]

Both sides of the relation between consideration and promise, and the conventional nature of that relation, may be illustrated by the case of the cask. Suppose that the truckman is willing to carry the cask, and the owner to let him carry it, without any bargain, and that each knows the other's state of mind; but that the truckman, seeing his own advantage in the matter, says to the owner, "In consideration of your delivering me the cask, and letting me carry it, I promise to carry it," and that the owner thereupon delivers it. I suppose that the promise would be binding. The promise is offered in terms as the inducement for the delivery, and the delivery is made in terms as the inducement for the promise. It may be very probable that the delivery would have been made without a promise, and that the promise would have been made in gratuitous form if it had not been accepted upon consideration; but this is only a guess after all. The delivery need not have been made unless the owner chose, and having

[12] *Ellis* v. *Clark*, 110 Mass. 389.

[13] *Fitch* v. *Snedaker*, 38 N. Y. 248, criticising *Williams* v. *Carwardine*, 4 Barn. & Ad. 621, where, however, it does not appear that the plaintiff did not know of the offer of a reward, but merely that the jury found that she was in fact actuated by other motives, a finding wholly beside the mark.

been made as the term of a bargain, the promisor cannot set up what might have happened to destroy the effect of what did happen. It would seem therefore that the same transaction in substance and spirit might be voluntary or obligatory, according to the form of words which the parties chose to employ for the purpose of affecting the legal consequences.

If the foregoing principles be accepted, they will be seen to explain a doctrine which has given the courts some trouble to establish. I mean the doctrine that an executed consideration will not sustain a subsequent promise. It has been said, to be sure, that such a consideration was sufficient if preceded by a request. But the objections to the view are plain. If the request was of such a nature, and so put, as reasonably to imply that the other person was to have a reward, there was an express promise, although not put in words, and that promise was made at the same time the consideration was given, and not afterwards. If, on the other hand, the words did not warrant the understanding that the service was to be paid for, the service was a gift, and a past gift can no more be a consideration than any other act of the promisee not induced by the promise.

The source of the error can be traced partially, at least, in history. Some suggestions touching the matter were made in the last Lecture. A few words should be added here. In the old cases of debt, where there was some question whether the plaintiff had shown enough to maintain his action, a "contract precedent" was spoken of several times as raising the duty. Thus, where a man had granted that he would be bound in one hundred shillings to pay his servant on a certain day for his services, and for payments made by the servant on his account, it was argued that there was no contract precedent, and that by parol the party is not obliged; and, further, that, so far as appeared, the payments were made by the servant out of his own head and at no request, from which no duty could commence.[14]

So when debt was brought on a deed to pay the plaintiff ten marks, if he would take the defendant's daughter to wife, and it was objected that the action should have been covenant,

[14] Y. B. 29 Ed. III. 25, 26.

it was answered that the plaintiff had a contract precedent which gave him debt.[15]

The first case in assumpsit[16] only meant to adopt this long familiar thought. A man went bail for his friend's servant, who had been arrested. Afterwards the master promised to indemnify the bail, and on his failure to do so was sued by him in assumpsit. It was held that there was no consideration wherefore the defendant should be charged unless the master had first promised to indemnify the plaintiff before the servant was bailed; "for the master did never make request to the plaintiff for his servant to do so much, but he did it of his own head." This is perfectly plain sailing, and means no more than the case in the Year Books. The report, however, also states a case in which it was held that a subsequent promise, in consideration that the plaintiff at the special instance of the defendant had married the defendant's cousin, was binding, and that the marriage was "good cause . . . because [it] ensued the request of the defendant." Whether this was intended to establish a general principle, or was decided with reference to the peculiar consideration of marriage,[17] it was soon interpreted in the broader sense, as was shown in the last Lecture. It was several times adjudged that a past and executed matter was a sufficient consideration for a promise at a later day, if only the matter relied on had been done or furnished at the request of the promisor.[18]

It is now time to analyze the nature of a promise, which is the second and most conspicuous element in a simple contract. The Indian Contract Act, 1872, § 2,[19] says:—

"(*a.*) When one person signifies to another his willingness to do or to abstain from doing anything, with a view to obtaining the assent of that other to such act or abstinence, he is said to make a proposal:

[15] 19 R. II., Fitzh. Abr. *Dett*, pl. 166.

[16] *Hunt* v. *Bate*, Dyer, 272, A. D. 1568.

[17] See *Barker* v. *Halifax*, Cro. Eliz. 741; S. C. 3 Dyer, 272 *a*, n. 32.

[18] *Sidenham* v. *Worlington*, 2 Leonard, 224; *Bosden* v. *Thinne*, Yelv. 40; *Lampleigh* v. *Brathwait*, Hobart, 105; Langdell, Cas. on Contr. (2d ed.), ch. 2, § 11, Summary, §§ 90 *et seq*. See above, Lecture VII. p. 224.

[19] Pollock, Contr. (1st ed.), p. 6.

"(*b.*) When the person to whom the proposal is made signifies his assent thereto, the proposal is said to be accepted. A proposal when accepted becomes a promise."

According to this definition the scope of promises is confined to conduct on the part of the promisor. If this only meant that the promisor alone must bear the legal burden which his promise may create, it would be true. But this is not the meaning. For the definition is of a promise, not of a legally binding promise. We are not seeking for the legal effects of a contract, but for the possible contents of a promise which the law may or may not enforce. We must therefore only consider the question what can possibly be promised in a legal sense, not what will be the secondary consequence of a promise binding, but not performed.

An assurance that it shall rain to-morrow,[20] or that a third person shall paint a picture, may as well be a promise as one that the promisee shall receive from some source one hundred bales of cotton, or that the promisor will pay the promisee one hundred dollars. What is the difference in the cases? It is only in the degree of power possessed by the promisor over the event. He has none in the first case. He has equally little legal authority to make a man paint a picture, although he may have larger means of persuasion. He probably will be able to make sure that the promisee has the cotton. Being a rich man, he is certain to be able to pay the one hundred dollars, except in the event of some most improbable accident.

But the law does not inquire, as a general thing, how far the accomplishment of an assurance touching the future is within the power of the promisor. In the moral world it may be that the obligation of a promise is confined to what lies within reach of the will of the promisor (except so far as the limit is unknown on one side, and misrepresented on the other). But unless some consideration of public policy intervenes, I take it that a man may bind himself at law that any future event shall happen.[b] He can therefore promise it in a legal sense. It may be said that when a man covenants that it shall rain to-morrow, or that A shall paint

[20] *Canham* v. *Barry*, 15 C. B. 597, 619; *Jones* v. *How*, 9 C. B. 1, 9; Com. Dig. *Condition*, D. 2; 1 Roll. Abr. 420 (D), pl. 1; Y. B. 22 Ed. IV. 26, pl. 6.

[b] [But even if he could not bind himself, as he could promise it.]

a picture, he only says, in a short form, I will pay if it does not rain, or if A does not paint a picture. But that is not necessarily so. A promise could easily be framed which would be broken by the happening of fair weather, or by A not painting. A promise, then, is simply an accepted assurance that a certain event or state of things shall come to pass.

But if this be true, it has more important bearings than simply to enlarge the definition of the word *promise.* It concerns the theory of contract.[e] The consequences of a binding promise at common law are not affected by the degree of power which the promisor possesses over the promised event. If the promised event does not come to pass, the plaintiff's property is sold to satisfy the damages, within certain limits, which the promisee has suffered by the failure. The consequences are the same in kind whether the promise is that it shall rain, or that another man shall paint a picture, or that the promisor will deliver a bale of cotton.

If the legal consequence is the same in all cases, it seems proper that all contracts should be considered from the same legal point of view. In the case of a binding promise that it shall rain tomorrow, the immediate legal effect of what the promisor does is, that he takes the risk of the event, within certain defined limits, as between himself and the promisee. He does no more when he promises to deliver a bale of cotton.

If it be proper to state the common-law meaning of promise and contract in this way, it has the advantage of freeing the subject from the superfluous theory that contract is a qualified subjection of one will to another, a kind of limited slavery. It might be so regarded if the law compelled men to perform their contracts, or if it allowed promisees to exercise such compulsion. If, when a man promised to labor for another, the law made him do it, his relation to his promisee might be called a servitude *ad hoc* with some truth. But that is what the law never does. It never interferes until a promise has been broken, and therefore

[e] [Whatever a man promise he can promise in a binding way, unless some consid. of pub. pol. interv. And all binding promises stand on the same legal footing, when the form of the obligation is the same. It does not matter to the theory of a simple contract whether it be to pay $1000 or that it shall rain tomorrow.]

cannot possibly be performed according to its tenor. It is true that in some instances equity does what is called compelling specific performance. But, in the first place, I am speaking of the common law, and, in the next, this only means that equity compels the performance of certain elements of the total promise which are still capable of performance. For instance, take a promise to convey land within a certain time, a court of equity is not in the habit of interfering until the time has gone by, so that the promise cannot be performed as made. But if the conveyance is more important than the time, and the promisee prefers to have it late rather than never, the law may compel the performance of that. Not literally compel even in that case, however, but put the promisor in prison unless he will convey. This remedy is an exceptional one. The only universal consequence of a legally binding promise is, that the law makes the promisor pay damages if the promised event does not come to pass. In every case it leaves him free from interference until the time for fulfilment has gone by, and therefore free to break his contract if he chooses.

A more practical advantage in looking at a contract as the taking of a risk is to be found in the light which it throws upon the measure of damages. If a breach of contract were regarded in the same light as a tort, it would seem that if, in the course of performance of the contract the promisor should be notified of any particular consequence which would result from its not being performed, he should be held liable for that consequence in the event of non-performance. Such a suggestion has been made.[21] But it has not been accepted as the law. On the contrary, according to the opinion of a very able judge, which seems to be generally followed, notice, even at the time of making the contract, of special circumstances out of which special damages would arise in case of breach, is not sufficient unless the assumption of that risk is to be taken as having fairly entered into the contract.[22] If a carrier should undertake to carry the machinery

[21] *Gee* v. *Lancashire & Yorkshire Railway Co.*, 6 H. & N. 211, 218, Bramwell, B. Cf. *Hydraulic Engineering Co.* v. *McHaffie*, 4 Q. B. D. 670, 674, 676.

[22] *British Columbia Saw-Mill Co.* v. *Nettleship*, L. R. 3 C. P. 499, 509, Willes, J.; *Horne* v. *Midland Railway Co.*, L. R. 7 C. P. 583, 591; s. c., L. R. 8 C. P. 131.

of a saw-mill from Liverpool to Vancouver's Island, and should fail to do so, he probably would not be held liable for the rate of hire of such machinery during the necessary delay, although he might know that it could not be replaced without sending to England, unless he was fairly understood to accept "the contract with the special condition attached to it." [23]

It is true that, when people make contracts, they usually contemplate the performance rather than the breach. The express language used does not generally go further than to define what will happen if the contract is fulfilled. A statutory requirement of a memorandum in writing would be satisfied by a written statement of the promise as made, because to require more would be to run counter to the ordinary habits of mankind, as well as because the statement that the effect of a contract is the assumption of the risk of a future event does not mean that there is a second subsidiary promise to assume that risk, but that the assumption follows as a consequence directly enforced by the law, without the promisor's co-operation. So parol evidence would be admissible, no doubt, to enlarge or diminish the extent of the liability assumed for non-performance, where it would be inadmissible to affect the scope of the promise.

But these concessions do not affect the view here taken. As the relation of contractor and contractee is voluntary, the consequences attaching to the relation must be voluntary. What the event contemplated by the promise is, or in other words what will amount to a breach of contract, is a matter of interpretation and construction. What consequences of the breach are assumed is more remotely, in like manner, a matter of construction, having regard to the circumstances under which the contract is made. Knowledge of what is dependent upon performance is one of those circumstances. It is not necessarily conclusive, but it may have the effect of enlarging the risk assumed.

The very office of construction is to work out, from what is expressly said and done, what would have been said with regard to events not definitely before the minds of the parties, if those events had been considered. The price paid in mercantile contracts generally excludes the construction that exceptional risks

[23] *British Columbia Saw-Mill Co.* v. *Nettleship*, L. R. 3 C. P. 499, 509.

were intended to be assumed. The foregoing analysis is believed to show that the result which has been reached by the courts on grounds of practical good sense, falls in with the true theory of contract under the common law.

The discussion of the nature of a promise has led me to analyze contract and the consequences of contract somewhat in advance of their place. I must say a word more concerning the facts which constitute a promise. It is laid down, with theoretical truth, that, besides the assurance or offer on the one side, there must be an acceptance on the other. But I find it hard to think of a case where a simple contract fails to be made, which could not be accounted for on other grounds, generally by the want of relation between assurance or offer and consideration as reciprocal inducements each of the other. Acceptance of an offer usually follows by mere implication from the furnishing of the consideration; and inasmuch as by our law an accepted offer, or promise, until the consideration is furnished, stands on no different footing from an offer not yet accepted, each being subject to revocation until that time, and each continuing until then unless it has expired or has been revoked, the question of acceptance is rarely of practical importance.

Assuming that the general nature of consideration and promise is understood, some questions peculiar to bilateral contracts remain to be considered. These concern the sufficiency of the consideration and the moment when the contract is made.

A promise may be a consideration for a promise, although not every promise for every other. It may be doubted whether a promise to make a gift of one hundred dollars would be supported by a promise to accept it. But in a case of mutual promises respectively to transfer and to accept unpaid shares in a railway company, it has been held that a binding contract was made. Here one party agrees to part with something which may prove valuable, and the other to assume a liability which may prove onerous.[24]

But now suppose that there is no element of uncertainty except in the minds of the parties. Take, for instance, a wager on a past horse-race. It has been thought that this would amount to an

[24] *Cheale* v. *Kenward*, 3 DeG. & J. 27.

absolute promise on one side, and no promise at all on the other.[25] But this does not seem to me sound. Contracts are dealings between men, by which they make arrangements for the future. In making such arrangements the important thing is, not what is objectively true, but what the parties know. Any present fact which is unknown to the parties is just as uncertain for the purposes of making an arrangement at this moment, as any future fact. It is therefore a detriment to undertake to be ready to pay if the event turns out not to have been as expected. This seems to be the true explanation why forbearance to sue upon a claim believed by the plaintiff to be good is a sufficient consideration, although the claim was bad in fact, and known by the defendant to be bad.[26] Were this view unsound, it is hard to see how wagers on any future event, except a miracle, could be sustained. For if the happening or not happening of the event is subject to the law of causation, the only uncertainty about it is in our foresight, not in its happening.

The question when a contract is made arises for the most part with regard to bilateral contracts by letter, the doubt being whether the contract is complete at the moment when the return promise is put into the post, or at the moment when it is received. If convenience preponderates in favor of either view, that is a sufficient reason for its adoption. So far as merely logical grounds go, the most ingenious argument in favor of the later moment is Professor Langdell's. According to him the conclusion follows from the fact that the consideration which makes the offer binding is itself a promise. Every promise, he says, is an offer before it is a promise, and the essence of an offer is that it should be communicated.[27] But this reasoning seems unsound. When, as in the case supposed, the consideration for the return promise has been put into the power of the offeree and the return promise has been accepted in advance, there is not an instant, either in time or logic, when the return promise is an offer. It is a promise and a term of a binding contract as soon as it is anything. An offer is a revocable and unaccepted communication of willingness to promise. When an offer of a certain bilateral contract has

[25] Langdell, Contr., §§ 89, 28.
[26] Langdell, Contr., § 57.
[27] Ibid., §§ 14, 15.

been made, the same contract cannot be offered by the other side. The so-called offer would neither be revocable nor unaccepted. It would complete the contract as soon as made.

If it be said that it is of the essence of a promise to be communicated, whether it goes through the stage of offer or not, meaning by *communicated* brought to the actual knowledge of the promisee, the law is believed to be otherwise. A covenant is binding when it is delivered and accepted, whether it is read or not. On the same principle, it is believed that, whenever the obligation is to be entered into by a tangible sign, as, in the case supposed, by letter containing the return promise, and the consideration for and assent to the promise are already given, the only question is when the tangible sign is sufficiently put into the power of the promisee. I cannot believe that, if the letter had been delivered to the promisee and was then snatched from his hands before he had read it, there would be no contract.[28] If I am right, it appears of little importance whether the post-office be regarded as agent or bailee for the offerer, or as a mere box to which he has access. The offeree, when he drops the letter containing the counter-promise into the letter-box, does an overt act, which by general understanding renounces control over the letter, and puts it into a third hand for the benefit of the offerer, with liberty to the latter at any moment thereafter to take it.

The principles governing revocation are wholly different. One to whom an offer is made has a right to assume that it remains open according to its terms until he has actual notice to the contrary. The effect of the communication must be destroyed by a counter communication. But the making of a contract does not depend on the state of the parties' minds, it depends on their overt acts. When the sign of the counter promise is a tangible object, the contract is completed when the dominion over that object changes.

[28] But see Langdell, Contr., §§ 14, 15.

LECTURE IX

CONTRACT.—III. VOID AND VOIDABLE

THE elements of fact necessary to call a contract into existence, and the legal consequences of a contract when formed, have been discussed. It remains to consider successively the cases in which a contract is said to be void, and those in which it is said to be voidable,—in which, that is, a contract fails to be made when it seems to have been, or, having been made, can be rescinded by one side or the other, and treated as if it had never been. I take up the former class of cases first.

When a contract fails to be made, although the usual forms have been gone through with, the ground of failure is commonly said to be mistake, misrepresentation, or fraud. But I shall try to show that these are merely dramatic circumstances, and that the true ground is the absence of one or more of the primary elements, which have been shown, or are seen at once, to be necessary to the existence of a contract.

If a man goes through the form of making a contract with A through B as A's agent, and B is not in fact the agent of A, there is no contract, because there is only one party. The promise offered to A has not been accepted by him, and no consideration has moved from him. In such a case, although there is generally mistake on one side and fraud on the other, it is very clear that no special doctrine need be resorted to, because the primary elements of a contract explained in the last Lecture are not yet present.

Take next a different case. The defendant agreed to buy, and the plaintiff agreed to sell, a cargo of cotton, "to arrive ex Peerless from Bombay." There were two such vessels sailing from Bombay, one in October, the other in December. The plaintiff meant the latter, the defendant the former. It was held that the defendant was not bound to accept the cotton.[1] It is commonly said that such a contract is void, because of mutual mistake as to the subject-matter, and because therefore the parties did not consent to the same thing. But this way of putting it seems to me misleading. The law has nothing to do with the actual state of the parties' minds. In contract, as elsewhere, it must go by externals, and judge parties by their conduct. If there had been but one "Peerless," and the defendant had said "Peerless" by mistake, meaning "Peri," he would have been bound. The true ground of the decision was not that each party meant a different thing from the other, as is implied by the explanation which has been mentioned, but that each said a different thing. The plaintiff offered one thing, the defendant expressed his assent to another.

A proper name, when used in business or in pleading,[2] means one individual thing, and no other, as every one knows, and therefore one to whom such a name is used must find out at his peril what the object designated is. If there are no circumstances which make the use deceptive on either side, each is entitled to insist on the meaning favorable to him for the word as used by him, and neither is entitled to insist on that meaning for the word as used by the other. So far from mistake having been the ground of decision, as mistake, its only bearing, as it seems to me, was to establish that neither party knew that he was understood by the other to use the word "Peerless" in the sense which the latter gave to it. In that event there would perhaps have been a binding contract, because, if a man uses a word to which he knows the other party attaches, and understands him to attach, a certain meaning, he may be held to that meaning, and not be allowed to give it any other.[3]

Next, suppose a case in which the offer and acceptance do not differ, and in which both parties have used the same words in the same sense. Suppose that A agreed to buy, and B agreed to sell, "these barrels of mackerel," and that the barrels in question turn out to contain salt. There is mutual mistake as to the contents

[1] *Raffles* v. *Wichelhaus*, 2 H. & C. 906. Cf. *Kyle* v. *Kavanagh*, 103 Mass. 356, 357.

[2] Cf. *Cocker* v. *Crompton*, 1 B. & C. 489.

[3] *Smith* v. *Hughes*, L. R. 6 Q. B. 597.

of the barrels, and no fraud on either side. I suppose the contract would be void.[4]

It is commonly said that the failure of the contract in such a case is due to the fact of a difference in kind between the actual subject-matter and that to which the intention of the parties was directed. It is perhaps more instructive to say that the terms of the supposed contract, although seemingly consistent, were contradictory in matters that went to the root of the bargain. For, by one of the essential terms, the subject-matter of the agreement was the contents of certain barrels, and nothing else, and, by another equally important, it was mackerel, and nothing else; while, as a matter of fact, it could not be both, because the contents of the barrels were salt. As neither term could be left out without forcing on the parties a contract which they did not make, it follows that A cannot be required to accept, nor B to deliver either these barrels of salt, or other barrels of mackerel; and without omitting one term, the promise is meaningless.

If there had been fraud on the seller's part, or if he had known what the barrels really contained, the buyer might have had a right to insist on delivery of the inferior article. Fraud would perhaps have made the contract valid at his option. Because, when a man qualifies sensible words with others which he knows, on secret grounds, are insensible when so applied, he may fairly be taken to authorize his promisee to insist on the possible part of his promise being performed, if the promisee is willing to forego the rest.

Take one more illustration like the last case. A policy of insurance is issued on a certain building described in the policy as a machine-shop. In fact the building is not a machine-shop, but an organ factory, which is a greater risk. The contract is void, not because of any misrepresentation, but, as before, because two of its essential terms are repugnant, and their union is insensible.[5]

Of course the principle of repugnancy last explained might be stretched to apply to any inconsistency between the different terms of a contract. It might be said, for instance, that if a piece of gold is sold as eighteen-carat gold, and it is in fact not so pure,

[4] See *Gardner* v. *Lane*, 12 Allen, 39; s. c. 9 Allen, 492, 98 Mass. 517.
[5] *Goddard* v. *Monitor Ins. Co.*, 108 Mass. 56.

or if a cow is sold as yielding an average of twelve quarts of milk a day, and in fact she yields only six quarts, there is no logical difference, according to the explanation which has just been offered, between those cases and that of the barrel of salt sold for mackerel. Yet those bargains would not be void. At the most, they would only be voidable, if the buyer chose to throw them up.

The distinctions of the law are founded on experience, not on logic. It therefore does not make the dealings of men dependent on a mathematical accuracy. Whatever is promised, a man has a right to be paid for, if it is not given; but it does not follow that the absence of some insignificant detail will authorize him to throw up the contract, still less that it will prevent the formation of a contract, which is the matter now under consideration. The repugnant terms must both be very important,—so important that the court thinks that, if either is omitted, the contract would be different in substance from that which the words of the parties seemed to express.

A term which refers directly to an identification by the senses has always this degree of importance. If a promise is made to sell this cow, or this mackerel, to this man, whatever else may be stricken from the contract, it can never be enforced except touching this object and by this man. If this barrel of salt is fraudulently sold for a barrel of mackerel, the buyer may perhaps elect to take this barrel of salt if he chooses, but he cannot elect to take another barrel of mackerel. If the seller is introduced by the name B, and the buyer supposes him to be another person of the same name, and under that impression delivers his written promise to buy of B, the B to whom the writing is delivered is the contractee, if any one is, and, notwithstanding what has been said of the use of proper names, I should suppose that a contract would be made.[6] For it is further to be said that, so far as by one of the terms of a contract the thing promised or the promisee is identified by sight and hearing, that terms so far preponderates over all others that it is very rare for the failure of any other

[6] See *Cundy* v. *Lindsay*, 3 App. Cas. 459, 469. Cf. *Reg.* v. *Middleton*, L. R. 2 C. C. 38, 55 *et seq.*, 62 *et seq.*; *Reg.* v. *Davies*, *Dearsly*, C. C. 640; *Rex* v. *Mucklow*, 1 Moody, C. C. 160; *Reg.* v. *Jacobs*, 12 Cox, 151.

element of description to prevent the making of a contract.[7] The most obvious of seeming exceptions is where the object is not in fact so identified, but only its covering or wrapper.

Of course the performance of a promise may be made conditional on all the terms stipulated from the other side being complied with, but conditions attaching to performance can never come into consideration until a contract has been made, and so far the question has been touching the existence of a contract in the first instance.

A different case may be suggested from any yet considered. Instead of a repugnancy between offer and assent which prevents an agreement, or between the terms of an agreement which makes it insensible on its face, there may be a like repugnancy between a term of the contract and a previous representation of fact which is not expressly made a part of the contract. The representation may have been the chief inducement and very foundation of the bargain. It may be more important than any of the expressed terms, and yet the contract may have been reduced to writing in words which cannot fairly be construed to include it. A vendor may have stated that barrels filled with salt contain mackerel, but the contract may be only for the barrels and their contents. An applicant for insurance may have misstated facts essential to the risk, yet the policy may simply insure a certain building or a certain life. It may be asked whether these contracts are not void also.

There might conceivably be cases in which, taking into account the nature of the contract, the words used could be said to embody the representation as a term by construction. For instance, it might be said that the true and well-understood purport of a contract of insurance is not, as the words seem to say, to take the risk of any loss by fire or perils of the sea, however great the risk may be, but to take a risk of a certain magnitude, and no other, which risk has been calculated mathematically from the

[7] "Præsentia corporis tollit errorem nominis." Cf. Byles, J., in *Way* v. *Hearne*, 32 L. J. N. S. C. P. 34, 40. But cf. the conflicting opinions in *Reg.* v. *Middleton*, L. R. 2 C. C. 38, 45, 57. It would seem that a proper name or other identification of an object or person as specific may have the same effect as an actual identification by the senses, because it refers to such an identification, although in a less direct way.

statements of the party insured. The extent of the risk taken is not specified in the policy, because the old forms and established usage are otherwise, but the meaning is perfectly understood.

If this reasoning were adopted, there would be an equal repugnancy in the terms of the contract, whether the nature of the risk were written in the policy or fixed by previous description. But, subject to possible exceptions of this kind, it would seem that a contract would be made, and that the most that could be claimed would be a right to rescind. Where parties having power to bind themselves do acts and and use words which are fit to create an obligation, I take it that an obligation arises. If there is a mistake as to a fact not mentioned in the contract, it goes only to the motives for making the contract. But a contract is not prevented from being made by the mere fact that one party would not have made it if he had known the truth. In what cases a mistake affecting motives only is a ground for avoidance, does not concern this discussion, because the subject now under consideration is when a contract is made, and the question of avoiding or rescinding it presupposes that it has been made.

I think that it may now be assumed that, when fraud, misrepresentation, or mistake is said to make a contract void, there is no new principle which comes in to set aside an otherwise perfect obligation, but that in every such case there is wanting one or more of the first elements which were explained in the foregoing Lecture. Either there is no second party, or the two parties say different things, or essential terms seemingly consistent are really inconsistent as used.

When a contract is said to be voidable, it is assumed that a contract has been made, but that it is subject to being unmade at the election of one party. This must be because of the breach of some condition attached to its existence either expressly or by implication.

If a condition is attached to the contract's coming into being, there is as yet no contract. Either party may withdraw, at will, until the condition is determined. There is no obligation, although there may be an offer or a promise, and hence there is no relation between the parties which requires discussion here. But some conditions seemingly arising out of a contract already made are conditions of this sort. Such is always the case if the condition of a promise lies within the control of the promisor's own will. For instance, a promise to pay for clothes if made to the customer's satisfaction, has been held in Massachusetts to make the promisor his own final judge.[8] So interpreted, it appears to me to be no contract at all, until the promisor's satisfaction is expressed. His promise is only to pay if he sees fit, and such a promise cannot be made a contract because it cannot impose any obligation.[9] If the promise were construed to mean that the clothes should be paid for provided they were such as ought to satisfy the promisor,[10] and thus to make the jury the arbiter, there would be a contract, because the promisor gives up control over the event, but it would be subject to a condition in the sense of the present analysis.

The conditions which a contract may contain have been divided by theorists into conditions precedent and conditions subsequent. The distinction has even been pronounced of great importance. It must be admitted that, if the course of pleading be taken as a test, it is so. In some cases, the plaintiff has to state that a condition has been performed in order to put the defendant to his answer; in others, it is left to the defendant to set up that a condition has been broken.

In one sense, all conditions are subsequent; in another, all are precedent. All are subsequent to the first stage of the obligation.[11] Take, for instance, the case of a promise to pay for work if done to the satisfaction of an architect. The condition is a clear case of what is called a condition precedent. There can be no duty to pay until the architect is satisfied. But there can be a contract before that moment, because the determination whether the promisor shall pay or not is no longer within his control. Hence the condition is subsequent to the existence of the obligation.

On the other hand, every condition subsequent is precedent to the incidence of the burden of the law. If we look at the law

[8] *Brown* v. *Foster*, 113 Mass. 136.

[9] Leake, Dig. Contr. 13, 14, 637; *Hunt* v. *Livermore*, 5 Pick. 395, 397; Langd. Contr. (2d ed.), § 36.

[10] Leake, Dig. Contr. 638; *Braunstein* v. *Accidental Death Ins. Co.*, 1 B. & S. 782.

[11] But cf. Langd. Contr. (2d ed.), § 29.

as it would be regarded by one who had no scruples against doing anything which he could do without incurring legal consequences, it is obvious that the main consequence attached by the law to a contract is a greater or less possibility of having to pay money. The only question from the purely legal point of view is whether the promisor will be compelled to pay. And the important moment is that at which that point is settled. All *conditions are precedent to that.*

But all conditions are precedent, not only in this extreme sense, but also to the existence of the plaintiff's cause of action. As strong a case as can be put is that of a policy of insurance conditioned to be void if not sued upon within one year from a failure to pay as agreed. The condition does not come into play until a loss has occurred, and the duty to pay has been neglected, and a cause of action has arisen. Nevertheless, it is precedent to the plaintiff's cause of action. When a man sues, the question is not whether he has had a cause of action in the past, but whether he has one then. He has not one then, unless the year is still running. If it were left for the defendant to set up the lapse of the year, that would be due to the circumstance that the order of pleading does not require a plaintiff to meet all possible defences, and to set out a case unanswerable except by denial. The point at which the law calls on the defendant for an answer varies in different cases. Sometimes it would seem to be governed simply by convenience of proof, requiring the party who has the affirmative to plead and prove it. Sometimes there seems to be a reference to the usual course of events, and matters belong to the defence because they are only exceptionally true.

The most logical distinction would be between conditions which must be satisfied before a promise can be broken, and those which, like the last, discharge the liability after a breach has occurred.[12] But this is of the slightest possible importance, and it may be doubted whether another case like the last could be found.

It is much more important to mark the distinction between a stipulation which only has the effect of confining a promise to certain cases, and a condition properly so called. Every condition,

[12] Langd. Contr. (2d ed.), § 29.

it is true, has this effect upon the promise to which it is attached, so that, whatever the rule of pleading may be,[13] a promise is as truly kept and performed by doing nothing where the condition of the stipulated act has been broken, as it would have been by doing the act if the condition had been fulfilled. But if this were all, every clause in a contract which showed what the promisor did not promise would be a condition, and the word would be worse than useless. The characteristic feature is quite different.

A condition properly so called is an event, the happening of which authorizes the person in whose favor the condition is reserved to treat the contract as if it had not been made,—to avoid it, as is commonly said,—that is, to insist on both parties being restored to the position in which they stood before the contract was made. When a condition operates as such, it lets in an outside force to destroy the existing state of things. For although its existence is due to consent of parties, its operation depends on the choice of one of them. When a condition is broken, the person entitled to insist on it may do so if he chooses; but he may, if he prefers, elect to keep the contract on foot. He gets his right to avoid it from the agreement, but the avoidance comes from him.

Hence it is important to distinguish those stipulations which have this extreme effect from those which only interpret the extent of a promise, or define the events to which it applies. And as it has just been shown that a condition need not be insisted on as such, we must further distinguish between its operation by way of avoidance, which is peculiar to it, and its incidental working by way of interpretation and definition, in common with other clauses not conditions.

This is best illustrated by taking a bilateral contract between A and B, where A's undertaking is conditional on B's doing what he promises to do, and where, after A has got a certain distance in his task, B breaks his half of the bargain. For instance, A is employed as a clerk by B, and is wrongfully dismissed in the middle of a quarter. In favor of A, the contract is conditional on B's keeping his agreement to employ him. Whether A insists on

[13] Cf. Bullen & Leake, Prec. of Plead. (3d ed.), 147, "Conditions Precedent."

the condition or not, he is not bound to do any more.[14] So far, the condition works simply by way of definition. It establishes that A has not promised to act in the case which has happened. But besides this, for which a condition was not necessary, A may take his choice between two courses. In the first place, he may elect to avoid the contract. In that case the parties stand as if no contract had been made, and A, having done work for B which was understood not to be gratuitous, and for which no rate of compensation has been fixed, can recover what the jury think his services were reasonably worth. The contract no longer determines the *quid pro quo*. But as an alternative course A may stand by the contract if he prefers to do so, and sue B for breaking it. In that case he can recover as part of his damages pay at the contract rate for what he had done, as well as compensation for his loss of opportunity to finish it. But the points which are material for the present discussion are, that these two remedies are mutually exclusive,[15] one supposing the contract to be relied on, the other that it is set aside, but that A's stopping work and doing no more after B's breach is equally consistent with either choice, and has in fact nothing to do with the matter.

One word should be added to avoid misapprehension. When it is said that A has done all that he promised to do in the case which has happened, it is not meant that he is necessarily entitled to the same compensation as if he had done the larger amount of work. B's promise in the case supposed was to pay so much a quarter for services; and although the consideration of the promise was the promise by A to perform them, the scope of it was limited to the case of their being performed in fact. Hence A could not simply wait till the end of his term, and then recover the full amount which he would have had if the employment had continued. Nor is he any more entitled to do so from the fact that it was B's fault that the services were not rendered. B's answer to any such claim is perfect. He is only liable upon a promise, and he in his turn only promised to pay in a case which

[14] Cf. *Cort* v. *Ambergate, Nottingham & Boston & Eastern Junction Railway Co.*, 17 Q. B. 127.

[15] *Goodman* v. *Pocock*, 15 Q. B. 576 (1850).

has not happened. He did promise to employ, however, and for not doing that he is liable in damages.

One or two more illustrations will be useful. A promises to deliver, and B promises to accept and pay for, certain goods at a certain time and place. When the time comes, neither party is on hand. Neither would be liable to an action, and, according to what has been said, each has done all that he promised to do in the event which has happened, to wit, nothing. It might be objected that, if A has done all that he is bound to do, he ought to be able to sue B, since performance or readiness to perform was all that was necessary to give him that right, and conversely the same might be said of B. On the other hand, considering either B or A as defendant, the same facts would be a complete defence. The puzzle is largely one of words.

A and B have, it is true, each performed all that they promised to do at the present stage, because they each only promised to act in the event of the other being ready and willing to act at the same time. But the readiness and willingness, although not necessary to the performance of either promise, and therefore not a duty, was necessary in order to present a case to which the promise of action on the other side would apply. Hence, although A and B have each performed their own promise, they have not performed the condition to their right of demanding more from the other side. The performance of that condition is purely optional until one side has brought it within the scope of the other's undertaking by performing it himself. But it is performance in the latter sense, that is, the satisfying of all conditions, as well as the keeping of his own promises, which is necessary to give A or B a right of action.

Conditions may be created by the very words of a contract. Of such cases there is nothing to be said, for parties may agree to what they choose. But they may also be held to arise by construction, where no provision is made in terms for rescinding or avoiding the contract in any case. The nature of the conditions which the law thus reads in needs explanation. It may be said, in a general way, that they are directed to the existence of the manifest grounds for making the bargain on the side of the rescinding party, or the accomplishment of its manifest objects. But that is not enough. Generally speaking, the disappointment must be caused by the wrong-doing of the person on the other side; and the most obvious cases of such wrong-doing are fraud and misrepresentation, or failure to perform his own part of the contract.

Fraud and misrepresentation thus need to be considered once more in this connection. I take the latter first. In dealing with it the first question which arises is whether the representation is, or is not, part of the contract. If the contract is in writing and the representation is set out on the face of the paper, it may be material or immaterial, but the effect of its untruth will be determined on much the same principles as govern the failure to perform a promise on the same side. If the contract is made by word of mouth, there may be a large latitude in connecting words of representation with later words of promise; but when they are determined to be a part of the contract, the same principles apply as if the whole were in writing.

The question now before us is the effect of a misrepresentation which leads to, but is not a part of, the contract. Suppose that the contract is in writing, but does not contain it, does such a previous misrepresentation authorize rescission in any case? and if so, does it in any case except where it goes to the height of fraud? The promisor might say, It does not matter to me whether you knew that your representation was false or not; the only thing I am concerned with is its truth. If it is untrue, I suffer equally whether you knew it to be so or not. But it has been shown, in an earlier Lecture, that the law does not go on the principle that a man is answerable for all the consequences of all his acts. An act is indifferent in itself. It receives its character from the concomitant facts known to the actor at the time. If a man states a thing reasonably believing that he is speaking from knowledge, it is contrary to the analogies of the law to throw the peril of the truth upon him unless he agrees to assume that peril, and he did not do so in the case supposed, as the representation was not made part of the contract.

It is very different when there is fraud. Fraud may as well lead to the making of a contract by a statement outside the contract as by one contained in it. But the law would hold the contract not less conditional on good faith in one case than in the other.

To illustrate, we may take a somewhat extreme case. A says to B, I have not opened these barrels myself, but they contain No. 1 mackerel: I paid so much for them to so and so, naming a well-known dealer. Afterwards A writes B, I will sell the barrels which you saw, and their contents, for so much; and B accepts. The barrels turn out to contain salt. I suppose the contract would be binding if the statements touching the contents were honest, and voidable if they were fraudulent.

Fraudulent representations outside a contract can never, it would seem, go to anything except the motives for making it. If outside the contract, they cannot often affect its interpretation. A promise in certain words has a definite meaning, which the promisor is presumed to understand. If A says to B, I promise you to buy this barrel and its contents, his words designate a person and thing identified by the senses, and they signify nothing more. There is no repugnancy, and if that person is ready to deliver that thing, the purchaser cannot say that any term in the contract itself is not complied with. He may have been fraudulently induced to believe that B was another B, and that the barrel contained mackerel; but however much his belief on those points may have affected his willingness to make the promise, it would be somewhat extravagant to give his words a different meaning on that account. "You" means the person before the speaker, whatever his name, and "contents" applies to salt, as well as to mackerel.

It is no doubt only by reason of a condition construed into the contract that fraud is a ground of rescission. Parties could agree, if they chose, that a contract should be binding without regard to truth or falsehood outside of it on either part.

But, as has been said before in these Lectures, although the law starts from the distinctions and uses the language of morality, it necessarily ends in external standards not dependent on the actual consciousness of the individual. So it has happened with fraud. If a man makes a representation, knowing facts which by the average standard of the community are sufficient to give him warning that it is probably untrue, and it is untrue, he is guilty of fraud in theory of law whether he believes his statement or not. The courts of Massachusetts, at least, go much further. They seem to hold that any material statement made by a man as of his own knowledge, or in such a way as fairly to be understood as made of his own knowledge, is fraudulent if untrue, irrespective of the reasons he may have had for believing it and for believing that he knew it.[16] It is clear, therefore, that a representation may be morally innocent, and yet fraudulent in theory of law. Indeed, the Massachusetts rule seems to stop little short of the principle laid down by the English courts of equity, which has been criticised in an earlier Lecture,[17] since most positive affirmations of facts would at least warrant a jury in finding that they were reasonably understood to be made as of the party's own knowledge, and might therefore warrant a rescission if they turned out to be untrue. The moral phraseology has ceased to be apposite, and an external standard of responsibility has been reached. But the starting-point is nevertheless fraud, and except on the ground of fraud, as defined by law, I do not think that misrepresentations before the contract affect its validity, although they lead directly to its making. But neither the contract nor the implied condition calls for the existence of the facts as to which the false representations were made. They call only for the absence of certain false representations. The condition is not that the promisee shall be a certain other B, or that the contents of the barrel shall be mackerel, but that the promisee has not lied to him about material facts.

Then the question arises, How do you determine what facts are material? As the facts are not required by the contract, the only way in which they can be material is that a belief in their being true is likely to have led to the making of the contract.

It is not then true, as it is sometimes said, that the law does not concern itself with the motives for making contracts. On the contrary, the whole scope of fraud outside the contract is the creation of false motives and the removal of true ones. And this consideration will afford a reasonable test of the cases in which

[16] *Fisher* v. *Mellen*, 103 Mass. 503. [17] *Supra*, p. 109.

fraud will warrant rescission. It is said that a fraudulent representation must be material to have that effect. But how are we to decide whether it is material or not? If the above argument is correct, it must be by an appeal to ordinary experience to decide whether a belief that the fact was as represented would naturally have led to, or a contrary belief would naturally have prevented, the making of the contract.

If the belief would not naturally have had such an effect, either in general or under the known circumstances of the particular case, the fraud is immaterial. If a man is induced to contract with another by a fraudulent representation of the latter that he is a great-grandson of Thomas Jefferson, I do not suppose that the contract would be voidable unless the contractee knew that, for special reasons, his lie would tend to bring the contract about.

The conditions or grounds for avoiding a contract which have been dealt with thus far are conditions concerning the conduct of the parties outside of the contract itself. Still confining myself to conditions arising by construction of law,—that is to say, not directly and in terms attached to a promise by the literal meaning of the words in which it is expressed,—I now come to those which concern facts to which the contract does in some way refer.

Such conditions may be found in contracts where the promise is only on one side. It has been said that where the contract is unilateral, and its language therefore is all that of the promisor, clauses in his favor will be construed as conditions more readily than the same words in a bilateral contract; indeed, that they must be so construed, because, if they do not create a condition, they do him no good, since *ex hypothesi* they are not promises by the other party.[18] How far this ingenious suggestion has had a practical effect on doctrine may perhaps be doubted.

But it will be enough for the purposes of this general survey to deal with bilateral contracts, where there are undertakings on both sides, and where the condition implied in favor of one party is that the other shall make good what he on his part has undertaken.

The undertakings of a contract may be for the existence of a

[18] Langd. Contr. (2d ed.), § 33.

fact in the present or in the future. They can be promises only in the latter case; but in the former, they may be equally essential terms in the bargain.

Here again we come on the law of representations, but in a new phase. Being a part of the contract, it is always possible that their truth should make a condition of the contract wholly irrespective of any question of fraud. And it often is so in fact. It is not, however, every representation embodied in the words used on one side which will make a condition in favor of the other party. Suppose A agrees to sell, and B agrees to buy, "A's seven-year-old sorrel horse Eclipse, now in the possession of B on trial," and in fact the horse is chestnut-colored, not sorrel. I do not suppose that B could refuse to pay for the horse on that ground. If the law were so foolish as to aim at merely formal consistency, it might indeed be said that there was as absolute a repugnancy between the different terms of this contract as in the case of an agreement to sell certain barrels of mackerel, where the barrels turned out to contain salt. If this view were adopted, there would not be a contract subject to a condition, there would be no contract at all. But in truth there is a contract, and there is not even a condition. As has been said already, it is not every repugnancy that makes a contract void, and it is not every failure in the terms of the counter undertaking that makes it voidable. Here it plainly appears that the buyer knows exactly what he is going to get, and therefore that the mistake of color has no bearing on the bargain.[19]

If, on the other hand, a contract contained a representation which was fraudulent, and which misled the party to whom it was made, the contract would be voidable on the same principles as if the representation had been made beforehand. But words of description in a contract are very frequently held to amount to what is sometimes called a warranty, irrespective of fraud. Whether they do so or not is a question to be determined by the court on grounds of common sense, looking to the meaning of the words, the importance in the transaction of the facts

[19] See the explanation of *Dimech* v. *Corlett*, 12 Moo. P. C. 199, in *Behn* v. *Burness*, 3 B. & S. 751, 760.

which the words convey, and so forth. But when words of description are determined to be a warranty, the meaning of the decision is not merely that the party using them binds himself to answer for their truth, but that their truth is a condition of the contract.

For instance, in a leading case[20] the agreement was that the plaintiff's ship, then in the port of Amsterdam, should, with all possible despatch, proceed direct to Newport, England, and there load a cargo of coals for Hong Kong. At the date of the charter-party the vessel was not in Amsterdam, but she arrived there four days later. The plaintiff had notice that the defendant considered time important. It was held that the presence of the vessel in the port of Amsterdam at the date of the contract was a condition, the breach of which entitled the defendant to refuse to load, and to rescind the contract. If the view were adopted that a condition must be a future event, and that a promise purporting to be conditional on a past or present event is either absolute or no promise at all, it would follow that in this case the defendant had never made a promise.[21] He had only promised if circumstances existed which did not exist. I have already stated my objections to this way of looking at such cases,[22] and will only add that the courts, so far as I am aware, do not sanction it, and certainly did not in this instance.

There is another ground for holding the charter-party void and no contract, instead of regarding it as only voidable, which is equally against authority, which nevertheless I have never been able to answer wholly to my satisfaction. In the case put, the representation of the lessor of the vessel concerned the vessel itself, and therefore entered into the description of the thing the lessee agreed to take. I do not quite see why there is not as fatal a repugnancy between the different terms of this contract as was found in that for the sale of the barrels of salt described as containing mackerel. Why is the repugnancy between the two terms,—first, that the thing sold is the contents of these barrels, and, second, that it is mackerel—fatal to the existence of a

[20] *Behn* v. *Burness*, 3 B. & S. 751.
[21] Langd. Contr. (2d ed.), § 28, p. 1000.
[22] See Lecture VIII.

contract? It is because each of those terms goes to the very root and essence of the contract,[23]—because to compel the buyer to take something answering to one, but not to the other requirement, would be holding him to do a substantially different thing from what he promised, and because a promise to take one and the same thing answering to both requirements is therefore contradictory in a substantial matter. It has been seen that the law does not go on any merely logical ground, and does not hold that every slight repugnancy will make a contract even voidable. But, on the other hand, when the repugnancy is between terms which are both essential, it is fatal to the very existence of the contract. How then do we decide whether a given term is essential? Surely the best way of finding out is by seeing how the parties have dealt with it. For want of any expression on their part we may refer to the speech and dealings of every day,[24] and say that, if its absence would make the subject-matter a different thing, its presence is essential to the existence of the agreement. But the parties may agree that anything, however trifling, shall be essential, as well as that anything, however important, shall not be; and if that essential is part of the contract description of a specific thing which is also identified by reference to the senses, how can there be a contract in its absence any more than if the thing is in popular speech different in kind from its description? The qualities that make sameness or difference of kind for the purposes of a contract are not determined by Agassiz or Darwin, or by the public at large, but by the will of the parties, which decides that for their purposes the characteristics insisted on are such and such.[25] Now, if this be true, what evidence can there be that a certain requirement is essential, that without it the subject-matter will be different in kind from the description, better than that one party has required and the other given a warranty of its presence? Yet the contract description of the specific vessel as now in the port of Amsterdam, although held to be an implied warranty, does not seem to have been regarded

[23] *Kennedy* v. *Panama, &c. Mail Co.*, L. R. 2 Q. B. 580, 588; *Lyon* v. *Bertram*, 20 How. 149, 153. Cf. Windscheid, Pand., § 76, nn. 6, 9.

[24] Windscheid, Pand., § 76 (4). See, generally, Ibid., nn. 6, 7; § 78, pp. 206, 207; § 82, pp. 216 *et seq.*

[25] Cf. Ihering, Geist d. Röm. Rechts, § 48, III. p. 116 (Fr. transl.).

as making the contract repugnant and void, but only as giving the defendant the option of avoiding it.[26] Even an express warranty of quality in sales does not have this effect, and in England, indeed, it does not allow the purchaser to rescind in case of breach. On this last point the law of Massachusetts is different.

The explanation has been offered of the English doctrine with regard to sales, that, when the title has passed, the purchaser has already had some benefit from the contract, and therefore cannot wholly replace the seller *in statu quo*, as must be done when a contract is rescinded.[27] This reasoning seems doubtful, even to show that the contract is not voidable, but has no bearing on the argument that it is void. For if the contract is void, the title does not pass.

It might be said that there is no repugnancy in the charterer's promise, because he only promises to load a certain ship, and that the words "now in the port of Amsterdam" are merely matter of history when the time for loading comes, and no part of the description of the vessel which he promised to load. But the moment those words are decided to be essential they become part of the description, and the promise is to load a certain vessel which is named the Martaban, and which was in the port of Amsterdam at the date of the contract. So interpreted, it is repugnant.

Probably the true solution is to be found in practical considerations. At any rate, the fact is that the law has established three degrees in the effect of repugnancy. If one of the repugnant terms is wholly insignificant, it is simply disregarded, or at most will only found a claim for damages. The law would be loath to hold a contract void for repugnancy in present terms, when if the same terms were only promised a failure of one of them would not warrant a refusal to perform on the other side. If, on the other hand, both are of the extremest importance, so that to enforce the rest of the promise or bargain without one of them would not merely deprive one party of a stipulated incident, but would force a substantially different bargain on him, the promise

[26] See, however, the language of Crompton, J. in s. c., 1 B. & S. 877. Cf. 2 Kent, Comm. (12th ed.), 479, n. 1, A (*c*).

[27] *Behn* v. *Burness*, 3 B. & S. 751, 755, 756.

will be void. There is an intermediate class of cases where it is left to the disappointed party to decide. But as the lines between the three are of this vague kind, it is not surprising that they have been differently drawn in different jurisdictions.

The examples which have been given of undertakings for a present state of facts have been confined to those touching the present condition of the subject-matter of the contract. Of course here is no such limit to the scope of their employment. A contract may warrant the existence of other facts as well, and examples of this kind probably might be found or imagined where it would be clear that the only effect of the warranty was to attach a condition to the contract, in favor of the other side, and where the question would be avoided whether there was not something more than a condition,—a repugnancy which prevented the formation of any contract at all. But the preceding illustrations are enough for the present purpose.

We may now pass from undertakings that certain facts are true at the time of making the contract, to undertakings that certain facts shall be true at some later time,—that is, to promises properly so called. The question is when performance of the promise on one side is a condition to the obligation of the contract on the other. In practice, this question is apt to be treated as identical with another, which, as has been shown earlier, is a distinct point; namely, when performance on one side is a condition of the right to call for performance on the other. It is of course conceivable that a promise should be limited to the case of performance of the things promised on the other side, and yet that a failure of the latter should not warrant a rescission of the contract. Wherever one party has already received a substantial benefit under the contract of a kind which cannot be restored, it is too late to rescind, however important a breach may be committed later by the other side. Yet he may be excused from going farther. Suppose a contract is made for a month's labor, ten dollars to be paid down, not to be recovered except in case of rescission for the laborer's fault, and thirty dollars at the end of the month. If the laborer should wrongfully stop work at the end of a fortnight, I do not suppose that the contract could be rescinded, and that the ten dollars could be recovered as money had and received; [28] but, on the other hand, the employer would not be bound to pay the thirty dollars, and of course he could sue for damages on the contract.[29]

But, for the most part, a breach of promise which discharges the promisee from further performance on his side will also warrant rescission, so that no great harm is done by the popular confusion of the two questions. Where the promise to perform on one side limited to the case of performance on the other, the contract is generally conditioned on it also. In what follows, I shall take up the cases which I wish to notice without stopping to consider whether the contract was in a strict sense conditioned on performance of the promise on one side, or whether the true construction was merely that the promise on the other side was limited to that event.

Now, how do we settle whether such a condition exists? It is easy to err by seeking too eagerly for simplicity, and by striving too hard to reduce all cases to artificial presumptions, which are less obvious than the decisions which they are supposed to explain. The foundation of the whole matter is, after all, good sense, as the courts have often said. The law means to carry out the intention of the parties, and, so far as they have not provided for the event which has happened, it has to say what they naturally would have intended if their minds had been turned to the point. It will be found that decisions based on the direct implications of the language used, and others based upon a remoter inference of what the parties must have meant, or would have said if they had spoken, shade into each other by imperceptible degrees.

Mr. Langdell has called attention to a very important principle, and one which, no doubt, throws light on many decisions.[30] This is, that, where you have a bilateral contract, while the consideration of each promise is the counter promise, yet *prima facie* the payment for performance of one is performance of the other. The performance of the other party is what each means to have in return for his own. If A promises a barrel of flour to B, and B

[28] Cf. *Anglo-Egyptian Navigation Co.* v. *Rennie*, L. R. 10 C. P. 271.

[29] *Ellen* v. *Topp*, 6 Exch. 424.

[30] Contracts (2d ed.), § 106, and *passim*.

promises him ten dollars for it, A means to have the ten dollars for his flour, and B means to have the flour for his ten dollars. If no time is set for either act, neither can call on the other to perform without being ready at the same time himself.

But this principle of equivalency is not the only principle to be drawn even from the form of contracts, without considering their subject-matter, and of course it is not offered as such in Mr. Langdell's work.

Another very clear one is found in contracts for the sale or lease of a thing, and the like. Here the qualities or characteristics which the owner promises that the thing furnished shall possess, go to describe the thing which the buyer promises to accept. If any of the promised traits are wanting in the thing tendered, the buyer may refuse to accept, not merely on the ground that he has not been offered the equivalent for keeping his promise, but also on the ground that he never promised to accept what is offered him.[81] It has been seen that, where the contract contains a statement touching the condition of the thing at an earlier time than the moment for its acceptance, the past condition may not always be held to enter into the description of the thing to be accepted. But no such escape is possible here. Nevertheless there are limits to the right of refusal even in the present class of cases. If the thing promised is specific, the preponderance of that part of the description which identifies the object by reference to the senses is sometimes strikingly illustrated. One case has gone so far as to hold that performance of an executory contract to purchase a specific thing cannot be refused because it fails to come up to the warranted quality.[82]

Another principle of dependency to be drawn from the form of the contract itself is, that performance of the promise on one side may be manifestly intended to furnish the means for performing the promise on the other. If a tenant should promise to make repairs, and the landlord should promise to furnish him

[81] *Chanter* v. *Hopkins*, 4 M. & W. 399, 404. Possibly *Behn* v. *Burness*, stated above, might have been dealt with in this way. The ship tendered was not a ship which had been in the port of Amsterdam at the date of the contract. It was therefore not such a ship as the contract called for.

[82] *Heyworth* v. *Hutchinson*, L. R. 2 Q. B. 447, criticised in Benj. Sales (2d ed.), pp. 742 *et seq.*

wood for the purpose, it is believed that at the present day, whatever may have been the old decisions, the tenant's duty to repair would be dependent upon the landlord's furnishing the material when required.[33]

Another case of a somewhat exceptional kind is where a party to a bilateral contract agrees to do certain things and to give security for his performance. Here it is manifest good-sense to hold giving the security a condition of performance on the other side, if it be possible. For the requirement of security shows that the party requiring it was not content to rely on the simple promise of the other side, which he would be compelled to do if he had to perform before the security was given, and thus the very object of requiring it would be defeated.[34]

This last case suggests what is very forcibly impressed on any one who studies the cases,—that, after all, the most important element of decision is not any technical, or even any general principle of contracts, but a consideration of the nature of the particular transaction as a practical matter. Suppose A promises B to do a day's work for two dollars, and B promises A to pay two dollars for a day's work. There the two promises cannot be performed at the same time. The work will take all day, the payment half a minute. How are you to decide which is to be done first, that is to say, which promise is dependent upon performance on the other side? It is only by reference to the habits of the community and to convenience. It is not enough to say that on the principle of equivalency a man is not presumed to intend to pay for a thing until he has it. The work is payment for the money, as much as the money for the work, and one must be paid for in advance. The question is, why, if one man is not presumed to intend to pay money until he has money's worth, the other

[33] See *Thomas* v. *Cadwallader*, Willes, 496; Langd. Contr. (2d ed.), §§ 116, 140. This is put as a case of equivalence by Mr. Langdell (Contr., § 116); but the above explanation is believed to be the true one. It will be noticed that this is hardly a true case of condition, but merely a limitation of the scope of the tenant's promise. So a covenant to serve as apprentice in a trade, which the other party covenants to teach, can only be performed if the other will teach, and must therefore be limited to that event. Cf. *Ellen* v. *Topp*, 6 Exch. 424.

[34] Langdell, Contracts (2d ed.), § 127. Cf. *Roberts* v. *Brett*, 11 H. L. C. 337.

is presumed to intend to give money's worth before he has money. An answer cannot be obtained from any general theory. The fact that employers, as a class, can be trusted for wages more safely than the employed for their labor, that the employers have had the power and have been the law-makers, or other considerations, it matters not what, have determined that the work is to be done first. But the grounds of decision are purely practical, and can never be elicited from grammar or from logic.

A reference to practical considerations will be found to run all through the subject. Take another instance. The plaintiff declared on a mutual agreement between himself and the defendant that he would sell, and the defendant would buy, certain Donskoy wool, to be shipped by the plaintiff at Odessa, and delivered in England. Among the stipulations of the contract was one, that the names of the vessels should be declared as soon as the wools were shipped. The defence was, that the wool was bought, with the knowledge of both parties, for the purpose of reselling it in the course of the defendant's business; that it was an article of fluctuating value, and not salable until the names of the vessels in which it was shipped should have been declared according to the contract, but that the plaintiff did not declare the names of the vessels as agreed. The decision of the court was given by one of the greatest technical lawyers that ever lived, Baron Parke; yet he did not dream of giving any technical or merely logical reason for the decision, but, after stating in the above words the facts which were deemed material to the question whether declaring the names of the vessels was a condition to the duty to accept, stated the ground of decision thus: "Looking at the nature of the contract, and the great importance of it to the object with which the contract was entered into with the knowledge of both parties, we think it was a condition precedent."[85]

[85] *Graves* v. *Legg*, 9 Exch. 709. Cf. Lang. Contr. (2d ed.), § 33, p. 1004. Mr. Langdell says that a bought note, though part of a bilateral contract, is to be treated as unilateral, and that it may be presumed that the language of the contract relied on was that of a bought note, and thus a condition in favor of the defendant, who made it. I do not quite understand how this can be assumed when the declaration states a bilateral contract, and the question arose on demurrer to a plea, which also states that the plaintiff "was by the agreement bound to declare" the names. How remote the explanation is from the actual ground of decision will be seen.

LECTURE X

SUCCESSIONS.—I. AFTER DEATH.—II. INTER VIVOS

In the Lecture on Possession, I tried to show that the notion of possessing a right as such was intrinsically absurd. All rights are consequences attached to filling some situation of fact. A right which may be acquired by possession differs from others simply in being attached to a situation of such a nature that it may be filled successively by different persons, or by any one without regard to the lawfulness of his doing so, as is the case where the situation consists in having a tangible object within one's power.

When a right of this sort is recognized by the law, there is no difficulty in transferring it; or, more accurately, there is no difficulty in different persons successively enjoying similar rights in respect of the subject-matter. If A, being the possessor of a horse or a field, gives up the possession to B, the rights which B acquires stand on the same ground as A's did before. The facts from which A's rights sprang have ceased to be true of A, and are now true of B. The consequences attached by the law to those facts now exist for B, as they did for A before. The situation of fact from which the rights spring is a continuing one, and any one who occupies it, no matter how, has the right attached to it.

But there is no possession possible of a contract. The fact that a consideration was given yesterday by A to B, and a promise received in return, cannot be laid hold of by X, and transferred from A to himself. The only thing which can be transferred is the benefit or burden of the promise, and how can they be separated from the facts which gave rise to them? How, in short, can a man sue or be sued on a promise in which he had no part?

Hitherto it has been assumed, in dealing with any special right or obligation, that the facts from which it sprung were true of the individual entitled or bound. But it often happens, especially in modern law, that a person acquires and is allowed to enforce a special right, although the facts which give rise to it are not true of him, or are true of him only in part. One of the chief problems of the law is to explain the machinery by which this result has been brought to pass.

It will be observed that the problem is not coextensive with the whole field of rights. Some rights cannot be transferred by any device or contrivance; for instance, a man's right to bodily safety or reputation. Others again are incident to possession, and within the limits of that conception no other is necessary. As Savigny said, "Succession does not apply to possession by itself." [1]

But the notion of possession will carry us but a very little way in our understanding of the modern theory of transfer. That theory depends very largely upon the notion of succession, to use the word just quoted from Savigny, and accordingly successions will be the subject of this and the following Lecture. I shall begin by explaining the theory of succession to persons deceased, and after that is done I shall pass to the theory of transfer between living people, and shall consider whether any relation can be established between the two.

The former is easily shown to be founded upon a fictitious identification between the deceased and his successor. And as a first step to the further discussion, as well as for its own sake, I shall briefly state the evidence touching the executor, the heir, and the devisee. In order to understand the theory of our law with regard to the first of these, at least, scholars are agreed that it is necessary to consider the structure and position of the Roman family as it was in the infancy of Roman society.

Continental jurists have long been collecting the evidence that, in the earlier periods of Roman and German law alike, the unit of society was the family. The Twelve Tables of Rome still recognize the interest of the inferior members of the family in the family property. Heirs are called *sui heredes*, that is, heirs of themselves or of their own property, as is explained by Gaius.[2] Paulus says that they are regarded as owners in a certain sense,

[1] Recht des Besitzes, § 11, p. 184, n. 1 (7th ed.), Eng. tr. 124, n. *t*.
[2] Inst. II. § 157.

even in the lifetime of their father, and that after his death they do not so much receive an inheritance as obtain the full power of dealing with their property.[3]

Starting from this point it is easy to understand the succession of heirs to a deceased *paterfamilias* in the Roman system. If the family was the owner of the property administered by a *paterfamilias,* its rights remained unaffected by the death of its temporary head. The family continued, although the head died. And when, probably by a gradual change,[4] the *paterfamilias* came to be regarded as owner, instead of a simple manager of the family rights, the nature and continuity of those rights did not change with the title to them. The *familia* continued to the heirs as it was left by the ancestor. The heir succeeded not to the ownership of this or that thing separately, but to the total *hereditas* or leadership of the family with certain rights of property as incident,[5] and of course he took this headship, or right of representing the family interests, subject to the modifications effected by the last manager.

The aggregate of the ancestor's rights and duties, or, to use the technical phrase, the total *persona* sustained by him, was easily separated from his natural personality. For this *persona* was but the aggregate of what had formerly been family rights and duties, and was originally sustained by any individual only as the family head. Hence it was said to be continued by the inheritance,[6] and when the heir assumed it he had his action in respect of injuries previously committed.[7]

[3] "In suis heredibus evidentius apparet continuationem dominii eo rem perducere, ut nulla videatur hereditas fuisse, quasi olim hi domini essent, qui etiam vivo patre quodammodo domini existimantur. unde etiam filius familias appellatur sicut pater familias, sola nota hac adiecta, per quam distinguitur genitor ab eo qui genitus sit. itaque post mortem patris non hereditatem percipere videntur, sed magis liberam bonorum administrationem consequuntur. hac ex causa licet non sint heredes instituti, domini sunt: nec obstat, quod licet eos exheredare, quod et occidere licebat." D. 28. 2. 11. Cf. Plato, Laws, *ια'*, vi. : *ἔγωγ' οὖν νομοθέτης ὢν οὔθ' ὑμᾶς ὑμῶν αὐτῶν εἶναι τίθημι οὔτε τὴν οὐσίαν ταύτην, ξύμπαντος δὲ τοῦ γένους ὑμῶν τοῦ τε ἔμπροσθεν καὶ τοῦ ἔπειτα ἐσομένου.*

[4] Cf. Laveleye, Propriété, 24, 202, 205, 211, n. 1, 232; Norton, L. C. Hindu Law of Inheritance, p. 193.

[5] D. 50. 16. 208. [6] D. 41. 1. 34. Cf. D. 41. 3. 40; Bract., fol. 8 *a*, 44 *a*.

[7] D. 43. 24. 13, § 5.

Thus the Roman heir came to be treated as identified with his ancestor for the purposes of the law. And thus it is clear how the impossible transfers which I seek to explain were accomplished in that instance. Rights to which B as B could show no title, he could readily maintain under the fiction that he was the same person as A, whose title was not denied.

It is not necessary at this point to study family rights in the German tribes. For it is not disputed that the modern executor derives his characteristics from the Roman heir. Wills also were borrowed from Rome, and were unknown to the Germans of Tacitus.[8] Administrators were a later imitation of executors, introduced by statute for cases where there was no will, or where, for any other reason, executors were wanting.

The executor has the legal title to the whole of the testator's personal estate, and, generally speaking, the power of alienation. Formerly he was entitled to the undistributed residue, not, it may fairly be conjectured, as legatee of those specific chattels, but because he represented the person of the testator, and therefore had all the rights which the testator would have had after distribution if alive. The residue is nowadays generally bequeathed by the will, but it is not even now regarded as a specific gift of the chattels remaining undisposed of, and I cannot help thinking that this doctrine echoes that under which the executor took in former times.

No such rule has governed residuary devises of real estate, which have always been held to be specific in England down to the present day. So that, if a devise of land should fail, that land would not be disposed of by the residuary clause, but would descend to the heir as if there had been no will.

Again, the appointment of an executor relates back to the date of the testator's death. The continuity of person is preserved by this fiction, as in Rome it was by personifying the inheritance *ad interim*.

Enough has been said to show the likeness between our executor and the Roman heir. And bearing in mind what was said about the *heres*, it will easily be seen how it came to be said, as it often was in the old books, that the executor "represents the

[8] Germania, c. 20.

person of his testator."[9] The meaning of this feigned identity has been found in history, but the aid which it furnished in overcoming a technical difficulty must also be appreciated. If the executor represents the person of the testator, there is no longer any trouble in allowing him to sue or be sued on his testator's contracts. In the time of Edward III., when an action of covenant was brought against executors, Persay objected: "I never heard that one should have a writ of covenant against executors, nor against other person but the very one who made the covenant, for a man cannot oblige another person to a covenant by his deed except him who was party to the covenant."[10] But it is useless to object that the promise sued upon was made by A, the testator, not by B, the executor, when the law says that for this purpose B is A. Here then is one class of cases in which a transfer is accomplished by the help of a fiction, which shadows, as fictions so often do, the facts of an early stage of society, and which could hardly have been invented had these facts been otherwise.

Executors and administrators afford the chief, if not the only, example of universal succession in the English law. But although they succeed *per universitatem*, as has been explained, they do not succeed to all kinds of property. The personal estate goes to them, but land takes another course. All real estate not disposed of by will goes to the heir, and the rules of inheritance are quite distinct from those which govern the distribution of chattels. Accordingly, the question arises whether the English heir or successor to real estate presents the same analogies to the Roman *heres* as the executor.

The English heir is not a universal successor. Each and every parcel of land descends as a separate and specific thing. Nevertheless, in his narrower sphere he unquestionably represents the person of his ancestor. Different opinions have been held as to whether the same thing was true in early German law. Dr. Laband says that it was;[11] Sohm takes the opposite view.[12] It is

[9] Littleton, § 337; Co. Lit. 209, *a*, *b*; Y. B. 8 Ed. IV. 5, 6, pl. 1; Keilway, 44 *a* (17 Hen. VII.); *Lord North* v. *Butts*, Dyer, 139 *b*, 140 *a*, top; *Overton* v. *Sydall*, Popham, 120, 121; *Boyer* v. *Rivet*, 3 Bulstr. 317, 321; *Bain* v. *Cooper*, 1 Dowl. Pr. Cas. N. S. 11, 14.

[10] Y. B. 48 Ed. III. 2, pl. 4.

[11] Vermögensrechtlichen Klagen, 88, 89.

[12] Proc. de la Lex Salica, tr. Thèvenin, p. 72 and n. 1.

commonly supposed that family ownership, at least of land, came before that of individuals in the German tribes, and it has been shown how naturally representation followed from a similar state of things in Rome. But it is needless to consider whether our law on this subject is of German or Roman origin, as the principle of identification has clearly prevailed from the time of Glanvill to the present day. If it was not known to the Germans, it is plainly accounted for by the influence of the Roman law. If there was anything of the sort in the Salic law, it was no doubt due to natural causes similar to those which gave rise to the principle at Rome. But in either event I cannot doubt that the modern doctrine has taken a good deal of its form, and perhaps some of its substance, from the mature system of the civilians, in whose language it was so long expressed. For the same reasons that have just been mentioned, it is also needless to weigh the evidence of the Anglo-Saxon sources, although it seems tolerably clear from several passages in the laws that there was some sort of identification.[13]

As late as Bracton, two centuries after the Norman conquest, the heir was not the successor to lands alone, but represented his ancestor in a much more general sense, as will be seen directly. The office of executor, in the sense of heir, was unknown to the Anglo-Saxons,[14] and even in Bracton's time does not seem to have been what it has since become. There is, therefore, no need to go back further than to the early Norman period, after the appointment of executors had become common, and the heir was more nearly what he is now.

When Glanvill wrote, a little more than a century after the Conquest, the heir was bound to warrant the reasonable gifts of his ancestor to the grantees and their heirs; [15] and if the effects of the ancestor were insufficient to pay his debts, the heir was bound to make up the deficiency from his own property.[16] Neither Glanvill nor his Scotch imitator, the Regiam Majestatem,[17] limits the liability to the amount of property inherited from the same

[13] Ethelred, II. 9; Cnut, II. 73; Essays in Ang. Sax. Law, pp. 221 *et seq.*
[14] 1 Spence, Eq. 189, note, citing Hickes, Dissert. Epist., p. 57.
[15] Glanv., Lib. VII. 3. 2 (Beames, p. 150).
[16] Ibid., c. 8 (Beames, p. 168). [17] Reg. Maj., Lib. II. c. 39.

source. This makes the identification of heir and ancestor as complete as that of the Roman law before such a limitation was introduced by Justinian. On the other hand, a century later, it distinctly appears from Bracton,[18] that the heir was only bound so far as property had descended to him, and in the early sources of the Continent, Norman as well as other, the same limitation appears.[19] The liabilities of the heir were probably shrinking. Britton and Fleta, the imitators of Bracton, and perhaps Bracton himself, say that an heir is not bound to pay his ancestor's debt, unless he be thereto especially bound by the deed of his ancestor.[20] The later law required that the heir should be mentioned if he was to be held.

But at all events the identification of heir and ancestor still approached the nature of a universal succession in the time of Bracton, as is shown by another statement of his. He asks if the testator can bequeath his rights of action, and answers, No, so far as concerns debts not proved and recovered in the testator's life. But actions of that sort belong to the heirs, and must be sued in the secular court; for before they are so recovered in the proper court, the executor cannot proceed for them in the ecclesiastical tribunal.[21]

This shows that the identification worked both ways. The heir was liable for the debts due from his ancestor, and he could recover those which were due to him, until the executor took his place in the King's Courts, as well as in those of the Church. Within the limits just explained the heir was also bound to warrant property sold by his ancestor to the purchaser and his heirs.[22]

[18] Fol. 61 *a*.

[19] Sachsensp., II. 60, § 2, cited in Essays in Ang. Sax. Law, p. 221; Grand Cust. de Norm., c. 88.

[20] Britt., fol. 64 *b* (Nich. ed. 163); Fleta, Lib. II. c. 62, § 10. Cf. Bract., fol. 37 *b*, § 10.

[21] Bracton, fol. 61 *a*, *b*. "Item quæro an testator legare possit actiones suas? Et verum est quod non, de debitis quæ in vita testatoris convicta non fuerunt nec recognita, sed hujusmodi actiones competunt hæredibus. Cum autem convicta sint et recognita, tunc sunt quasi in bonis testatoris, et competunt executoribus in foro ecclesiastico. Si autem competant hæredibus, ut prædictum est, in foro seculari debent terminari, quia antequam communicantur et in foro debito, non pertinet ad executores, ut in foro ecclesiastico convincantur."

[22] Bract., fol. 62 *a*.

It is not necessary, after this evidence that the modern heir began by representing his ancestor generally, to seek for expressions in later books, since his position has been limited. But just as we have seen that the executor is still said to represent the person of his testator, the heir was said to represent the person of his ancestor in the time of Edward I.[23] So, at a much later date, it was said that "the heir is in representation in point of taking by inheritance *eadem persona cum antecessore*,"[24] the same *persona* as his ancestor.

A great judge, who died but a few years ago, repeats language which would have been equally familiar to the lawyers of Edward or of James. Baron Parke, after laying down that in general a party is not required to make profert of an instrument to the possession of which he is not entitled, says that there is an exception "in the cases of heir and executor, who may plead a release to the ancestor or testator whom they respectively represent; so also with respect to several tortfeasors, for in all these cases there is a privity between the parties which constitutes an identity of person."[25]

But this is not all. The identity of person was carried farther still. If a man died leaving male children, and owning land in fee, it went to the oldest son alone; but, if he left only daughters, it descended to them all equally. In this case several individuals together continued the *persona* of their ancestor. But it was always laid down that they were but one heir.[26] For the purpose of working out this result, not only was one person identified with another, but several persons were reduced to one, that they might sustain a single *persona*.

What was the *persona*? It was not the sum of all the rights and duties of the ancestor. It has been seen that for many centuries his general status, the sum of all his rights and duties except

[23] Y. B. 20 & 21 Ed. I. 232; cf. ib. 312.

[24] *Oates* v. *Frith*, Hob. 130. Cf. Y. B. 5 Hen. VII. 18, pl. 12; Popham, J., in *Overton* v. *Sydall*, Poph. 120, 121 (E. 39 El.); *Boyer* v. *Rivet*, 3 Bulstr. 317, 319–322; *Brooker's Case*, Godb. 376, 380 (P. 3 Car. I.).

[25] *Bain* v. *Cooper*, 1 Dowl. Pract. Cas. N. S. 11, 14. Cf. Y. B. 14 Hen. VIII. pl. 5, at fol. 10.

[26] Bract., fol. 66 *b*, 76 *b*, and *passim;* Y. B. 20 Ed. I. 226, 200; Littleton, § 241. The same thing was said where there were several executors: "They are only in the place of one person." Y. B. 8 Ed. IV. 5, pl. 1.

those connected with real property, has been taken up by the executor or administrator. The *persona* continued by the heir was from an early day confined to real estate in its technical sense; that is, to property subject to feudal principles, as distinguished from chattels, which, as Blackstone tells us,[27] include whatever was not a feud.

But the heir's *persona* was not even the sum of all the ancestor's rights and duties in connection with real estate. It has been said already that every fee descends specifically, and not as incident to a larger *universitas*. This appears not so much from the fact that the rules of descent governing different parcels might be different,[28] so that the same person would not be heir to both, as from the very nature of feudal property. Under the feudal system in its vigor, the holding of land was only one incident of a complex personal relation. The land was forfeited for a failure to render the services for which it was granted; the service could be renounced for a breach of correlative duties on the part of the lord.[29] It rather seems that, in the beginning of the feudal period under Charlemagne, a man could only hold land of one lord.[30] Even when it had become common to hold of more than one, the strict personal relation was only modified so far as to save the tenant from having to perform inconsistent services. Glanvill and Bracton [31] tell us that a tenant holding of several lords was to do homage for each fee, but to reserve his allegiance for the lord of whom he held his chief estate; but that, if the different lords should make war upon each other, and the chief lord should command the tenant to accompany him in person, the tenant ought to obey, saving the service due to the other lord for the fee held of him.

We see, then, that the tenant had a distinct *persona* or *status* in respect of each of the fees which he held. The rights and duties incident to one of them had no relation to the rights and duties incident to another. A succession to one had no connection with

[27] 2 Comm. 385.

[28] Cf. Glanv., Lib. VII. c. 3; F. N. B. 21 L; Dyer, 4 *b*, 5 *a*.

[29] Cf. Bract., fol. 80 *b*.

[30] Charta Divis. Reg. Franc., Art. IX. & VIII. Cf. 3 Laferrière, Hist. du Droit Français, 408, 409.

[31] Glanv., Lib. IX. c. 1 (Beames, pp. 218, 220); Bract., fol. 79 *b*.

the succession to another. Each succession was the assumption of a distinct personal relation, in which the successor was to be determined by the terms of the relation in question.

The *persona* which we are seeking to define is the estate. Every fee is a distinct *persona*, a distinct *hereditas*, or inheritance, as it has been called since the time of Bracton. We have already seen that it may be sustained by more than one where there are several heirs, as well as by one, just as a corporation may have more or less members. But not only may it be divided lengthwise, so to speak, among persons interested in the same way at the same time: it may also be cut across into successive interests, to be enjoyed one after another. In technical language, it may be divided into a particular estate and remainders. But they are all parts of the same fee, and the same fiction still governs them. We read in an old case that "he in reversion and particular tenant are but one tenant." [32] This is only a statement of counsel, to be sure; but it is made to account for a doctrine which seems to need the explanation, to the effect that, after the death of the tenant for life, he in reversion might have error or attaint on an erroneous judgment or false verdict given against the tenant for life.[33]

To sum up the results so far, the heir of modern English law gets his characteristic features from the law as it stood soon after the Conquest. At that time he was a universal successor in a very broad sense. Many of his functions as such were soon transferred to the executor. The heir's rights became confined to real estate, and his liabilities to those connected with real estate, and to obligations of his ancestor expressly binding him. The succession to each fee or feudal inheritance is distinct, not part of the sum of all the ancestor's rights regarded as one whole. But to this day the executor in his sphere, and the heir in his, represent the person of the deceased, and are treated as if they were one with him, for the purpose of settling their rights and obligations.

The bearing which this has upon the contracts of the deceased has been pointed out. But its influence is not confined to contract; it runs through everything. The most striking instance, however, is the acquisition of prescriptive rights. Take the case of a

[32] *Brooker's Case*, Godbolt, 376, 377, pl. 465.
[33] Dyer, 1 *b*. Cf. *Bain* v. *Cooper*, 1 Dowl. Pr. C. N. S. 11, 12.

right of way. A right of way over a neighbor's land can only be acquired by grant, or by using it adversely for twenty years. A man uses a way for ten years, and dies. Then his heir uses it ten years. Has any right been acquired? If common sense alone is consulted, the answer must be no. The ancestor did not get any right, because he did not use the way long enough. And just as little did the heir. How can it better the heir's title that another man had trespassed before him? Clearly, if four strangers to each other used the way for five years each, no right would be acquired by the last. But here comes in the fiction which has been so carefully explained. From the point of view of the law it is not two persons who have used the way for ten years each, but one who has used it for twenty. The heir has the advantage of sustaining his ancestor's *persona*, and the right is acquired.

I now reach the most difficult and obscure part of the subject. It remains to be discovered whether the fiction of identity was extended to others besides the heir and executor. And if we find, as we do, that it went but little farther in express terms, the question will still arise whether the mode of thought and the conceptions made possible by the doctrine of inheritance have not silently modified the law as to dealings between the living. It seems to me demonstrable that their influence has been profound, and that, without understanding the theory of inheritance, it is impossible to understand the theory of transfer *inter vivos*.

The difficulty in dealing with the subject is to convince the sceptic that there is anything to explain. Nowadays, the notion that a right is valuable is almost identical with the notion that it may be turned into money by selling it. But it was not always so. Before you can sell a right, you must be able to make a sale thinkable in legal terms. I put the case of the transfer of a contract at the beginning of the Lecture. I have just mentioned the case of gaining a right by prescription, when neither party has complied with the requirement of twenty years' adverse use. In the latter instance, there is not even a right at the time of the transfer, but a mere fact of ten years' past trespassing. A way, until it becomes a right of way, is just as little susceptible of being held by a possessory title as a contract. If then a contract can be sold, if a buyer can add the time of his seller's adverse user to his own, what is the machinery by which the law works out the result?

The most superficial acquaintance with any system of law in its earlier stages will show with what difficulty and by what slow degrees such machinery has been provided, and how the want of it has restricted the sphere of alienation. It is a great mistake to assume that it is a mere matter of common sense that the buyer steps into the shoes of the seller, according to our significant metaphor. Suppose that sales and other civil transfers had kept the form of warlike capture which it seems that they had in the infancy of Roman law,[34] and which was at least partially retained in one instance, the acquisition of wives, after the transaction had, in fact, taken the more civilized shape of purchase. The notion that the buyer came in adversely to the seller would probably have accompanied the fiction of adverse taking, and he would have stood on his own position as founding a new title. Without the aid of conceptions derived from some other source, it would have been hard to work out a legal transfer of objects which did not admit of possession.

A possible source of such other conceptions was to be found in family law. The principles of inheritance furnished a fiction and a mode of thought which at least might have been extended into other spheres. In order to prove that they were in fact so extended, it will be necessary to examine once more the law of Rome, as well as the remains of German and Anglo-Saxon customs.

I will take up first the German and Anglo-Saxon laws which are the ancestors of our own on one side of the house. For although what we get from those sources is not in the direct line of the argument, it lays a foundation for it by showing the course of development in different fields.

The obvious analogy between purchaser and heir seems to have

[34] In the American Law Review for October, 1872, VII. 49, 50, I mentioned one or two indications of this fact. But I have since had the satisfaction of finding it worked out with such detail and learning in Ihering's Geist des Römischen Rechts, §§ 10, 48, that I cannot do better than refer to that work, only adding that for my purposes it is not necessary to go so far as Ihering, and that he does not seem to have been led to the conclusions which it is my object to establish. See, further, Clark, Early Roman Law, 109, 110; Laferrière, Hist. du Droit Franç., I. 114 *et seq.*; D. 1. 5. 4, § 3; Gaii Inst. IV. § 16; ib. II. § 69.

been used in the folk-laws, but mainly for another purpose than those which will have to be considered in the English law. This was to enlarge the sphere of alienability. It will be remembered that there are many traces of family ownership in early German, as well as in early Roman law; and it would seem that the transfer of property which originally could not be given outside the family, was worked out through the form of making the grantee an heir.

The history of language points to this conclusion. *Heres*, as Beseler [35] and others have remarked, from meaning a successor to the property of a person deceased, was extended to the donee *mortis causa*, and even more broadly to grantees in general. *Hereditare* was used in like manner for the transfer of land. Hévin is quoted by Laferrière [36] as calling attention to the fact that the ancient usage was to say *hériter* for purchase, *héritier* for purchaser, and *déshériter* for sell.

The texts of the Salic law give us incontrovertible evidence. A man might transfer the whole or any part of his property [37] by delivering possession of it to a trustee who, within twelve months, handed it over to the beneficiaries.[38] To those, the text reads, whom the donor has named *heredes* (*quos heredes appellavit*). Here then was a voluntary transfer of more or less property at pleasure to persons freely chosen, who were not necessarily universal successors, if they ever were, and who nevertheless took under the name *heredes*. The word, which must have meant at first persons taking by descent, was extended to persons taking by purchase.[39] If the word became enlarged in meaning, it is probably because the thought which it conveyed was turned to new uses. The transaction seems to have fallen half-way between the institution of an heir and a sale. The later law of the Ripuarian Franks treats it more distinctly from the former point of view. It permits a man who has no sons to give all his property to whomsoever he chooses, whether relatives or

[35] Erbverträge, I. 15 *et seq*. [36] Hist. du Droit Franç., IV. 500.

[37] "Quantum dare voluerit aut totam furtunam cui voluerit dare . . . nec minus nec majus nisi quantum ei creditum est." Lex Sal. (Merkel), XLVI.

[38] Lex Sal. (Merkel), Cap. XLVI., *De adfathamire;* Sohm, Fränk. Reichs- u. Gerichtsverfassung, 69.

[39] Beseler, Erbverträge, I. 101, 102, 105.

strangers, as inheritance, either by way of *adfathamire,* as the Salic form was called, or by writing or delivery.[40]

The Lombards had a similar transfer, in which the donee was not only called *heres,* but was made liable like an heir for the debts of the donor on receiving the property after the donor's death.[41] By the Salic law a man who could not pay the *wergeld* was allowed to transfer formally his house-lot, and with it the liability. But the transfer was to the next of kin.[42]

The house-lot or family curtilage at first developed strictly within the limits of the family. Here again, at least in England, freedom of alienation seems to have grown up by a gradually increased latitude in the choice of successors. If we may trust the order of development to be noticed in the early charters, which it is hard to believe accidental, although the charters are few, royal grants at first permitted an election of heirs among the kindred, and then extended it beyond them. In a deed of the year 679, the language is, "as it is granted so do you hold it and your posterity." One a century later reads, "which let him always possess, and after his death leave to which of his heirs he will." Another, "and after him with free power (of choice) leave to the man of his kin to whom he wishes to" (leave it). A somewhat earlier charter of 736 goes a step further: "So that as long as he lives he shall have the power of holding and possessing (and) of leaving it to whomsoever he choose, either in his lifetime, or certainly after his death." At the beginning of the ninth century

[40] "Omnem facultatem suam . . . seu cuicunque libet de proximis vel extraneis, adoptare in hereditatem vel in adfatimi vel per scripturarum seriem seu per traditionem." L. Rib., Cap. L. (al. XLVIII.); cf. L. Thuring. XIII. So Capp. Rib. § 7: "Qui filios non habuerit et alium quemlibet heredem facere sibi voluerit coram rege . . . traditionem faciat."

[41] Ed. Roth., cap. 174, 157; cf. ib. 369, 388; Liutpr. III. 16 (al. 2), VI. 155 (al. 102). Cf. Beseler, Erbverträge, I. 108 *et seq.*, esp. 116–118. Compare the charter of A. D. 713, "Offero . . . S. P. ecclesia quam mihi heredem constitui." (Mem. di Lucca V. b. No. 4.) Troya III. No. 394, cited Heusler, Gewere, 45, 46. Cf. ib. 484. This, no doubt, was due to Roman influence, but it recalls what Sir Henry Maine quotes from Elphinstone's History of India (I. 126), as to sale by a member of one of the village communities: "The purchaser steps exactly into his place, and takes up all his obligations." Ancient Law, ch. 8, pp. 263, 264.

[42] (Merkel) Cap. LVIII., *De chrene cruda.* Sohm, Fränk. R. u. G. Verf. 117.

the donee has power to leave the property to whomsoever he will, or, in still broader terms, to exchange or grant in his lifetime, and after his death to leave it to whom he chooses,—or to sell, exchange, and leave to whatsoever heir he chooses.[43] This choice of heirs recalls the *quos heredes appellavit* of the Salic law just mentioned, and may be compared with the language of a Norman charter of about the year 1190: "To W. and his heirs, to wit those whom he may constitute his heirs." [44]

A perfect example of a singular succession worked out by the fiction of kinship is to be found in the story of Burnt Njal, an Icelandic saga, which gives us a living picture of a society hardly more advanced than the Salian Franks, as we see them in the *Lex Salica*. A lawsuit was to be transferred by the proper plaintiff to another more versed in the laws, and better able to carry it on, —in fact, to an attorney. But a lawsuit was at that time the alternative of a feud, and both were the peculiar affair of the family concerned.[45] Accordingly, when a suit for killing a member of the family was to be handed over to a stranger, the innovation had to be reconciled with the theory that such suit belonged only to the next of kin. Mord is to take upon himself Thorgeir's suit

[43] A. D. 679: "Sicuti tibi donata est ita tene et *posteri tui*." Kemble, Cod. Dip., I. 21, No. XVI. Uhtred, A. D. 767: "Quam is semper possideat et post se *cui voluerit heredum relinquat*." Ib. I. 144, CXVII. ("Cuilibet heredi voluerit relinquat" is very common in the later charters; ib. V. 155, MLXXXII.; ib. VI. 1, MCCXVIII.; ib. 31, MCCXXX.; ib. 38, MCCXXXIV.; and *passim*. This may be broader than *cui voluerit heredum*.) Offa, A. D. 779: "Ut se vivente habe . . . deat. et post se *suæ propinquitatis homini cui ipse vo* . . . possidendum libera utens potestate relinquat." Ib. I. 164, 165, CXXXVII. Æthilbald, A. D. 736: "Ita ut quamdiu vixerit potestatem habeat tenedi ac possidendi *cuicumque voluerit* vel eo vivo vel certe post obitum suum *relinquendi*." Ib. I. 96, LXXX.; cf. ib. V. 53, MXIV. Cuthred of Kent, A. D. 805: "*Cuicumque hominum voluerit* in æternam libertatem *derelinquat*." Ib. I. 232, CXC. "Ut habeat libertatem commutandi vel donandi in vita sua et post ejus obitum teneat facultatem relinquendi cuicumque volueris." Ib. I. 233, 234, CXCI.; cf. ib. V. 70, MXXXI. Wiglaf of Mercia, Aug. 28, A. D. 831: "Seu vendendum aut commutandum ł cuicumque ei herede placuerit derelinquendum." Ib. I. 294, CCXXVII.

[44] "W. et heredibus suis, videlicet quos heredes constituerit." Memorials of Hexham, Surtees Soc. Pub., 1864, II. 88.

[45] Cf. Y. B. 27 Ass., fol. 135, pl. 25. Under the Welsh laws the champion in a cause decided by combat acquired the rights of the next of kin, the next of kin being the proper champion. Lea, Superstition and Force (3d ed.), 165. Cf. ib. 161, n. 1; ib. 17.

against Flosi for killing Helgi, and the form of transfer is described as follows.

"Then Mord took Thorgeir by the hand and named two witnesses to bear witness, 'that Thorgeir Thorir's son hands me over a suit for manslaughter against Flosi Thord's son, to plead it for the slaying of Helgi Njal's son, with all those proofs which have to follow the suit. Thou handest over to me this suit to plead and to settle, and to enjoy all rights in it, *as though I were the rightful next of kin*. Thou handest it over to me by law; and I take it from thee by law.'" Afterwards, these witnesses come before the court, and bear witness to the transfer in like words: "He handed over to him then this suit, with all the proofs and proceedings which belonged to the suit, he handed it over to him to plead and to settle, and to make use of all rights, as though he were the rightful next of kin. Thorgeir handed it over lawfully, and Mord took it lawfully." The suit went on, notwithstanding the change of hands, as if the next of kin were plaintiff. This is shown by a further step in the proceedings. The defendant challenges two of the court, on the ground of their connection with Mord, the transferee, by blood and by baptism. But Mord replies that this is no good challenge; for "he challenged them not for their kinship to the true plaintiff, the next of kin, but for their kinship to him who pleaded the suit." And the other side had to admit that Mord was right in his law.

I now turn from the German to the Roman sources. These have the closest connection with the argument, because much of the doctrine to be found there has been transplanted unchanged into modern law.

The early Roman law only recognized as relatives those who would have been members of the same patriarchal family, and under the same patriarchal authority, had the common ancestor survived. As wives passed into the families of their husbands, and lost all connection with that in which they were born, relationship through females was altogether excluded. The heir was one who traced his relationship to the deceased through males alone. With the advance of civilization this rule was changed. The prætor gave the benefits of the inheritance to the blood relations, although they were not heirs, and could not be admitted to the succession according to the ancient law.[46] But the change was not brought about by repealing the old law, which still subsisted under the name of the *jus civile*. The new principle was accommodated to the old forms by a fiction. The blood relation could sue on the fiction that he was an heir, although he was not one in fact.[47]

One of the early forms of instituting an heir was a sale of the *familia* or headship of the family to the intended heir, with all its rights and duties.[48] This sale of the *universitas* was afterwards extended beyond the case of inheritance to that of bankruptcy, when it was desired to put the bankrupt's property into the hands of a trustee for distribution. This trustee also could make use of the fiction, and sue as if he had been the bankrupt's heir.[49] We are told by one of the great jurisconsults that in general universal successors stand in the place of heirs.[50]

The Roman heir, with one or two exceptions, was always a universal successor; and the fiction of heirship, as such, could hardly be used with propriety except to enlarge the sphere of universal successions. So far as it extended, however, all the consequences attached to the original fiction of identity between heir and ancestor followed as of course.

To recur to the case of rights acquired by prescription, every universal successor could add the time of his predecessor's adverse use to his own in order to make out the right. There was no addition, legally speaking, but one continuous possession.

The express fiction of inheritance perhaps stopped here. But when a similar joinder of times was allowed between a legatee or devisee (*legatarius*) and his testator, the same explanation was offered. It was said, that, when a specific thing was left to

[46] D. 38. 8. 1, pr.

[47] "Cum is, qui ex edicto bonorum possessionem petiit, ficto se herede agit." Gaii Inst. IV. § 34. Cf. Ulp. Fragm. XXVIII. § 12; D. 37. 1. 2. So the *fidei commissarius*, who was a prætorian successor (D. 41. 4. 2, § 19; 10. 2. 24), "in similitudinem heredis consistit." Nov. 1. 1, § 1. Cf. Just. Inst. 2, 24, pr., and then Gaius, II. §§ 251, 252.

[48] Gaii Inst. II. §§ 102 *et seq*. Cf. ib. §§ 252, 35.

[49] Gaii Inst. IV. § 35: "Similiter et bonorum emptor ficto se herede agit." Cf. ib. §§ 144, 145. Keller, Römische Civilprocess, § 85, III. But cf. Scheurl, Lehrb. der Inst., § 218, p. 407 (6th ed.).

[50] Paulus in D. 50. 17. 128.

a person by will, so far as concerned having the benefit of the time during which the testator had been in possession for the purpose of acquiring a title, the legatee was in a certain sense quasi an heir.[51] Yet a *legatarius* was not a universal successor, and for most purposes stood in marked contrast with such successors.[52]

Thus the strict law of inheritance had made the notion familiar that one man might have the advantage of a position filled by another, although it was not filled, or was only partially filled, by himself; and the second fiction, by which the privileges of a legal heir in this respect as well as others had been extended to other persons, broke down the walls which might otherwise have confined those privileges to a single case. A new conception was introduced into the law, and there was nothing to hinder its further application. As has been shown, it was applied in terms to a sale of the *universitas* for business purposes, and to at least one case where the succession was confined to a single specific thing. Why, then, might not every gift or sale be regarded as a succession, so far as to insure the same advantages?

The joinder of times to make out a title was soon allowed between buyer and seller, and I have no doubt, from the language always used by the Roman lawyers, that it was arrived at in the way I have suggested. A passage from Scævola (B.C. 30) will furnish sufficient proof. Joinder of possessions, he says, that is, the right to add the time of one's predecessor's holding to one's own, clearly belongs to those who succeed to the place of others, whether by contract or by will: for heirs and those who are treated as holding the place of successors are allowed to add their testator's possession to their own. Accordingly, if you sell me a slave I shall have the benefit of your holding.[53]

The joinder of times is given to those who succeed to the place

[51] "In re legata in accessione temporis quo testator possedit, legatarius quodammodo quasi heres est." D. 41. 3. 14, § 1.

[52] D. 41. 1. 62; 43. 3. 1, § 6; Gaii Inst. II. § 97; Just. Inst. 2. 10. § 11.

[53] "[Accessiones possessionum] plane tribuuntur his qui in locum aliorum succedunt sive ex contractu sive voluntate: heredibus enim et his, qui successorum loco habentur, datur accessio testatoris. Itaque si mihi vendideris servum utar accessione tua." D. 44. 3. 14, §§ 1, 2.

of another. Ulpian cites a like phrase from a jurisconsult of the time of the Antonines,—"to whose place I have succeeded by inheritance, or purchase, or any other right."[54] *Succedere in locum aliorum,* like *sustinere personam,* is an expression of the Roman lawyers for those continuations of one man's legal position by another of which the type was the succession of heir to ancestor. *Succedere* alone is used in the sense of "inherit,"[55] and *successio* in that of "inheritance."[56] The succession *par excellence* was the inheritance; and it is believed that scarcely any instance will be found in the Roman sources where "succession" does not convey that analogy, and indicate the partial assumption, at least, of a *persona* formerly sustained by another. It clearly does so in the passage before us.

But the succession which admits a joinder of times is not hereditary succession alone. In the passage which has been cited Scævola says that it may be by contract or purchase, as well as by inheritance or will. It may be singular, as well as universal. The jurists often mention antithetically universal successions and those confined to a single specific thing. Ulpian says that a man succeeds to another's place, whether his succession be universal or to the single object.[57]

If further evidence were wanting for the present argument, it would be found in another expression of Ulpian's. He speaks of the benefit of joinder as derived from the *persona* of the grantor. "He to whom a thing is granted shall have the benefit of joinder from the *persona* of his grantor."[58] A benefit cannot be derived from a *persona* except by sustaining it.

[54] "Ab eo . . . in cujus locum hereditate vel emptione aliove quo iure successi." D. 43. 19. 3, § 2.

[55] D. 50. 4. 1, § 4. Cf. Cic. de Off. 3. 19. 76; Gaii Inst. IV. § 34.

[56] C. 2. 3. 21; C. 6. 16. 2; cf. D. 38. 8. 1, pr.

[57] "In locum successisse accipimus sive per universitatem sive in rem sit successum." D. 43. 3. 1, § 13. Cf. D. 21. 3. 3, § 1; D. 12. 2. 7 & 8; D. 39. 2, 24, § 1.

[58] D. 41. 2. 13, § § 1, 11. Other cases put by Ulpian may stand on a different fiction. After the termination of a *precarium,* for instance, *fingitur fundus nunquam fuisse possessus ab ipso detentore.* Gothofred, note 14 (Elz. ed.). But cf. Puchta, in Weiske, R. L., art. *Besitz,* p. 50, and D. 41. 2. 13, § 7.

It farther appears pretty plainly from Justinian's Institutes and the Digest, that the benefit was not extended to purchasers in all cases until a pretty late period.[59]

Savigny very nearly expressed the truth when he said, somewhat broadly, that "every *accessio*, for whatever purpose, presupposes nothing else than a relation of juridical succession between the previous and present possessor. For succession does not apply to possession by itself." [60] And I may add, by way of further explanation, that every relation of juridical succession presupposes either an inheritance or a relation to which, so far as it extends, the analogies of the inheritance may be applied.

The way of thinking which led to the *accessio* or joinder of times is equally visible in other cases. The time during which a former owner did not use an easement was imputed to the person who had succeeded to his place.[61] The defence that the plaintiff had sold and delivered the thing in controversy was available not only to the purchaser, but to his heirs or to a second purchaser, even before delivery to him, against the successors of the seller, whether universal or only to the thing in question.[62] If one used a way wrongfully as against the predecessor in title, it was wrongful as against the successor, whether by inheritance, purchase, or any other right.[63] The formal oath of a party to an action was conclusive in favor of his successors, universal or singular.[64] Successors by purchase or gift had the benefit of agreements made

[59] Inst. 2. 6, §§ 12, 13. Cf. D. 44. 3. 9. See, for a fuller statement, 11 Am. Law Rev. 644, 645.

[60] Recht des Besitzes, § 11 (7th ed.), p. 184, n. 1, Eng. tr. 124, n. *t*.

[61] Paulus, D. 8. 6. 18, § 1. This seems to be written of a rural servitude (*aqua*), which was lost by mere disuse, without adverse user by the servient owner.

[62] Hermogenianus, D. 21. 3. 3; Exc. rei jud., D. 44. 2. 9, § 2; ib. 28; ib. 11, §§ 3, 9; D. 10. 2. 25, § 8; D. 46. 8. 16, § 1; Keller, Röm. Civilproc., § 73. Cf. Bracton, fol. 24 *b*, § 1 *ad fin*.

[63] "Recte a me via uti prohibetur et interdictum ei inutile est, quia a me videtur vi vel clam vel precario possidere, qui ab auctore meo vitiose possidet. nam et Pedius scribit, si vi aut clam aut precario ab eo sit usus, in cuius locum hereditate vel emptione aliove quo iure successi, idem esse dicendum: cum enim successerit quis in locum eorum, æquum non est nos noceri hoc, quod adversus eum non nocuit, in cuius locum successimus." D. 43. 19. 3, § 2. The variation *actore*, argued for by Savigny, is condemned by Mommsen, in his edition of the Digest,—it seems rightly.

[64] D. 12. 2. 7 & 8.

with the vendor.[65] A multitude of general expressions show that for most purposes, whether of action or defence, the buyer stood in the shoes of the seller, to use the metaphor of our own law.[66] And what is more important than the result, which often might have been reached by other ways, the language and analogies are drawn throughout from the succession to the inheritance.

Thus understood, there could not have been a succession between a person dispossessed of a thing against his will and the wrongful possessor. Without the element of consent there is no room for the analogy just explained. Accordingly, it is laid down that there is no joinder of times when the possession is wrongful,[67] and the only enumerated means of succeeding *in rem* are by will, sale, gift, or some other right.

The argument now returns to the English law, fortified with some general conclusions. It has been shown that in both the systems from whose union our law arose the rules governing conveyance, or the transfer of specific objects between living persons, were deeply affected by notions drawn from inheritance. It had been shown previously that in England the principles of inheritance applied directly to the singular succession of the heir to a specific fee, as well as to the universal succession of the executor. It would be remarkable, considering their history, if the same principles had not affected other singular successions also. It will soon appear that they have. And not to be too careful about the order of proof, I will first take up the joinder of times in prescription, as that has just been so fully discussed. The Eng-

[65] Ulpian, D. 39. 2. 24, § 1. Cf. D. 8. 5. 7; D. 39. 2. 17, § 3, n. 79 (Elzevir ed.); Paulus, D. 2. 14. 17, § 5.

[66] "Cum quis in alii locum successerit non est æquum ei nocere hoc, quod adversus eum non nocuit, in cujus locum successit. Plerumque emptoris eadem causa esse debet circa petendum ac defendendum, quæ fuit auctoris." Ulp. D. 50. 17. 156, §§ 2, 3. "Qui in ius dominiumve alterius succedit, iure ejus uti debet." Paulus, D. 50. 17. 177. "Non debeo melioris condicionis esse, quam auctor mens, a quo ius in me transit." Paulus, D. 50. 17. 175, § 1. "Quod ipsis qui contraxerunt obstat, et successoribus eorum obstabit." Ulp. D. 50. 17. 143. "Nemo plus iuris ad alium transferre potest, quam ipse haberet." Ulp. D. 50. 17. 54; Bract., fol. 31 *b*. Cf. Decret. Greg. Lib. II. Tit. XIII. c. 18, *De rest. spoliat.*: "Cum spoliatori quasi succedat in vitium." Bruns, R. d. Besitzes, p. 179. Windscheid, Pand., § 162 *a*, n. 10.

[67] "Ne vitiosæ quidam possessioni ulla potest accedere: sed nec vitiosa ei, quæ vitiosa non est." D. 41. 2. 13, § 13.

lish law of the subject is found on examination to be the same as the Roman in extent, reason, and expression. It is indeed largely copied from that source. For servitudes, such as rights of way, light, and the like, form the chief class of prescriptive rights, and our law of servitudes is mainly Roman. Prescriptions, it is said, "are properly personal, and therefore are always alleged in the person of him who prescribes, viz. that he and all those whose estate he hath, &c.; therefore, a bishop or a parson may prescribe, . . . for there is a perpetual estate, and a perpetual succession, and the successor had the very same estate which his predecessor had, for that continues, though the person alters, like the case of the ancestor and the heir."[68] So in a modern case, where by statute twenty years' dispossession extinguished the owner's title, the Court of Queen's Bench said that probably the right would be transferred to the possessor "if the same person, or several persons, claiming one from the other by descent, will or conveyance, had been in possession for the twenty years." "But . . . such twenty years' possession must be either by the same person, or several persons claiming one from the other, which is not the case here."[69]

In a word, it is equally clear that the continuous possession of privies in title, or, in Roman phrase, successors, has all the effect of the continuous possession of one, and that such an effect is not attributed to the continuous possession of different persons who are not in the same chain of title. One who dispossesses another of land cannot add the time during which his disseisee has used a way to the period of his own use, while one who purchased can.[70]

The authorities which have been quoted make it plain that the

[68] *Hill* v. *Ellard*, 3 Salk. 279. Cf. *Withers* v. *Iseham*, Dyer, 70 *a*, 70 *b*, 71 *a*; *Gateward's Case*, 6 Co. Rep. 59 *b*, 60 *b*; Y. B. 20 & 21 Ed. I. 426; 34 Ed. I. 205; 12 Hen. IV. 7.

[69] *Doe* v. *Barnard*, 13 Q. B. 945, 952, 953, per Cur., Patteson, J. Cf. *Asher* v. *Whitlock*, L. R. 1 Q. B. 1, 3, 6, 7.

[70] See, further, *Sawyer* v. *Kendall*, 10 Cush. 241; 2 Bl. Comm. 263 *et seq.*; 3 Ch. Pl. 1119 (6th Am. ed.); 3 Kent, 444, 445; Angell, Limitations, ch. 31, § 413. Of course if a right had already been acquired before the disseisin different considerations would apply. If the right claimed is one of those which are regarded as incident to land, as explained in the following Lecture, the disseisor will have it. Jenk. Cent. 12, First Cent. Case 21.

English law proceeds on the same theory as the Roman. One who buys land of another gets the very same estate which his seller had. He is in of the same fee, or *hereditas*, which means, as I have shown, that he sustains the same *persona*. On the other hand, one who wrongfully dispossesses another,—a disseisor,—gets a different estate, is in of a new fee, although the land is the same; and much technical reasoning is based upon this doctrine.

In the matter of prescription, therefore, buyer and seller were identified, like heir and ancestor. But the question remains whether this identification bore fruit in other parts of the law also, or whether it was confined to one particular branch, where the Roman law was grafted upon the English stock.

There can be no doubt which answer is most probable, but it cannot be proved without difficulty. As has been said, the heir ceased to be the general representative of his ancestor at an early date. And the extent to which even he was identified came to be a matter of discussion. Common sense kept control over fiction here as elsewhere in the common law. But there can be no doubt that in matters directly concerning the estate the identification of heir and ancestor has continued to the present day; and as an estate in fee simple has been shown to be a distinct *persona*, we should expect to find a similar identification of buyer and seller in this part of the law, if anywhere.

Where the land was devised by will, the analogy applied with peculiar ease. For although there is no difference in principle between a devise of a piece of land by will and a conveyance of it by deed, the dramatic resemblance of a devisee to an heir is stronger than that of a grantee. It will be remembered that one of the Roman jurists said that a *legatarius* (legatee or devisee) was in a certain sense *quasi heres*. The English courts have occasionally used similar expressions. In a case where a testator owned a rent, and divided it by will among his sons, and then one of the sons brought debt for his part, two of the judges, while admitting that the testator could not have divided the tenant's liability by a grant or deed in his lifetime, thought that it was otherwise with regard to a division by will. Their reasoning was that "the devise is *quasi* an act of law, which shall inure without attornment, and shall make a sufficient privity, and so it may well be apportioned by this means."[71] So it was said by Lord Ellenborough, in a case where a lessor and his heirs were entitled to terminate a lease on notice, that a devisee of the land as *heres factus* would be understood to have the same right.[72]

But wills of land were only exceptionally allowed by custom until the reign of Henry VIII., and as the main doctrine of conveyancing had been settled long before that time, we must look further back and to other sources for their explanation. We shall find it in the history of warranty. This, and the modern law of covenants running with the land, will be treated in the next Lecture.

[71] *Ards* v. *Watkin*, Cro. Eliz. 637; s. c., ib. 651. Cf. Y. B. 5 Hen. VII. 18, pl. 12; Dyer, 4 *b*, n. (4).

[72] *Roe* v. *Hayley*, 12 East, 464, 470 (1810).

LECTURE XI

SUCCESSIONS.—II. INTER VIVOS

The principal contracts known to the common law and suable in the King's Courts, a century after the Conquest, were suretyship and debt. The heir, as the general representative of his ancestor's rights and obligations, was liable for his debts, and was the proper person to sue for those which were due the estate. By the time of Edward III. this had changed. Debts had ceased to concern the heir except secondarily. The executor took his place both for collection and payment. It is said that even when the heir was bound he could not be sued except in case the executor had no assets.[1]

But there was another ancient obligation which had a different history. I refer to the warranty which arose upon the transfer of property. We should call it a contract, but it probably presented itself to the mind of Glanvill's predecessors simply as a duty or obligation attached by law to a transaction which was directed to a different point; just as the liability of a bailee, which is now treated as arising from his undertaking, was originally raised by the law out of the position in which he stood toward third persons.

After the Conquest we do not hear much of warranty, except in connection with land, and this fact will at once account for its having had a different history from debt. The obligation of warranty was to defend the title, and, if the defence failed, to give to the evicted owner other land of equal value. If an ancestor had conveyed lands with warranty, this obligation could not be fulfilled by his executor, but only by his heir, to whom his other lands had descended. Conversely as to the benefit of warranties made to a deceased grantee, his heir was the only person inter-

[1] *Boyer* v. *Rivet*, 3 Bulstr. 317, 321.

ested to enforce such warranties, because the land descended to him. Thus the heir continued to represent his ancestor in the latter's rights and obligations by way of warranty, after the executor had relieved him of the debts, just as before that time he had represented his ancestor in all respects.

If a man was sued for property which he had bought from another, the regular course of litigation was for the defendant to summon in his seller to take charge of the defence, and for him, in turn, to summon in his, if he had one, and so on until a party was reached in the chain of title who finally took the burden of the case upon himself. A contrast which was early stated between the Lombard and the Roman law existed equally between the Anglo-Saxon and the Roman. It was said that the Lombard presents his grantor, the Roman stands in his grantor's shoes,—*Langobardus dat auctorem, Romanus stat loco auctoris.*[2]

Suppose, now, that A gave land to B, and B conveyed over to C. If C was sued by D, claiming a better title, C practically got the benefit of A's warranty,[3] because, when he summoned B, B would summon A, and thus A would defend the case in the end. But it might happen that between the time when B conveyed to C, and the time when the action was begun, B had died. If he left an heir, C might still be protected. But supposing B left no heir, C got no help from A, who in the other event would have defended his suit. This no doubt was the law in the Anglo-Saxon period, but it was manifestly unsatisfactory. We may conjecture, with a good deal of confidence, that a remedy would be found as soon as there was machinery to make it possible. This was furnished by the Roman law. According to that system, the buyer stood in the place of his seller, and a fusion of the Roman with the Anglo-Saxon rule was all that was needed.

Bracton, who modelled his book upon the writings of the mediæval civilians, shows how this thought was used. He first puts the case of a conveyance with the usual clause binding the grantor and his heirs to warrant and defend the grantee and his heirs. He then goes on: "Again one may make his gift greater and make other persons quasi heirs [of his grantee], although, in

[2] Essays in A. S. Law, 219.

[3] "Per medium," Bracton, fol. 37 *b*, § 10 *ad fin.*

fact, they are not heirs, as when he says in the gift, to have and to hold to such a one and his heirs, or to whomsoever he shall choose to give or assign the said land, and I and my heirs will warrant to the said so and so, and his heirs, or to whomsoever he shall choose to give or assign the said land, and their heirs, against all persons. In which case if the grantee shall have given or assigned the land, and then have died without heirs, the [first] grantor and his heirs begin to hold the place of the first grantee and his heirs, and are in place of the first grantee's heir (*pro herede*) so far as concerns warranting to his assigns and their heirs according to the clause contained in the first grantor's charter, which would not be but for the mention of assigns in the first gift. But so long as the first grantee survives, or his heirs, they are held to warranty, and not the first grantor." [4]

Here we see that, in order to entitle the assign to the benefit of the first grantor's warranty, assigns must be mentioned in the original grant and covenant. The scope of the ancient obligation was not extended without the warrantor's assent. But when it was extended, it was not by a contrivance like a modern letter of credit. Such a conception would have been impossible in that stage of the law. By mentioning assigns the first grantor did not offer a covenant to any person who would thereafter purchase the land. If that had been the notion, there would have been a contract directly binding the first grantor to the assign, as soon as the land was sold, and thus there would have been two warranties arising from the same clause,—one to the first grantee, a second to the assign. But in fact the assign recovered on the original warranty to the first grantee.[5] He could only come on the first grantor after a failure of his immediate grantor's heirs. The first grantor by mentioning assigns simply enlarged the limits of his grantee's succession. The assign could vouch the first grantor only on the principles of succession. That is to say, he could only do so when, by the failure of the first grantee's blood, the first grantee's feudal relation to the first grantor, his *persona*, came to be sustained by the assign.[6]

[4] Bract., fol. 17 *b*. Cf. Fleta, III. c. 14, § 6.

[5] See, further, *Middlemore* v. *Goodale*, Cro. Car. 503, stated *infra*, p. 379.

[6] See also Bract., fol. 380 *b*, 381. "Et quod de hæredibus dicitur, idem dici poterit de assignatis. . . . Et quod assignatis fieri debet warrantia per

This was not only carrying out the fiction with technical consistency, but was using it with good sense, as fictions generally have been used in the English law. Practically it made little difference whether the assign got the benefit of the first grantor's warranty mediately or immediately, if he got it. The trouble arose where he could not summon the mesne grantor, and the new right was given him for that case alone. Later, the assign did not have to wait for the failure of his immediate grantor's blood, but could take advantage of the first grantor's warranty from the beginning.[7]

If it should be suggested that what has been said goes to show that the first grantor's duty to warrant arose from the assign's becoming his man and owing homage, the answer is that he was not bound unless he had mentioned assigns in his grant, homage or no homage. In this Bracton is confirmed by all the later authorities.[8]

Another rule on which there are vast stores of forgotten learning will show how exactly the fiction fell in with the earlier law. Only those who were privy in estate with the person to whom the warranty was originally given, could vouch the original warrantor. Looking back to the early procedure, it will be seen that of course only those in the same chain of title could even mediately get the benefit of a former owner's warranty. The ground on which a man was bound to warrant was that he had conveyed the property to the person who summoned him. Hence a man could summon no one but his grantor, and the successive vouchers came to an end when the last vouchee could not call on another from whom he had bought. Now when the process was abridged,

---

modum donationis: probatur in itinere W. de Ralegh in Com. Warr. circa finem rotuli, et hoc maxime, si primus dominus capitalis, et primus feoffator, ceperit homagium et servitium assignati." Cf. Fleta, VI. c. 23, § 6; Moore, 93, pl. 230; Sheph. Touchst. 199, 200. As to the reason which led to the mention of assigns, cf. Bract., fol. 20 *b*, § 1; 1 Britt. (Nich.), 223, 312.

[7] I do not stop to inquire whether this was due to the statute of Quia Emptores, by which the assign was made to hold directly of the first grantor, or whether some other explanation must be found. Cf. Bract., fol. 37 *b;* Fleta, III. c. 14, §§ 6, 11; VI. c. 28, § 4; 1 Britton (Nich.), 256, [100 *b*].

[8] Fleta, III. c. 14, § 6, fol. 197; 1 Britton (Nich.), 223, 233, 244, 255, 312; Co. Lit. 384 *b;* Y. B. 20 Ed. I. 232; Abbr. Placit., fol. 308, 2d col., Dunelm, rot. 43; Y. B. 14 Hen. IV. 5, 6.

no persons were made liable to summons who would not have been liable before. The present owner was allowed to vouch directly those who otherwise would have been indirectly bound to defend his title, but no others. Hence he could only summon those from whom his grantor derived his title. But this was equally well expressed in terms of the fiction employed. In order to vouch, the present owner must have the estate of the person to whom the warranty was made. As every lawyer knows, the estate does not mean the land. It means the *status* or *persona* in regard to that land formerly sustained by another. The same word was used in alleging a right by prescription, "that he and those whose estate he hath have for time whereof memory runneth not to the contrary," &c.; and it will be remembered that the word corresponds to the same requirement of succession there.

To return to Bracton, it must be understood that the description of assigns as *quasi heredes* is not accidental. He describes them in that way whenever he has occasion to speak of them. He even pushes the reasoning drawn from the analogy of inheritance to extremes, and refers to it in countless passages. For instance: "It should be noted that of heirs some are true heirs and some quasi heirs, in place of heirs, &c.; true heirs by way of succession, quasi heirs, &c. by the form of the gift; such as assigns," &c.[9]

If it should be suggested that Bracton's language is only a piece of mediæval scholasticism, there are several answers. In the first place it is nearly contemporaneous with the first appearance of the right in question. This is shown by his citing authority for it as for something which might be disputed. He says, "And that warranty must be made to assigns according to the form of the gift is proved [by a case] in the circuit of W. de Ralegh, about the end of the roll," &c.[10] It is not justifiable to assume that a contemporary explanation of a new rule had nothing to do with its appearance. Again, the fact is clear that the assign got the benefit of the warranty to the first grantee, not of a new one to himself, as has been shown, and Bracton's explanation of how this was worked out falls in with what has been seen of the course of the German and Anglo-Saxon law, and with the pervading thought of the Roman law. Finally, and most important,

[9] Fol. 67 *a*; cf. 54 *a*.

[10] Fol. 381; *supra*, p. 291, n. 6.

the requirement that the assign should be in of the first grantee's estate has remained a requirement from that day to this. The fact that the same thing is required in the same words as in prescription goes far to show that the same technical thought has governed both.

As I have said, Glanvill's predecessors probably regarded warranty as an obligation incident to a conveyance, rather than as a contract. But when it became usual to insert the undertaking to warrant in a deed or charter of feoffment, it lost something of its former isolation as a duty standing by itself, and admitted of being generalized. It was a promise by deed, and a promise by deed was a covenant.[11] This was a covenant having peculiar consequences attached to it, no doubt. It differed also in the scope of its obligation from some other covenants, as will be shown hereafter. But still it was a covenant, and could sometimes be sued on as such. It was spoken of in the Year Books of Edward III. as a covenant which "falls in the blood," [12] as distinguished from those where the acquittance fell on the land, and not on the person.[13]

The importance of this circumstance lies in the working of the law of warranty upon other covenants which took its place. When the old actions for land gave way to more modern and speedier forms, warrantors were no longer vouched in to defend, and if a grantee was evicted, damages took the place of a grant of other land. The ancient warranty disappeared, and was replaced by the covenants which we still find in our deeds, including the covenants for seisin, for right to convey, against incumbrances, for quiet enjoyment, of warranty, and for further assurance. But the principles on which an assign could have the benefit of these covenants were derived from those which governed warranty, as any one may see by looking at the earlier decisions.

For instance, the question, what was a sufficient assignment to give an assign the benefit of a covenant for quiet enjoyment, was argued and decided on the authority of the old cases of warranty.[14]

[11] Cf. *Pincombe* v. *Rudge*, Hobart, 3; Bro. *Warrantia Carte*, pl. 8; s. c., Y. B. 2 Hen. IV. 14, pl. 5.

[12] Y. B. 50 Ed. III. 12 *b* & 13.

[13] Y. B. 42 Ed. III. 3, pl. 14, per Belknap, *arguendo*.

[14] *Noke* v. *Awder*, Cro. Eliz. 373; s. c., ib. 436. Cf. *Lewis* v. *Campbell*, 8 Taunt. 715; s. c., 3 J. B. Moore, 35.

The assign, as in warranty, came in under the old covenant with the first covenantee, not by any new right of his own. Thus, in an action by an assign on a covenant for further assurance, the defendant set up a release by the original covenantee after the commencement of the suit. The court held that the assignee should have the benefit of the covenant. "They held, that although the breach was in the time of the assignee, yet if the release had been by the covenantee (who is a party to the deed, and from whom the plaintiff derives) before any breach, or before the suit commenced, it had been a good bar to the assignee from bringing this writ of covenant. But the breach of the covenant being in the time of the assignee, . . . and the action brought by him, and so attached in his person, the covenantee cannot release this action wherein the assignee is interested."[15] The covenantee even after assignment remains the legal party to the contract. The assign comes in under him, and does not put an end to his control over it, until by breach and action a new right attaches in the assign's person, distinct from the rights derived from the *persona* of his grantor. Later, the assign got a more independent standing, as the original foundation of his rights sunk gradually out of sight, and a release after assignment became ineffectual, at least in the case of a covenant to pay rent.[16]

Only privies in estate with the original covenantee can have the benefit of covenants for title. It has been shown that a similar limitation of the benefits of the ancient warranty was required by its earlier history before the assign was allowed to sue, and that the fiction by which he got that right could not extend it beyond that limit. This analogy also was followed. For instance, a tenant in tail male made a lease for years with covenants of right to let and for quiet enjoyment, and then died without issue male. The lessee assigned the lease to the plaintiff. The latter was soon turned out, and thereupon brought an action upon the covenant against the executor of the lessor. It was held that he could not recover, because he was not privy in estate with the original covenantee. For the lease, which was the original cov-

[15] *Middlemore* v. *Goodale*, Cro. Car. 503; *s. c.*, ib. 505, Sir William Jones, 406.

[16] *Harper* v. *Bird*, T. Jones, 102 (Pasch. 30 Car. II.). These cases show an order of development parallel to the history of the assignment of other contracts not negotiable.

enantee's estate, was ended by the death of the lessor and termination of the estate tail out of which the lease was granted, before the form of assignment to the plaintiff.[17]

The only point remaining to make the analogy between covenants for title and warranty complete was to require assigns to be mentioned in order to enable them to sue. In modern times, of course, such a requirement, if it should exist, would be purely formal, and would be of no importance except as an ear-mark by which to trace the history of a doctrine. It would aid our studies if we could say that wherever assigns are to get the benefit of a covenant as privies in estate with the covenantee, they must be mentioned in the covenant. Whether such a requirement does exist or not would be hard to tell from the decisions alone. It is commonly supposed not to. But the popular opinion on this trifling point springs from a failure to understand one of the great antinomies of the law, which must now be explained.

So far as we have gone, we have found that, wherever one party steps into the rights or obligations of another, without in turn filling the situation of fact of which those rights or obligations are the legal consequences, the substitution is explained by a fictitious identification of the two individuals, which is derived from the analogy of the inheritance. This identification has been seen as it has been consciously worked out in the creation of the executor, whose entire status is governed by it. It has been seen still consciously applied in the narrower sphere of the heir. It has been found hidden at the root of the relation between buyer and seller in two cases at least, prescription and warranty, when the history of that relation is opened to a sufficient depth.

But although it would be more symmetrical if this analysis exhausted the subject, there is another class of cases in which the transfer of rights takes place upon a wholly different plan. In explaining the succession which is worked out between buyer and seller for the purpose of creating a prescriptive right, such as a right of way over neighboring land to the land bought and sold, it was shown that one who, instead of purchasing the land, had wrongfully possessed himself of it by force, would not be treated as a successor, and would get no benefit from the previous

[17] *Andrew* v. *Pearce*, 4 Bos. & Pul. 158 (1805).

use of the way by his disseisee. But when the former possessor has already gained a right of way before he is turned out, a new principle comes into operation. If the owner of the land over which the way ran stopped it up, and was sued by the wrongful possessor, a defence on the ground that the disseisor had not succeeded to the former owner's rights would not prevail. The disseisor would be protected in his possession of the land against all but the rightful owner, and he would equally be protected in his use of the way. This rule of law does not stand on a succession between the wrongful possessor and the owner, which is out of the question. Neither can it be defended on the same ground as the protection to the occupation of the land itself. That ground is that the law defends possession against everything except a better title. But, as has been said before, the common law does not recognize possession of a way. A man who has used a way ten years without title cannot sue even a stranger for stopping it. He was a trespasser at the beginning, he is nothing but a trespasser still. There must exist a right against the servient owner before there is a right against anybody else. At the same time it is clear that a way is no more capable of possession because somebody else has a right to it, than if no one had.

How comes it, then, that one who has neither title nor possession is so far favored? The answer is to be found, not in reasoning, but in a failure to reason. In the first Lecture of this course the thought with which we have to deal was shown in its theological stage, to borrow Comte's well-known phraseology, as where an axe was made the object of criminal process; and also in the metaphysical stage, where the language of personification alone survived, but survived to cause confusion of reasoning. The case put seems to be an illustration of the latter. The language of the law of easements was built up out of similes drawn from persons at a time when the *noxæ deditio* was still familiar; and then, as often happens, language reacted upon thought, so that conclusions were drawn as to the rights themselves from the terms in which they happened to be expressed. When one estate was said to be enslaved to another, or a right of way was said to be a quality or incident of a neighboring piece of land, men's minds were not alert to see that these phrases were only so many personifying metaphors, which explained nothing unless the figure of speech was true.

Rogron deduced the negative nature of servitudes from the rule that the land owes the services, not the person,—*Prædium non persona servit*. For, said Rogron, the land alone being bound, it can only be bound passively. Austin called this an "absurd remark." [18] But the jurists from whom we have inherited our law of easements were contented with no better reasoning. Papinian himself wrote that servitudes cannot be partially extinguished, because they are due from lands, not persons.[19] Celsus thus decides the case which I took for my illustration: Even if possession of a dominant estate is acquired by forcibly ejecting the owner, the way will be retained; since the estate is possessed in such quality and condition as it is when taken.[20] The commentator Godefroi tersely adds that there are two such conditions, slavery and freedom; and his antithesis is as old as Cicero.[21] So, in another passage, Celsus asks, What else are the rights attaching to land but qualities of that land? [22] So Justinian's Institutes speak of servitudes which inhere in buildings.[23] So Paulus speaks of such rights as being accessory to bodies. "And thus," adds Godefroi, "rights may belong to inanimate things." [24] It easily followed from all this that a sale of the dominant estate carried existing easements, not because the buyer succeeded to the place of the seller, but because land is bound to land.[25]

All these figures import that land is capable of having rights, as Austin recognizes. Indeed, he even says that the land "is

[18] Austin, Jurisprudence, II. p. 842 (3d ed.).

[19] "Quoniam non personæ, sed prædia deberent, neque adquiri libertas neque remitti servitus per partem poterit." D. 8. 3. 34, pr.

[20] "Qui fundum alienum bona fide emit, itinere quod ei fundo debetur usus est: retinetur id ius itineris: atque etiam, si precario aut vi deiecto domino possidet fundus enim qualiter se habens ita, cum in suo habitu possessus est, ius non deperit, neque refert, iuste nec ne possideat qui talem eum possidet." D. 8. 6. 12.

[21] Elzevir ed., n. 51, *ad loc. cit.;* Cicero de L. Agr. 3. 2. 9.

[22] D. 50. 16, 86. Cf. Ulpian, D. 41. 1. 20, § 1; D. 8. 3. 23, § 2.

[23] Inst. 2. 3, § 1.

[24] D. 8. 1. 14, pr. Cf. Elzevir ed., n. 58, "Et sic jura . . . accessiones esse possunt corporum."

[25] "Cum fundus fundo servit." D. 8. 4. 12. Cf. D. 8. 5. 20, § 1; D. 41. 1. 20, § 1.

erected into a legal or fictitious *person*, and is styled 'prædium *dominans*.'"[26] But if this means anything more than to explain what is implied by the Roman metaphors, it goes too far. The dominant estate was never "erected into a legal person," either by conscious fiction or as a result of primitive beliefs.[27] It could not sue or be sued, like a ship in the admiralty. It is not supposed that its possessor could maintain an action for an interference with an easement before his time, as an heir could for an injury to property of the *hereditas jacens*. If land had even been systematically treated as capable of acquiring rights, the time of a disseisee might have been added to that of the wrongful occupant, on the ground that the land, and not this or that individual, was gaining the easement, and that long association between the enjoyment of the privilege and the land was sufficient, which has never been the law.

All that can be said is, that the metaphors and similes employed naturally led to the rule which has prevailed, and that, as this rule was just as good as any other, or at least was unobjectionable, it was drawn from the figures of speech without attracting attention, and before any one had seen that they were only figures, which proved nothing and justified no conclusion.

As easements were said to belong to the dominant estate, it followed that whoever possessed the land had a right of the same degree over what was incidental to it. If the true meaning had been that a way or other easement admits of possession, and is taken possession of with the land to which it runs, and that its enjoyment is protected on the same grounds as possession in other cases, the thought could have been understood. But that was not the meaning of the Roman law, and, as has been shown, it is not the doctrine of ours. We must take it that easements have become an incident of land by an unconscious and unreasoned assumption that a piece of land can have rights. It need not be said that this is absurd, although the rules of law which are based upon it are not so.

Absurd or not, the similes as well as the principles of the Roman law reappear in Bracton. He says, "The servitude by which

[26] Jurisprudence, II. p. 847 (3d ed.).
[27] Cf. Windscheid, Pand., § 57, n. 10 (4th ed.), p. 150.

land is subjected to [other] land, is made on the likeness of that by which man is made the slave of man."[28] "For rights belong to a free tenement, as well as tangible things. . . . They may be called rights or liberties with regard to the tenements to which they are owed, but servitudes with regard to the tenements by which they are owed. . . . One estate is free, the other subjected to slavery."[29] "[A servitude] may be called an arrangement by which house is subjected to house, farm to farm, holding to holding."[30] No passage has met my eye in which Bracton expressly decides that an easement goes with the dominant estate upon a disseisin, but what he says leaves little doubt that he followed the Roman law in this as in other things.

The writ against a disseisor was for "so much land and its appurtenances,"[31] which must mean that he who had the land even wrongfully had the appurtenances. So Bracton says an action is *in rem* "whether it is for the principal thing, or for a right which adheres to the thing, . . . as when one sues for a right of way, . . . since rights of this sort are all incorporeal things, and are quasi possessed and reside in bodies, and cannot be got or kept without the bodies in which they inhere, nor in any way had without the bodies to which they belong."[32] And again, "Since rights do not admit of delivery, but are transferred with the thing in which they are, that is, the bodily thing, he to whom they are transferred forthwith has a quasi possession of those rights as soon as he has the body in which they are."[33]

There is no doubt about the later law, as has been said at the outset.

We have thus traced two competing and mutually inconsistent principles into our law. On the one hand is the conception of succession or privity; on the other, that of rights inhering in a thing. Bracton seems to have vacillated a little from a feeling of the possibility of conflict between the two. The benefit of a warranty was confined to those who, by the act and consent of the grantee, succeeded to his place. It did not pass to assigns

[28] Fol. 10 *b*, § 3.
[29] Fol. 220 *b*, § 1.
[30] Fol. 221.
[31] Fol. 219 *a*, *b*.
[32] Fol. 102 *a*, *b*.
[33] Fol. 226 *b*, § 13. All these passages assume that a right has been acquired and inheres in the land.

unless assigns were mentioned. Bracton supposes grants of easements with or without mention of assigns, which looks as if he thought the difference might be material with regard to easements also. He further says, that if an easement be granted to A, his heirs and assigns, all such by the form of the grant are allowed the use in succession, and all others are wholly excluded.[84] But he is not speaking of what the rights of a disseisor would be as against one not having a better title, and he immediately adds that they are rights over a corporeal object belonging to a corporeal object.

Although it may be doubted whether the mention of assigns was ever necessary to attach an easement to land, and although it is very certain that it did not remain so long, the difficulty referred to grew greater as time went on. It would have been easily disposed of if the only rights which could be annexed to land were easements, such as a right of way. It then might have been said that these were certain limited interests in land, less than ownership in extent, but like it in kind, and therefore properly transferred by the same means that ownership was. A right of way, it might have been argued, is not to be approached from the point of view of contract. It does not presuppose any promise on the part of the servient owner. His obligation, although more troublesome to him than to others, is the same as that of every one else. It is the purely negative duty not to obstruct or interfere with a right of property.[85]

But although the test of rights going with the land may have been something of that nature, this will not help us to understand the cases without a good deal of explanation. For such rights might exist to active services which had to be performed by the person who held the servient estate. It strikes our ear strangely to hear a right to services from an individual called a right of property as distinguished from contract. Still this will be found to have been the way in which such rights were regarded. Bracton argues that it is no wrong to the lord for the tenant to alienate land held by free and perfect gift, on the ground that the *land* is bound and

[84] Fol. 53 *a;* cf. 59 *b, ad fin.,* 242 *b.*

[85] "Nihil praescribitur nisi quod possidetur," cited from Hale de Jur. Maris, p. 32, in *Blundell* v. *Catterall,* 5 B. & Ald. 268, 277.

charged with the services into whose hands soever it may come. The lord is said to have a fee in the homage and services; and therefore no entry upon the land which does not disturb them injures him.[36] It is the tenement which imposes the obligation of homage,[37] and the same thing is true of villein and other feudal services.[38]

The law remained unchanged when feudal services took the form of rent.[39] Even in our modern terms for years rent is still treated as something issuing out of the leased premises, so that to this day, although, if you hire a whole house and it burns down, you have to pay without abatement, because you have the land out of which the rent issues, yet if you only hire a suite of rooms and they are burned, you pay rent no longer, because you no longer have the tenement out of which it comes.[40]

It is obvious that the foregoing reasoning leads to the conclusion that a disseisor of the tenant would be bound as much as the tenant himself, and this conclusion was adopted by the early law. The lord could require the services,[41] or collect the rent[42] of any one who had the land, because, as was said in language very like Bracton's, "the charge of the rent goes with the land."[43]

Then as to the right to the rent. Rent was treated in early law as a real right, of which a disseisin was possible, and for which a possessory action could be brought. If, as was very frequently the case, the leased land lay within a manor, the rent was parcel of the manor,[44] so that there was some ground for saying that one who was seised of the manor, that is, who possessed the lands occupied by the lord of the manor, and was recognized by the tenants as lord, had the rents as incident thereto. Thus Brian, Chief Justice of England under Henry VII., says, "If I am disseised of a manor, and the tenants pay their rent to the disseisor, and then I re-enter, I shall not have the back rent of my tenants

[36] Bract., fol. 46 *b;* cf. 17 *b,* 18, 47 *b,* 48. [37] Fol. 81, 81 *b,* 79 *b,* 80 *b.*

[38] Fol. 24 *b,* 26, 35 *b,* 36, 208 *b,* &c. Cf. F. N. B. 123, E; Laveleye, Propriété, 67, 68, 116.

[39] Abbr. Plac. 110, rot. 22, Devon. (Hen. III.).

[40] *Stockwell* v. *Hunter,* 11 Met. (Mass.) 448.

[41] Keilway, 130 *b,* pl. 104. [42] Keilway, 113 *a,* pl. 45; Dyer, 2 *b.*

[43] Keilway, 113 *a,* pl. 45. Cf. Y. B. 33–35 Ed. I. 70; 45 Ed. III. 11, 12.

[44] Litt. § 589.

which they have paid to my disseisor, but the disseisor shall pay for all in trespass or assize."[45] This opinion was evidently founded on the notion that the rent was attached to the chief land like an easement. *Sic fit ut debeantur rei a re.*[46]

Different principles might have applied when the rent was not parcel of a manor, and was only part of the reversion; that is, part of the landlord's fee or estate out of which the lease was carved. If the lease and rent were merely internal divisions of that estate, the rent could not be claimed except by one who was privy to that estate. A disseisor would get a new and different fee, and would not have the estate of which the rent was part. And therefore it would seem that in such a case the tenant could refuse to pay him rent, and that payment to him would be no defence against the true owner.[47] Nevertheless, if the tenant recognized him, the disseisor would be protected as against persons who could not show a better title.[48] Furthermore, the rent was so far annexed to the land that whoever came by the reversion lawfully could collect it, including the superior lord in case of escheat.[49] Yet escheat meant the extinction of the fee of which the lease and rent were parts, and although Bracton regarded the lord as coming in under the tenant's title *pro herede,* in privity, it was soon correctly settled that he did not, but came in paramount. This instance, therefore, comes very near that of a disseisor.

Services and rent, then, were, and to some extent are still, dealt with by the law from the point of view of property. They were things which could be owned and transferred like other property. They could be possessed even by wrong, and possessory remedies were given for them.

No such notion was applied to warranties, or to any right which was regarded wholly from the point of view of contract. And when we turn to the history of those remedies for rent which sounded in contract, we find that they were so regarded. The actions of debt and covenant could not be maintained without

[45] Keilway, 2 *a,* pl. 2 *ad fin.* (12 Hen. VII.). But cf. Y. B. 6 Hen. VII. 14, pl. 2 *ad fin.*

[46] 4 Laferrière, Hist. du Droit. Franç. 442; Bracton, fol. 53 *a.*

[47] Cf. Co. Lit. 322 *b, et seq.;* Y. B. 6 Hen. VII. 14, pl. 2 *ad fin.*

[48] *Daintry* v. *Brocklehurst,* 3 Exch. 207.

[49] Y. B. 5 Hen. VII. 18, pl. 12.

privity. In the ninth year of Henry VI.[50] it was doubted whether an heir having the reversion by descent could have debt, and it was held that a grantee of the reversion, although he had the rent, could not have that remedy for it. A few years later, it was decided that the heir could maintain debt,[51] and in Henry VII.'s reign the remedy was extended to the devisee,[52] who, as has been remarked above, seemed more akin to the heir than a grantee, and was more easily likened to him. It was then logically necessary to give assigns the same action, and this followed.[53] The privity of contract followed the estate, so that the assignee of the reversion could sue the person then holding the term.[54] On like grounds he was afterwards allowed to maintain covenant.[55] But these actions have never lain for or against persons not privy in estate with the lessor and lessee respectively, because privity to the contract could never be worked out without succession to the title.[56]

However, all these niceties had no application to the old freehold rents of the feudal period, because the contractual remedies did not apply to them until the time of Queen Anne.[57] The freehold rent was just as much real estate as an acre of land, and it was sued for by the similar remedy of an assize, asking to be put back into possession.

The allowance of contractual remedies shows that rent and feudal services of that nature, although dealt with as things capable of possession, and looked at generally from the point of view of property rather than of contract, yet approach much nearer to the nature of the latter than a mere duty not to interfere with a way. Other cases come nearer still. The sphere of prescription and custom in imposing active duties is large in early law. Sometimes the duty is incident to the ownership of certain land; sometimes the right is, and sometimes both are, as in the case of an easement. When the service was for the benefit

[50] Y. B. 9 Hen. VI. 16, pl. 7.
[51] Y. B. 14 Hen. VI. 26, pl. 77.
[52] Y. B. 5 Hen. VII. 18, pl. 12.
[53] Cf. Theloall, Dig. I. c. 21, pl. 9.
[54] *Buskin* v. *Edmunds*, Cro. Eliz. 636.
[55] *Harper* v. *Bird*, T. Jones, 102 (30 Car. II.).
[56] *Bolles* v. *Nyseham*, Dyer, 254 *b; Porter* v. *Swetnam*, Style, 406; s. c., ib. 431.
[57] 3 Bl. Comm. 231, 232.

of other land, the fact that the burden, in popular language, fell upon one parcel, was of itself a reason for the benefit attaching to the other.

Instances of different kinds are these. A parson might be bound by custom to keep a bull and a boar for the use of his parish.[58] A right could be attached to a manor by prescription to have a convent sing in the manor chapel.[59] A right might be gained by like means to have certain land fenced by the owner of the neighboring lot.[60] Now, it may readily be conceded that even rights like the last two, when attached to land, were looked at as property, and were spoken of as the subject of grant.[61] It may be conceded that, in many cases where the statement sounds strange to modern ears, the obligation was regarded as falling on the land alone, and not on the person of the tenant. And it may be conjectured that this view arose naturally and reasonably from there having been originally no remedy to compel performance of such services, except a distress executed on the servient land.[62] But any conjectured distinction between obligations for which the primitive remedy was distress alone, and others, if it ever existed, must soon have faded from view; and the line between those rights which can be deemed rights of property, and those which are mere contracts, is hard to see, after the last examples. A covenant to repair is commonly supposed to be pure matter of contract. What is the difference between a duty to repair, and a duty to fence? The difficulty remains almost as great as ever of finding the dividing line between the competing principles of transfer,—succession on the one side, and possession of dominant land on the other. If a right in the nature of an easement could be attached to land by prescription,

[58] *Yielding* v. *Fay*, Cro. Eliz. 569.

[59] *Pakenham's Case*, Y. B. 42 Ed. III. 3, pl. 14; *Prior of Woburn's Case*, 22 Hen. VI. 46, pl. 36; *Williams's Case*, 5 Co. Rep. 72 *b*, 73 *a*; *Slipper* v. *Mason*, Nelson's Lutwyche, 43, 45 (top).

[60] F. N. B. 127; *Nowel* v. *Smith*, Cro. Eliz. 709; *Star* v. *Rookesby*, 1 Salk. 335, 336; *Lawrence* v. *Jenkins*, L. R. 8 Q. B. 274.

[61] Dyer, 24 *a*, pl. 149; F. N. B. 180 N.

[62] F. N. B. 128 D, E; Co. Lit. 96 *b*. It is assumed that, when an obligation is spoken of as falling upon the land, it is understood to be only a figure of speech. Of course rights and obligations are confined to human beings.

it could equally be attached by grant. If it went with the land in one case, even into the hands of a disseisor, it must have gone with it in the other. No satisfactory distinction could be based on the mode of acquisition,[63] nor was any attempted. As the right was not confined to assigns, there was no need of mentioning assigns.[64] In modern times, at least, if not in early law, such rights can be created by covenant as well as by grant.[65] And, on the other hand, it is ancient law that an action of covenant may be maintained upon an instrument of grant.[66] The result of all this was that not only a right created by covenant, but the action of covenant itself, might in such cases go to assigns, although not mentioned, at a time when such mention was essential to give them the benefit of a warranty. Logically, these premises led one step farther, and not only assigns not named, but disseisors, should have been allowed to maintain their action on the contract, as they had the right arising out of it. Indeed, if the plaintiff had a right which when obtained by grant would have entitled him to covenant, it was open to argument that he should be allowed the same action when he had the right by prescription, although, as has been seen in the case of rent, it did not follow in practice from a man's having a right that he had the contractual remedies for it.[67] Covenant required a specialty, but prescription was said to be a sufficiently good specialty.[68] Where, then, was the line to be drawn between covenants that devolved only to successors, and those that went with the land?

The difficulty becomes more striking upon further examination of the early law. For side by side with the personal warranty

[63] Keilway, 145 *b*, 146, pl. 15; *Sir Henry Nevil's Case*, Plowd. 377, 381; *Chudleigh's Case*, 1 Co. Rep. 119 *b*, 122 *b*.

[64] F. N. B. 180 N; Co. Lit. 385 *a*; *Spencer's Case*, 5 Co. Rep. 16 *a*, 17 *b*; *Pakenham's Case*, Y. B. 42 Ed. III. 3, pl. 14; Keilway, 145 *b*, 146, pl. 15; Comyns's Digest, *Covenant* (B, 3).

[65] *Holms* v. *Seller*, 3 Lev. 305; *Rowbotham* v. *Wilson*, 8 H. L. C. 348; *Bronson* v. *Coffin*, 108 Mass. 175, 180. Cf. Bro. *Covenant*, pl. 2.

[66] Y. B. 21 Ed. III. 2, pl. 5; F. N. B. 180 N.

[67] The action is case in the *Prior of Woburn's Case*, Y. B. 22 Hen. VI. 46, pl. 36. In F. N. B. 128 E, n. (*a*), it is said that a *curia claudenda* only lay upon a prescriptive right, and that if the duty to fence was by indenture the plaintiff was put to his writ of covenant. But see below, pp. 308, 310–311.

[68] Y. B. 32 & 33 Ed. I. 430.

which has been discussed hitherto, there was another warranty which has not yet been mentioned, by which particular land alone was bound.[69] The personal warranty bound only the warrantor and his heirs. As was said in a case of the time of Edward I., "no one can bind assigns to warranty, since warranty always extends to heirs who claim by succession and not by assignment." [70] But when particular land was bound, the warranty went with it, even into the hands of the King, because, as Bracton says, the thing goes with its burden to every one.[71] Fleta writes that every possessor will be held.[72] There cannot be a doubt that a disseisor would have been bound equally with one whose possession was lawful.

We are now ready for a case [73] decided under Edward III., which has been discussed from the time of Fitzherbert and Coke down to Lord St. Leonards and Mr. Rawle, which is still law, and is said to remain still unexplained.[74] It shows the judges hesitating between the two conceptions to which this Lecture has been devoted. If they are understood, I think the explanation will be clear.

Pakenham brought covenant as heir of the covenantee against a prior, for breach of a covenant made by the defendant's predecessor with the plaintiff's great-grandfather, that the prior and convent should sing every week in a chapel in his manor, for him and his servants. The defendant first pleaded that the plaintiff and his servants were not dwelling within the manor; but, not daring to rest his case on that, he pleaded that the plaintiff was not heir, but that his elder brother was. The plaintiff replied that he was tenant of the manor, and that his great-grandfather enfeoffed a stranger, who enfeoffed the plaintiff and his wife; and that thus the plaintiff was tenant of the manor by purchase, and privy to the ancestor; and also that the services had been rendered for a time whereof the memory was not.

[69] Y. B. 20 Ed. I. 360. [70] Y. B. 32 & 33 Ed. I. 516.

[71] "Quia res cum homine [obviously a misprint for *onere*] transit ad quemcunque." Fol. 382, 382 *b*.

[72] Lib. VI. c. 23, § 17. [73] *Pakenham's Case*, Y. B. 42 Ed. III. 3, pl. 14.

[74] Sugd. V. & P. (14th ed.), 587; Rawle, Covenants for Title (4th ed.), p. 314. Cf. *Vyvyan* v. *Arthur*, 1 B. & C. 410; *Sharp* v. *Waterhouse*, 7 El. & Bl. 816, 823.

It is evident from these pleadings that assigns were not mentioned in the covenant, and so it has always been taken.[75] It also appears that the plaintiff was trying to stand on two grounds; first, privity, as descendant and assign of the covenantee; second, that the service was attached to the manor by covenant or by prescription, and that he could maintain covenant as tenant of the manor, from whichever source the duty arose.

Finchden, J. puts the case of parceners making partition, and one covenanting with the other to acquit of suit. A purchaser has the advantage of the covenant. Belknap, for the defendants, agrees, but distinguishes. In that case the acquittance falls on the land, and not on the person.[76] (That is to say, such obligations follow the analogy of easements, and, as the burden falls on the quasi servient estate, the benefit goes with the dominant land to assigns, whether mentioned or not, and they are not considered from the point of view of contract at all. Warranty, on the other hand, is a contract pure and simple, and lies in the blood,—falls on the person, not on the land.[77])

Finchden: *a fortiori* in this case; for there the action was maintained because the plaintiff was tenant of the land from which the suit was due, and here he is tenant of the manor where the chapel is.

Wichingham, J.: If the king grants warren to another who is tenant of the manor, he shall have warren, &c.; but the warren will not pass by the grant [of the manor], because the warren is not appendant to the manor. No more does it seem the services are here appendant to the manor.

Thorpe, C. J., to Belknap: "There are some covenants on which no one shall have an action, but the party to the covenant, or his heir, and some covenants have inheritance in the land, so that whoever has the land by alienation, *or in other manner*, shall have action of covenant; [or, as it is stated in Fitzherbert's Abridgment,[78] the inhabitants of the land as well as *every one who has the land*, shall have the covenant;] and when you say he is not heir, *he is privy of blood, and may be heir:* [79] and *also he is tenant*

[75] Co. Lit. 385 *a*. [76] Cf. Finchden as to rent in Y. B. 45 Ed. III. 11, 12.
[77] Cf. Y. B. 50 Ed. III. 12, 13, pl. 2. [78] *Covenant*, pl. 17.
[79] There is a colon here in both editions of the Year Books, marking the beginning of a new argument.

of the land, and it is a thing which is annexed to the chapel, which is in the manor, and so annexed to the manor, *and so he has said that the services have been rendered for all time whereof there is memory, whence* it is right this action should be maintained." Belknap denied that the plaintiff counted on such a prescription; but Thorpe said he did, and we bear record of it, and the case was adjourned.[80]

It will be seen that the discussion followed the lines marked out by the pleading. One judge thought that the plaintiff was entitled to recover as tenant of the manor. The other puisne doubted, but agreed that the case must be discussed on the analogy of easements. The Chief Justice, after suggesting the possibility of sufficient privity on the ground that the plaintiff was privy in blood and might be heir, turns to the other argument as more promising, and evidently founds his opinion upon it.[81] It would almost seem that he considered a prescriptive right enough to support the action, and it is pretty clear that he thought that a disseisor would have had the same rights as the plaintiff.

In the reign of Henry IV., another case [82] arose upon a covenant very like the last. But this time the facts were reversed. The plaintiff counted as heir, but did not allege that he was tenant of the manor. The defendant, not denying the plaintiff's descent, pleaded in substance that he was not tenant of the manor in his own right. The question raised by the pleadings, therefore, was whether the heir of the covenantee could sue without being tenant of the manor. If the covenant was to be approached from the side of contract, the heir was party to it as representing the covenantee. If, on the other hand, it was treated as amounting to the grant of a service like an easement, it would naturally go with the manor if made to the lord of the manor. It seems to have been thought that such a covenant might go either way, according as it was made to the tenant of the manor or to a stranger. Markham, one of the judges, says: "In a writ of covenant one must be privy to the covenant if he would have a writ of covenant or aid by the covenant. But, peradventure, if the covenant had been made with the lord of the manor, who had

[80] *Pakenham's Case,* Y. B. 42 Ed. III. 3, pl. 14.
[81] Bro. *Covenant,* pl. 5. Cf. *Spencer's Case,* 5 Co. Rep. 16 *a,* 17 *b,* 18 *a.*
[82] *Horne's Case.* Y. B. 2 Hen. IV. 6, pl. 25.

inheritance in the manor, *ou issint come determination poit estre fait*, it would be otherwise," which was admitted.[83] It was assumed that the covenant was not so made as to attach to the manor, and the court, observing that the service was rather spiritual than temporal, were inclined to think that the heir could sue.[84] The defendant accordingly pleaded over and set up a release. It will be seen how fully this agrees with the former case.

The distinction taken by Markham is stated very clearly in a case reported by Lord Coke. In the argument of *Chudleigh's Case* the line is drawn thus: "Always, the warranty as to voucher requires privity of estate to which it was annexed," (i. e. succession to the original covenantee), "and the same law of a use. . . . But of things annexed to land, it is otherwise, as of commons, advowsons, and the like appendants or appurtenances. . . . So a disseisor, abator, intruder, or the lord by escheat, &c., shall have them as things annexed to the land. So note a diversity between a use of warranty, and the like things annexed to the estate of the land in privity, and commons, advowsons, and other hereditaments annexed to the possession of the land."[85] And this, it seems to me, is the nearest approach which has ever been made to the truth.

Coke, in his Commentary on Littleton (385 *a*), takes a distinction between a warranty, which binds the party to yield lands in recompense, and a covenant annexed to the land, which is to yield but damages. If Lord Coke had meant to distinguish between warranties and all covenants which in our loose modern sense are said to run with the land, this statement would be less satisfactory than the preceding.

A warranty was a covenant which sometimes yielded but damages, and a covenant in the old law sometimes yielded land. In looking at the early cases we are reminded of the still earlier German procedure, in which it did not matter whether the plaintiff's claim was founded on a right of property in a thing, or simply on a contract for it.[86] Covenant was brought for a freehold

[83] "Quod conceditur." Cf. *Spencer's Case*, 5 Co. Rep. 16 *a*, 18 *a*.

[84] It was quite possible that two liabilities should exist side by side. Bro. *Covenant*, pl. 32; *Brett* v. *Cumberland*, Cro. Jac. 521, 523.

[85] 1 Co. Rep. 122 *b;* s. c., *sub nom. Dillon* v. *Fraine*, Popham, 70, 71.

[86] Essays in Ang. Sax. Law, 248.

under Edward I.,[87] and under Edward III. it seems that a mill could be abated by the same action, when maintained contrary to an easement created by covenant.[88] But Lord Coke did not mean to lay down any sweeping doctrine, for his conclusion is, that "a covenant is *in many cases* extended further than the warrantie." Furthermore, this statement, as Lord Coke meant it, is perfectly consistent with the other and more important distinction between warranties and rights in the nature of easements or covenants creating such rights. For Lord Coke's examples are confined to covenants of the latter sort, being in fact only the cases just stated from the Year Books.

Later writers, however, have wholly forgotten the distinction in question, and accordingly it has failed to settle the disputed line between conflicting principles. Covenants which started from the analogy of warranties, and others to which was applied the language and reasoning of easements, have been confounded together under the title of covenants running with the land. The phrase "running with the land" is only appropriate to covenants which pass like easements. But we can easily see how it came to be used more loosely.

It has already been shown that covenants for title, like warranties, went only to successors of the original covenantee. The technical expression for the rule was that they were annexed to the estate in privity. Nothing was easier than to overlook the technical use of the word "estate," and to say that such covenants went with the land. This was done, and forthwith all distinctions became doubtful. It probably had been necessary to mention assigns in covenants for title, as it certainly had been to give them the benefit of the ancient warranty; [89] for this seems to have been the formal mark of those covenants which passed only to privies. But it was not necessary to mention assigns in order to attach easements and the like to land. Why should it be necessary for one covenant running with the land more than another? and if necessary for one, why not for all? [90] The necessity of such

[87] Y. B. 22 Ed. I. 494, 496.

[88] Y. B. 4 Ed. III. 57, pl. 71; s. c., 7 Ed. III. 65, pl. 67.

[89] Bract., fol. 17 *b*, 37 *b;* Fleta, III. c. 14, § 6; 1 Britton (Nich.), 223, 233, 244, 255, 312; Abbrev. Plac. p. 308, col. 2, Dunelm, rot. 43 (33 Ed. I.); Y. B. 20 Ed. I. 232; Co. Lit. 384 *b*.

[90] *Hyde* v. *Dean of Windsor*, Cro. Eliz. 552.

mention in modern times has been supposed to be governed by a fanciful rule of Lord Coke's.[91] On the other hand, the question is raised whether covenants which should pass irrespective of privity are not governed by the same rule which governs warranties.

These questions have not lost their importance. Covenants for title are in every deed, and other covenants are only less common, which, it remains to show, belong to the other class.

Chief among these is the covenant to repair. It has already been observed that an easement of fencing may be annexed to land, and it was then asked what was the difference in kind between a right to have another person build such structures, and a right to have him repair structures already built. Evidence is not wanting to show that the likeness was perceived. Only, as such covenants are rarely, if ever, made, except in leases, there is always privity to the original parties. For the lease could not, and the reversion would not be likely to, go by disseisin.

The *Dean of Windsor's Case* decides that such a covenant binds an assignee of the term, although not named. It is reported in two books of the highest authority, one of the reporters being Lord Coke, the other Croke, who was also a judge. Croke gives the reason thus: "For a covenant which runs and rests with the land lies for or against the assignee at the common law, *quia transit terra cum onere,* although the assignees be not named in the covenant." [92] This is the reason which governed easements, and the very phrase which was used to account for all possessors being bound by a covenant binding a parcel of land to warranty. Coke says, "For such covenant which extends to the support of the thing demised is *quo-dammodo* appurtenant to it, and goes with it." Again the language of easements. And to make this plainer, if need be, it is added, "If a man grants to one estovers to repair his house, it is appurtenant to his house." [93] Estovers for

[91] *Spencer's Case,* 5 Co. Rep. 16 *a.* Cf. *Minshull* v. *Oakes,* 2 H. & N. 793, 807.

[92] *Hyde* v. *Dean of Windsor,* Cro. Eliz. 552, 553; s. c., ib. 457. Cf. *Bally* v. *Wells,* 3 Wilson, 25, 29.

[93] *Dean of Windsor's Case,* 5 Co. Rep. 24 *a;* s. c., Moore, 399. Cf. Bro. *Covenant,* pl. 32. Cf. further, *Conan* v. *Kemise,* W. Jones, 245 (7 Car. I.).

repair went with the land, like other rights of common,[94] which, as Lord Coke has told us, passed even to disseisors.

In the next reign the converse proposition was decided, that an assignee of the reversion was entitled in like manner to the benefit of the covenant, because "it is a covenant which runs with the land."[95] The same law was applied, with still clearer reason, to a covenant to leave fifteen acres unploughed for pasture, which was held to bind an assignee not named,[96] and, it would seem, to a covenant to keep land properly manured.[97]

If the analogy which led to this class of decisions were followed out, a disseisor could sue or be sued upon such covenants, if the other facts were of such a kind as to raise the question. There is nothing but the novelty of the proposition which need prevent its being accepted. It has been mentioned above, that words of covenant may annex an easement to land, and that words of grant may import a covenant. It would be rather narrow to give a disseisor one remedy, and deny him another, where the right was one, and the same words made both the grant and the covenant.[98]

The language commonly used, however, throws doubt and darkness over this and every other question connected with the subject. It is a consequence, already referred to, of confounding covenants for title, and the class last discussed, under the name of covenants running with the land. According to the general opinion there must be a privity of estate between the covenantor and covenantee in the latter class of cases in order to bind the assigns of the covenantor. Some have supposed this privity to be tenure; some, an interest of the covenantee in the land of the covenantor; and so on.[99] The first notion is false, the second misleading, and the proposition to which they are applied is unfounded. Privity of estate, as used in connection with covenants at common law, does not mean tenure or easement; it means suc-

[94] F. N. B. 181 N; *Sir Henry Nevil's Case*, Plowden, 377, 381.

[95] *Ewre* v. *Strickland*, Cro. Jac. 240. Cf. *Brett* v. *Cumberland*, 1 Roll. R. 359, 360 "al comen ley"; s. c., Cro. Jac. 399, 521.

[96] *Cockson* v. *Cock*, Cro. Jac. 125.

[97] *Sale* v. *Kitchingham*, 10 Mod. 158 (E. 12 Anne).

[98] *Supra*, pp. 306, 308, 310–311. Cf., however, Lord Wensleydale, in *Rowbotham* v. *Wilson*, 8 H. L. C. 348, 362, and see above, p. 304, as to rents.

[99] 4 Kent (12th ed.), 480, n. 1.

cession to a title.[100] It is never necessary between covenantor and covenantee or any other persons, except between the present owner and the original covenantee. And on principle it is only necessary between them in those cases—such as warranties, and probably covenants for title—where, the covenants being regarded wholly from the side of contract, the benefit goes by way of succession, and not with the land.

If now it should be again asked, at the end of this long discussion, where the line is to be drawn between these two classes of covenants, the answer is necessarily vague in view of the authorities. The following propositions may be of some service.

A. With regard to covenants which go with the land:—

(1.) Where either by tradition or good sense the burden of the obligation would be said, elliptically, to fall on the land of the covenantor, the creation of such a burden is in theory a grant or transfer of a partial interest in that land to the covenantee. As the right of property so created can be asserted against every possessor of the land, it would not be extravagant or absurd to allow it to be asserted by the action of covenant.

(2.) Where such a right is granted to the owner of a neighboring piece of land for the benefit of that land, the right will be attached to the land, and go with it into all hands. The action of covenant would be allowed to assigns not named, and it would not be absurd to give it to disseisors.

(3.) There is one case of a service, the burden of which does not fall upon land even in theory, but the benefit of which might go at common law with land which it benefited. This is the case of singing and the like by a convent. It will be observed that the service, although not falling on land, is to be performed by a corporation permanently seated in the neighborhood. Similar cases are not likely to arise now.

B. With regard to covenants which go only with the estate in the land:—

In general the benefit of covenants which cannot be likened

[100] It is used in a somewhat different sense in describing the relation between a tenant for life or years and reversioner. Privity between them follows as an accidental consequence of their being as one tenant, and sustaining a single *persona* between them.

to grants, and the burden of which does not fall on land, is confined to the covenantee and those who sustain his *persona,* namely, his executor or heir. In certain cases, of which the original and type was the ancient warranty, and of which the modern covenants for title are present examples, the sphere of succession was enlarged by the mention of assigns, and assigns are still allowed to represent the original covenantee for the purposes of that contract. But it is only by way of succession that any other person than the party to the contract can sue upon it. Hence the plaintiff must always be privy in estate with the covenantee.

C. It is impossible, however, to tell by general reasoning what rights will be held in English law to belong to the former class, or where the line will be drawn between the two. The authorities must be consulted as an arbitrary fact. Although it might sometimes seem that the test of the first was whether the service was of a nature capable of grant, so that if it rested purely in covenant it would not follow the land,[101] yet if this test were accepted, it has already been shown that, apart from tradition, some services which do follow the land could only be matter of covenant. The grant of light and air, a well-established easement, is called a covenant not to build on the servient land to the injury of the light, by Baron Parke.[102] And although this might be doubted,[103] it has been seen that at least one well-established easement, that of fencing, cannot be considered as a right granted out of the servient land with any more propriety than a hundred other services which would be only matter of contract if the law allowed them to be annexed to land in like manner. The duty to repair exists only by way of covenant, yet the reasoning of the leading cases is drawn from the law of easement. On the other hand, a covenant by a lessee to build a wall upon the leased premises was held, in *Spencer's Case,* not to bind assigns unless mentioned;[104] but Lord Coke says that it would have bound them if it had purported to. The analogy of warranty makes its appearance, and throws a doubt on the fundamental principle of the case. We can only say that the application of the law is

[101] *Rowbotham* v. *Wilson,* 8 H. L. C. 348, 362 (Lord Wensleydale).
[102] *Harbidge* v. *Warwick,* 3 Exch. 552, 556.
[103] *Rowbotham* v. *Wilson,* 8 El. & Bl. 123, 143, 144.
[104] 5 Co. Rep. 16, *a*

limited by custom, and by the rule that new and unusual burdens cannot be imposed on land.

The general object of this Lecture is to discover the theory on which a man is allowed to enjoy a special right when the facts out of which the right arises are not true of him. The transfer of easements presented itself as one case to be explained, and that has now been analyzed, and its influence on the law has been traced. But the principle of such transfers is clearly anomalous, and does not affect the general doctrine of the law. The general doctrine is that which has been seen exemplified in prescription, warranty, and such covenants as followed the analogy of warranty. Another illustration which has not yet been mentioned is to be found in the law of uses.

In old times a use was a chose in action,—that is, was considered very nearly from the point of view of contract, and it had a similar history to that which has been traced in other cases. At first it was doubted whether proof of such a secret trust ought to be allowed, even as against the heir.[105] It was allowed, however, in the end,[106] and then the principle of succession was extended to the assign. But it never went further. Only those who were privies in estate with the original feoffee to uses, were bound by the use. A disseisor was no more bound by the confidence reposed in his disseisee, than he was entitled to vouch his disseisee's warrantor. In the time of Henry VIII. it was said that "where a use shall be, it is requisite that there be two things, *sc.* confidence, and privity: . . . as I say, if there be not privity or confidence, then there can be no use: and hence if the feoffees make a feoffment to one who has notice of the use, now the law will adjudge him seised to the first use, since there is sufficient privity between the first feoffer and him, for if he [i. e. the first feoffer] had warranted he [the last feoffee] should vouch as assign, which proves privity; and he is in in the *per* by the feoffees; but where one comes into the land in the *post,* as the lord by escheat or the disseisor, then the use is altered and changed, because privity is wanting." [107]

[105] Y. B. 8 Ed. IV. 5, 6, pl. 1; 22 Ed. IV. 6, pl. 18. Cf. 5 Ed. IV. 7, pl. 16.
[106] Cf. Keilway, 42 *b*, 46 *b*; 2 Bl. Comm. 329.
[107] Y. B. 14 Hen. VIII. 6, pl. 5. Cf. *Chudleigh's Case,* 1 Co. Rep. 120 *a*, 122 *b*; s. c., *nom. Dillon* v. *Fraine,* Popham, 70–72.

To this day it is said that a trust is annexed in privity to the person and to the estate[108] (which means to the *persona*). It is not regarded as issuing out of the land like a rent, so that while a rent binds every one who has the land, no matter how, a disseisor is not bound by the trust.[109] The case of the lord taking by escheat has been doubted,[110] and it will be remembered that there is a difference between Bracton and later authors as to whether he comes in as *quasi heres* or as a stranger.

Then as to the benefit of the use. We are told that the right to sue the *subpœna* descended indeed to the heir, on the ground of *heres eadem persona cum antecessore*, but that it was not assets.[111] The *cestui que use* was given power to sell by an early statute.[112] But with regard to trusts, Lord Coke tells us that in the reign of Queen Elizabeth all the judges in England held that a trust could not be assigned, "because it was a matter in privity between them, and was in the nature of a *chose in action*."[113] Uses and trusts were both devisable, however, from an early day,[114] and now trusts are as alienable as any form of property.

The history of early law everywhere shows that the difficulty of transferring a mere right was greatly felt when the situation of fact from which it sprung could not also be transferred. Analysis shows that the difficulty is real. The fiction which made such a transfer conceivable has now been explained, and its history has been followed until it has been seen to become a general mode of thought. It is now a matter of course that the buyer stands in the shoes of the seller, or, in the language of an old law-book,[115] that "the assign is in a manner quasi successor to his assignor." Whatever peculiarities of our law rest on that assumption may now be understood.

[108] Lewin, Trusts, Ch. I. (7th ed.), pp. 16, 15.

[109] 4 Inst. 85; Gilb. Uses (Sugd.), 429, n. (6); Lewin, Trusts (7th ed.), pp. 15, 228.

[110] *Burgess* v. *Wheate*, 1 Eden, 177, 203, 246.

[111] Lewin, Trusts, Introd. (7th ed.), p. 3.

[112] 1 Rich. III. c. 1. Cf. *Rex* v. *Holland*, Aleyn, 14, Maynard's arg.; Bro. *Feoffements al Uses*, pl. 44; Gilb. Uses, 26 * (Sugd. ed., 50).

[113] 4th Inst. 85; s. c., Dyer, 369, pl. 50; Jenk. Cent. 6, c. 30. Cf. Gilb. Uses, 198 * (Sugd. ed. 399).

[114] Gilb. Uses, 35 * (Sugd. ed. 70).

[115] Theloall's Dig., I. 16, pl. 1.

GLOSSARY OF LEGAL TERMS

Appeals de pace et plagis: In the early English law persons wronged by crime could initiate a private proceeding for redress known as an appeal. When the charge concerned a breach of the peace and wounding the appeal was known as an appeal "de pace et plagis."

Assize and jurata: By legislation of Henry II, certain important proprietary actions were henceforth to be tried by assize—by a sworn inquest responsible for the decision of defined and designated issues. The *jurata*, by contrast, was the body of men summoned to decide questions of fact which might incidentally arise in the course of the trial of a nonproprietary action. With time, the assize was swallowed up, as it were, in the *jurata*. It is to the latter that the origin of the jury may be traced.

Commodatum: By this term the Roman law described the transaction by which a gratuitous loan of a specific chattel to be used by the transferee was effected. See also *Depositum; Pignus.*

Depositum: By this term the Roman law described the gratuitous transaction by which an owner of movable property, for his own benefit alone, transferred it to the care of another.

Hereditas jacens: By the Roman law certain heirs could refuse their inheritance. During the time which passed before they decided whether to accept or reject the inheritance the goods were described as an "hereditas jacens"—a vacant inheritance. To this estate the law ascribed an incomplete personification.

Lex Aquilia: This law, of uncertain date, contained two important provisions for a civil remedy for damage to property. One provided that whoever killed another's slave or beast should pay the owner the highest value which the property had within the previous year. The other dealt with unlawful damage done to property not within the classification of the first provision.

Noxae deditio: By the Roman law the noxal actions (*Noxales Actiones*) were made available to persons who had been injured by another's slave or another's son. The proceeding was against the owner or the father, and if successful, concluded with the surrender (deditio) of the slave or son to the injured person or the payment of all damages. Another class of noxal action was permitted when injury was done by an animal.

Pignus: A pledge or security for a debt or demand. As distinguished from another security device, the *hypotheca,* the *pignus* required a transfer of the property to the pledgee.

Salic Law: The Lex Salica, one of the earliest extant statements of Germanic custom, dating from the fifth century, consisted largely of a tariff of offenses and atonements.

Secta: It was a requirement of the early English law that the plaintiff in a civil action should produce a body of witnesses—the *secta*—who would testify, not to the facts in issue, but to the genuineness of the plaintiff's cause of complaint.

TABLE OF CASES

YEAR BOOKS AND EARLY CASES

INDEX

For Product Safety Concerns and Information please contact our EU
representative GPSR@taylorandfrancis.com
Taylor & Francis Verlag GmbH, Kaufingerstraße 24, 80331 München, Germany

www.ingramcontent.com/pod-product-compliance
Ingram Content Group UK Ltd.
Pitfield, Milton Keynes, MK11 3LW, UK
UKHW022206190926
475702UK00003B/234

* 9 7 8 1 1 3 8 5 3 4 7 8 0 *